To Evelyn Abrahams

I know of your deep
friendship for Ruth, & of
her admiration of you

H. S. Rubiner

PEPPER, RICE, AND ELEPHANTS

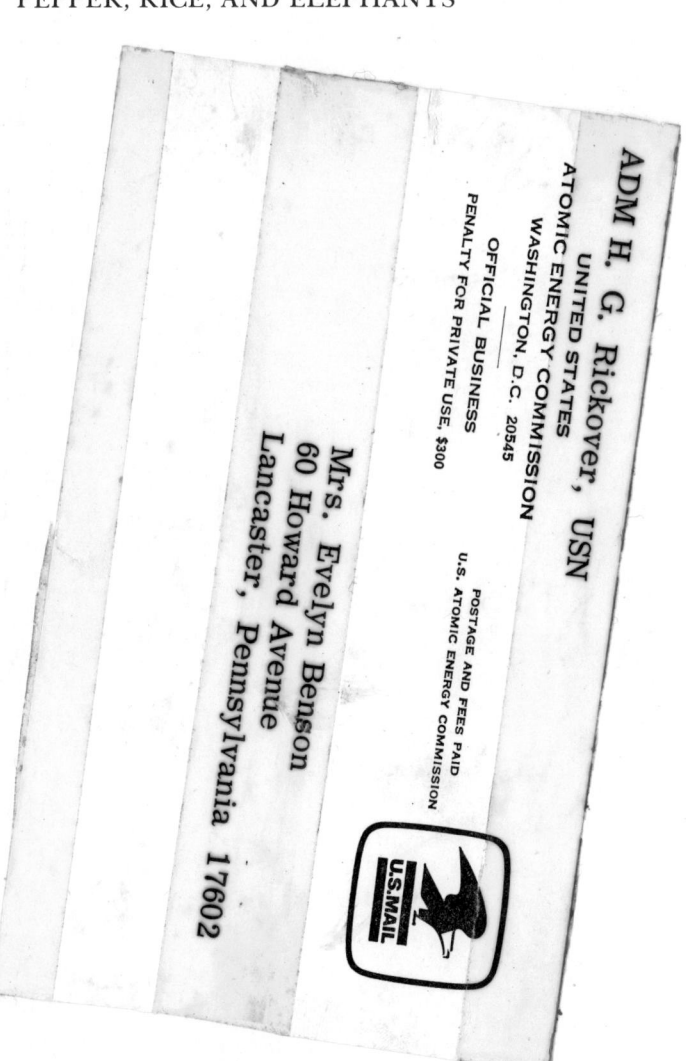

NAVAL INSTITUTE PRESS   Annapolis, Maryland

Pepper, Rice, and Elephants

A SOUTHEAST ASIAN JOURNEY FROM CELEBES TO SIAM

by Ruth Masters Rickover

Copyright © 1975 by the United States Naval Institute, Annapolis, Maryland.

All rights reserved. No part of this book may be reproduced without written permission from the publisher.

Library of Congress Catalogue Card No. 74-77974.

ISBN 0-87021-509-4.

Printed in the United States of America.

Contents

Foreword vii
Prologue ix
1 The *Tjinegara* 1
2 Bali 13
3 Java 45
4 Sumatra 67
5 Malaya 101
6 Angkor 124
7 Muang Thai 157
8 Siamese Laos 182
9 Back to Bangkok 215
10 French Laos 229
11 Annam 246
12 Yunnan 258
13 Tonkin 282
Epilogue 297
Bibliography 299
Index 301

Foreword

Ruth Masters Rickover studied international law at Columbia University where she received her master's degree in 1930 and her doctorate in 1932. Under her maiden name, she was the author of *International Law in National Courts; A Study of the Enforcement of International Law in German, Swiss, French, and Belgian Courts,* published by the Columbia University Press (1932), and the *Handbook of International Organizations in the Americas* published by the Carnegie Endowment for International Peace (1945). In addition, she wrote several articles, among them "International Organization of European Rail Transport," published by the Carnegie Endowment for International Peace in *International Conciliation* (May 1937) and "International Agencies in the Western Hemisphere," which appeared in the *American Journal of International Law*, Volume 39 (1945).

Subsequently, she devoted her efforts to the upbringing and education of our son, Robert Masters Rickover, and to giving me immeasurable assistance in my work. She was at once the most human and intelligent person I ever knew, the greatest influence on my life and career. She died May 25, 1972.

> Give her of the fruit of her hands; and let her own works praise her in the gates. *Proverbs 31:31*

H. G. Rickover

Prologue

One Sunday afternoon, last summer, I sat in my garden watching a hummingbird buzzing ecstatically among the white and pink hollyhocks, for all the world like a miniature helicopter. The zinnias were coming along splendidly and there would soon be many tomatoes for the salad bowl. I had just gone through the usual turmoil of seeing my husband off on one of his all-too-frequent plane trips. Robert, our son, had been trying to squeeze the maximum attention from his father—submerged in shaving cream—before he again escaped the family into his own atomic world. The telephone rang incessantly and, while I relayed messages, I tried in vain to pin my husband down to a definite date for the next dinner party. Now he was gone. Peace descended—but it did not last for long.

A most indignant young man appeared on the scene. "You've just got to come upstairs, Mother, and tend to that phone. It's ringing and ringing and I have to do my Morse Code practice. I just can't be bothered with all those characters crying for Daddy."

I sighed and got up, thinking how completely our life had become enslaved to those pesky nuclear reactors. They'd elbowed their way into the family and become its most important members. Though my husband got involved in atomic submarines ten years ago, my knowledge of atomic power plants remains rudimentary. All I know is that there are problems in developing nuclear reactors—difficulties often arise in the middle of the night, resulting in the telephone ringing at all hours and making the lesser members of the family resentful.

We are rushing into the atomic age in a spirit of restless speed and deadly seriousness. Most of us worry at times lest we prove incapable of controlling the mighty forces we are unleashing. But I have a more personal concern. While we in this country and the technically advanced countries are groping our way into the new push-button era, the gulf between us and that large portion of mankind, politely termed "undeveloped," is broadening alarmingly. We remain tied to our brothers whose lives are lived in a handicraft age or earlier. Mutual understanding is vital yet becomes daily more difficult to achieve as our paths diverge and barriers—iron, bamboo, and bureaucratic—come crashing down between the peoples of the world. Parts of the world are gradually becoming closed to the individual merchant and traveler and only government trade missions and government-conducted tours cross the boundaries. Fewer and fewer individual visitors can wander as they will, make their own contacts, and reach their own conclusions on the basis of what they see and hear.

It seems to me that the world is reverting to the state it was in before the Portuguese, the Dutch, and the English blasted their way into forbidden countries, forcing trade upon them. As I write today—less than two decades later—the pleasant, secure, and highly unconventional type of travel which my husband and I enjoyed in the late thirties would be impossible. In 1937 he was ordered to duty in the Orient and in the next two years we were lucky enough to see much of the countries of that area, particularly Southeast Asia. Besides fun and friendships with many different types of people, we gained primarily an understanding of the great variety of living patterns fashioned by mankind. And this, in turn, made current events more interesting and comprehensible.

As I left the garden—my own pre-atomic world—I wondered how atomic power plants would affect the people we had met and liked on our travels. I saw them in my mind as climbing slowly up the ladder of civilization. There had been the Negritos—Stone Age people—who, clad in G-strings, hunted for food with bone arrows; eternal wanderers through the jungle, sleeping in the ashes of their campfires and knowing no man-made shelter. Then, a little higher, the Igorots, marvelously competent rice farmers, living in ordered little villages surrounded by lush green rice terraces which had been literally carved by hand from solid rock thousands of years ago. Though they had been somewhat softened by contact with civilization, we still read occasionally of forays made from their mountain villages for the purpose of hunting the heads of peaceful Filipino peasants. After all, since time immemorial, the young Igorot swain proved his virility by bringing home a head to hang under the low eaves of his bride's new home.

In towns and villages we had seen modern replicas of the medieval artisan world. In Silk Street, Copper Street, Gold Street, and many others, owners and apprentices labored in tiny shops, slowly turning out handsome products for the local market. We often saw them at mealtime, companionably seated around a low table, master and servants eating from the same bowl. Yet we had also seen the end of this world and the harsh beginnings of an industrial revolution similar to the one England went through two centuries ago. A dark barn in Tonkin, into which were crowded as many hand looms as possible, each tended by a narrow-chested weaver assisted by a little boy helper, all working away feverishly from dawn to dusk to enrich a small native capitalist—exactly as depicted in economic textbooks and vividly brought to life in the novels of Dickens. Thinking of these people and wondering about their place in the new world my husband was helping to usher in, I decided to write this book.

It tells of our travels through Southeast Asia on the eve of Pearl Harbor. Without suspecting it, we witnessed the end of an era that has since been swept away in the turbulence of war and Japanese conquest, emancipation from colonial rule, and the desperate struggle to ward off the tide of Communism. After thousands of years of misgovernment by native rulers, and centuries of struggles between rival colonial powers, the area was enjoying a long period of peace, a sort of modern *Pax Romana*, maintained by a small, almost invisible corps of competent administrators and soldiers led by modern proconsuls of diverse European origins.

In retrospect, the European peace, which in those days seemed indestructible, appears to have had more solid advantages for the mass of colonial subjects than was evident to us—or them—at the time. Irksome though foreign rule must be, sooner or later it must end. But most of the people of this vast area did benefit from domestic peace, responsible government, good roads, absence of arbitrary exactions, and that uniquely Western invention—equality and security of law. Certainly we, as travelers, enjoyed a comfort and security never known before the white man came and not likely to reappear for many years to come.

We talked with everyone—natives as well as resident whites—and collected many interesting data on their colonial and pre-colonial history. I took shorthand notes and later incorporated them into a diary from which this book has been fashioned. I have changed nothing except to omit purely personal matters and subjects which were timely then but are of little interest today. I have checked facts and added bits of history to round out my narrative. Because of the upheavals of the last two decades, this travelogue has turned into a "swan song" for a vanished era which may make it of interest today. I hope that it sheds a light upon friendly people whom we came to know and love.

December 1954 *Ruth Masters Rickover*

PEPPER, RICE, AND ELEPHANTS

1
The *Tjinegara*

Being shrewd and practical burghers, the Dutch ran their Indonesian Empire on the time-honored principle that colonies must benefit the motherland and foreigners should be kept out. Shipping to and from the ports of *onze Indië* (our India)—as they called Indonesia,—was restricted to Dutch merchantmen, so we could not go to Bali on an American Silver Line freighter as we had planned. But, once on board the JCJL* liner *Tjinegara*, we were quickly reconciled to traveling under the Dutch flag. She was a lovely ship, well built for tropical cruising, immaculately clean, with excellent cuisine and congenial ship's company. We sat at the captain's table, almost submerged among huge Hollanders with enormous appetites and ear-splitting voices. There were a retired Shanghai pilot captain, Mr. Huyser, with his plump and cozy wife; Mr. Hendricus M. Spit, tourist manager of the JCJL; and Mr. Nater, importer of Japanese cottons.

This being the summer of 1938, the conversation inevitably veered towards the Sino-Japanese War. Mr. Nater, who had just spent one and a half years in Japan representing a Batavian import firm, reported that the war was unpopular in Japan—the people were apathetic and big businessmen grumbled, frankly calling the war a mistake. Japan, so they said, was like a man who owned a factory and a private car. He foolishly spent all his money on the car, leaving nothing to run the factory, and would soon go bankrupt. Mr. Huyser said he "felt it in his bones" that Japan would win the war against China and also drive out the white man from all of East Asia; hence he had sold his pilot's license† and decided to return home to a peaceful life in Holland. Mr. Nater was certain that the war would

---

*The Java-China-Japan Line, all of whose ships have names starting with "Tj," for some obscure reason.

†Navigation on the Whangpoo River from Shanghai to Wusung, where the river empties into the East China Sea, is difficult and ships must take on a pilot. In those days the Shanghai Pilots' Association kept its membership limited. Anyone wishing to join not only had to pass a stiff examination but also had to wait for a vacant membership, for which a high price was asked.

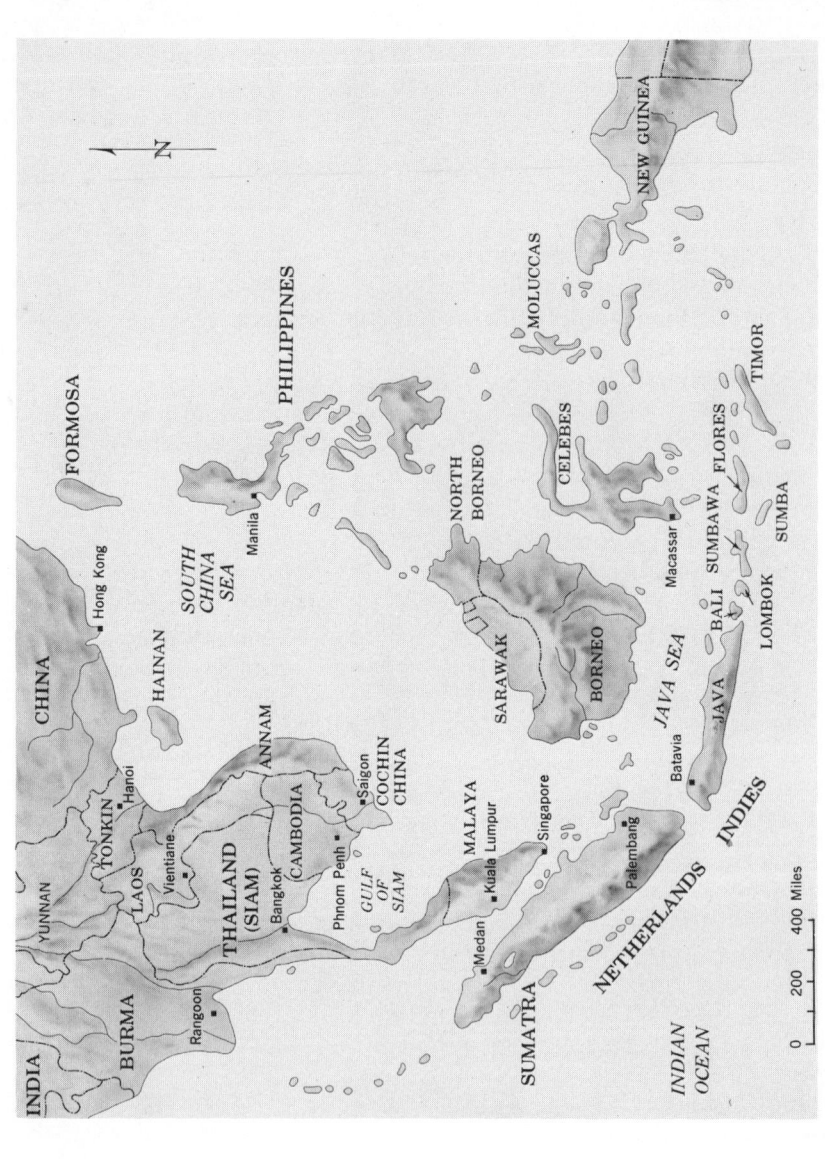

not end with a compromise. Japan would lose too much face and the military rulers knew their own safety was at stake. He felt this introduced a dangerous element of hysteria, and "crazy" things would be done if they felt they were not winning.

My husband, George, wanted to know whether Mr. Nater thought we could prevent Japan's taking eventual control of the entire oriental market. On our trips through the Philippines we had noticed a steady increase of Japanese goods on the shelves of native stores, while European and American brands were increasingly hard to obtain. Even if you picked up a familiar bar of Lux soap, Palmolive shave cream, or the like, they turned out to be clever Japanese imitations. Nater said he was certain that nothing Europe or America could do would prevent Japan from outselling Western goods. He said oriental shopkeepers had little cash and preferred to stock cheap goods, even if they were inferior; they could sell four flimsy Japanese suits at 2.50 guilders each* more readily than one Dutch-made garment at 5 guilders, even though the Dutch suit would outlast four Japanese suits. Psychologically, he felt, it was impossible to compete with Japanese goods since the Dutch had no home market for such shoddy goods and nobody had yet been able to export successfully products that were not used at home. "No," he said, "artificial barriers can't stem the flow of Japanese goods forever."

One evening the conversation turned to Austria, which had just been incorporated into the Third Reich, and George asked jokingly: "Well, when do you Dutch figure Hitler will gobble you up?" This aroused much deep-throated laughter. One of the giant Dutchmen remarked: "Haven't you heard of the dog that choked to death when he swallowed too big a bone?" Mr. Spit submitted airily, "The question is, when are we going to swallow up Hitler?" Whereupon we were treated to an earnest and Teutonic lecture on the basic differences between the Dutch and the Germans. "We love liberty and we're democratic; the Germans must always have someone tell them what to do." "But," said George, "since the Dutch look like Germans, both peoples must be racially related." Great indignation! "Not at all. Why you only have to look at our women—how much *finer* they are." We suppressed incipient chuckles at this most laudable sentiment; all the Dutch ladies present were anything but delicate, which is what was meant by the word *finer*. However, we listened gravely to the argument that the Dutch resembled Scandinavians and that, while once the Germans were almost like these worthy peoples, they had of late become so mixed up with Slavs and other nationalities that now

---

*At that time, one Dutch guilder, which contained 100 Dutch cents, was worth 58 American cents.

they were entirely different. Their language, too, was not as pure and melodious as Dutch which, of course, was the mother tongue; German being a later aberration. Since Dutch sounds rather raucous to the non-Dutch ear, and remarkably Germanic in inflection, we were not convinced.

Since we were Americans and traveling for the first time to a European colony, we were the recipients of much good advice on how to conduct ourselves appropriately. This advice went in one ear and out the other for, by inclination and by reason of our limited financial resources, we had planned our trip carefully to get the maximum of sightseeing for minimum expenditure, disregarding all obligations to carry the white man's burden of dignified and costly deportment. In this we received moral support only from an American missionary, Mr. George A. Campbell, who was traveling on behalf of the Seventh Day Adventists and was concerned primarily with the task of translating their religious tracts into as many native dialects as possible. He was an experienced traveler and gave us many hints on how to make ourselves comfortable without paying exorbitantly for the white man's comforts.

He confided that his great ambition was to reach the Balinese, whose women were "crying out" for conversion to his particular creed. They would have been converted long ago, were it not for the despicable greed of the Dutch government which would not let missionaries into Bali for fear they might ruin the delightful native costume and thus lessen Bali's attraction for tourists. Our Dutch friends were highly amused by what they called "The Great War" between the government/KPM* forces and the missionaries who were supported furtively by the textile industry. At issue was the exposed upper half of the Balinese women which the government and KPM wished to keep that way in the interest of the tourist trade. Though the missionaries had so far been beaten off, Mr. Campbell remained optimistic, placing his faith in the power of the Balinese women who were clamoring, so he said, to become converted.

We found the *Tjinegara* a good place to find out more about the life of the white man in the East. Mrs. Huyser told me long sad stories of her life in Shanghai. All the wives, she said, were terribly spoiled and equally dissatisfied. Nobody ever did anything useful. Day followed day in a dreary round of perpetual shopping, bridge, mahjong, dancing, and going to the races, with some mild adultery for spice. Still, anyone who had lived a while in the East could not

---

*Koninklijke Paketvaart Maatschappij, or Royal Packet Navigation Company, a government-owned steamship line, which monopolized inter-island trade and had a quasi-monopoly on tourism.

readjust to life back home either. This was true everywhere in the Orient. In the Indies, the men were paid high salaries and the women had hordes of servants. Every five years they received eight months' leave and a free trip home. They dreamed about this vacation all these years but, when they got home, Holland seemed too small and life too petty; they had dropped out of their former circle of friends and felt uncomfortable. Most could not wait to get back to the Indies where they promptly fell to grumbling again, and so on ad infinitum. Yet this sad life paid well, and love of money made exile preferable to a more soul-satisfying life at home. The Dutch profited from an empire which cost them nothing except additional expenditures on armaments for defense of the islands. About ten percent of the population of the Netherlands lived directly or indirectly off the Indies.

Another passenger, Mr. Smith, told how grim life could be for a young man in the Indies. He had spent much of his time in British colonies and so had a basis for comparison. Curiously, he had found it easier to make social contacts among the supposedly reserved British. Once you were admitted to a good club—usually through business contacts—and you played a decent game of tennis and golf, you found yourself directly in the midst of things. While the Dutch also had clubs, theirs were not social clubs giving one entree into family life, but specialized ones devoted to a single sport, such as tennis, golf, bowling, etc. You joined for the sport and didn't necessarily combine it with sociability. The Dutch were mostly involved with their families and not inclined to open their homes to lonely bachelors. This was also the French system. Smith preferred the English way—in fact we had a hard time remembering he was Dutch because he spoke English without an accent.

George and Mr. Huyser were getting to be fast friends—on the basis of a common nautical background, I guess. Both were on the Whangpoo River during the 1937 Japanese attack on Shanghai and enjoyed reminiscing. Having spent most of his adult life in the East, Mr. Huyser had witnessed the gradual decline of white prestige and of courteous international relations among the Great Powers. One of the last times the treaty powers comported themselves with the grave dignity customary in the good old days occurred during the summer months of 1937 when the Whangpoo was lined with the warships of the treaty powers, among them those of Japan; the Japanese shooting over the ships of the Chinese, setting the city of Shanghai on fire. Each morning at eight, the bands of the warships lined up on deck and greeted the new day with a series of national anthems: first their own, next that of the territorial sovereign—China, then in the process of deteriorating—and finally those of all the other warships in the order of the seniority of their commanders. With all the bands playing at the same time, the resultant cacophony was a fitting requiem to a vanishing era. Needless to say, the Japanese bands courteously played the Chinese anthem while their planes bombed Shanghai.

Inevitably George and Mr. Huyser turned to the subject of merchant marines and their relative worth. After some polite hemming and hawing, Huyser ventured that the American merchant marine was the worst in the world, barring the Chinese. He thought this was because we had no maritime tradition and ran our shipping companies on purely financial lines and for quick profit: "You can't build up a good merchant marine if the shipping lines are owned by financiers who use them as pawns in their stockmarket juggling. A tradition has to be built slowly and you can do it only if you treat crew, passengers, and shippers decently. Your ships have atrocious quarters for the crew; officers are treated little better than the men and, since they usually come up from the ranks, have little education. When your ships are laid up in port, you often force the captain to take an unpaid vacation. The worst of your companies is the Dollar Line. This could be a well-paying concern since it has an excellent freight run. Instead, it is a mess. You have a fine law requiring ships to give merchant marine cadets a few trial cruises, but the company directors circumvent the law by sending their sons and nephews on pleasure trips, calling them 'cadets.' You evade the law requiring seventy-five percent of the crew to be citizens and you cheat your shipyards of work by having repairs done cheaply in foreign ports. You do all this, despite the fact that the government pays large subsidies in order to have a trained merchant marine reserve in case of war." He was quite indignant. It wasn't pleasant to take this criticism but he obviously knew what he was talking about. Remembering a deck steward on a Dollar Line ship who had called an admiral's dignified wife "tootsie," and another steward who refused (because this was not his specific duty) when I asked him politely to help me push open my porthole, and a dozen more instances of poor service, we didn't have much to say to refute Mr. Huyser.

He told us that Dutch merchant marine officers are trained in special schools and usually remain with the same company—even on the same ship—for years at a time. If they do their jobs well, they can count on keeping their berth and advancing steadily; after twenty-five years they receive a decent pension. The pay is good and they get a percentage of profits. There are many competitions between ships for greater efficiency, satisfaction of passengers and shippers, lowering of costs, etc., which keep them on their toes despite the security of their jobs. Some of the KPM captains, cruising around the islands of the Indies on inter-island runs, made as much as five hundred guilders ($290.00) a month in bonuses alone based on the freight they carried.

According to Huyser, most other countries have similar systems. He felt that the Dutch maritime and air services were better than those of the British. They had to be, if they were to offset the advantages the British Empire afforded British enterprise in those days. For example, the Dutch air service from the Orient to Europe was then faster than the British, but the British made the Dutch unload all mail for India in Karachi, whence it had to be forwarded by train, thus offsetting the benefit of the shorter air run and giving British planes a chance to beat the competition. I don't know, but from what I saw of the Dutch, I suspect they engaged in similar practices, for never had I seen anything so tightly sewn up for the home interests as the Dutch East Indies!

George asked Mr. Huyser why the Japanese merchant marine, with its low wages, had not succeeded in ousting all other merchant marines. I was interested in his reply because I had not thought along these lines before. Huyser said Japan had a good merchant marine and treated officers and crews well, but it was curious how merchant marines always reflect their countries. No matter how much the Japanese tried to imitate foreign standards, their own ways of life invariably surfaced. People act in different ways and, more importantly, food is a very national affair. You can only cook good food if you like the food yourself. The Dutch liners served Dutch food and most people found it delicious; also their kind of cleanliness was liked by other white people. The Japanese tried hard but, he remarked, "They haven't got beyond fried chicken." For these reasons there was room for other shipping lines, particularly in passenger traffic.

The *Tjinegara* was certainly Dutch in every way and reminded me of what Samuel de Champlain said in *Les Voyages de la Nouvelle France*: Everything on a ship should be very neat and clean, after the fashion of the Flemings, who by common consent take first place in this respect over all seafaring nations. The ship positively glittered with cleanliness and was permeated with a certain Germanic atmosphere, as evidenced by the many long printed regulations tacked up everywhere. I found these useful for practicing Dutch. It is a language that surpasses even German in the length of individual words—one reason being the Dutch predilection for doubling vowels. The first few days I had a tantalizing sense of catching on when I heard Dutch spoken; a word now and then would be either completely German or completely English, for Dutch seems to be a curious amalgam of both these languages. After a week on board, I could understand much of the conversation and most of the radio bulletins posted by the purser.

When we got into our cabin, we were amused to see a large sign tacked above a contraption that resembled a baggage rack. It read *ALLEEN VOOR HOEDEN*, which means "for hats only." The idea of telling passengers that they could put only hats on this rack! We naturally piled lots of other things on it.

The bathroom was splendid and full of printed instructions on how to wash oneself and what not to do in the line of messing things up; it also contained a large wooden box filled with fresh water and covered with a wooden slab—somewhat reminiscent of old-fashioned outhouses, only much shinier. There was a large brass dipper for splashing oneself. This is the regulation way of taking a bath in both the Indies and Malaya, copied from the Malayan bath. Even when they bathe in a river, the Malays use a pail and splash the water over themselves, hair and all. It is the most refreshing way to bathe in the tropics. Another sidelight on Dutch cleanliness: the swimming tank on deck was constantly being emptied and filled with fresh water. There was seldom any time left for swimming.

Under the benevolent supervision of my new Dutch friends, I labored a little each day on improving my knowledge of Malay.* I had started to tackle this quaint language with its unfamiliar combinations of vowels and consonants before we left Manila. But all I had to work with was a small phrase book put out by the Dutch and a brief vocabulary of Malay as spoken in British Malaya. Although both taught *pasar* (bazaar) Malay, there were some differences in pronunciation and spelling. We had been unable to locate a proper grammar or textbook in Manila and were therefore delighted to find people who actually knew the language. I had trouble at first and it took me several days to learn the numbers from one to ten but then, all of a sudden, things went fast for this is really a simple language. Bazaar Malay is not difficult to learn. It is a sort of pidgin Malay which is spoken throughout the Malay Archipelago and British Malaya, though not in the Philippines. The language spoken by cultivated Malays, however, differs considerably in the different parts of this large area and is difficult to learn.

Malay is a charming language with few grammatical rules. One merely strings words along as they come naturally. You don't have to learn any irregular verbs. All verbs form the past tense by prefixing the word *sudah* (already), the future by adding *nanti* (wait). Dou-

*Malay is the name most commonly given to the brown-skinned branch of the Mongoloid or yellow race who inhabit the Malay Peninsula and the Malay Archipelago from Sumatra in the west to New Guinea in the east, and from the Philippines in the north to the Lesser Sunda Islands in the south. In this area the predominant race calls itself *orang melayu*—Malay man—and speaks a variety of languages belonging to the Malayo-Polynesian linguistic stock. Although these languages differ about as much as do those of Europe, communication is made easy by the widespread knowledge among these peoples of a sort of pidgin Sumatran Malay—which is called *pasar* or bazaar Malay, a modified form of the Malay language with a number of Portuguese, Chinese, and Dutch words altered to conform to Malayan pronunciation.

bling a noun puts it into the plural and, as a modern innovation—probably to save time—you may simply put the arabic numeral "2" beside a noun instead of doubling it. Thus *gigi* (tooth) becomes *gigi*^{2} for teeth and also indicates a dentist's office.

The Malays have a fine sense of humor. I like the way they have adapted their vocabulary, developed in a pre-industrial society, to such modern inventions as the telegram, which they call *surat kawat* (letter wire), the railroad, which they call *djalan keréta api* (fire wagon), and so forth. Some of their expressions are quite apt. The sun is *mata hari* (eye of the day), a spring of water is *mata ayer* (eye of water); the heart is *hati*, to have courage *berhati*, and to be careful *hati-hati*. If you want to insult someone, call him "less polite"—this is more cutting than calling him a *sapi* (cow). A person who likes to stuff himself is a "basket with a hole"; a successful man is one with "cold hands"; and a lucky home is a "cold house"—very expressive in a hot country!

The Malays are accustomed to making a slogan of the initials of well-known firms or brand names. The Koninklijke Nederlandsh-Indische Luchtvaart Maatschappij (KNILM)* was known as *Kalau naik ini lebih mati*, which means, "If you go up in this you will be dead." The Japanese, who had been trying to cause trouble for the Dutch in the islands, sometimes made effective use of this custom. A well-known medicine by the name of Dyintan was widely advertised with the picture of a hearty Japanese general. Presumably he became a general, and one in such obvious good health, by diligently imbibing Dyintan. The Japanese made a slogan of the initials, *Djenderal yan ini nanti tulung anak negri*, which means "This general will help the children of this country." Mr. Nater rather discounted these Japanese shenanigans, claiming that the Sino-Japanese War had lessened Malay enthusiasm for liberation by the Japanese. He said that the Chinese merchants—all loyal admirers of Chiang Kai-shek—were doing their best to squeeze out Japanese competitors. Anyone trying to compete with a Chinese storekeeper might just as well give up before trying.

One of the difficulties with Malay is that, like many primitive languages, it dispenses with most adjectives. Instead, it has a different word for almost every conceivable aspect of a single subject. For example, there are a hundred words for rice depicting its various stages of growth in the field or different ways of preparation in the cooking pot—things we would express with modifying adjectives.

Another vexing problem is the manner of addressing the person to whom one speaks. Not only is there a difference between formal

*Royal Netherlands Indies Airways

and informal "you"—the French *vous* and *tu*—but the whole mode of speaking varies, depending upon whether equals are speaking to one another, an inferior is addressing a superior, or vice versa. Of course, this applies more to high-class Malay than to bazaar Malay. Still, in view of the complications involved in getting the proper form of address, I usually dispensed with "you," speaking somewhat stiltedly in the third person. This is satisfying to the ego of the person to whom you speak—somewhat like addressing royalty. I had been warned not to talk bazaar Malay with upper-class Malays as they were apt to regard this as an insult. Whenever I spoke to a native not positively in rags, I was careful to try English first before switching to Malay. The Malays are a polite people and are appreciative when one tries to conform to their etiquette.

On the fourth day out, we had our first glimpse of the "Indies." We stopped at Menado, at the tip of Celebes. The people there look exactly like the Moros of the Southern Philippines, except that the women wear multi-colored sarongs "made in Japan" and, over these, tight-fitting white blouses with much lace around the edges. One could easily recognize in them a sanitized version of the black tight-fitting bodices of the Moro ladies we saw in Jolo.

The houses were on the ground, not on stilts, and cleaner than in Moroland—Dutch influence, no doubt. Those of the Dutch and wealthy Chinese were large, airy, surrounded by spacious, shady grounds, and had the entire front wall taken off so that they resembled stage settings. The open front room, in which Dutch householders used to spend most of their time, was called the *voorgalerij*.

It was still early when we wandered around Menado (7:00 a.m.) and we saw many pajama-clad figures sipping coffee, as they reclined in split-reed chairs. The Dutch morning in the colonies invariably began with early coffee in the *voorgalerij*—everyone in his night clothes. After that they bathed and shaved and had a real honest-to-goodness breakfast.

This northerly leg of Celebes (the island looks somewhat like a crab with long, crooked legs) is inhabited by the Minahassa, a tribe which embraced Christianity and is highly thought of by the Dutch. We were told that these people were almost like whites and so loyal that their country was often called the "twelfth province"—Holland proper having eleven provinces.

The next day we sailed into Macassar which I found disappointing because I had read so much about its alleged picturesqueness. The harbor is, in fact, attractive with its hundreds of graceful praus—their high sterns crowded against each other. Macassar is the capital of Celebes and the center of an important entrepôt trade with the islands, from which spices, copra, and fruit are brought by native praus for shipment abroad in freighters. One of the native peoples, the Buginese of Macassar, are excellent sailors and, like their distant cousins the Philippine Moros, are recently reformed pirates. Also like the Moros, they are quick to take offense and tend to run amok. The government has forbidden them to carry weapons, but nobody pays any attention to this rule. Personally, I think the Filipinos handle the Moros more sensibly, merely demanding that weapons be left at the entrance of the weekly market so that business can proceed undisturbed. This much can be accomplished, but to try and disarm permanently the fierce Moslem Buginese would obviously be impossible.

The Dutch took Macassar from a Portuguese trade monopoly, almost three hundred years ago, by defeating native forces in 1667. But as late as 1905 they still had trouble with the native rajas. In that year the whole Dutch population was ordered for the last time inside the walls of Fort Rotterdam, where so often in the past they had sought refuge from native attack. The fort dates from the time of the Portuguese, with whose assistance it was built by the Macassars. It was captured from the King of Goa by the Dutch under Admiral Cornelis Speelman in 1667. Inside its walls is found a most authentic bit of the Holland of that period. There is an old church surrounded by several high-gabled buildings which look oddly medieval with their many-paned, shuttered windows. The walls are thick and in the center court there are wells and shady old trees. When the Dutch drove the Portuguese out (as they had driven them from so many outposts in this area), the entire Dutch population lived in Fort Rotterdam. Now it is but a relic, guarded by native soldiers wearing strange green uniforms with Napoleonic tricorn hats.

We arrived in time for the changing of the guard. The soldiers marched in German goose-step manner. When we teased our Dutch friends on the *Tjinegara* later that evening, they said that only the native troops did the goose-step, but we remained skeptical. The discipline of the guard was magnificent and suffered only slightly when we got in the way to take pictures of their complicated evolutions. They, like the fort, seemed authentic seventeenth century and as out of place in this modern world as all the more spectacular manifestations of colonialism.

One of the major handicrafts of Macassar was gold and silver filigree work. We saw a great deal of it; all finely done but in execrable taste and as outdated as the antimacassars with which Victorian ladies used to protect their upholstery against male heads drenched in Macassar oil. Come to think of it, Victorian ladies wore filigree brooches! Without question, Macassar hadn't caught up with the times.

We felt less depressed when we saw our first Malay dentist shops. The garish signs of *GIGI GIGI* or *GIGI*² above hideous giant-sized replicas of parts of the human jaw enlivened the slightly decayed atmosphere of past glory that permeated the city. We were intrigued with exhibits of black artificial teeth, although a moment's reflection showed us how indispensable these would be among a people whose standards of beauty called for pitch-black teeth and blood-red gums dripping betel juice. Best of all were the displays of gold crowns with cutout stars or crescents. A gold tooth was the great ambition of every native—for about 75 cents (American) he could have a thin layer of gold leaf cemented on a healthy tooth. Through the cutout stars or crescents, the good tooth would then shine in black splendor. Dentists were obviously doing a thriving business.

We thought Macassar was too clean, too orderly, too Dutch, and not at all as we had pictured it from Joseph Conrad's stories. We looked at the Oranje Hotel which was the Sunda Hotel in *Almayer's Folly*. It had been renovated and did not look the way I had imagined it. There were many fine old solid stone buildings in the city—Dutch warehouses for the most part. Once the city teemed with life and commerce. It had been the meeting place and vacation spot of many adventurers sailing about in this somewhat lawless part of the world. The Dutch imposed law and order, the Depression ruined the spice and copra trade, and many of the whites brought their wives with them. Macassar is now a tame place and Conrad would be disappointed if he saw it today.

2
Bali

When we saw the first faint outline of Bali, I felt somewhat disillusioned for it looked like hundreds of other tropical islands we had seen. Foolishly, I had expected it would be different, that somehow we should recognize it right away as Bali. There was an air of excitement on board the *Tjinegara* and suddenly, for the first time on the entire trip, people grouped themselves according to nationality. The time of easy shipboard friendship was over.

We discovered that the Dutch are highly resentful when foreigners disregard their efficient tourist services. Mr. Spit almost lost his good manners when we mentioned casually that we were not planning to use the KPM services but intended to set out on our own. Although he was a JCJL man, and hence one of KPM's competitors, his tourist-manager heart could not bear to see us travel about independently. "I can't understand why people who spend thousands of dollars on a trip around the world try to save a few guilders by not using a service that can offer so much since it specializes in showing tourists around. The KPM goes to all the trouble of making Bali accessible and easy to travel in and people won't use it." When we gently reminded him there were other reasons besides saving guilders that might induce people to want to see Bali on their own—such as a constitutional dislike for being herded like sheep—he quickly saw his slip and hastened to assure us that he could quite understand our attitude and that he, himself, rather liked to be on his own. But this sudden outburst of the otherwise staid and impeccably courteous gentleman revealed to us Dutch touchiness in a matter which we should never have guessed to be of such importance to them.

The day we boarded the *Tjinegara*, the purser asked us whether we had made reservations at *the* hotel in Bali—the KPM hostelry at Den Pasar—since it was likely to be crowded. He also handed us a printed request for the standard KPM tour of Bali. With the pilot boat at Buleleng, Bali's northern harbor, there arrived a representative of that admirable organization and he almost succeeded in bundling us into one of the KPM cars by sheer willpower. However, we managed

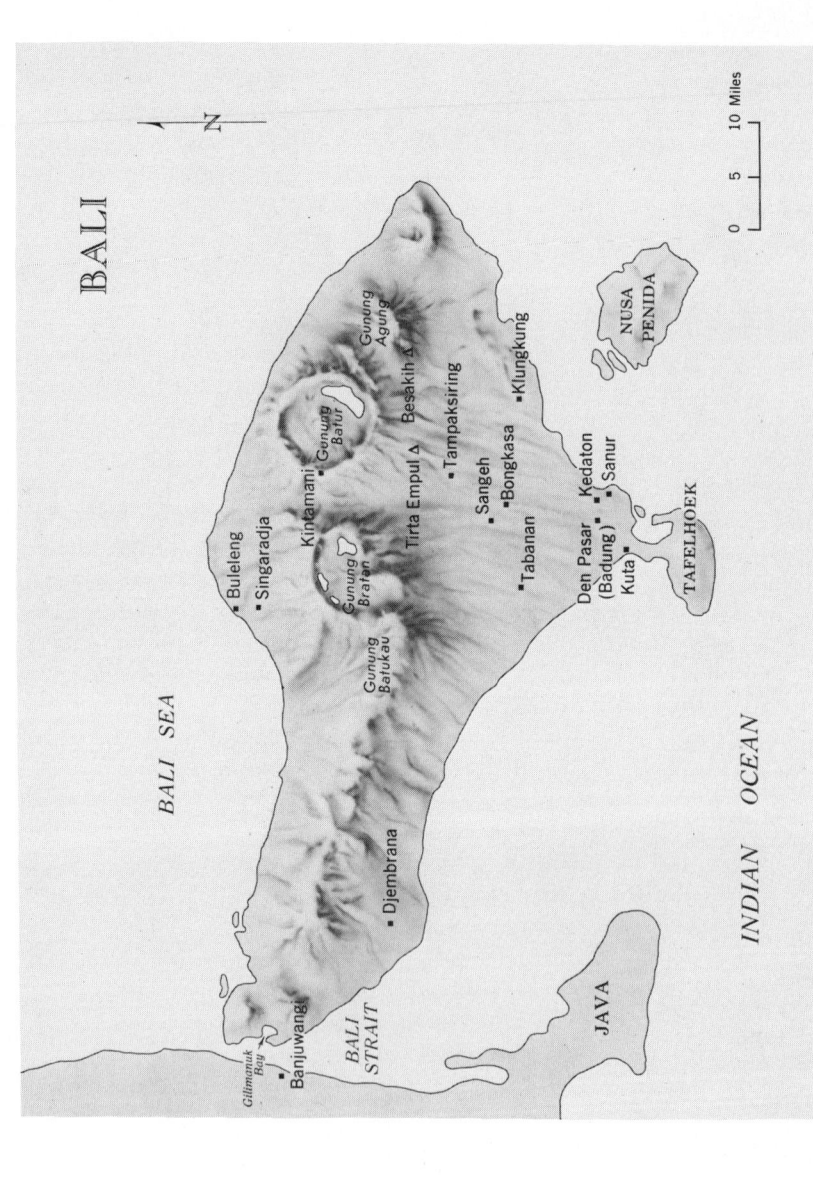

to escape him, though not without having been made to feel cheap and wicked. Our worst crime was that we spurned the KPM hotel in Den Pasar. We had decided to stay at a recently opened hotel run by Americans that had been highly recommended by friends who had stayed there.

The Dutch have a preference for systematizing everything. For a long time they resented the intrusion of foreigners into their island kingdom. They wanted to exploit it themselves. Slowly it became obvious that money might be made from tourists. So, in their own methodical way, they proceeded to publicize the islands, putting out beautiful folders with artistically perfect photographs and interesting material on native life. They worked out splendid itineraries, covering everything of historic or artistic interest they felt should be seen, and built hotels to look after the foreign tourists' comfort—at a good price, of course. Having put much earnest effort into this scheme, they were resentful if one did not take advantage of it. Personal loss of tourist dollars was not the whole reason either. Virtually all the Netherlanders we met resented our resistance to the Dutch tourist service, though they themselves disliked the autocratic behavior of KPM, which used its monopoly to charge exorbitant prices. One of their less endearing capers was to refuse sale of anything but first-class tickets to white persons, allegedly to uphold Dutch prestige but also to increase KPM profits, no doubt. Some of the Dutch were clever and sent their native servants to buy second-class tickets; then KPM could only fuss and fume. We were quite proud of never once using their services on any of our trips—they just were not for us.

The *Tjinegara* stopped at Buleleng only long enough for us to disembark into a small motorboat, then immediately steamed off to Surabaja, Java. There is no natural harbor in Bali; hence big ships must anchor some distance from shore.

It was a sunny, hot day and our first glimpse of Bali showed nothing worth traveling halfway around the world to see. There were a small customs shed and a KPM office with a row of motorcars lined up in front. Now came my first chance to practice what I had so laboriously learned. My Dutch friends had drilled me in the proper way to hire a car and I had my sentences pat. The principal thing was to appear nonchalant. George stood aside to let me do my bargaining and I knew he didn't expect much so I took extra trouble to do things right. I wandered along the cars, inspecting them carefully, pointing out worn tires or cracked windows, showing no interest if addressed in English, and replying firmly *terlalu mahal* (too much) whenever a price was mentioned. First they wanted 17 guilders for the 100-kilometer trip to Den Pasar. I said I might possibly pay eight, at which they threw up their hands in dismay, telling me a long sad tale of how expensive gas was. This had no effect on me. Finally, one car-owner remarked that the problem was the empty run back from Den Pasar; if he didn't have to consider that, he could rent us a car for 7½ cents a kilometer plus food for the driver. This was, of course, exactly what we wanted but he had not intended it for a bid. I hastily nailed him down and, before he knew what was happening, he had rented us a fairly good Chevrolet and a serious chauffeur in a faded sarong and slightly rakish, ragged turban who did all our driving for us during our stay in Bali. The owner hadn't expected me to understand him or to overwhelm him with a flood of Malay and he still looked dazed when we drove off. This was a good bargain and I felt proud of myself. Sitting beside the driver, I showed off by ordering him to slow down, speed up, or stop. I was a "pain in the neck" in the first flush of triumph at actually speaking a language of which I had not known a single word two weeks before!

The driver's name was long and unpronounceable so George baptized him Abdullah. Throughout our trip we called all our drivers Abdullah—it was wonderful how quickly they got used to the new name.

We stopped at a *pura* (temple) en route—the first of a long procession of *puras*, all intricately carved of greyish stone and usually placed in some lovely grove. Then we drove into the mountains at Kintamani Pass where there is a splendid view of Lake Batur and the Guning Agung and Gunung Batur—two still-active volcanoes that dominate almost every scene in Bali. At first we were disappointed in the villages we passed for they looked like typical native villages and we had expected better. But as soon as we started downhill from the pass, we came into southern Bali where the real Balinese life centers around Den Pasar and the villages took on an entirely different character. They lined both sides of the road and were often hidden behind long, grey, moss-topped walls, interspersed at regular intervals by high, intricately carved doorways. These doorways opened into courtyards with several balés (straw-covered pavilions), each inhabited by one family. Such Balinese families include all manner of relatives, and so a courtyard may house a considerable number of people.

Many villages were noticeable because of their *waringin* (banyan) tree, the sacred tree of the Hindus. They grow to a large size, often shading the entire village square, and spread by aerial roots from the branches that, upon touching the ground, also grow into trees. Sometimes we saw village councils meeting under the widespread branches of these huge old trees. More often, the sudden appearance of grey walls indicated the presence of a village. As we drove along by the walls, we got an occasional glimpse into a narrow passageway branching off the main road and leading to village temple, village green, or velvety green *sawah* (rice field). These paths, flanked by mossy grey walls, were deeply shaded, quiet, and mysterious. Clumps of coconut palms stood about the terraced rice fields, giving them a park-like effect. There were many deep ravines, for the soil is so soft that rivers sink down quickly. The *sawahs* often perch as precariously on the terraced hillsides along the rivers as do those of the Igorots in northern Luzon. But in Bali everything is graceful and delicate, not grand as in Luzon. There are two mountain complexes. In the central highland a volcanic formation rises over 7,000 feet on Gunung Batukau, or Tabanan Peak, and the volcanic crater of Bratan. The eastern highland has the 10,308-foot volcanic cone of Gunung Agung, or Peak of Bali, with its smaller active companion, the crater of Gunung Batur. The remainder of Bali is mostly gentle hillsides and undulating plains. The country is unbelievably lovely and everything done by humans has enhanced its natural beauty.

Often we saw in the rice fields small shrines, directed to the harvest deities. There was always an offering of flowers or grain artistically arranged. Each field had a small shelter built into a tree where we sometimes saw small Balinese boys watching for the white rice birds. Strings were drawn across the ripening fields to which weird contraptions of tin and wood were attached. The boys were supposed to shake the strings when birds appeared, to scare them away with the noise. This would be a good system were it not for the well-known propensity of small boys to doze in the warm sun. Still, enough rice grows on this lovely island to feed both the birds and the Balinese.

As we drove on, we passed many temples built of crumbling grey sandstone, a conglomerate of volcanic ash called *paras*, and we were impressed with the fantastic intricacy of the stone carvings. The temples were not so much buildings as enclosed courtyards. Many had a strange split entrance gateway called *tjandi-bentar*. The ceremonial gateway to the inner courtyard was called *padu-raksa* and was guarded by two fearful *raksasas* (giants)—its temple-watchers. The *tjandi-bentar* looked as if a regular stone temple gate had been split down the center and the two parts moved apart to form an opening. The one or more outer courtyards were often used for village purposes of a non-religious nature, such as council meetings and storage of food. In Bali, life is permeated with religion and there is no clear delineation between the spiritual and the mundane. The inner courtyard was reserved for the gods to whom offerings were made on several *merus*—slender, wooden, pagoda-like structures that faintly resemble Chinese pagodas. They consist of an uneven number (from three to eleven) of superimposed, curved roofs made from thick layers of palm fiber. We were told that they were symbolic of the mountains

A village street in Bali

Sawahs

Merus

whose summits the Balinese believe to be the abode of their gods. But it seems likely to me that, if there were such an indigenous concept, it had been merged with the Hindu idea of a mythical Mount Meru where dwell Brahma and Vishnu with their wives Sarasvati and Lakshmi. Indian temples were looked upon as symbols of Mount Meru.

The temples, with their moss-covered crumbling stones, appeared to be incredibly old but they were not old at all. The stone is volcanic and so soft that it breaks up after a few years, looking ancient and beautiful. This is fortunate because it has kept the Balinese continually busy carving new temples so that their art has remained living and never in danger of being lost.

Whenever we came to a crossroads, we would find a small grassy plot enclosed by stones with a carved god on a sort of altar in the center. Abdullah pointed to one of them and said it was Gana. This is the Hindu guardian of travelers who sees to it that they find the right way and arrive home safely. Thus well-protected, we always got where we wanted to go on our wanderings through Bali.

Robert Koke, part owner of the Kuta Beach Hotel, awaited us when we arrived there in the fast growing dusk and said he could put us up. We found ourselves presently in a small cottage, strongly reminiscent of shelters along the Appalachian Trail. Everything needed was there but no unnecessary frills. We used kerosene lamps because the hotel had no electricity. The washing facilities and WC were in a small building. To get there one wandered through a coconut grove with a beautiful beach on one side where the surf rumbled constantly. It was all most satisfying and exactly what one would like to find on a tropical island.

Koke had been a technical advisor for the Hollywood production *Mutiny on the Bounty* which was filmed in Bali; when the others left he decided to remain. He and a Mrs. Garrett, a divorcee, had financed and now managed the Kuta Beach Hotel. I think they must have planned the hotel with the typical American longing for tropical romance in mind. The guests slept in individual small cottages nestled in a coconut grove. Each had a charming front porch overlooking the beach and a high-ceilinged bedroom. With windows and doors open—all of them screened, of course, for this was an American enterprise—it was wonderfully cool at night. The KPM victims in Den Pasar, on the other hand, sweltered in a splendidly modern hotel with all the latest conveniences and the hottest climate in all Bali. That we had no running water was no hardship and fitted well into the "life on a tropical isle" game we were playing. The regular Malay-type bath was just the right thing after a hot and tiring day of sightseeing.

Later we heard that the KPM and the Dutch officials in Bali were at first hostile to the would-be American hoteliers, but realized gradually that the Kuta Beach Hotel catered to a different kind of tourist and brought in trade that might otherwise not come at all. Even so, Koke found it necessary to kowtow assiduously to Dutch officialdom.

Dinner was served on the lawn facing the beach at small tables lighted by kerosene lamps with fantastic Balinese shades. All the *djongos* (male waiters or houseboys) were tall, handsome youths in sarongs who *dok-doked* (crouched on the ground) whenever they served us and played soft tinkly music between courses.

Mrs. Garrett, attractive in the dim light, was a gracious hostess but she did not have much success in promoting a companionable atmosphere because everybody was tired from sightseeing. A middle-aged American couple with rather tight mouths frowned upon the brown nakedness around them and clearly did not approve of waiters wearing hibiscus blossoms behind the ear and women with no covering from the waist up. On the other hand, an elderly English lady with a kindly face proclaimed loudly and firmly that only the Balinese knew true art. She was a painter and intrigued us with her costume—evening clothes as befitted an English lady—even in regions where others might easily let down standards, but of what period? George thought perhaps 1900. Two American businessmen traveling through the Indies to inspect various branches of their firm ate rapidly and discussed business without a glance at their exotic surroundings. An old woman with purple-tinted hair and her face a mask of whitish makeup, ropes of pearls around her wrinkled neck, and an air of insufferable boredom amused herself throwing money to the *djongos*, preening herself as Lady Bountiful.

That evening a native opera was being staged in a village some twenty miles away. Although it had been a long day, we decided to see it. The performance was scheduled to begin at ten o'clock but when we arrived at eleven o'clock there was still no sign of a show. The entire village had congregated in the square and an impromptu market was going full swing. The Balinese always have a market when such festivities as village councils, shadow plays, concerts, dances, or funerals are in progress. The women bring out their simple paraphernalia, consisting of a board or table covered with various dishes containing unknown edibles, a wooden bowl, and a spoon. They sit behind their display and have a gay time gossiping, flirting, and watching the crowds while making a little pin money. They look quite handsome, with a towel twisted around their heads from which a long black bunch of hair cascades to one side of their smooth heart-shaped faces. Their eyes are large, lustrous, and shaded with long lashes; their small cupid's bow mouths with the two front teeth protruding slightly are attractive. In the flickering light of small kerosene lamps, they enhance the colorful scene. One vivacious belle in a red blouse, flanked by two gallants courting her strenuously, made an especially attractive picture. The love-making was frank and open, yet somehow nothing the Balinese do becomes offensive. We found out later that only *Sudra* women, members of the fourth, or lowest, Hindu caste go about bare above the waist. This girl must have been of a higher caste. On her the red blouse was more enticing than bareness.

A man with a simple soda fountain caught our fancy. He stood behind a small table which held four bottles containing strongly colored liquids—red, purple, blue, green—a plate with a medium-sized piece of ice, a rusty tin can of water, and several cracked glasses; none clean. For two kepengs—at that time, about one quarter of one American penny—you could buy a sweet drink. For this moderate price you could choose any one or a mixture of all the colored sirups and he would squirt a little into your glass. Then he would carefully shave a tiny sliver off his piece of ice and fill the glass with water from the tin can. His movements were exactly like those of an American soda fountain clerk—the same elegant swish of the hand as it dips into the various containers; the same deft movement as the glass is placed before the customer and the coins are swept into the till. A perfect tropical replica! The man must have watched the authentic thing in a movie.

We waited and waited for the opera to begin. George and I wandered down the village street and into one of the side paths. It was foggy, the moon was full, and we had the sensation of walking into a fairy story. Suddenly a figure materialized out of the fog and, for an instant, I actually felt scared and thought it was Rangda, the Witch. Rangda is a fearful creature with a great shock of white hair, an enormous tongue, and long white fangs. She appears in almost every Balinese dance and I had seen many pictures of her. One, an especially fearful likeness in Covarrubias' book *Island of Bali* must have made a deep impression on me for I am not normally an imaginative person. That night the spell of Bali was upon me and I could have believed almost anything.

At twelve-thirty we gave up. The Balinese have no sense of time and, once started on dissipation, they don't care if it lasts until morning. Loss of sleep can always be made up during the hot midday. We were told the opera could not begin since they still had a lot of food. Quite sensibly it was felt that, as long as the women had a chance to sell their concoctions, one ought not to interfere. The men, in the meantime, had found plenty to occupy them. Those not making love were crowded around two gaming tables in back of the square, having a wonderful time losing all the kepengs their wives were slowly collecting out front.

In Bali you are never at a loss for entertainment at almost any time of the night. We had heard that there was a puppet shadow play (*wayang kulit*) going on somewhere else and, since we did not wish to miss it, we reluctantly gave up the opera. Just to see the market had been worth motoring 20 miles, especially since driving on a moonlit night through Bali is heaven itself.

The shadow play was in full swing when we arrived. The audience sat in the road in front of a flimsy wooden stage. Should a car wish to pass, the stage could quickly be moved and the audience would goodnaturedly scramble up and disperse. As soon as it had passed, the play would resume.

The shadow plays are based on old Hindu tales handed down unchanged for generations. Everybody knows the tales by heart and the hundreds of figures that take part in the plays are known to every Balinese child. The *kulit* (leather) figures, cut out of gilded or painted water-buffalo hide, have fragile legs and arms and are controlled by attached sticks. The puppet master sits in a small hut raised on poles and manipulates the figures between an oil lamp and a transparent screen stretched across one open side of the hut. His musicians sit behind him and a boy acts as propman.

Our arrival made hardly a ripple in the stirring drama going on among the shadows. People smiled at us and grinned approval when we indicated we wanted to climb into the hut and see things backstage. The puppet master, who is also called the *dalang* (storyteller), was an emaciated old man apparently in the last stages of TB but such a marvelous actor that you forgot him completely in the fascination of his performance. He was completely absorbed in his stories and gave every bit of himself. Great rumbling noises issued from his frail body when some terrible ogre appeared on the stage, and furious shrieks shook his slender frame when a hapless puppet was beaten senseless. We could not understand a word—and probably not many in the audience could either, since the language was high Malay—but the stories were so adeptly portrayed that we were able to follow them quite well. We could have listened for hours. Occasionally, the puppet master took a long drink from a bottle and deftly spat betel juice into a hole in the floor. His wonderfully expressive, seamed old face broke into a radiant smile when we thanked him politely at the end of the show. It had been a full day and I fell asleep as we drove through the quiet moonlit villages.

We had planned a busy day. At breakfast a guest greeted us with a smile and asked if we had noticed our audience. "I guess you are the most interesting couple here, so no wonder the *djongos* had their eyes glued to your cottage window this morning." "Oh, we know," said George, "Ruth asked them to bring warm shaving water and they did." We had lived long enough in the Orient not to be disconcerted at evidences of the overwhelming curiosity of the natives. Compared to them, we whites are simply bundled up in clothes and so, of course, they are curious to see how we really look.

The Sacred Forest near Sangeh was the first item on our program that morning. On the way we passed through Den Pasar—a neat little town, full of Indian, Chinese, and Arab shops, and dominated by the KPM hotel. It was the scene of the heroic *puputan* of the Prince of Badung. A *puputan* (the end or, more accurately, the last stand) is a distinctly Balinese occurrence, a suicidal stand usually led by a raja or Balinese prince against an overwhelming enemy in which his household or village participates and everyone dies, either at the enemy's or his own hand.

The *puputan* of the Prince of Badung came as the climax to a series of incidents between the Dutch and the Balinese rajas that lasted from 1904 to 1906. The Dutch, though willing to rule with a light hand, insisted on the maintenance of certain minimum standards of order and humaneness which the rajas refused to accept. The Dutch insisted that *suttee* (the burning of widows on the funeral piles of their husbands) be stopped, and this the princes had promised to do. Nevertheless *suttees* of three widows occurred in Tabanan during this period. In another instance, the Dewa Agung of Klungkung offended Dutch notions of justice by meting out stern punishment to two of his daughters who had erred from the path of virtue in company with two young men he considered totally unfit to become their husbands. The Dewa had the hands of the daughters tied behind their backs and their live bodies thrown to the sharks. One of the men was tortured to death but the other escaped. The princes were often cruel but, since they seldom interfered with normal village life, the people did not object to their cruelties. What finally brought these and other frictions to a head and induced the Dutch to send an expedition to subdue the Balinese princes was the plunder of a Chinese schooner, the *Sri Koemala* at Sanur in May of 1904. This was an affair of such insignificance that it can hardly be regarded as justification for war, but it was the proverbial straw that broke the camel's back and Dutch patience had worn thin.

As has been their custom, the Balinese considered that anything thrown on their shores by the sea was legitimate loot. The *Sri Koemala* was wrecked in a storm and foundered offshore. The Balinese helped the crew to safety and even set a guard to watch over the property that had been salvaged by the ship's crew. Apparently the guard fell asleep and some boxes were stolen. The Chinese owner assessed these at 200 ringgits, or about 500 guilders. While the wreck was lying offshore, abandoned by its crew, some wood and brass fittings were removed from the ship. The Chinese owner lodged an official complaint, but was refused payment by the Prince of Badung. The dickering went on for two years. By the time the owner submitted his figures to the Dutch, the estimated losses had grown to 3,000 guilders. Later, after South Bali had been conquered, he received from the Dutch government the sum of 7,500 guilders. It was good business for the Chinese owner but his profit strikes one as excessive, considering the mass immolation to which it led.

Faced with overwhelming Dutch military might, the Prince of Badung decided on *puputan*. On the morning of September 20, 1906, he burned his *puri* (palace), then he and his entire court marched forth to meet the Dutch. The men wore red and black sarongs and each, even the small boys, carried his most precious, jewel-encrusted *kris* (sacred ancestral dagger). The women put on their best clothes and all their jewels. Mothers carried their babies and led their older children by the hand. Bruce Lockhart describes the scene in these eloquent words:

> At nine o'clock, when the first news of the Dutch advance was received, the little band, barely 250 strong, moved forward along what is now the main road. According to custom the prince went first, carried on the shoulders of one of his household. Not even the Persians advancing on Leonidas's seven hundred at Thermopylae could have been more astonished than was the Dutch infantry company when on that September morning it caught its glimpse of this glittering array moving slowly forward to a certain death. Only three hundred paces separated the two forces, and the Dutch had a machine-gun. To do him justice, the Dutch captain did all he could by signs and shouting to persuade the Balinese to surrender. But they had already committed their souls to heaven.
>
> Unheeding, they advanced until they were so close that the captain dared no longer endanger the lives of his own men. At seventy yards the Balinese charged, and the Dutch captain gave the order to fire. Many fell. Those who survived pressed forward until they, too, were shot down. Women, afraid lest they might be spared, bared their breasts and pointed to their heart in order that they might die a warrior's death. The wounded committed suicide or begged their companions to finish them off. One old man, jumping nimbly over the heap of corpses, krissed all who remained alive until he himself was shot dead.
>
> While the slaughter was at its height, a second force of Balinese approached. It was headed by the prince's half-brother, a youth of twelve scarcely able to carry his lance. The captain summoned him to surrender. For a moment he hesitated. Then, urged on by his followers,

he gave the order to charge. All met the same fate, When the firing ceased, a few children were seen crawling away from the heaps of corpses. They were the only survivors. . . . The body of the prince was found at the very bottom of the highest heap. He had led the way and had fallen first. His dead followers had made a human cairn over him.*

Lockhart based this description on the historic facts reported in a book by Dr. van Weede, a Dutch member of the expedition of 1906 who witnessed the *puputan*.

Vicki Baum, in her *Tale of Bali*, gives a vivid picture of life in Bali in the years preceding the final conquest in 1906. Perhaps because her book is based on a manuscript left her by Dr. Fabius, a long-time Dutch resident in Bali, she has succeeded better than anyone I know in penetrating native life and making it understandable to the Westerner. Though she leaves the reader deeply stirred by her story of the heroic *puputan* of Badung, she is fair to the Dutch. The great mass of the Balinese were probably better off under the light Dutch rule than they were under their rajas. As Vicki Baum says in the foreword to her book: ". . . the Dutch have carried out an achievement in colonization that reflects the highest credit on them. Scarcely anywhere in the world are natives free to live their own lives under white rule so happily and with so little interference and change as in Bali; and I would like to believe . . . that the self-sacrifice of so many Balinese at that time . . . had a deep significance, since it impressed upon the Dutch the need of ruling this proud and gentle island people as considerately as they have, and kept Bali the paradise it is even today."

Bali, slightly smaller than the state of Delaware and with a population of over a million, was ruled from Dutch headquarters in Singaradja by a Dutch Resident, two Assistant Residents, seven Controleurs, and a few police—a handful of Dutch of whose presence one was hardly conscious.

We could find nothing in Den Pasar to remind us of these historic events. Where the *puri* of the ill-fated Prince of Badung once stood we found a museum and a football field. Of the princely gardens only two huge *waringin* trees remained; they grew near the main street intersection where a modern clock had been installed for the convenience of tourists. On the spot where the palace temple once stood, the KPM hotel had been erected, and the road where the gallant band marched to their death had become a drab street of garages, Japanese photo studios, and Hindu curio shops selling the famous carved wooden Balinese heads.

---

*R. H. Bruce Lockhart, *Return to Malaya*, pp. 327–328.

As soon as we got out of our car at Sangeh we were surrounded by dozens of small grey monkeys, incredibly tame and determined to extract their proper quota of peanuts and bananas from each visitor. They were so eager to get these that they climbed up our legs and pulled at my dress. They ate out of our hands without fear. I could have watched them for hours. Their most intimate family affairs could be observed, giving us an excellent view of monkey life. Oddly enough, there were distinct resemblances between monkey life and Malayan life. As did Malayan mothers, monkey mothers were busy delousing their offspring and occasionally spanking them; a few thoughtful males sat on their haunches staring into space; females sat together gossiping and picking lice out of each other's hair—the monkey females ate the lice and so got more enjoyment out of this daily routine than did the Malays. The young males chased the young females and the big ones got all the best peanuts. All very human.

As we walked through the split temple door, the monkeys followed, one faithful (or greedy) character holding on firmly to my skirt all the while. We were greeted by a wonderfully handsome and dignified old gentleman with a most expressive face. He was the temple priest. We walked through a quiet lovely forest, reaching a temple which stood in a sacred spot—one of the most peaceful places I have ever seen. Huge old trees shaded the small stone altars with their odd grinning little gods before whom flower and fruit offerings had been laid. Our dignified guide showed us around and demonstrated how one should pray to the gods. He didn't object to our photographing him or the temple. When we had finished, he suggested that we might wish to sacrifice to the gods which we did while he looked discreetly away. In their paternal way, the Dutch forbade solicitations in temples; one paid instead a fixed fee for which a receipt was given. We were amused by the old Brahman's ingenious way of getting around this rule. The Balinese look on their gods in a practical way. They offer them fruits and flowers, but the gods are supposed to take only the essence of the food; the faithful eat what is left. Something like this undoubtedly happened to our money offering, too.

From Sangeh we drove to the village of Bongkasa, where we saw a *waringin* tree whose branches spread over an area at least an acre in extent. The tree has been regarded as sacred since before the advent of Hinduism, which is tolerant of older faiths. It had its own small temple, beside which sat a fat gentleman with a book in his lap surrounded by villagers. We started a conversation involving an exchange of information about our respective names, ages, origins, and destinations. This was well-covered by the list of useful phrases Mr. Nater had made me write out and memorize. It was more difficult to discuss what we all did for a living. I suspected the man of being a

Monkeys at Sangeh

Split entrance gate (tjandi-bentar) at Sangeh

tax collector and he nodded delightedly when I said to him "You ask money these men; put money this pocket; write money this book; go *raja belanda* (white king); give money to *raja belanda*." Basic Malay, that's what it was. When he wanted to know what George did for a living, I first thought of calling him an *orang laut*, which means man of the sea. I thought, "Heck, let's do this up proud." "This one *raja laut*," I said. Everyone was impressed to be entertaining such illustrious foreigners and so we took photographs and left, with many expressions of mutual regard. Later I found out that *Orang Laut* is the name given to the Sea Gypsies, a somewhat disreputable Malay tribe of roving folk who spend their lives on boats and live by fishing and, until recently, piracy.

After lunch we set out to visit a temple perched high upon a cliff at the southeastern tip of Bali on a peninsula called at that time Tafelhoek. Part of the way we drove over short grass which looked like a lawn. We stopped at a pretty grove and ascended the steep stairs. At the top we had a magnificent view over the Pacific—we could have seen clear to Australia, had our eyes been good enough to see that far. The temple was built at the edge of a precipice above foaming surf. Some young men who were working on the temple gladly stopped to help us photograph each other and to ask the usual personal questions. They got a great kick out of watching the surf through the viewfinder in our camera.

On the way home we were in high spirits and everything threw us into fits of laughter. George saw some carabao, or water buffalo, with tinkling wooden bells around their necks. We had seen these animals many times in the Philippines—in fact, George had ridden on one. He decided he had to have the bells and made Abdullah stop the car. Disdaining my help, he went to interview the cowherd. Pointing at a carabao, George offered ten cents. (By this time he had learned to say in Malay: "ten cents," "bring shave water quickly," and "go away.") The cowherd, thinking George wanted to buy the carabao for ten cents, thought this a huge joke and shrieked with laughter. George then ran after the carabao and, catching the beast, pointed to the bells and repeated his offer. This seemed to the cowherd an even better joke for the bells were not worth a tenth of the price offered. These doings had attracted the entire village which found our wanting to buy cowbells hilarious. The carabao didn't like the whole business and ran away, with George, the cowherd, and the village in hot pursuit. Finally, George got back into the car with the bells which we draped in the windows. They made quite a racket, causing the Balinese in each village great amusement. Even dignified Abdullah grinned from ear to ear. I am sure everyone was more than ever convinced that all Americans were crazy.

A ride on a carabao

Every Friday evening there was a Balinese dance at the KPM hotel in Den Pasar and we went and sat brazenly among the exploited "schedule" tourists, with all of native Den Pasar crowded around and behind us. The dancers wore beautifully embroidered garments of gold cloth. Their performance struck me as at once artistically perfect yet not wholly satisfying, because the audience and the setting were artificial and out of place. Even so, we enjoyed watching the graceful movements of hands and head, and the tinkling music of the *gamelan*—a native orchestra composed almost entirely of percussion instruments.* The dance movements were made from the waist upwards and the legs were either crossed or straight and, if the latter, they remained in identical posture throughout the dance.

Saturday was our fullest day and the high point of the entire visit. In the morning we drove to Kedaton, near Den Pasar, where another KPM-inspired dance took place. The setting was quite right this time—a square in front of a temple, shaded by large old trees. But the time of day and the audience were even less appropriate than the night before. It was too hot and the group of bored tourists must have had a depressing effect on the dancers. People were constantly getting up and wandering about, taking photographs of the dancers from every angle; it was a wonder the dance could continue.

We saw a *djanger*—a dance dating back only to about 1920 and popular with the young people—in which the dancers form a square with girls facing girls and boys facing boys. The girls wore elaborate and attractive headdresses and the boys wore around their handsome heads the usual picturesque rag—purple at this particular dance. Both tied their sarongs just below the armpits and remained in a sitting position through most of the dance, moving only their upper bodies, especially hands, heads, and eyes. A *dag* (dancemaster) sat in the center and directed the movements of the dance and the singing of the groups—somewhat like the fiddler who calls the figures in a Virginia Reel. A Hindu epic was enacted, some of the members of the group impersonating heroes and monsters.

We also saw a *legong*, an intricate, fast-moving dance performed by three richly dressed small girls, who seemed to be in a trance. Often it is explained by a *dalang* who introduces the various characters represented. Girls stop dancing the *legong* when they reach adolescence. The baby faces of the performers retain the same fixed expression throughout the dance while their agile fingers flutter and their heads, necks, and eyes move jerkily in a most fascinating manner.

---

*Gongs, drums, cymbals, xylophones, bells, flutes, and two-stringed lutes. The stands that supported these instruments were beautifully carved.

Their expression is infinitely sophisticated; a half-smile or rather the ghost of a smile, perhaps a little arrogant. When we saw the temple of Besakih the next day, we were intrigued to discover the smile of our delicate little dancing girls carved in sandstone on dozens of fantastic gods guarding the entrance stairs of the temple. The Balinese evidently are partial to this half-smile.

At the end of the dance Rangda, the witch, appeared and a fearful monster she was. One was filled with admiration for the delicate girls who put her to rout with their small jewelled *krises*. Our own ideas of witches are tame compared to those of the Balinese. Had I stayed long enough in Bali I think I should have come to believe in Rangda and to fear her!

After the dance we drove to the Aquarium near Sanur. It belonged to two young Germans, Hans Neuhaus and his brother, who had collected beautiful specimens of tropical fish which could be viewed for a fee of 50 cents. We had been given a letter of introduction and were told that the way to win their hearts was to speak German. So I greeted the first one we met in German and, in a little while, he warmed up and became friendly and chatty. He and his brother also owned a curio shop with superb Balinese wood carvings and paintings. One brother was the secretary—and the only white member—of a Balinese wood-carvers' union which sought to evade the middleman and get more for their work. We bought some lovely things there; much more authentic and no more expensive than the things in the Den Pasar shops.

We mentioned that we should like to plan for a *ketjak* dance that evening. They said they were arranging one with some friends and would be delighted to share expenses with us. It was therefore decided that we should call at eight that evening and that Hans, the blond, handsome brother, would ride with us and explain things.

We had a cremation on our list for the afternoon and also a visit to the weekly market in Den Pasar, so we had to hurry. The market was not nearly as interesting as the improvised one we saw on our first evening in the village where they were going to have an opera. The cremation also was disappointing. We had heard so much about these elaborate funerals that we probably expected too much. To save expenses, cremations are usually mass affairs. This one was for poor *Sudras* and therefore a relatively inexpensive affair. In the morning on our way to the dance we had seen the funeral towers lined along the road, in the process of being decorated with tinsel and flowers.

The Balinese believe that the dead must be twice purified, once through fire and once through water, before their souls fly to heaven for a short stay prior to being reincarnated. Those who have been good and have made proper offerings to the gods will return to the

Djanger

Legong

Exorcising Rangda with a kris

happiest place on earth, Bali. Those whose behavior has not been up to standard must wait longer before being reincarnated into a Balinese. The wicked are condemned to reincarnation as members of some other race, to live miserably and far from Bali—the worst fate that could be imagined by a Balinese. It is a pretty idea and robs death of all terror. Cremations are particularly joyous affairs since finally enough money has been scraped together to purify the souls of loved ones and thus release them for speedy return to Bali. Until this double purification has been carried out, the souls of the departed hover uneasily about their old homes and are apt to cause trouble for the living; thus it is a happy event for the family when they are able finally to free their homes from the potentially dangerous wandering souls of their departed kin.

The day before the funeral, the family goes to the cemetery and digs up the bones of their dead, often buried for years in temporary graves, for the improvident and carefree Balinese find it difficult to save the substantial sum required for even the simplest cremation. The bones are placed in gaudily decorated towers built of rattan and bamboo. The height and size of these towers depend upon the position of the deceased and the pocketbook of the family—some are 100 feet tall. Brightly colored decorations made of paper, silk, or glass are attached to the towers. In the center is a paper or wooden animal, usually a bull,* into which the corpse is placed just before it is consigned to the flames. At the last moment, the mourners strip the decorations in a jolly free-for-all, for they are supposed to bring good luck. The entire ceremony is a joyful one. The digging of the bones, building of the towers, burning, etc., are accompanied by laughter and skirmishing over the bones to show how much they are valued. Also, it is necessary to make much noise and to take sudden unexpected turns while carrying the funeral towers in order to fool and scare away the evil spirits.

We didn't see the whole ceremony. Such cremations are all-day affairs and it was very hot that day. However, we arrived in time to watch a curious dance by a number of elderly gentlemen, dressed in square-checked trousers and tall peaked hats, who were carrying lances and eggs. As the dancing became more frenzied, the old men began to throw the eggs on the ground. These were for the evil spirits who, having been fed, would then do no harm. There was almost no space in which to dance and many of the tourists pressing in close to take pictures were splattered by the raw eggs.

The cremation took place in a large meadow on the road from Kuta Beach to Den Pasar. Many towers were burning slowly when

---

*A bull seemed such an odd creature to serve as a casket, but possibly he is symbolic of Nandi, Siva's bull. Siva is the God of Death, the Destroyer.

we came and the smoke was dense. Of course a market was going on right beside the burning bulls and the whole was reminiscent of a country fair. Later that night the Balinese took the ashes of their dead to the sea and cast them on the waves. After that they undoubtedly felt virtuous and happy for they had done everything they could to help their dear departed.

Despite our full days, we always managed to have a short swim before dinner and found this refreshing. In fact, if we hadn't stayed at Bob Koke's where there was coolness and quiet and the music of the surf, we shouldn't have been able to accomplish all we did. As it was, we were a source of constant surprise to everybody at the hotel. A year later friends told us that we were still being cited as examples of the most astonishing endurance. Everyone admitted that we hadn't missed a thing worth seeing in all Bali during the five short days we were there. I do believe that, unless we had remained half a year or so, we could not have retained more out of our visit.

We had taken several drives through the moonlit country and that evening we took quite a long one. First we went to pick up Hans—not without some difficulty. The road through a village on our way to his house was completely blocked by a *gamelan* concert. We were already late so it was a bit trying to watch the leisurely clearing away of all the *gamelan* paraphernalia. Wordbook in hand, I managed to convey to the villagers that it would be a splendid idea if they remained off the road for ten minutes, as we should presently be returning. They naturally tried to get us involved in the usual exchange of personal data but we finally convinced them that we really had to hurry—a concept difficult for Balinese to grasp.

We got to Hans in time and then drove some twenty miles along narrow roads that led us far from the usual tourist haunts and into the interior of the island. When we finally reached the village where the dance was to have been held, we discovered there had been a mix-up and they had no idea they were to give a performance. Even so, it took them only ten minutes to make their simple preparations. The *gamelan* orchestra was set up, a few torches were lighted, and the show began.

We sat on a raised platform and had a marvelous view of the performers and the audience. It was hard to decide which was the more fascinating. The entire village had come, even the tiniest tots, and they all watched with complete abandon and delight. Never had I seen such truly folk art. Yet, strangely enough, it was sophisticated, highly developed art performed and, in part, even created by simple peasants.

We were lucky for they had one of the best orchestra leaders and the best woman dancer in Bali. She was no longer young and she was a little too heavy and not really handsome, but could she dance! It was her job to be able to dance with any man in the audience who might choose to enter the arena, and each man danced with his own personal kind of dance. But, while allowing for complicated variations, the fundamentals are definite and must be memorized. Every member of the audience knew them well and was a keen critic. At times the woman danced alone and then she would hop from one musician to another, stopping in front of each and dancing *at* him in a most provocative manner. There were moments when we were relieved to know that the instruments separated them. The musician would keep on playing but make dance movements with his body from the waist upward. The music was wild and stirring.

The woman's dance changed almost imperceptibly into a warrior's dance; first a few men entered the circle to dance with her, then an old man rose from the audience and improvised a story which covered the transition while she gradually danced away. Then the men began to dance. They had magnificent bodies and their poses were like those of Greek statues. They fenced and attacked and the children's eyes nearly popped out of their heads when it looked as if surely one warrior or more would be killed.

The final dance was the famous *ketjak*, sometimes called the monkey dance, from one of the legends of the *Ramayana*.* It was quite the most stirring dance of all we saw. The audience retreated, leaving a large open space. The orchestra was cleared away. Then some 150 men seated themselves around a fire in concentric circles. They were naked except for loincloths and the inevitable colored rags wound around their heads. First they leaned forward until their heads touched ground, then they lay back almost flat. They kept doing this in perfect unison to the accompaniment of a sort of humming and soft chatter. At times they sang all together, at times they syncopated. Always the human spiral moved in perfect harmony forwards, backwards, then sideways—like a field of grain swept by the wind. The sound of their humming rose and fell, became wildly exciting, then subsided and became as soft as a sigh. Some of the humming sounded like "K'cha, k'cha," also "tch, tch, tch," sort of susurrant, imitating the sound of the jungle animals. It is hard to describe the effect of this mass performance, which apparently had no leadership. It was elemental and showed how perfectly each individual fitted into the whole, naturally and without direction. Only a people whose entire life is lived communally could have done it.

A storyteller then began to tell the ancient tale and the intonations and movements of the men who formed the chorus were

---

*The *Ramayana* is a collection of epic poems described in detail in Chapter 6.

sometimes angry, often frightening. Occasionally the storyteller (acting the part of Hanuman, king of the monkeys) would jump into the center of the mass of revolving bodies, and while the circle swayed to and fro, now swiftly in passion, now slowly in languorous ecstasy, the torches threw weird shadows and the full moon shot rays of silver through the leafy canopy above. Suddenly the demon, Ravana, appeared and tried to enter the circle. The half circle at his side cowered in fear while, from across the circle, the storyteller exorcised him, half the men rising like a wave against him, the foremost ones hunched up part way, the ones farther out rising in graduated rings to the outermost ones who extended their arms and fiercely intoned some strange adjuration. Then Ravana would try to enter from the opposite side and the whole process reversed itself, the half circles rising and subsiding like waves. It was a terrific dance and we were completely unaware that it lasted almost an hour. We could have watched forever.

When the performance was over, we were considerably shaken up emotionally. I simply couldn't tear myself away and told Hans I wished this would go on all night. The leader of the musicians who had throughout been our gracious host asked Hans why I looked so unhappy—hadn't I liked the dance? Hans told him it was quite the contrary; I loved it so much that I did not want to leave. Whereupon this nice Balinese gentleman assured me that they wouldn't think of letting us go if we wanted to stay, and to come along into the *puri* (palace) of the raja nearby where they would set up the raja's *gamelan* orchestra and have more music for us.

We walked through a quiet grove—Hans removing his sandals, probably to be more perfectly in tune with the Balinese setting. Soon we reached a courtyard surrounded by wooden houses on stilts with veranda-like structures facing inward. The prince's family *gamelan* orchestra was swiftly assembled—some of the small children had to be pulled out of bed but didn't mind—and soon we were treated to more of the charming Balinese music. The courtyard was bathed in moonlight. No artificial illumination marred the natural setting. Shadowy figures could be seen on the verandas and occasionally a dog or a cat would slink by. Our host regaled us with bananas and rice wine. In our honor, the wine was served in glasses, which he carefully wiped with an incredibly dirty rag. George and I simply could not offend such a wonderfully gracious and delightful host so we swished the wine around our glasses, hoping the alcohol would at least weaken the germs, and drank bravely.

It was a beautiful night. Hans explained a lot about Bali to us. Glad, I think, to be able to speak German and to find congenial people of his own kind (which he would not have admitted), he opened up and gave us an interesting talk on Bali, Balinese art, and the Balinese people.

Art and music, he said, are natural functions of the Balinese; things entirely divorced from intellect and operating by instinct alone. It seems strange that there can be great sophistication, great artistic delicacy, without great intellect. The Balinese are constantly inventing new forms of art; they compose new music, think up new dances, and vary their carvings. All their music is composed by the group, although one man, usually the orchestra leader, may contribute the largest share. They sit around and experiment with new melodies and, when they like one, adopt it. This is the way new compositions evolve. The dancers operate in similar manner. This reminded me of a ditty composed by Noel Coward during a visit to Bali:

> As I said this morning to Charlie,
> There's far too much music in Bali
> And though as a place it's entrancing
> There's also, I thought, too much dancing.
> It seems that the average native
> From the womb to the tomb is creative,
> Although the result is quite clever
> There's too much artistic endeavor.

The wood-carvers are a little more individual, as are the painters, but still they work in groups, no doubt influencing each other subtly. All are part-time artists, their main occupation being farming. Each belongs to a village organization of like-minded neighbors. In fact, every Balinese is a member of some association—the village itself, a subdivision of the village, trade associations, artistic associations; there is even an association for those belonging to no other club. Life is lived communally.

This elaborate community organization was not consciously thought out. It just happened, as everyone always took the way that caused least friction. Balinese seldom quarrel. There are few, if any, social misfits. Everyone has a place in the community and does something useful while he is capable of work; even the children and the old make themselves useful. When the latter are no longer able to work, they are lovingly taken care of by the family, the association, or the village.

The fertile soil of Bali, where every field yields two rice crops annually as well as an intermediate crop of peanuts or corn, does not require long working hours. After everyone has contributed his share of work, there is plenty of time left for play. Practically everybody does something artistic in his free time. The Balinese are thoroughly happy, gentle, loving people. Anyone who gets to know them even as little as we did cannot help but be charmed by them. I think, however, that their peaceful existence is predicated on factors that could not be duplicated elsewhere: the extraordinary fertility of the soil, the mild climate, the absence of plentiful natural resources which might have tempted outsiders to exploit them and, most important of all, their gentle unaffected personalities. Where there is economic plenty and little differentiation in intellectual ability, a free communal society can flourish.

Lockhart gives an interesting example of the way the Balinese guild system works. There is little or no attempt to evade the rules of the guild and no provision for punishing a possible wrongdoer. When Baron von Plessen made the movie *Black Magic*, he engaged a handsome young Balinese cement worker to play a leading part. The young man was paid what to a Balinese must have been a fabulous salary. He did not touch it until the movie was finished and then gave everything to his guild. The money we paid for the dance performance also went to the guild. It was used to pay for new instruments and costumes.

Hans concluded his lecture with the sad comment that he felt the golden age of Bali was fast coming to an end. You could not blame the Dutch or the tourists. It was inevitable, once the island had come into contact with Western civilization. The young men had already begun to prefer bicycles to dance costumes. Only one family in all Bali still knew the art of weaving the beautiful Balinese brocades, with the gold and silver embroidery, used in such dances as the *legong*. The young people still danced the *djanger* but the movies were beginning to draw them away. To me it seemed incredible that the Balinese could prefer the inferior Westerns that were the usual movie fare thereabouts to their own beautiful music, plays, and dances. Fortunately, this dismal trend was faintly discernible only to pessimists like Hans. I hope what he feared will not happen for a long time.

Sunday we took a picnic lunch and drove to Besakih on the slopes of Gunung Agung. It is the most sacred temple of Bali, which every Balinese is supposed to visit once a year. On the way we passed through Klungkung, the scene of another famous *puputan* in 1908 in which the Dewa Agung of Klungkung was killed. It was a pleasant little town with few reminders of the princely era. The palace had been razed; where it had stood there was a grassy square fronting the residence of the Dutch Controleur. We were amused by two odd Balinese sculptures; one depicting a Dutchman counting his guilders, the other a Dutchman drinking beer—rather a commentary on Balinese opinion of the colonial Dutch! Nevertheless, Dutch influence was seen at its best in the healthy youngsters playing football on a new athletic field—a much better pastime, we thought, than cock-fighting or gambling.

The road began to rise and soon we were driving up a steep mountain with many sharp curves and breathtaking views across the green *sawahs* rising tier upon tier. Near the top, the road ended and we drove on a grass track which led to a parklike landscape of almost northerly aspect. The air was fresh and bracing and when we reached the temple at 3,000 feet we had a superb view of the Peak of Bali and the active volcano Gunung Batur. Far below us, all Bali was spread before our eyes. No wonder this is the national shrine of the island.

There were three temples built upon terraces like huge steps of a giant staircase. Many graceful black-roofed *merus* gave Besakih its distinctive air. What made this *pura* unique, however, was its mountainous setting, great height, and solitude. For some time we had been pleasantly aware of an absence of *desas* (villages), people, and carabao—a welcome change from populous Bali.

Koke had invited some of the Dutch officials in Den Pasar for dinner at the Kuta Beach Hotel, and afterward there was a dance on the beach. A small boy performed the *kebiyar*, a dance which does not tell a story but seeks to interpret by facial expressions and body movements the music of the orchestra. The boy dancer sat on a mat and occasionally hopped around in a circle between the members of the *gamelan* orchestra. He wore a brocaded sarong wound tightly around the upper part of his slender body and extending to his ankles. It had a train which he manipulated with one hand, while delicately fluttering a fan with the other. The Dutch gentlemen and their wives looked bored and poor Koke hovered anxiously around, trying to keep his guests in good humor. We didn't like this evidence of Dutch power over a well-run American establishment.

On our last day we did a lot of photographing and visited the nine royal graves at Tampaksiring. We walked down a steep path to a quiet spot where a small river had dug itself a bed and, on its shore, an old temple seemed to sleep. There were caves with curiously carved tombstones, supposedly dating back to the ninth century. A little farther on we came to the sacred springs of Tirta Empul where many Balinese were bathing. These were natural warm springs believed to have miraculous healing powers.

And so our Bali visit came to an end. Except for the *sapis* (cows), everyone had been charming to us. The *sapis* didn't like our car and refused to make way so that frequently we almost ran them down. The geese along the way also were something of a traffic hazard. They are a feature of the Balinese landscape. They are seen mostly in the morning and in the evening being driven by boys who carry a stick at the end of which flutters a piece of white cloth. The geese are trained

Preparations for a Balinese cremation

Kebiyar as danced by Mario, its originator

to remain with the white flag so that if the herder wishes to leave them for a short time, he simply puts the stick into the ground and the geese will wait patiently until he returns.

I think the main reason our visit in Bali was successful was the fact that I knew enough Malay so that we could be independent. Armed with a map, we needed no one's help to get anywhere we pleased. Also, we didn't have to uphold Dutch prestige and could be friendly with the Balinese, who are a delightful people. Abdullah was an ideal companion who contributed much to the congenial spirit which made our stay such fun.

Once, however, George really made me angry. I was carefully explaining to our *djongos* that we wanted some washing done when George came up, took the laundry and, rubbing it between his hands, said, "Washee, washee—you understand?" The *djongos* grinned and answered in English, "Yes, sir." George has a tendency at times to put me in my place if he feels that I am getting above myself, especially in matters linguistic; he likes to show that he can get along quite well with plain English or with sign language.

On our last day in Bali, we got up at 3:00 a.m. and had a sketchy breakfast of oranges, bananas, and mangosteens on the porch. Our only illumination was a kerosene torch stuck in the wall, and the moon riding high in the sky. The breakers were rolling in from the sea, glittering like liquid silver. We were still slightly damp from a quick farewell dip at Kuta Beach—the best way to wash the sleep from one's eyes so early in the morning.

An hour later we were off on the long ride to Gilimanuk Bay where the Strait of Bali is only one mile wide and a ferry takes you to Banjuwangi in Java. Bali was still asleep as we rode for the last time past the grey stone walls of the *desas* and *puras*—homesick before we had even left the island. Once we saw several women, marching in single file, led by one woman carrying a torch, apparently bent for a nearby cemetery. Another time we came upon a procession carrying umbrellas; we had no idea what this meant, but one always sees processions of one kind or another. This one, suddenly emerging from a side street, startled us—we narrowly avoided a collision. Finally the moon disappeared, the sun rose, and we found ourselves on the desolate Djembrana Plateau of western Bali. Occasionally we had a glimpse of the ocean at our left. The aspect of the country began to change and we saw evidences of Islam: mosques instead of *puras*, Malay-type *kampongs* (villages consisting of thatch-roofed huts or houses) instead of the familiar walled-in villages. The people looked different, too—poorer and not so gay. Finally we reached the ferry at Gilimanuk and said farewell to Abdullah, whose honest face beamed when he saw his tip.

The KPM took good care to keep this passage to Java a secret, so that they could extract fat fees for transporting unwary tourists the short trip from Buleleng in Bali to Surabaja in Java. No travel agency ever told us about the Gilimanuk passage; we found it ourselves. The Dutch have a Teutonic love of accuracy and they do make beautiful maps. On the Bali folder we noticed a fine dotted line across the strait between Bali and Java and a NITOUR (Netherlands India Tourist Office) clerk, after much evasion, finally admitted that there was indeed a ferry between Bali and Java. A small motor launch took us across for one and a half guilders. Had we lived up to the proper white man's standard, we could have had the same accommodation for two and a half guilders and it would then have been called first-class. Either way, one sits in an open launch and is tossed and turned about so much that, unless you are a good *orang laut* like George you might prefer the comfort of the KPM boat. We had a rough passage and I turned progressively greener but, with a supreme effort, managed to hold on to my dignity.

I imagine the roughness of the strait and the fact that the northwestern part of Bali is barren and almost uninhabited accounts for the centuries of Balinese isolation which preserved its Hindu civilization while the rest of the Malay Archipelago was being converted to Islam.* These natural barricades, in addition to the inaccessible coastlines which are steep and mountainous or protected by coral reefs, may also have helped to delay establishment of Dutch rule over Bali. Although as long ago as 1743, the Susuhunan of Surakarta in Java, who claimed suzerainty over Bali, had been induced to cede the island to the Dutch, the Balinese rajas remained to all intents and purposes independent until 1906. The Dutch merely tried through treaties to modify some of the more objectionable Balinese customs, such as *suttee*, slavery, piracy, and "shore rights," i.e. the right claimed by the islanders to salvage whatever the sea threw upon their shores. If the rajas had not constantly violated these treaties and endlessly quarrelled among themselves, the Dutch might not have sent the expedition to conquer Bali which culminated in the *puputan* of Badung.

Before we set out on our trip I had tried to find out something about the history of the Indies before their European colonization. This was difficult because not only is our historical knowledge completely Europe-centered, with hardly any attention given to the Far East, but the Eastern peoples themselves have done little to

---

*The Dutch East Indies were almost 90 percent Moslem. Bali was the only Hindu enclave and there were some Christian communities, such as the Minahassa in Celebes and the Batak in Sumatra.

preserve knowledge of their own past. They seem to lack Western man's predilection to record his doings for the edification of future generations. We have few concrete facts to chart that astonishing phenomenon—the terrific impact Indian civilization has had on Southeast Asia. We have to fit together bits of information gleaned from stone inscriptions, tales of traveling Chinese Buddhist monks who passed through the Indies on their way to India, medieval legends, chronicles and poems written by official scribes of the courts of various Javanese princes. Also, such factual evidence as Indian monuments and temples, Indian art, music and drama, Indian words in the Malay languages and Malayanized versions of Sanskrit once used as script in various parts of the archipelago. Western historians have collected these bits and pieces and built them into a history of the Malay people. I could find no Malay historian doing this, which may mean that the Malays are missing a great opportunity; if you want to build a modern independent state, history is a valuable tool.

Although I had read that Indian merchants, priests, and adventurers had been going to the Malay Archipelago since the first century of the Christian era, bringing with them their religion, arts, and crafts, I was surprised to find Bali a small replica of India, including even the caste system. I had never thought of India as a maritime and colonizing nation. Of course, she never was that in the sense that Spain and Portugal or later Holland, France, and England were. Indian colonization was not government-supported; small bands of Indians sailed eastward, probably in search of spices and trade with China. Navigationally this was quite a feat: more than a thousand years before Columbus, Indian seafarers traversed distances almost two-thirds as great as that from Spain to America. It is 1,800 miles from the Coromandel Coast to the Straits of Malacca, and 2,100 miles from Ceylon to Java. Indian colonization was slow and tolerant of indigenous ways of life. Buddhism and Hinduism absorbed the more primitive native religions. Individual Indians made themselves rulers of native tribes but did not change the basic social organization of the Malays. They brought with them the caste system but it seems to have softened when superimposed on the essential democracy of Malay tribal society. In Bali, where the caste system still exists nominally, it forms far less rigid barriers than it does in India. Wherever Indian civilization penetrated, it raised the simple tribal society and the primitive agricultural practices of the native population to a higher level than had been achieved by the Malay peoples on their own. This is evident when one compares the Hinduized Javanese and Balinese with their cousins in the mountain fastnesses which remained untouched by Indian migration—the Bataks in Sumatra, the Igorots in Luzon, or even with Malay tribes in outlying parts of the archipelago, such as the Philippines, where Indian influence was slight. The Malays absorbed Indian civilization to an astonishing degree. Perhaps this was because the material bases of life of the two races were not far apart. Indian civilization was indeed more highly developed, but the overwhelming majority of Indians were peasants like the Malays, and their life did not differ greatly from that of the peasants in the archipelago. The Indians introduced the plow, they brought their arts and crafts, their literature and script, and their more highly developed religion. In adopting these, the Malays enriched their own civilization without suffering the severe break with tradition that occurs when an invading civilization is vastly more productive and powerful than the inherent culture, as was Western culture compared with that of the East.

We were impressed with the beneficent results of the merging of Indian civilization with the indigenous culture of the Balinese—a predominantly Malay people with some Papuan and Polynesian admixture. The harsher aspects of Indian religion and social organization did not take root in this gentle island, but its spiritual and artistic aspects blended smoothly with the innate ways of Balinese life, giving it a gaiety and charm which we found completely absent in the Moslem parts of Indonesia. In truth, Bali owes much to its natural barricades which made it difficult for invaders to attack the island.

3
Java

All the tourist literature made it clear that the only possible way to travel in the Indies was first-class. Not only are we natural nonconformists, but we had to budget ourselves within the somewhat limited income granted by Uncle Sam, especially since lack of time made it necessary to do some expensive flying to get back in time to Cavite, so we decided that second-class would have to do for us. When we reached Banjuwangi, however, we noticed that our train had the usual open European coaches with a passage running down one side of the car and seats placed opposite each other to form semiprivate sections. The seats were straw-covered and identical in second- and third-class; the only difference being that the sections were roomier in second. At a saving of about 50 percent, it seemed advisable to use third. We found it suitable and traveled that way throughout Java. We always had a section to ourselves; the natives being too polite to intrude on a *tuan* and a *nyonya* (Malay titles of respect for a gentleman and a lady). There are some personal advantages to traveling in a country where the ruling whites insist on their prerogatives! While traveling in comfortable seclusion, we could still watch native life in the open coach and, if we wished, engage in conversation with our Javanese co-passengers whom we found uniformly neat, clean, and polite.

In Surabaja we transferred to the daily express for Batavia.* Since this was an extra-fare train, the third-class coach was almost entirely filled with whites—presumably of the lower social order! We found them quite as amusing to watch as the natives, because of the amazing manner in which they mixed strong emotions of grief at parting with the rapid consumption of enormous quantities of solid

---

*This city was founded in 1527 when a Javanese warrior, Faletehan, conquered a coastal village called Sunda Kelapa, which was already trading with the Portuguese, and changed its name to Djayakarta (complete victory). Later, after the town was destroyed, the Dutch under Governor General Jan Pieterzoon Coen, built the city of Batavia in 1619. When the Indonesians gained their independence in 1949, they renamed the city Djakarta, a contraction of the name given it by Faletehan.

JAVA

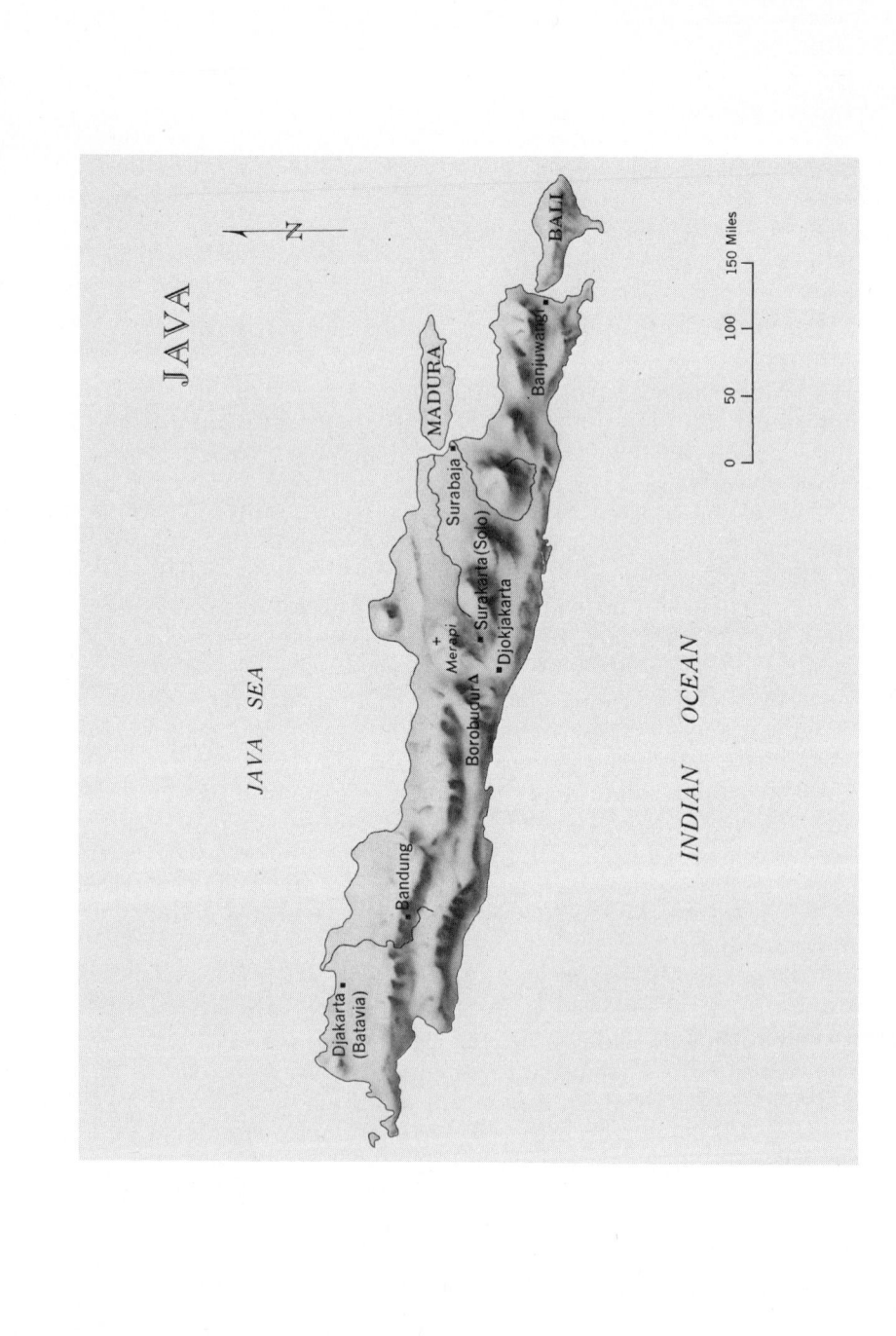

Djakarta (Batavia)
Bandung
Borobudur
Merapi
Surakarta (Solo)
Djokjakarta
Surabaja
MADURA
Banjuwangi
BALI

JAVA SEA

INDIAN OCEAN

0 50 100 150 Miles

Dutch food packed in large hampers—possibly the emotional jab whetted their appetites. As we were boarding the train, a large lady with tears streaming down her face fell around my neck and poured a torrent of incomprehensible Dutch upon me. At the moment I was tired and anxious to get to my seat, so this unexpected encounter unnerved me a bit. I gathered later that she was confiding to everyone at the station that her two teen-age sons were leaving for Batavia. Oh, horror! practically to the end of the world, and all alone, too. The sons, as well as all the other passengers, hung weeping out of the windows as the train slowly gathered speed, but as soon as the fluttering handkerchiefs of the grieving friends and families could no longer be seen, the boys pulled down their hampers and began eating huge sausages between slabs of bread, their appetites quite unimpaired. All the other people in the coach did the same. The eating capacity of these Dutch is terrific. On the *Tjinegara*, Mr. Huyser used to eat clear down the menu, which was gigantic in itself. Then, time and again, he would start in at the top, with soup, and go once more down the line. Everyone at our table kept urging us to eat more and expressed grave doubt that on our starvation diet we would have enough energy to do *onze Indië* justice.

It was a long trip but luckily it turned cool soon after we left Surabaja. In the middle of the day Java is hot, but the nights are comfortable. What we could see from the train looked attractive—mostly rice fields, terraced as in Bali and climbing up steep mountains. Sated with impressions of Bali, we were inclined to regard Java as an anticlimax—which it proved to be—chiefly because it was too "Dutchified." Still, if we had seen Java first and had not been spoiled by the charms of Bali, we should have found native life there fascinating. The people resembled the Filipinos somewhat, although they were not as handsome, gay, or lively as the Balinese.

It had been a long day, from 3:00 a.m., when we arose sleepily by the light of the Balinese moon, until past midnight when we crawled wearily into our enormous becurtained beds at the Mataram Hotel in Djokja* after having most inconsiderately wakened the *tuan besar* (manager) who, clad in striped pajamas of a delicate pink hue, came to dicker with us. We had a list of hotels with minimum and maximum accommodations put out by NITOUR, but throughout our trip we found its minimum prices nonexistent, even when we were the only guests at a hotel.

We could spend only three days in Java. It seemed best, therefore, to concentrate upon central Java where the only native sul-

---

*The name of this important old city is written indiscriminately on various official signs as Jogja, Jocja, Djogja, Djokja, and Djokjakarta—karta meaning city.

tanates were situated and where native life was said to be still fairly unspoiled. We had a letter from a friend in Manila to the principal police officer of Java, who had his headquarters in Djokja. His name was Otto Coerper, a naturalized Hollander of German origin—we were always running into Germans in the Indies. I telephoned him in the morning and he came over right away. From then on we were entirely in the hands of the hospitable Coerpers who drove us about in their official car and told us many fascinating stories about Java and the Javanese. Without them we should never have seen so much in so short a time.

We received two principal impressions of Java. One, its fantastic overpopulation—about the size of the State of New York, it had then forty million inhabitants.* Crowds were everywhere but especially on the roads, which were never without humans, day or night. The other was the poverty of the natives—a direct result of overpopulation. Most were too poor to use animals for transport and therefore they, themselves, had become beasts of burden. Nowhere else had we seen men—and women, too—carrying such back-breaking loads. Often these loads were taller than the slender natives who carried them long distances. The heaviest loads were transported by bullocks, pulling huge wooden carts with steep roofs. Both the lumbering carabao and the carts with their squeaking wheels had a prehistoric air about them. We had seen the first of these ancient vehicles in Banjuwangi, and thereafter met them wherever we went in Java. Sensibly, whenever the Javanese had to travel long distances, they rested during the day and drove their carabao carts at night. We encountered several of these carts one evening when we were returning to Djokja by car. It was weird to see our headlights reflected in the big eyes of the carabao, as they trudged along to the monotonous clapping of the bells around their necks.

The Coerpers took us to Kota Gedeh, near Djokja, where the famous Djokja silversmiths live. As everywhere in the Orient, each trade had its own street. It was not difficult to locate that of the silversmiths for the noise of the hammering could be heard from afar. Everything was hammered out by hand. It was hard to believe that

---

*Wherever the Dutch, British, French, or Americans have taken political control, they have established law and order, put an end to the continuous tribal warfare of the indigenous populations, and brought modern sanitation, with consequent drastic reduction of the death rate. In Java, the Dutch have contributed much to increase agricultural productivity, too. As a result population has increased tenfold from 4.5 million in 1815 to approximately 45 million in the late 1930's. In the Outer Islands where Dutch influence has been less strongly felt, there has been not nearly as large an increase in population. Before the Dutch came, population density was about even throughout the archipelago, but thereafter Java acquired the lion's share.

people could live all day in this terrific din. We were almost deafened. The silver was good and work creditable but, though individual items were pleasing, we thought it too stereotyped; the patterns too elaborate. There were too many raised garlands of flowers and fruits and altogether too many *garudas*, mythical birds of good fortune.*

We found the same stereotyped repetition of a few ancient Hindu motifs in everything artistic in Java. Of course, all oriental art is given to repetition; even such highly developed art as that of the Chinese has fewer variations than comparable European or American art. I suppose this is a result of the group life of Oriental man, which contrasts strongly with the individualism of the West. Educated Orientals are inclined to condemn the West, especially America, for materialism and standardization. Well, as to standardization, we never saw anything approaching the extreme observed in native markets throughout the East—the same few patterns in the cottons and silks, the same shapes and colors of pottery, identical metal work, basket work, sandals, hats, etc. This is not surprising when one remembers that sons follow their fathers' footsteps and seldom move out of the economic niche into which they were born. To Westerners, the Orient looks fascinatingly colorful because everything there is unfamiliar; because the people like gorgeous colors not often seen in the West; and because the people, having but few worldly possessions, often lavish great artistic beauty on simple utensils of daily life. Because transportation facilities are poor, there is much diversity even between neighboring localities. Villages on the opposite sides of a mountain often have completely different costumes and customs, but within a community there is an astonishing degree of standardization in handicraft products—comparable in fact to Western machine standardization.

Still, there are degrees, and Javanese art is certainly more conventionalized and stereotyped than Balinese art. We thought this might have been the result of Java's religion—Islam. The prophet forbade the portrayal of human and animal forms. There is an element of puritanism in Islam, not conducive to developing individualistic art other than architecture. Since the Moslems were not artistic people, this puritanism was natural. Later, as they acquired control over half the known world, they began to crave the luxuries of the more highly civilized peoples they conquered, and Moslem princes often became patrons of such handicrafts as gold- and silverwork, fine silks and brocades, carpets, pottery, and carved ivories. The need to erect houses of worship for the new religion developed a

*In Hindu mythology, the garuda was a half-human bird that carried the god, Vishnu. The garuda, without human elements, is today the symbol of Indonesia.

distinct and beautiful architecture. In the Indies, the Moslems showed an admirable tolerance for the use of Hindu motifs in the handicrafts, while ferociously destroying the magnificent monuments of Hindu religion built of stone. All Javanese art is concerned with Hindu gods and heroes and the legends of *Ramayana* and *Mahabharata*,* even though the Javanese are devout Moslems who obey the Koran, maintain a famed religious school at Mecca, and ruin themselves economically to make the prescribed pilgrimage to Mecca.

We bought some silver in Kota Gedeh and searched around for choice batiks. Djokja was famous for its handmade batiks and the government maintained a craft school there which taught the special dyeing method. Batik is an ancient craft calling for a steady hand and much patience. Intricate designs are drawn with softened wax on a piece of cloth, after which the cloth is dipped into dye which colors all but the area covered by the wax. Then the wax is removed and a new design drawn, the cloth dipped in a different color, and so on, until the material is overlaid with a mass of intricately drawn and harmoniously blended designs. Unfortunately, sarongs made of such batiks are far too expensive for the average Javanese who wears cheap imitations—made in Japan.

I was anxious to buy one of the old handmade sarongs and, after much searching, was lucky to acquire a princely one that came from the *kraton* (palace) of the Sultan of Djokja. The original owner, like all Javanese aristocrats—so Coerper told us—probably lived beyond his income; it was the thing to do. When he found himself in straitened circumstances he pawned the sarong, no doubt expecting to redeem it eventually. When he failed to do this, his elegant costume was bought by us.

The pawnshops were run by the government. Though often criticized for making too much money, the government in fact operated the shops efficiently and honestly, unlike the Chinese who had previously controlled the pawnshop business. In a society where no one plans ahead, pawnshops are indispensable. They function as a sort of savings bank in reverse. Clothing and jewels are usually bought with a view to their value in the pawnshop and they will move in and out of these shops with fair regularity as family income ebbs and flows. When we were in Java, we were told that the pawnshop estimators had the reputation of being the best judges of batik in the country. Loans up to 50 percent of the market value were allowed, but the amount asked was usually smaller. Since the Javanese were inherently incapable of saving, small emergencies kept recurring and this was where the pawnshops were used. Most articles

*For descriptions of these legends, *see* Chapter 6.

were redeemed within the prescribed time limits; those that were not were put up for auction and sold.

In Djokja the court sarongs differed from those worn by ordinary mortals by being double the width and having so-called royal designs. While the humble Malay simply wound the sarong around himself at the waist, the aristocratic gentleman at the sultan's court had to spend at least one hour draping his voluminous sarong around himself in big loops. We considered this time wasted, since the court sarongs did not look nearly as graceful as the ordinary ones. Even if the busy Javanese farmer could have spent as much time on dressing himself, he would have had no use for the court sarongs since *adat* (customary law) forbade his wearing them. There was, therefore, only a limited market for pawned court sarongs and they could often be obtained for a song.

In the afternoon the Coerpers drove us to the Borobudur temple. We had originally planned to arrive at sunset, have dinner there, and wait for the moon to rise, but the sky was overcast and we didn't want to risk waiting half the night for a problematical moon, perhaps keeping the small Coerper children out of bed unnecessarily. So we missed what is said to be a miraculous sight—the view from the top of the temple in moonlight. Even so, it was lovely to look down on the mellow landscape in the fading light of the short tropical dusk.

We questioned our kind host about Javanese history and found him most knowledgeable. He was one of those rare white administrators who possessed intellectual curiosity about the people whom he ruled. I suppose he knew more Javanese history than most educated Javanese. This history, unfortunately, has a big element of speculation, since it was reconstructed by Europeans on the basis of inadequate source materials. "Isn't it too bad," he said, "that Buddhist monasteries never set themselves the task of preserving the cultural heritage of their native countries, the way this was done by the medieval monasteries in Europe after the fall of Rome. They were then the only institutions that kept historical records, but the Malays never developed universities or similar centers of learning. As it is, what we call 'history' is largely guesswork."

The evidence is strong that Malay civilization lacked the concept of the state and Malay political organization never rose above the clan level; i.e. the only governments that developed indigenously were those of village or tribe—groups of people living under a headman to whom they were related or whose slaves they were. These groups were small and did not combine or coalesce into larger units.* Except for

---

*Good examples of indigenous Malay society were the *barangay* which the Spaniards found and described when they occupied the northern and central Philippine Islands. Because of their geographic position at the extreme northern end of the

the rudimentary dispensation of justice by the headman, in consultation with a council of elders, there seems to have been no governmental machinery. But there was a well-defined body of *adat* that was probably more conscientiously obeyed than is law in more highly developed communities, for primitive people are always more strictly bound by convention than are civilized people. Besides this strong sanction of general acceptance, enforcement of law apparently depended on fear of reprisal by the injured party and his family.

When the Indians came to the archipelago they brought with them a concept of political organization only slightly more developed—the princely state. Without disturbing the existing clan society, individual Indians acquired control over a number of clans and set up a princely state on the Indian model. They built palaces and temples, brought in retainers, and armed followers and a host of artisans to serve the needs of the court. The princes and their relations became an hereditary aristocracy supported by taxes levied on the population. They kept Brahmans to conduct services in the new temples and chroniclers and poets to cater to their self-esteem. All this was a burden on the people but it also enriched and beautified life. Under Indian instruction, the Malays became artisans and artists. An Indianized native literature and drama developed. Away from the courts, village life went on in its old accustomed way.

As happened in India, some princely houses were able to bring others under control as tribute-paying vassals and to expand their domains through advantageous marriages. These loose conglomerations seldom lasted long, because they depended entirely upon the personality of the ruler. A few, however, grew into empires as important in their own corner of the world as the Greek, Persian, and other empires of antiquity, about which we learned in school. Though George and I flattered ourselves on having a good knowledge of history, we had never heard of the Indianized empires of Sri Vijaya, Mataram, or Madjapahit. Yet Sri Vijaya lasted seven hundred years and at the height of its power controlled Malaya, Sumatra, and parts of Java; Mataram was strong enough to defeat a Chinese invading force sent by Kublai Khan, and Madjapahit conquered both Sri Vijaya and Mataram and all the rest of the princely states of the archipelago from Malaya clear across to Bali and northward to the southern part of the Philippines.

Malay Archipelago, these islands retained the original Malay way of life. It was the smallness of the *barangay* and their inability to federate that made Spanish conquest easy. In contrast, the Moros of the southern Philippines, who had received Islam and the Indian concept of state through Indianized Malays—i.e., at second hand—had a stronger political organization which successfully resisted Spanish efforts at subjugation.

Sri Vijaya interested us especially since, through intermarriage with the rulers of what is now Djokja and Solo, it ruled in central Java when the Borobudur was built. Sri Vijaya was a Buddhist Malay empire which rose in Sumatra in the seventh century and waxed rich and powerful through its control of the trade between India, China, and the Spice Islands (Moluccas). It held strong points in Malaya which gave it a grip on shipping through the Straits of Malacca and, through possession of Palembang, also controlled the Sunda Strait (between Java and Sumatra). For centuries Sri Vijaya levied toll on all ships sailing between the Indian Ocean and the South China Sea and hence the more lucrative route to the spice-growing Moluccas. It succumbed in the late thirteenth century when it was attacked simultaneously by the Thai from the north, Madjapahit from the east, and Islam from the west, leaving little but an evil legacy of piracy in the Straits of Malacca which persisted until Western warships eliminated the pirate nests some 80 years ago.

The last and greatest of the Indianized Malay empires was Madjapahit, which rose in Java and spread eastward by conquest of Mataram and westward by absorption of Sri Vijaya. Madjapahit was a Hindu Malay empire—Hinduism having by that time replaced and absorbed Buddhism.* It flourished through the fourteenth and fifteenth centuries and brought the entire Malay Archipelago under vassalage, even claiming suzerainty over the distant Philippines. Under its rule Malay civilization reached its highest point. But even as it expanded in power, there arose the threat of Islam in the West. As early as the thirteenth century, Moslem missionaries and traders from Arabia and India had obtained a foothold in Sumatra by converting the Raja of Atjeh. The principalities in Sumatra and Malaya that owed allegiance to Madjapahit were rapidly converted to Islam and, fortified by their new and intolerant religion, turned on their overlords and gradually splintered the Madjapahit empire. Whatever fragile unity Indonesia had possessed under Madjapahit rule disappeared and in its place arose innumerable independent Moslem principalities, perpetually at war with each other and hence

---

*The intricacies of Indian religious concepts are baffling. It appears that the early Indian religion is known as Vedism or, in its more developed form, Brahmanism. Buddhism was a reform movement that lost out in India to a revived Brahmanism, which incorporated many of the basic concepts of Buddhism. This latter religion is generally designated Hinduism. Hinduism preserves the system of caste and the huge mass of religious rites of worship of numberless gods—there are said to be over 300 million of these—while adopting Buddhist ethics and concepts of asceticism and reverence for all living things. Buddha was adopted into the Hindu hierarchy of gods, his position varying at different times. All Indian religions are extremely tolerant of other religious beliefs and can find room for the most primitive animism as well as for the loftiest concept of one God.

an easy prey for the Europeans who made their appearance hard on the heels of Islam.*

With its usual ruthlessness and fanatical intolerance, Islam destroyed most of the marvelous temples and monuments that had been built during a thousand years of Buddhism and Hinduism. Only a few survived. Some were hidden by faithful priests and devotees; others were saved by their isolated locations and were soon buried in jungle growth. White men discovered them and dug them out with care. Of these perhaps the greatest is the Borobudur. It is unique. One can compare it only with some of the ruins in Angkor (Cambodia) which also were built by Indianized native principalities—an outgrowth of the same Indian migration eastward that penetrated the Malay Archipelago.

The Borobudur is a Buddhist monument rather than a temple, and may at one time have contained the ashes of Buddha or of one of his saintly followers.† Such monuments are called *stupas*. The Borobudur was built in the eighth or ninth century and represents the culmination of the *stupa* style of architecture. Later *stupas* have molded bases and high conical towers. Borobudur has the shape of a hemisphere erected on a plinth, and consists of seven terraced galleries, the four lower ones polygonal (almost square), the three top ones round. The ancient Javanese chose to erect this 135-foot-high edifice on an uncertain foundation of natural hill supplemented by clay and sand landfill. Thus the temple sits unsteadily upon a potential rock slide—in an area where as much as eight inches of rain can pour down in twenty-four hours. The plinth or base platform seems to have been added after the temple was partly finished, when it was found that the base would not be strong enough to support the whole structure. Excavations have disclosed partly finished bas-reliefs under the platform.

---

*We have an eye-witness account of the break-up of Madjapahit in *Suma Oriental*, a recently re-discovered Portuguese account of the Malay Archipelago and Peninsula written between 1512 and 1515 by Tomé Pires. It was lost from sight for centuries and seems never to have received the attention it deserves. In 1944 the *Suma Oriental* was published both in the original Portuguese, and in an English translation by the Hakluyt Society. When Tomé Pires wrote, the Hindu ruler still held sway in the mountain fastnesses of Java but all the seaports had fallen to Islam. His descriptions of these countries are as interesting as those of Marco Polo.

†The ashes of Buddha were distributed by Asoka to "all parts of the world" when this most famous of Indian emperors (third century B.C.) turned from military aggression to "conquest" of the world through Buddhism. His edicts establishing foreign missions were inscribed on rocks and may still be seen. At his behest, Buddhist missionaries carried the word of Buddha to all of Asia. Although Buddhism disappeared from India, having been absorbed into Hinduism, it became the religion of Burma, Siam, Indo-China, Tibet, China, Japan, and Korea. It seems probable that the great Indian migration into Southeast Asia was originally spurred by Buddhist missionary zeal, for the earlier Indian religion (Vedism, Brahmanism) forbade caste Indians to cross the ocean.

Carrying load of baskets in Djokja

Borobudur

The galleries are adorned with latticework niches containing images of the Buddha; originally there were over 500 but more than half this number are missing or badly damaged. Those that remain intact show the Buddha in a serene mood and are exceedingly pleasing to the Western eye.

The four lower galleries are enclosed by balustrades. The inner sides of the balustrades and the inner walls of the galleries are covered with intricate, beautifully executed bas-reliefs. In the center of each of the four sides of the building are flights of stairs guarded by sitting lions of ferocious mien. Where the stairs cross the galleries you pass through carved stone gates. The *stupa*-shaped monument is topped by a huge bell-like structure which is likewise called a *stupa*.

We liked Coerper's explanation of the meaning of the Borobudur. The pilgrim, he said, would begin walking around the first gallery where scenes of daily life and strife in bas-relief remind him that life is short and often full of misery. Then would come extremely realistic carvings of the Buddhist hell and heaven and scenes showing the many ways redemption had been sought before the advent of Buddha. Ascending the galleries, the pilgrim could see the life and death of Buddha depicted in great detail. Hot, thirsty, and weary he would tramp the galleries, observing more than two miles of bas-reliefs, until suddenly he reached the top, fresh air, the cloudless sky above, and saw himself surrounded by a circle of smiling statues of the Buddha. Coerper looked on the pilgrimage as a symbol of the devout Buddhist's life.

We were fascinated with the bas-reliefs, especially those illustrating daily life as it was lived by the Javanese of these early centuries. Nothing had changed radically in a thousand years. Most of the people frozen in stone could be seen any day on the roads of Java, pursuing activities very like those depicted in stone. The scenes of Buddha's life were charming and full of little homely touches, such as one showing his mother reclining on a couch and being massaged by her serving women to comfort her while she awaited the birth of her illustrious son. Another charming vignette that we liked especially showed two comical grinning cats which had obviously just that moment swallowed some canaries. There were also thrilling battle scenes and graceful sailing vessels riding stormy seas. I wanted to stay for hours wandering through the galleries and letting my imagination transplant me to Sri Vijaya or Madjapahit, but we had to leave.

Of the history of the Borobudur nothing definite is known. One legend has it that there once was a local prince whose daughter was lost. Though he mobilized all his retainers to search for her, she could not be found. Many years later he met and married a beautiful young lady and they had a son. As they were rejoicing in the birth of the eagerly awaited heir, a revengeful courtier taunted the prince, claiming that he was the one who had stolen the prince's young daughter years ago and—to repay the prince for some fancied insult—had arranged for the prince to marry her. Horror-stricken, the prince consulted the priests, who ruled that he, his wife, and son must be put into a walled cell there to die penitently; in no other way could they attain forgiveness for their heinous crime, unless, within ten days the prince built a temple according to their specifications. Whereupon he assembled all his subjects and set them to work day and night, but when the time was up the temple lacked one statue of Buddha. So the prince, his daughter-wife, and son had to die.

Another legend tells of a foreign prince who wanted to marry the daughter of the local potentate. He was told that he could have her only if, in a single night, he built a temple to the royal father's design. Again the task was almost accomplished, but again one thing was missing—one *stupa*. So the poor prince did not marry the lady.

Coerper said he wasn't sure whether these legends actually applied to the Borobudur or to another, much smaller temple—the exquisite Tjandi Mendut. This temple, which contains quite the loveliest statue of Buddha I ever saw, is a beautifully designed little gem of a temple and, like Borobudur, full of bas-reliefs done with great artistry.

I was struck by the similarity of these legends to many European fairy tales in which impossible tasks also are almost—but not quite—performed by heroes or heroines. Perhaps these similarities give us a faint glimpse of some far-off time when the present races of mankind, each so prone to claim superiority of all others, were all part of a single prehistoric people.

Borobudur is one of the temples that had been hidden by faithful Javanese when the Moslems were on their rampage of destruction. Sir Stamford Raffles discovered it in 1814, and it has since been dug out and carefully restored.* The Dutch have written intelligently about it so that even a tourist can get a good idea of its meaning. If you are an American tourist, a guide will follow your every step, as it is claimed that Americans immediately proceed to chip off parts of the figures.

Next morning Coerper took us to the royal cemetery of the Sultans of Djokja and the Susuhunans of Surakarta, or Solo, as it is more commonly called. We climbed a long steep staircase only to find

---

*During the Napoleonic wars, the British occupied the Dutch colonies. Raffles, an employee of the British East India Company, was made Governor of Java, where he initiated many important reforms, subsequently continued by the Dutch when the Indies were returned to them by the peace settlement at Vienna in 1815.

Buddha at Borobudur

Bas-relief sculpture at Borobudur

Tjandi Mendut

that ordinary mortals were not permitted to visit the actual tombs without proper permits. All we were allowed to see were the magnificently carved doors leading to the cemetery which were guarded by elegant courtiers dressed in the widely looped court sarong with a carved *kris* stuck into the belt in the middle of the back. They showed us a sacred fishpond and assured us that any unauthorized person daring to fish in it would be poisoned if he ate what he caught. They also told us that the Sultans of Djokja lie buried at the right, the Susuhunans of Solo at the left, and that no prince ever visits the tombs until he is carried there after death.

Djokja and Solo, the two principal native states in Java, had lesser potentates titled, respectively, the Paku Alam of Djokja and the Mangkunegoro of Solo. The Susuhunan of Solo was the highest ranking prince in Java. Although he took precedence at official functions, he and the Sultan of Djokja were otherwise equal. Both retained much influence over their people, in spite of the fact that each state had a Dutch Governor, a Resident, an Assistant Resident, and a Translateur (the go-between for the Dutch and the princes). The princes acted as agents of the Dutch government, carrying out its orders on the local level.

The Sultan of Djokja and the Susuhunan of Solo were forever competing with each other, to the great amusement of the Dutch. In this continual race for prestige, the two lesser princes joined with gusto. It made life interesting for rulers who must have been irked at times by Dutch restraints; their forebears, after all, were absolute kings whose word was law within the four corners of their domain and whose power over their subjects was absolute. When we were there, the favorite story was of a recent feud. The number two Djokja prince—an intelligent person with modern ideas—built a motor road into the mountains with a pavilion at the end for dispensing refreshments. When he invited the Susuhunan of Solo to send a delegation for the initiation festivities, that potentate—a cranky, old-fashioned, rude, and coarse man—showed his contempt for new-fangled things by sending seven blind men.

One of the titles of the Susuhunan is "Nail of the World," the idea being that at Solo there is a nail that pins down Java and with it the rest of our globe. Coerper remarked that this little dictator could teach some of the more powerful Europeans of this species a thing or two. He insisted, for example, that his race horses must win all races, and when he played cards he was accompanied by a special retainer who went around looking at the cards of his guests. But once a year even he was on his own; that was during the bridge match in Solo between the Sultan and Governor of Djokja and their counterparts.

Coerper was surprised when we asked him whether he knew of the magic black stone of the "white monkey." Apparently we were the only visitors who knew of it. I read the story in a magazine and was so intrigued that I had put a visit to the stone at the top of our list for Java. After some difficulty we found it but, alas, someone had spoiled everything by cutting down the old *waringin* trees and enclosing the stone in an ugly cement building. It used to lie in a small clearing shaded by four huge banyans, in a quiet place which invited repose and thoughts upon the vanity of life and the cruel tricks sometimes played on us by fate. Now the place is locked; one pays a fee to a functionary and all the atmosphere has gone.

Even so we were glad to see it. The stone is black and shiny, of oblong shape, about three feet wide and a little over four feet long. It must have been brought from a considerable distance for nothing like it can be found in this part of Java. The story goes that long, long ago there was a frightful storm which raged for days. When the sun reappeared, two fishermen went to look at what the sea had cast upon the shore. They found strange wreckage—articles of wood and iron such as they had never seen before. Suddenly one of the fishermen called out: "Look what I've found. A white monkey!" They were puzzled by the appearance of the strange animal and thought at first it would die because it was so exhausted. But it recovered. Not knowing what else to do with it, they took it to the *kraton* and showed it to the sultan. They thought it might amuse him and he could decide what to do with this odd creature. The sultan was intrigued and said: "Never before have I seen anything like this white monkey. Clearly it must have aroused the anger of some god who punished it by expelling it from the sea. Let the animal be made secure and every day it shall have two full meals as long as it lives." Accordingly, the white monkey was chained to a heavy stone and given bananas and such other food as happened to be at hand. It lived for thirty years. The children sometimes played with it and, although a morose and angry creature, it was gentle with the little ones. Sometimes the monkey could be seen scratching with a small stone on the rock to which it was chained. These scratches are still fairly legible. In the center of a rough circle, it says in capital letters: *Ad aeternam memoriam sortis infelicis*; underneath are the letters I G M and something that may be the date 1669. Around this is written: *Zoo gaat de wereld/ Cosi va il mondo/ ita movetur mundus/ ainsi va le monde.* In an even larger circle it says: *In fortuna consortis digni valete quid stupearis insani videte ignari et ridete/ contemnite vos contemptu digni.** Poor white

---

*The white monkey was not a good classical scholar or perhaps we read the almost illegible words incorrectly but here is what the writing on the stone *seems* to say: "To the everlasting memory of one (those) whose fortune was unhappy—

monkey. His was a bitter heart. It is believed that he was a Dutch doctor whose ship was stranded: a doctor, for only doctors knew that many languages in those days; and Dutch, for only a Netherlander would know Dutch. The time of the unfortunate man's imprisonment was probably 1669 and I G M are believed to have been his initials. We found the story intriguing because of its gentle mockery of white notions of superiority; no one at the Sultan's court had ever seen a European.

Of course, what really happened will never be known. Another version, perhaps more probable but not as appealing, has it that the prisoner was a Dutchman, but not a doctor. On the basis of the date 1669 and of a number of historically recorded facts, some Dutch investigators came to the conclusion that he was a Franciscan monk. At that time there were such monks in Java, and we have historical evidence that three Franciscans set out from Java for Timor in 1669. Soon after their departure there was a great storm in the vicinity. Nothing was heard of the ship or the monks until many years later when word reached Batavia from the Resident in Bantam that a renegade monk lived at the court of the Susuhunan of Mataram, where he had risen from a lowly position to become the ruler's principal adviser. The monk was said to have renounced his faith and embraced Islam. Having gained the prince's confidence, he lived in wealth and splendor. Then the son of the Susuhunan fell in love with the daughter of the Sultan of Bantam and the renegade monk was sent to ask for the hand of the princess. She refused and, as was customary in those days, failure of his mission meant disgrace for the luckless emissary, even possible death. The Susuhunan, however, was merciful and allowed him to live, though tied to a big stone. This might explain the lament, "So goes the world," which the prisoner appears to have been anxious to preserve at all costs for posterity, since he took the trouble to scratch it laboriously in Dutch, Italian, Latin, and French. What surprised us was that he did not leave us more interesting data. The sentiments are hardly worth all that trouble. Carving them with a rude stone must have been a time-consuming task.

That afternoon the Coerpers took us to Kaliurang, a small resort on Mount Merapi near Djokja, where we had tea on a terrace overlooking the beautiful Djokja plain. On the way back we stopped at their house and were regaled with honest-to-goodness fresh cow's milk—a treat which we had not enjoyed in over a year. We drank a quart and a half between the two of us.

IGM—1669—So goes the world—Farewell comrades—Why are you stupefied, you fools—Look and laugh—ignorant ones—You who are yourselves deserving of scorn, be scornful if you wish."

The most beautiful item in the house was a lovely silver vase—a bequest from Coerper's uncle, who had been an admiral in the German Asiatic Fleet before World War I. He bought the vase in Bali when he was a young lieutenant and the island was still ruled by its rajas. Coerper used to listen to his uncle's tales of the Far East, never guessing he would wind up policing central Java. He also had been a naval officer (class of 1913). By accident he was transferred from the ill-fated cruiser *Scharnhorst*, which went down with her entire crew off the west coast of South America, to the gunboat *Jaguar*, which was in Tsingtao during its seige by the Japanese in 1914. He told us amusing stories of the battle, in which for three months some 60,000 Japanese battered at the town, which was defended by a small German force. In their methodical way, the Japanese waged war according to textbooks they had bought in Europe; each morning it was merely a question of finding on which page they were, to anticipate every move. "They used to bombard us from their warships whose guns had a greater range than our shore batteries," said Coerper, "so at first we were pretty helpless. But then someone discovered that the Japanese ships steamed to their firing positions by taking bearings on a particular buoy in the bay. One night two of our men went out and moved the buoy half a mile inshore. The Japs never verified their findings by other bearings and so thereafter they invariably came close enough for us to hit them. We really did some damage to their ships with our few batteries." The Germans held off the Japanese as long as they had ammunition and did not capitulate until the last bullet had been fired. The day before the surrender, one lone flyer left Tsingtao and made a fantastically adventurous trip home, returning in time to do some more fighting for Germany before the war ended.

Coerper spent from 1915 to 1920 in Japan as a prisoner of war, learning Japanese and nearly starving to death on the pay of a Japanese lieutenant, junior grade. Under the Hague Convention, prisoners of war had to be given pay equivalent to that of corresponding personnel of the country that had captured them. In those days the saying was: A Japanese admiral gets as much pay as a German lieutenant and a German lieutenant gets as much as an American enlisted man. At first the German prisoners of war were well treated but, oddly enough, when they wrote home to that effect, the Japanese became stricter with them. At that time Japan was still anxious to be recognized as a modern power and behaved accordingly. Still, the Japanese had no high regard for a man who let himself be taken prisoner; I suppose they didn't want to overdo the humanitarianism.

The Japanese were inordinately proud of having taken Tsingtao. They felt that they, alone, had defeated Imperial Germany while their allies—the French and British—had not won any conspicuous victories. Coerper showed us a book of official photographs issued by Japan to commemorate their victory at Tsingtao. One lone German machine gun figured in a dozen or more pictures. First you saw the gun alone; then a group of German prisoners standing around it; then a Japanese general inspecting it; then various groups of victorious Japanese draped in front of, beside, and in back of the gun. A few stacked rifles were likewise used in a number of ways to show how much booty had been captured by the Japanese.

The prisoners of war were not released immediately after the armistice, as they had hoped to be, but were kept until 1920. At that time Coerper and some two hundred other German prisoners received an offer from the Dutch government to enter the Dutch colonial service. To men whose world had crashed about them and whose careers were finished, the terms seemed princely. Of course, it meant becoming Dutch citizens, but many probably wondered whether there was any Germany left to claim their allegiance. At any rate, most of them accepted. Coerper was the last one still in Dutch service.

At that time the Netherlands government was in desperate need of civil servants to man their colonial service. People in Holland were making large fortunes in shipping and other businesses connected with postwar reconstruction and nobody wanted to go out to the Indies. Those already there were no longer content with government pay and resigned in droves to become rubber or oil millionaires. But to the Germans in Japanese prisoner-of-war camps the prospect of work in the Dutch colonial service looked good. Coerper wrote home and asked his childhood sweetheart to come out and marry him. Mrs. Coerper—a charming blond lady—told me that it seemed to her then like a fairy tale to leave shattered Germany, where it was cold and nobody could get coal, and where people were hungry and little food was to be had. She said with a smile that merely the word *Orient* thrilled her and she thought it a dream to sail into this peaceful, warm, and lovely country. They had their honeymoon in a scenic spot in Sumatra and soon settled down to their new life. By the time we met them, they all spoke Dutch like natives. The children were the most patriotic little Netherlanders, but we wondered what would happen if ever loyalty to Germany and Holland should come into conflict. The hotels were full of beautifully printed booklets and pamphlets praising the "new" Germany and urging the Dutch to lose themselves "in a larger country of the same race where they would have much greater freedom than in the Netherlands." We were told that there was a strong Nazi movement among the Germans in the Indies; members of the movement went around to all hotels leaving their literature. The hotel-keepers didn't want to risk their ill will, so they let the pamphlets lie about the lobbies; we didn't see anyone reading them.

Since Coerper knew Japanese and Javanese people and had lived in both countries, we were interested in how he compared the two peoples. He thought them totally different. He considered the Japanese reserved, devious, cruel, and said their politeness was only a thin veneer. On the other hand, he liked the Javanese immensely and felt that they were far closer to Europeans than were the Japanese. But, while he liked them, Coerper did not regard the Javanese too highly, looking upon them as happy-go-lucky children, frank, open, and lovable. The longer he lived in Japan, the farther he felt himself from the Japanese, while every year he spent in Java brought him closer to the Javanese. He thought it fortunate that the more competent Japanese cannot stand tropical climates. They cannot even adapt themselves as well as Europeans to the heat of the Indies. Still less are they a match in this respect for their chief competitors in Southeast Asia—the Chinese. There were some Japanese photograph studios, beauty shops, and dentists in most Indonesian towns, but the retail trade was solidly in Chinese hands.

Our own observations led us to believe that there must be Malay blood in the common people of Japan, though the upper classes are of lighter skin and look more Chinese. We thought we detected a number of similarities in the customs of the peasants, and that level of society is preponderant in both countries. We noticed that the sliding-door walls of Indonesian houses were similar to the sliding panels of Philippine houses; the two peoples used similar pumps to raise water into their rice fields; and there were other similarities. Many Japanese peasant women looked to us like Filipinos, a racial similarity possibly reinforced by similarity of character. In both races the women are hardworking, responsible, cheerful, and pleasant—far more admirable members of society than their men. The Japanese peasants struck us as industrious, skillful agriculturists, but the ridiculous illusions of masculine superiority that make up so large a part of Japanese males spoil their character. The Filipino man—not similar at all to the Japanese man—is fortunately free of these illusions and is even apt to be a little henpecked. He is a light-hearted character, *muy simpatico*, but somewhat shiftless, indolent, and inclined to gamble away the family funds.

During our trip through the Japanese countryside we had found the people as helpful and friendly as the Malays, but it is true that we had no affection for Japanese officials. Possibly Coerper's views were colored by his experiences with Japanese bureaucrats. Country people the world over are generally pleasant and friendly.

We questioned Coerper closely on the subject of mixed marriages. The Dutch intermarried freely with the Malays, and officially they regarded anyone with a drop of European blood as European, provided he had been acknowledged by his European father; legitimacy was not required. In all government positions, such persons were theoretically on a par with the Dutch and received the same pay, if found capable of holding a job hitherto reserved to Dutchmen. In hotels, trains, theatres, there was no color bar and we saw a number of mixed couples. Still, there were apparently certain social bars. It all depended upon the individual; if he was desirable, his antecedents were not held against him.

We were amused to observe the determination with which half-castes identified themselves with the ruling whites and the contempt they expressed towards the "inferior" natives. If we got into trouble with native servants, shopkeepers, or guides, we could always locate a half-caste who was eager to come to the rescue, highly apologetic at the "dishonesty of these natives" but, oddly, himself seldom averse to fleecing the unwary tourist. Still, if we appealed to them as fellow whites, they always came through. Thus while the hotel manager in Djokja had to be encouraged by strenuous bargaining on our part to stick to the official rates, he, in turn, was indignant when we reported that the bank teller had quoted us an outrageous rate on our dollars. He went to the bank in person, and got us the correct rate. Strange how oriental bazaar customs found their way into such nominally Dutch institutions as banks and hotels. At home the Dutch would never have tolerated these petty dishonesties.

Perhaps this came about because the Dutch leaned so heavily on their *mandurs* (native superintendents or foremen)—their number one boys, as we called them in China. The average Dutchman in the Indies was astonishingly uninformed about the country he lived in and, while always most willing to help a stranger, rarely knew the location of famous landmarks in his vicinity or the history of some well-known show place. Automatically he turned to his *mandur* who usually had the information. At Gilimanuk Bay we had found a Dutch official who knew no English but whose *mandur* spoke it fluently. He was an exception, however. The Dutch are usually good linguists and we never had much trouble finding one who could speak English. What surprised us was that some seemed to live with closed eyes in this interesting country.

We thought many Dutch customs amusing, such as the absence of soap—you must bring your own—in the hotels of these excessively clean people, and the generous display of posters with "don't" on them. Our hotel room in Djokja was simply plastered with them and everywhere you walked you saw *djangan masoek* (forbidden entry) signs. And then the beds: Dutch beds are generously constructed to support this race of giants and they are provided with ample folds of mosquito netting, but they do not have the proper number of sheets. They give you a hard bolster, called a *Dutch wife*, one sheet, and one blanket. You are expected to lie on the sheet, drape your legs around the Dutch wife so that air can circulate and keep you cool, and, if it gets too cold, pull up the blanket. We had the dickens of a time getting the *djongos* to bring us a second sheet. In the morning the floor in our room was always covered with unwanted pillows and Dutch wives, and I do not doubt that the *djongos* were shocked. George was intrigued by the small, embroidered bags which we found at our place in the dining room and into which we were supposed to tuck our soiled napkins for use the next day; he called them *pillow slips*.

We left Djokja for Bandung early in the morning. No sooner had we installed ourselves comfortably on the train, when we saw the Coerpers, complete with uniformed chauffeur, and carrying two bottles of milk for us, coming down the platform at the station. We were touched by this thoughtfulness and much distressed to have put our gracious hosts to the embarrassment of being seen by the natives with people who traveled third-class. But they carried it off beautifully and their official splendor gave us much face among the natives with their chickens who shared our coach. Next morning we flew from Bandung to Batavia, where we transferred to our plane for Sumatra.

4
Sumatra

We had booked passage to Pakanbaru without knowing what it would be like there or how we would get away from it. Despite the many beautifully printed folders on Sumatra, in which NITOUR had mapped out elaborate itineraries for cross-country drives in private cars, we could not obtain any real information about Sumatra anywhere. All the pamphlets stressed the wildness of the country and the danger of having a breakdown and being stranded in the midst of jungles populated by fearsome wild beasts. It was intimated that such breakdowns were apt to occur if one did not use the dependable (and outrageously expensive) NITOUR tour cars. Nobody knew whether there were any buses in Sumatra; in fact, the mere suggestion that we might wish to travel by native bus distressed the young gentlemen in the travel agencies so much that we did not have the heart to press them for information. We figured that there were but a handful of whites in the central part of Sumatra and that the natives must have some way to move about. Obviously, they could not afford to travel NITOUR. Very well, we would chance it. We looked at the map of Sumatra and, figuring backwards from the time we had to be in Medan to catch our steamer to Penang, we decided to take the KNILM plane to the farthest point east, which was Pakanbaru, trusting to our luck to find some way out from this tiny place in the midst of the jungle. We felt quite adventurous that morning, having braved all the dire predictions of danger and discomfort from everyone whose advice we had sought.

The early morning plane from Bandung deposited us at the Batavia airfield only forty-five minutes before the weekly plane for Sumatra left. We had, therefore, no time to see Batavia. The only stop before we reached our destination was Palembang, center of the ancient Sri Vijayan empire, where the plane seemed to dive straight into the forest. At the last moment we noticed a small clearing and felt reassured. The airport was primitive—a wooden shack where you could buy little more than Dutch chocolates. Fortunately, they served a good picnic lunch on the plane; this was our last proper meal for some time to come.

SUMATRA

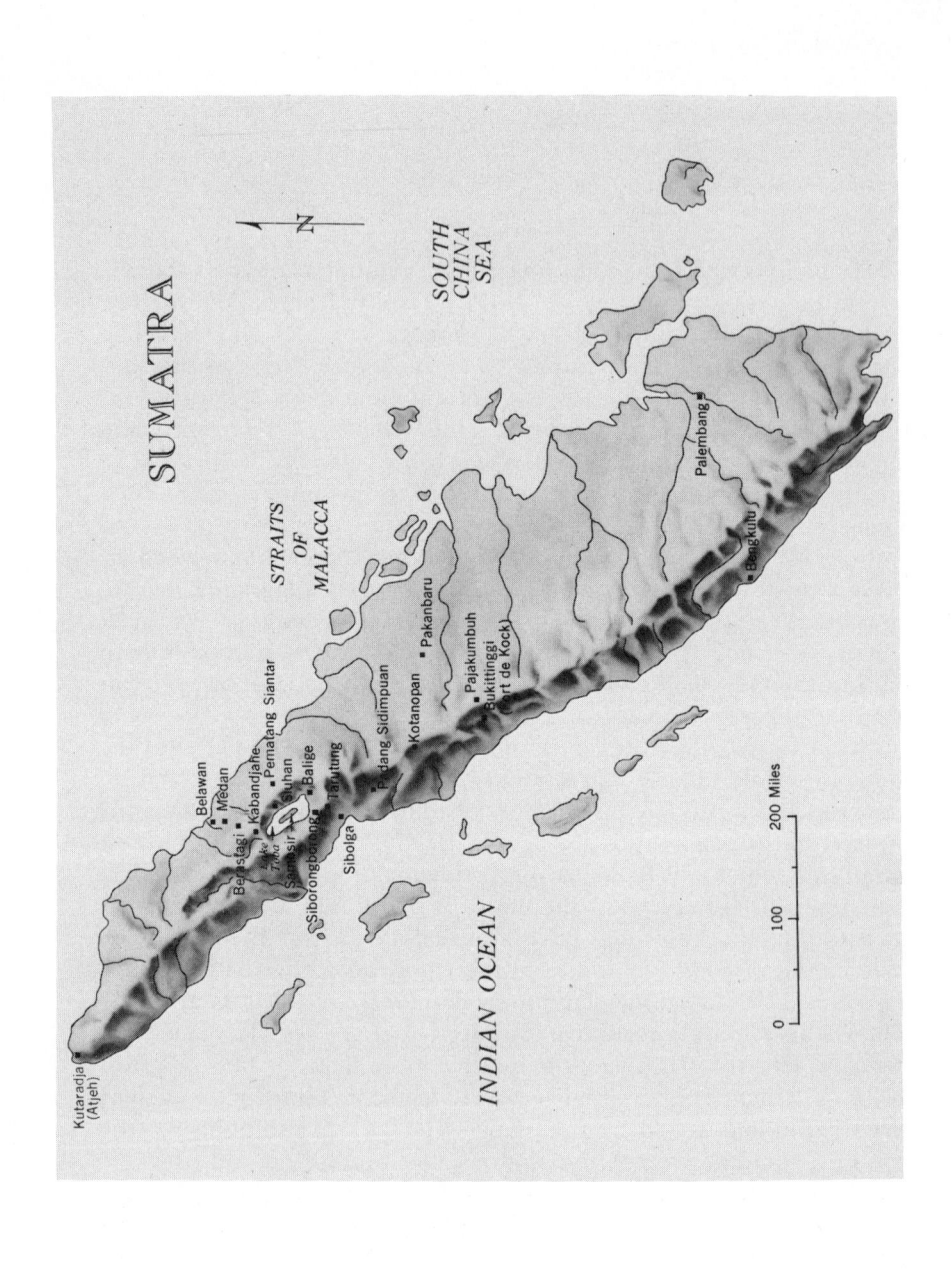

STRAITS OF MALACCA

SOUTH CHINA SEA

INDIAN OCEAN

- Kutaradja (Atjeh)
- Belawan
- Medan
- Kabandjahee
- Berastagi
- Pematang Siantar
- Sibuhan
- Sandosir
- Balige
- Siborongborong
- Tarutung
- Sibolga
- Padang Sidimpuan
- Kotanopan
- Pakanbaru
- Pajakumbuh
- Bukittinggi (Fort de Kock)
- Palembang
- Bengkulu

Lake Toba

0   100   200 Miles

We flew for two and a half hours above a green sea of trees in which we could not discern the slightest sign of human habitation. As we looked down into the green jungle, we began to feel apprehensive, but the captain of the plane said he thought that there was a bus line from Pakanbaru to Fort de Kock,* our goal for that day. He was dubious, however, whether the buses were fit for white people and shook his head at our casual attitude towards travel in jungles.

When the ship nosed down, we were quite excited and looked eagerly around, but all we saw was a small shed with the letters KNILM painted on its roof. One could buy bottled drinks there and wash up. I did a thorough job knowing it would be the last chance I would get that day. It was noon and hot. In the excitement I had forgotten to drink all the water I could before leaving the plane and, as soon as I remembered this, I began to get thirsty. There was no drinking water to be had; nothing but bottles of sweet drinks that merely increased your thirst.

We were cheered, however, to discover that there was indeed a bus to Fort de Kock; it ran once a week and this was the day. We hired a taxi to a nearby village where the bus was loading at the moment. For two and half guilders we were driven about half a mile down the road where we found an exceedingly ramshackle bus already so tightly packed that we wondered if we would be able to squeeze in. But this can always be managed thereabouts. We transferred ourselves and, after an interminable time, drove off. Soon we noticed that we were headed back to the flying field. When we arrived there, we took the official sternly to task for sending us about the country in the heat when we could have awaited the bus at the airfield. He was embarrassed and muttered something about wanting to make sure we should get a seat. We knew that he had been given a rake-off on the taxi fare but could not afford to quarrel with him because we needed him in our fight with the bus driver—who had overcharged us scandalously for seats in the third row which he had the nerve to call first-class. A manifest lie, since we knew by then that only the first row is considered first-class. The half-caste official gave the native bus driver a rough talking-to and extracted several guilders from him which he handed to us triumphantly. It still left both of them a nice illegal profit but we decided to call it a bargain. Although I had used my worst Malay words on the driver, he bore us no resentment and in no time we became good friends. These little disagreements are part of business deals in that part of the world and nobody bears you a grudge when he is prevented from swindling you.

*The name of this city was changed to Bukittinggi when Dutch occupation of the East Indies ceased.

Though everything had worked out better than we had any right to expect, we weren't too enthusiastic at first over our new mode of transportation. The seats were hard and we were terribly crowded. Most of the passengers were local people—Minangkabaus—a handsome people considered by the Dutch to be the crème de la crème of the Malay race. There were also three Chinese women who traveled first-class and kept to themselves. They obviously felt like *pukkah memsahibs* surrounded by aborigines. George and I were of absorbing interest to all the passengers and everything we did aroused their curiosity. They smiled at us in an exceedingly friendly way and soon had us answering the usual personal questions. As happens when one speaks a foreign language badly, I must have committed a number of malapropisms for some of my most harmless remarks produced gales of laughter and were later repeated to all the people we met when stopping on the way. I remember one incident that pleased them inordinately although I shall never understand why it was so amusing.

In that part of the world no man does more than a meager job of work. The bus driver drove. He had no concern with the motor. He had assistants to see that it ran and that the oil and gas were checked. One man had the sole duty of seeing that there was enough water in the radiator. Every so often the bus stopped and he ran to a spring to fetch water. When I made some comment about his pouring water—*tuang ayer*—the passengers burst into loud giggles and it was a long time before they quieted down. After everyone had dried his tears and regained his composure, somebody would murmur *tuang* and off they were again in paroxysms of laughter. Even a poor chap who had been carsick most of the time—doing his struggling quietly and unobtrusively—cheered up and began to join in the fun. It was obviously necessary to teach me better Malay and the entire bus earnestly turned to it. I learned quite a lot on that long, hot drive. Not to be outdone, we taught them English; it was a most profitable trip for all concerned.

If I hadn't been so infernally thirsty, I should have enjoyed myself enormously. But with every mile I felt more miserable. Soon the other passengers noticed what was wrong and great efforts were made to help me. First, they ordered the driver to detour to a well and pointed it out to me, but I was afraid it might be polluted. Then they made him take us to a native rest house where I was offered a glass of water. But it looked so much like the one offered us by the Balinese raja that I could not bring myself to drink it; there wasn't any rice wine to control the germs. Much distress among my kindly fellow passengers! Now they brought out bananas which I ate gratefully; they helped a little but not enough. The sun beat down and my mouth got dryer and dryer.

Finally, after considerable discussion among themselves, a decision was reached and resolutely put into effect. The driver took George into a store where he bought several bottles of soda water—known as *ayer belanda* (white man's water). We did not have a cup and I hesitated to put my mouth to the bottle. By now we must have appeared like helpless children to the people on the bus. They stopped at a native restaurant and all of them trooped in with us. The innkeeper was told to boil water in a pot and lower a cup into the water, swish it around and lift it out with a long spoon. Then the *ayer belanda* was poured into the cup and everyone looked on with great satisfaction while I downed the sweet liquid. To my surprise it helped quite a bit.

At every village, while loading and unloading freight, we stopped for a little chat. The passengers immediately told all they knew about us to the villagers, who smiled at us in the most friendly fashion. In my best Malay I would ask if I could wash my hands and, in this way, I saw the interiors of many native homes. They were all clean and neat.

On and on we chugged in our creaking vehicle, stopping every few miles so that water could be poured into the radiator. Twice we had to get out to ford rivers. The ferries were primitive—merely three boats connected together by a few planks. I shouldn't like to depend upon them in bad weather. As the day wore on, we became more and more one big family. Even the Chinese ladies gradually thawed and joined in the conversation; one offered me her smelling salts, another lent me her fan. The driver, who evidently felt responsible for our welfare, questioned us closely on our travel plans. People gave us advice and we took photographs. All the while the scenery became more and more beautiful.

First we drove through flat country. The road was new and we could see how it had been cut out of the jungle. There were no cars and few people. Those we saw looked handsome and healthy and no one carried heavy loads. Sumatra was pioneer country. We passed many rice fields that had been planted for the first time on land which had not yet been properly cleared. The young rice plants grew among half-charred tree stumps. The Dutch were indignant at the natives' unscientific deforestation of Sumatra, but we felt that this was a chance for a better way of life for them and worth the sacrifice of some jungle trees. Hadn't we done the same in America? The difference between the looks and bearing of the people in Sumatra and those in Java was striking. Sumatra was a land of opportunity and only carabao carried loads and not very heavy ones at that. Gradually we came into mountainous country. The scenery was majestic and quite untouched by man. Particularly dramatic was the gorge of a river which we followed for some time. Up and down the mountains the road wound, the jungle reaching closely on both sides so that in the high-slung bus we felt as if we were blazing a trail straight through the forest. We saw few human habitations until we approached Pajakumbuh, a fairly large town.

We were now in Minangkabau country and soon we saw their unusual gabled housetops peeping through banana groves, which they also plant around their houses. Their roofs, which sloped down in the center and rose at both ends into sharp points, reminded one of Malay praus. Most houses had two such curved roofs superimposed upon each other and of different lengths. Unlike most other Malay houses, these were not on stilts. They were well-constructed and substantial. Unfortunately the modern trend is away from these picturesque roofs and towards unattractive sheet iron monstrosities.

It was dark when we reached Pajakumbuh, where we changed buses. Sadly we said goodbye to all our new friends. By now my thirst had become truly great and we walked all around the town trying to find water. Ordinarily this would not be difficult in a large town with a considerable number of white residents, but although it was an up-to-date town with asphalt avenues and pretty European villas, Pajakumbuh lacked anything resembling a drug store or café. We finally met a Dutch couple and asked them where we could get some drinking water. As usual they were helpless—eager to be of assistance but simply incapable of dealing with such an unexpected problem. They were on their way to a dinner party at the home of a Dutch official; in fact, they were standing right in front of his house when we accosted them. It never occurred to them to invite us in or even to go in themselves and carry a glass out to us. Instead they said they thought there was a government rest house somewhere and looked around frantically wondering where it could be. Finally they left us, full of regrets at not having been able to help. George then decided to disregard my protests and to simply walk up to a house and ask for water. We looked for one that had the appearance of European occupation and knocked on the door. A surprised young Dutchman, holding in his hand a book on French night life, opened the door. In a medley of French, English, and German, we were able to make known our need and he immediately ordered his boy to bring *ayer belanda*. We should have preferred plain water but this evidently was not to be had that day. Even the *ayer belanda* tasted like nectar. Despite language difficulties we carried on a pleasant conversation, and our Good Samaritan insisted on taking us personally to the bus. He was probably puzzled at our unconventional manner of traveling but too well-mannered to comment. Meeting him did much to counterbalance our somewhat sour opinion of Dutch hospitality.

The ride to Fort de Kock in the cool of the night was pleasant, especially since the road was hard-surfaced and the bus, therefore, did not shake us up. Above there was the clearest starlit sky I ever saw and all around were high, dark mountains, covered with dense forest. Once we stopped at a crossroads to let a procession of carabao carts pass. These carts looked like the Minangkabau houses; their roofs also were steep and curved downwards in the center and had pointed ends. The wheels were often five feet high. The carts moved slowly, creaking, their bells tinkling, and tiny lights dangling from their roofs. This was one of the most picturesque sights in Sumatra.

We were glad when we finally drew up in front of the Park Hotel and, after a little dickering, were led to a large, clean, comfortable room. It was heaven to pour water over our tired, dusty selves, and then eat a good dinner with plenty of real water.

One of the most exciting features of hotel life was watching the lively little lizards frisk gaily over the furniture and across the walls. If we caught one by the tail, the tail came off in our fingers. Apparently they were able to grow replacements, for many tails were of odd lengths.

We stayed a day at Fort de Kock to rest after our strenuous bus ride. In the morning we walked over to Carabao Canyon. Hundreds of monkeys ran across our path and swung from the trees on each side, gibbering at us. These cunning creatures never failed to give us a special thrill for they were a visible confirmation that we were indeed wandering in exotic lands.

We photographed groups of Minangkabaus and their carabao carts. In the afternoon we took a drive to the famous Minangkabau village of Puntjak Bukit, which was *de rigeur* for tourists. The village consisted of several houses with lavishly carved and painted sides and gracefully curved horn-ridged roofs. These houses were as sturdily built and substantial as the homes of the average American farmer, though lacking their amenities. We entered one by its wide, stone staircase and found that it had large well-appointed rooms, covered with fine mats, and furnished with tables and chairs. At each end there was a large bed on a raised platform with clean mosquito netting and a profusion of embroidered pillows. We noticed a huge picture of Princess Juliana and her husband Prince Bernhard.

Only women were at home. They had regular features, attractive by our own standards. Their costumes consisted of a sarong and over it a long, straight coat. All wore heavy gold bracelets and looked well fed. Their head covering was odd indeed, resembling nothing so much as a flat pillow, dented in the middle and puffed out at the ends; this was folded neatly into an embroidered shawl hanging down in back, the

Ferry in Sumatra

Carabao cart near Fort de Kock

Minangkabau village

long fringes at each end dangling below the shoulders. Though cumbersome, the outfit was dignified and handsome. Some of the ladies wore numerous long, bead necklaces and rings on their fingers.

The Minangkabau district is believed to have been the "cradle of the Malay race" from which, it is said, the Malays spread northwestward and eastward throughout the Malay Archipelago.* We were always amused by the tendency of ethnologists to search everywhere for the countries whence any given people are supposed to have come. Here, for the first time, they stated that a people actually originated where they are found today! Just why the Minangkabaus, rather than the Javanese, Buginese, Filipinos, or such mountain tribes as the Igorots or Bataks, should be thought to be the original Malays is not clear to us. Ethnologists do plunge into the most amazing theories on the flimsiest of evidence. We could see no good reason why the Dutch should consider the Minangkabaus the most highly civilized of all the people in the Indies. In fact, if one must grade them—always an arbitrary and dangerous proceeding—we should give this encomium to the Balinese. Even Javanese civilization seems to us richer and more sophisticated. In this connection, it is worth noting that the Minangkabaus formerly wrote in Javanese script, never having developed one of their own, and now use Arabic script. Be that as it may, these people are pleasant-looking and intelligent, their homes solid and handsome, their villages clean and well-run, their bearing dignified. All this may in large part be the result of living in a splendid climate, on land that provides ample harvests. Also, the

*Another theory is that the present Malays originated in southern Asia and migrated to Malaya and the Malay Archipelago when the later was still connected with the mainland of Asia. They drove into the mountains and forests the aborigine dwarf negroes, descendants of a more ancient negroid race, who are still to be found in a few isolated areas in Malaya (where they are called Semang or Pangan), the Philippines (where they are called Aetas or Negritos), and other parts of the Archipelago. These shy people live on what must be the lowest level of civilization. They have no shelter other than trees or a few branches pulled together to form an open windbreak, and depend for their food on what they can gather or kill with their blowguns and poisoned arrows. There is little intercourse or intermarriage between the Malays and the dwarf negroes.

Among the Malays proper there are two distinct types, and it is believed that they came in two separate waves of migration. The Proto-Malays are shorter than the Malays proper; their skin is darker, their hair is slightly wavy, their faces are cruder and they are of a more stocky build. They were the first to inhabit the Archipelago. When the second wave of Malays, the Deutero-Malays, came, the Proto-Malays were driven into the mountains. They retained their animist religion and were touched neither by Hinduism nor by Islam. Cannibalism and headhunting, once common among them, are disappearing. The two examples of this racial type with whom we became acquainted—the Igorot and Ifugao of northern Luzon in the Philippines and the Batak in Sumatra—appealed to us as frank and open mountain people, excellent farmers, and interesting because, in their social organization, they probably represent the primitive Malay type, unaffected by foreign influences.

mountains have protected the Minangkabaus against foreign invasions and allowed them to work out their destiny in relative peace.

Although Sumatra must have been the first of the islands of the archipelago to receive Indian migrants and was indeed the country of origin of the great Sri Vijayan empire, we were surprised to find it virtually bare of Indian temple ruins or sculptures, possibly because Sumatra also was the first to receive Islam which may have been particularly successful in destroying the hated edifices of the heathen. A curious reminder of a far-off, Indian-influenced period is the claim made even today by the Minangkabau princes that they are descended from Sultan Iskander—Alexander the Great! The people are solidly Moslem but have retained their curious matriarchal social organization. Name, property, and legal status derive from the wife who, after marriage, remains with her own people, the husband visiting her occasionally; he lives with his mother's people. Land cannot be sold and remains in the family. Several families with the same name live in one large house; a few of these houses, together with their well-built storehouses, the mosque, the school, a community house, and an inn make up a Minangkabau village. The houses are always surrounded by trees, usually banana palms, through which their fantastic roofs peek like something out of a fairy tale. In the village we visited there was a small square with a beautiful community house, where court convened and village business and entertainments took place. A big drum, used to call the villagers to meetings, was kept in a small house nearby. The Minangkabaus are excellent farmers and their women must be splendid housekeepers, judging by the well-filled storehouses and the neat appearance of this village.

On our way back, we contacted the local Chinese agent of LIM (the government bus service) and found him, like all Chinese we met, efficient and businesslike. He told us the exact bus rate—one cent per kilometer, second-class—and thenceforth we were never again cheated by bus drivers. We merely handed them what we had calculated as the correct fare and they were so surprised they did not know what to say. They thought it rather a joke and liked us the more for it.

In our hotel garden, I cut off a tiny bit of bark from a cinnamon tree. It always gave me a thrill to see where our familiar kitchen staples came from; by then I was thoroughly familiar with the botanical facts about sugar, rice, rubber, coffee, tea, coconut, pepper, hemp, banana, pineapple, mango, and many more I cannot name at the moment. But this was our first cinnamon tree. It had red leaves and we saw entire hillsides covered with these trees, as with a red veil. The hotelkeeper showed us a small cage covered by a tasseled cloth containing a singing dove. The Minangkabaus enjoy competitions

Minangkabau girl

Courthouse at Puntjak Bukit

with their singing birds and bet on them like the Filipinos and the Balinese do on cock fights. The birds are kept in dark cages and, when the cloth is removed, they sing joyously.

Next morning we started off by bus for Kotanopan, halfway between Fort de Kock and the port of Sibolga. It was a rickety bus, and for the first time we had a poor driver. He drove fast on curves and slow on straight level stretches, apparently trying to keep at a steady rate of speed all the time. Like all native drivers, he saved gasoline by going downhill in neutral. As the road wound steeply around sharp curves, we had several unpleasant moments when we thought he no longer had the bus under control. However, the brakes held miraculously and we only got shaken up, the springs having long ago given up the ghost. Though the bus was old and decrepit, its interior at least was enlivened by a picture of Juliana and Bernhard walking through a canopy of swords after their wedding. It hung above the driver's head and swayed to and fro. Pictures of Juliana were much in evidence throughout the Dutch East Indies.

The Dutch felt that white prestige required them to travel in private cars. If they wanted to go somewhere and had no car, they just didn't go. But, if it was absolutely necessary to use a bus, there was a way of preventing too severe a loss of face: you paid three times as much as the natives for exactly the same accommodation, and throughout the trip you maintained a cool, reserved attitude, never saying a word to anyone. We could observe this at leisure in our companion of that day. She was an elderly Dutch lady traveling from Bengkulu to Tarutung—a long trip. She didn't talk with us until almost the end of the day. When the ice was finally broken she was quite pleasant. But her presence in the bus cast a shadow on us; we were so well-behaved that we did not have any fun.

The scenery, however, was even lovelier and more majestic than on the road from Pakanbaru to Fort de Kock. There were many wild rivers, gorges, high mountains, and deep valleys. As the landscape became wilder, the villages began to look less prosperous and clean. We were leaving the Minangkabau villages and coming to Batak country. We saw fewer people with light skin, heart-shaped faces, bee-stung mouths and finely drawn eyebrows. Instead we began to notice stocky men and women, strangely like our Philippine Igorots. These were the Bataks who live around Lake Toba, the great inland lake in north central Sumatra.

Traveling by bus may not be convenient, but we were able to see bits of native life we might otherwise have missed. In one village we came upon preparations for a funeral. A young woman had just died. She was being laid out in a shroud with many women busily washing her and getting her ready, while the menfolk were congregated a small distance away. All this went on right in the village street and we could see it with ease since the bus had stopped there. In another village a young lad got off the bus and literally fell into the arms of a congregation of relatives who rushed out of an attractive house when we drew up in front of it. As soon as he tumbled into their arms, everyone set up terrific wailing and weeping while he was helped into the house. The bus waited patiently—everybody sympathetic. The young man, we were told, had just been called home from Java, where he was studying. His mother had died suddenly. Presently someone came to get his luggage. Besides many bags and bundles, it included a camp bed, a huge washbasket full of fruit and other victuals, a lunch container with a red rose painted on it, and a covered cage with a singing dove—no books.

It was dark when we arrived at the *pasanggrahan* (government rest house) in Kotanopan. We had time only for a short stroll before dinner was served. There was the inevitable *nasi goreng* (fried rice), a common food in government rest houses. It is a simplified form of *rijsttafel* (rice table) and by far the safest thing to eat. As the Dutch served it in their colony, this dish consisted of a huge platter of rice upon which one heaped innumerable meats, condiments, spices, and sauces, which were brought by a line of *djongos* in white coats. A truly elegant *rijsttafel* required twenty-two boys, each with two platters of things to put on the rice. A good Dutchman used to wash this down with copious draughts of beer and go back to his office and many more hours of hard work. Shows what a hardy race the Dutch are! One orders a meal for *satu orang* (one person) and two people have a hard time doing away with it (unless they are Dutch, of course!). We found the rest house satisfactory, though not luxurious. These *pasanggrahans* were built in out-of-the-way places for the convenience of government officials who had to travel where there were no proper hotels. Others were accepted if there was room. Prices were high for what was received but one was grateful to find a place to sleep in these places. They were run by native *mandurs* who kept them passably clean.

The next day we warmed somewhat to our Dutch lady companion, and she told us that she would be met by her brother's car in Padang Sidimpuan whence a new road leads directly to Tarutung. This was our destination also. I felt a little under the weather, so when she urged us to hire a car to take us directly to Tarutung, bypassing Sibolga, we thought it a good idea. The bus really was uncomfortable. When we got to Padang Sidimpuan, the Dutch lady did her very best trying to find a taxi for us but none could be located. Her brother's car arrived, and she climbed into its huge emptiness without once even *thinking* of offering us a lift. It just never entered her head. We should have been only too glad to pay the cost of the gasoline. Naturally we didn't say anything to her but it puzzled us. We couldn't imagine an American, traveling for two days with the only two white people in an area several thousand miles square, not offering a lift when no native car was to be had. The lady obviously had the friendliest feelings for us. She felt quite sorry about my traveling farther in the rickety bus and not feeling well at that. Her last action before we got off the bus was to pour a generous portion of eau de cologne on my head.

We arrived in Sibolga at four in the afternoon and found it hot and uninteresting. We had been told that the local hotel was abominable and were, therefore, anxious to get away as fast as possible. We wandered around town trying to find a bus leaving for Tarutung, in the mountains, that evening. As usual, the Chinese merchants were our best and most helpful friends. George located an English-speaking one at the mail-bus agency. After George told him that he had been in Shanghai during the Japanese attack on that city in 1937 and had found the Chinese extremely brave fighters, the most amiable diplomatic relations were established. The Chinese grinned broadly and said: "America very good friend China. Must help China win war from Japanese. Me must help you." It is nice to come from a popular country.

He telephoned around and found a Chinese grocery truck on the point of leaving for Tarutung and the driver was willing to take us along for one guilder apiece. Thus it happened that we sank so low as to be bundled into an ancient Chevrolet truck, half-filled with copra, gasoline, bananas, and all manner of queerly shaped baskets with groceries, evil-smelling dried fish, and what not. The forward half of the truck carried a dozen or so passengers, all apparently friends of our driver. He was a jolly lad with decidedly American mannerisms and a fair command of English. He had been taught a little English at a missionary school and must have seen some American movies, because he knew interesting slang expressions as well as odd bits of poetry and several hymns which I doubt he recognized for what they were.

The road to Tarutung goes up steep mountains in two hundred hairpin curves. Our driver, who was good though perhaps somewhat exuberant, dashed at forty miles an hour around these curves on the narrow road, singing lustily: "Come to Jesus, come to Jesus"—at times we feared we might. He varied this with "Jesus love me, dat I know, for de Bible tell me so" combined with something a bit garbled about the hula-hula girls in Waikiki. When we remonstrated with him and urged a little caution, the rear wheels having just barely got back on the road after hanging for a moment above the abyss, he would grin and yell, "Okey, dokey; keep you shirt on." Everyone in the truck joined in the singing and reassured us that it usually got down to Tarutung all right.

At frequent intervals we would come to a *veldpolitie* (rural police) station where all vehicles must stop to be weighed. The Dutch laid down careful regulations concerning maximum weight of buses and trucks, but they might as well have saved themselves the expense and bother of the weighing stations. Whenever there was doubt as to the weight of a truck, all passengers, with their possessions, got off a few hundred yards before the station and rejoined the truck a few hundred yards beyond it.

Our driver told us frankly he wasn't fond of the Dutch, but liked Americans. All Americans, he said, were rich; presumably even those traveling in grocery trucks. "America fine country. They take away from rich, give to poor," he said, thus summing up tersely the philosophy of the New Deal. In one village we saw pigs and were startled. We had been traveling in Moslem territory for so long that we weren't used to seeing these "unclean animals." When questioned, the driver said loftily: "Where there's pigs, there's Christians." He pointed to a small church, saying: "This Martin Luther propaganda." Strange as his words sounded to our ears, they were quite natural for a Moslem, who probably looked upon non-Moslems as contemptible non-believers. We had come into Batak country where a German mission was busily converting natives to Christianity. Our driver had no use for the missionaries. "They say God love us, but put money in pocket. German clever man." was his verdict. As to the Japanese, he hated them because "They kill baby" referring to the sack of Nanking. He was a young man of pronounced opinions.

Wherever we stopped, we had to explain in detail who we were, where we came from, and where we were going. George once started to enumerate all the places we had visited but when he mentioned New York it was too much and our audience laughed good-humoredly, one man remarking with a twinkle in his eye: "I come from Hindustan." Another said: "I come from Siam." It turned into a game as to who could think of the most outlandish places to have visited. If we were going to lie about our travels, they felt they could lie as well. It struck us as odd that New York should seem so strange a place that they couldn't believe we'd been there.

George and the driver kept up a continuous conversation which was translated, word for word, for the benefit of the other passengers. It got dark and we stopped at a village where we had time to wander about. Soon the usual group of retainers followed us and again we answered many questions about ourselves. At one place we found an open fire. The children jumped over it to show off and we gave the winner a copper penny which brought forth the most delightful smile of happiness. When we came back to the truck we found that all the groceries, gasoline, and fish had been unloaded and we were now taking on a load of firewood, at four local cents a bundle. The loading took place by the uncertain light of a single tiny oil lamp, which reminded us forcefully of Alice Hobart's *Oil for the Lamps of China*. An ancient crone held the lamp. I wish we could have photographed her. When we drove off, the whole village ran alongside the bus crying *horas*—the Batak farewell.

It was nine o'clock when we arrived at the *pasanggrahan* at Tarutung. We were dumbfounded when the *mandur* said *"tidak ada"*—no rooms. There was no other inn or hotel in this small place and we were dead tired. I sank exhausted into a chair and asked if I might not keep that chair for the night, but this couldn't be done; it was against regulations. We asked whether there were any cars for hire to drive us to the next *pasanggrahan*. There were none. Somebody suggested seeing the Controleur. The Dutch had a touching faith in this official and always told you to see him when you were in any difficulty. Wearily we tramped over to the Controleur's house, but all he could tell us was that there was no room in the Tarutung *pasanggrahan* and that we must go to the next one in Siborongborong, 38 miles away. This we knew already. When we explained that we could find no transportation and were very tired and asked if we could stay in the rest house living room, he said regretfully "No, it is against regulations," and quietly closed the door. We were disheartened as we trudged back to the *pasanggrahan*, but there we met an unusually resourceful Dutchman, Mr. de Jong, who had lined up two gentlemen who not only owned a car but were actually willing to give us a ride in it. One was even Dutch! The car, however, belonged to his companion, an Englishman. These two had also wanted to spend the night at Tarutung and were now leaving for Siborongborong. They were representatives of a tobacco company and we are eternally thankful to them for rescuing us from this unpleasant situation. It was our own fault. Heedlessly, we had neglected to reserve a room as the Dutch had told us we should, since this was one of the best and hence most popular *pasanggrahans*.

This was the first and only lift we ever got in the Dutch East Indies. It felt wonderful to be traveling in the luxury of an elegant car. We were fortunate to have caught it just before leaving. That night at Siborongborong was the most primitive on the trip. The *pasanggrahan* was small and badly kept; the mattress of our bed as hilly as the country through which we had just traveled. However, we did succeed in wresting two sheets from the *mandur* and were so tired we slept wonderfully well. In the morning, after a sketchy breakfast of bananas and tea, we saw our Good Samaritan friends off to Sibolga.

It rained and looked too dreary for words. Left alone, we set out to find a helpful Chinese. But we couldn't find one and had to depend on the Dutch official for information about buses. He promised to send his *mandur* and have the bus call for us and take us to Balige on Lake Toba. When we asked him the fare, stating ungraciously that we had frequently been cheated and would like to know the correct price, he must have taken our complaint to heart, for a little later the village constable arrived and gravely told us he had contacted the bus, it would stop for us, and the fare was 35 cents.

Since the rest house in Balige looked comfortable, in fact, luxurious, after Siborongborong we decided to stay there for a day of rest. Our helpful friend, Mr. de Jong, stopped by to inquire about us. We thanked him once more and told him he had provided us with the greatest surprise of our trip—a free ride in a private car. He looked nonplussed as he drove off.

In the afternoon we walked to the Batak village through fields where the rice harvest was in progress. The Batak houses stood on high stilts and had incredibly steep, gabled roofs tilting crazily forward. Actually each house was just one big roof. The space between the stilts was enclosed by latticework and housed the domestic animals. Ladders were used to enter into the houses. Batak villages center around a common square where the village life takes place—women weaving, men gambling, children playing. The houses stand in rows with the steep roofs abutting on the square.

Everything looked more aboriginal than in Minangkabau villages; cruder and not as clean or as prosperous. The women wore shorter jackets than those of the Minangkabaus and fewer ornaments. On their heads they had the weirdest "pillow" yet, wrapped entirely into a shawl and kept in place by two large silver pins with spirals at the ends. This headgear looked as if it would tumble down any minute and, with the diagonal stripes of their sarongs, somehow made them look like the Red Queen of *Alice in Wonderland*. The men also wore high-necked jackets and sarongs but their turbans were of a more conventional type. Batak faces are not as open and friendly as those of the Minangkabaus. Until fifty years or so ago, these people were cannibals and they still have the look of such.

After we left the village we wandered aimlessly on a shady path which meandered through a bamboo grove. Suddenly we came upon several European villas as well as a number of buildings with an obvious institutional look. We decided this must be the German mission our driver had mentioned. When we saw two ladies of

Germanic aspect in the garden of one of the villas we stopped and spoke with them. They were Mrs. Dannert, wife of the German head surgeon, and a nurse; both gracious ladies. When we indicated our interest in the mission they invited us in, showed us around the girls' dormitory, and took us to the singing class, which was practicing for a concert and gave us a charming performance. The ladies told us that the mission had been founded by the Rhënish missionary Ludwig Nommensen, who came to the Batak country in 1864 and by great tact and the force of his remarkable character succeeded in winning over the chiefs to the Evangelical faith. Not much earlier, two American missionaries had failed in their endeavor to convert the Bataks and had been killed and eaten by them. This was not done in anger or greed, but because the Bataks believed the strength of the men they ate would be passed on to them. It must be admitted that there was also not ample meat available. The Dutch erected a monument to the American missionaries, on which the disgraceful story was spelled out in detail. The Bataks, of whom about 10 percent have now become good Christians eating dogs and pigs instead of humans, not unnaturally resented this record of past transgression. They chiseled out the word *eaten* and substituted *killed*.

Nommensen, we were told, was a large blond man with powerful blue eyes and a fine sense of humor. The Bataks were firmly convinced he could look into their hearts with his stethoscope. Once, a German dignitary from the Rhënish mission came on an inspection tour and gave the Sunday sermon. He wasn't much of a speaker and every word he said had to be translated. Nommensen noticed that the audience was quietly sinking into what Mrs. Dannert called a "healthy church slumber." Quick-witted, Nommensen got up and stood behind the speaker, taking the false teeth out of his mouth and waving them above that gentleman's head while making faces at the audience. The dignitary later complimented Nommensen on the rapt attention with which the congregation had listened to the sermon.

Mrs. Dannert was interested when we remarked on the resemblance of the Bataks to the Igorots in Luzon. Even their handwoven sarongs had similar patterns. For a long time, both these peoples have lived isolated from the rest of the world and, like mountain people everywhere, they were strong and unspoiled. Mrs. Dannert said they had found the Bataks intelligent and eager to learn; certainly the girls in the mission school looked wide-awake and attractive. We were told that the mission had just begun a school for the daughters of Batak chiefs and other upper-class girls. This was done because many of the wealthier families were giving their boys a good education; the educated men, in turn, wanted educated wives. At first, there was great opposition, especially from the older women, to sending girls to school, but this had gradually disappeared. Eventually, Mrs. Dannert thought, the unbalance between educated boys and old-fashioned girls—so noticeable where Western schools had been introduced into primitive native life—would vanish.

The Bataks have a talent for mathematics; they also have lovely voices and a musical bent. The little girls sang Bach for us, polyphonic and beautiful. It sounded strange coming from their brown Batak faces. They loved school and their unspoiled minds absorbed knowledge rapidly. The Dannerts thought them every bit as fine a people as the Minangkabaus and scoffed at the idea that the latter were the most highly civilized people of the Indies. The Dannerts, however, were in a minority. Not only did the Dutch disagree with their views, but the Minangkabaus themselves felt so superior that they would not eat at the same table with Bataks or even touch Batak food. In all the larger villages we saw signs saying: Minangkabau Restaurant.

As it was getting dark, we parted and the Dannerts promised to show us more the next day. They recommended that we make our next overnight stop at a Swiss hotel in Siuhan and promised to telephone the hotel for reservations and to ask that our bus be met by the hotel car. The hotel owner was a Mr. Dinker, a friend of the Dannerts.

Next day we saw more of the school. A class of small girls danced for us and we photographed the water pumper, a Batak boy whose job it was to push a large wheel with his bare feet. The wheel worked a pump. All delightfully primitive but, as the Dannerts said, it never went out of order.

On our bus rides through Sumatra we had visited a number of schoolhouses and it had seemed to us that the Dutch were doing their best to educate the children of the Indies. At one school we saw a number of small huts and were told that they were for children whose homes were too far away for them to come daily to school—a sort of tropical boarding school. By this time, the government acknowledged the mission schools, i.e., it controlled the curriculum, paid the teachers—as was the case in Holland for religious schools—and fixed the fees of the mission hospital, but it could not make funds available for urgently needed new buildings. Nevertheless, the Dannerts' mission had started an ambitious building program expected to cost 125,000 guilders, of which they had only 50,000 on hand. They had gone into debt for the remainder, trusting in God for help. The support they had previously obtained had been stopped by the Nazis but they went right ahead with their plans. The German administrator had once been an architect and gave his free time to planning and supervising construction. Everyone else gave as much time and money as they could spare. In fact, everyone's last penny had been sunk into the venture.

Although the school could not have been kept going without it, government support had its drawbacks. One problem was the monthly fee of 25 local cents (12 American cents) which the government required the school to collect from each child. The Bataks were anxious to send their children to school and willing to pay, but often could not afford the 25 cents it cost them to give their children an education. In the end the teachers usually dug into their own pockets, though they could ill afford it. A new threat to the school, said Mr. Dannert, was competition from a Catholic school which, being private, charged only 20 cents. The Catholics had recently come to the Batak country but were already a severe threat to the Evangelical mission. The natives, ready to try anything once, were only too ready to try a new faith, go to a new church with much more gold inside than the plain Evangelical church, and send their children to a school charging a lesser fee. We gathered that what riled the good Dannerts was that they felt it wasn't cricket for the Catholic mission to go after good Evangelical Bataks instead of converting the heathen of whom there were still large numbers about.

After we had inspected the school, the Dannerts took us to their home where we found cold drinks and delicious cakes served on the lawn. The Dinkers, who had come to seek medical advice, had also been invited. They offered to take us to their hotel that evening but, before we left, Dr. Dannert wanted to show us the hospital. He was an extremely interesting person and knew a lot about the Bataks, for whom he had a warm spot in his generous heart.

He called them a "clean-living race" and said that almost no VD was to be found among them. Very sensibly, their *adat* required that any Batak who left his village to work away from Batak country must submit to a medical examination before marrying a Batak girl. The Bataks seldom intermarried with strangers; they were a proud tribe. The girls were virtuous and practically always *virgo intacta* when they married. For one thing, they were never left alone; for another, they knew that if they slipped from the path of virtue, their parents could get no marriage price for them. The girls were bought by the young men after prolonged negotiations between the families and with strict attention to the class and wealth of the prospective mates. Sometimes a poor lad would fall in love with the daughter of a rich man whose marriage price he could never hope to pay. One way out of the difficulty was to start a rumor in the village that all was not as it should be with the girl. Such a rumor ruins a girl's reputation and she can then be bought for a song. Here is where Dr. Dannert was of invaluable help to the Batak parents. Girls were sent to him for examination if there was the slightest doubt as to their virtue. He then issued one of three well-known and generally accepted types of certificates: (1) Absolutely certain virgin; (2) Definitely no longer virgin; or (3) Could be there was a slip from the path of virtue but this is not definite; there might have been an accidental hurt. This system put an end to the scheming of the village lovers.

Mrs. Dannert told us they were careful never to interfere with *adat*, since outside it a girl had no place in Batak life. Therefore, they did not teach Western cooking but trained the girls in better preparation of the usual Batak fare and taught them the rudiments of nutrition, cleanliness, and first aid. She showed us the school kitchen where only Batak utensils were used. This struck us as eminently sensible. One of the defects of the otherwise admirable educational work of missions in Asia was that they prepared their students for a Western way of life, making them misfits and disgruntled rebels fitting neither into the East nor the West.

Batak women had a subordinate role, for this was a patriarchy —another difference between the Bataks and the Minangkabaus. Strange how these differences will exist among people living near to each other for thousands of years. The women had no place in the village except within the rules of *adat*. Hence the missionaries did not try to undermine it in the girls' eyes. Still, the girls had managed to absorb Western ideas of hygiene, sanitation, even of the proper place of women, views that were in conflict with *adat*. Their high marriage price makes them more influential in practice than *adat* would lead one to expect. As their most expensive property, Batak women naturally are important to their husbands. A Batak will not lightly part from his expensive wife, for he must pay her parents damages if he discards her. So when she insists on making changes in the household that accord with her newly found modern ideas, though denounced by the older women as contrary to *adat*, the husband is apt to side with his wife. Thus wives manage gradually to change *adat*, modernize family life, and carry their husband's families along with them. Even when we were there, there was an occasional love match.

We asked how much the average Batak bride cost and were amazed to hear that prices varied between 150 and 200 guilders. These were fantastic sums, for Bataks earned on the average only about 30 cents a day. Unfaithfulness is exceedingly rare, but a case had occurred when we were in Balige. A wife ran away with another Batak; he was brought before the village elders and made to pay the injured husband the price that had originally been paid her parents. This was considered sufficient restitution and no other punishment was meted out to the guilty pair.

The Bataks do not have appendicitis but suffer much from malaria which Dr. Dannert cured with the German drug *atabrine*. He claimed wonderful results and was indignant that, because of their large stake in quinine plantations, the Dutch wouldn't allow it to be advertised. "Believe me they know quinine isn't nearly as effective," he said, "for when they themselves get malaria, they invariably ask for *atabrine*."

About the incidence of leprosy he said: "There is quite a bit of it here and we have an excellent leprosarium in Balige. Unfortunately, we still do not know how to cure it. Even chaulmoogra oil is not an effective medication. Leprosy is like TB. As soon as a nominally cured patient gets run down, the disease flares up again. We usually release some 3 percent of our 500 lepers after they have reacted negatively for two years. The government pays their fare for periodical physical examinations and if we find they have lost weight, we put them to bed and feed them until they have filled out again. This is valuable as a preventative." When we asked him what became of the cured lepers, he said that the Bataks had absolute trust in the white doctors and unhesitatingly took the cured patients back into the village. This seemed to us a much more humane system than the Philippine custom of building so-called "negative *barrios*" (villages) for the cured lepers, where these poor people were almost as much outcasts as they were in the leprosarium itself.

The pride of the Dannerts in their hospital and school was a joy to watch. The good doctor told us with beaming face that he felt sure the Bataks would soon abandon their *datos* (medicine men), who worked principally with spells, magic wands, and incantations. More and more women were coming to the hospital to have their babies, he said, and these infants were growing up to be healthy boys and girls. We were impressed with the good job the German mission was accomplishing and felt that our grocery-truck driver had been most unfair in his criticism.

The Dinkers, who took us in their car to their hotel at Siuhan, were typically Swiss. He had been a planter for eighteen years—rubber, tobacco, and sugar. I suppose, like the careful Swiss he was, he managed his finances well for he was now evidently a rich man. He had bought a rugged, hilly peninsula jutting into Lake Toba and on it built a private residence, tennis courts, swimming pool, boathouse, garages, servants' quarters, and what not, besides the hotel proper which looked as if it had been taken bodily from Lucerne or Interlaken and put beside just such a lake as one finds everywhere in Switzerland. I have no doubt Dinker looked all around to find the spot in Sumatra that looked most nearly like home and settled there to practice that most Swiss of professions—the hotel business. His little kingdom was off the main road and, to reach it, he had to build a mile-long mountain road with numerous sharp curves. He set himself to do the job with seventy natives, and this took seven months. The road was hewn from solid rock and struck us as a most remarkable job, but Dinker nonchalantly waved away this compliment saying that "we planters have to learn a lot of trades; road-building isn't the hardest by far." We thought he had probably settled on Lake Toba to end his years in this lovely spot and had put up the hotel merely to have something to do. He obviously didn't need more money.

Even so, we felt certain that his hotel would soon become known all over the Indies as one of the most delightful places to spend a vacation. It had a thoroughly Swiss atmosphere. Just as clean as the best Dutch hotels in the Indies but not nearly as stolid and without those annoying rules and regulations and posters with *djangan* (forbidden) on them. Dinker personally planted a fine park with deep green lawns and shady trees around the hotel. Beautiful purple bougainvillea grew in profusion over the balconies, and the view from every window was lovely. Our room was light and pleasant and the food delicious. They had the best bread we had ever eaten.

We told the Dinkers we would like to visit the island of Samosir, in the middle of Lake Toba, which is the last preserve of the truly unspoiled and unconverted Bataks. The island is famous for its many stone sarcophagi of great age. These are curious stone vessels resembling boats in which the ancient Bataks buried their chiefs. On one sarcophagus, larger than the others, a large human face was carved into the stone at one end, and a small seated female figure was carved at the other end. Many Malay tribes believed that the souls of the dead travel to heaven in so-called soul ships driven by a personage not unlike Charon, who ferried the dead across the River Styx to Hades. These Batak sarcophagi looked as if they might be such soul ships. It was strange to find among these simple mountain folk notions of the hereafter similar not only to those of the Greeks, but also to those of the Egyptians who built elaborate ships for their dead pharaohs, so they might follow the sun god in his daily round across the heavens.

Dinker offered to accompany us and we gladly accepted. Piet, a young Dutch planter who was staying at the hotel, came along. We set forth for Samosir at 7:30 in a small motor launch. When we got there, Dinker bargained for a long time—much longer than we ever did—to get an ancient Chevrolet truck to take us to the largest village on the island, where we visited the house of an old raja who owned 100 *kampongs* and lived in the finest house. It was decorated with beautiful carvings and looked fully as grand as the best Minangkabau houses we saw in Fort de Kock. However, the entry through a hole in the floor, via a rickety ladder, was more primitive. It was, after all, merely a deluxe Batak house and differed from the general run only in being larger, more sturdily built, more elegantly carved, and better furnished. The old man had no intention of putting up some outlandish building to show his wealth; in this he showed himself much wiser than most Malay sultans who go in for European-style palaces and rococo furniture as soon as they are rich enough.

Like all Batak houses, the raja's house was all roof and no windows. We were courteously bidden to enter and at first could see nothing. After our eyes got accustomed to the darkness, we discovered a number of dignified gentlemen sitting in a circle and were told that these were village elders meeting to settle a boundary dispute. Disputes were always decided by *adat*, as administered by village councils. Dutch legal machinery wasn't needed.

We were struck by a large diploma, in which Queen Wilhelmina attested to the faithful services of the raja, that was tacked to the wall. The raja was a splendid old man with a serene countenance. As we shook hands, we had difficulty believing that in his youth he had eaten three men. He was now eighty and all that lay far behind. We bought a knife in a silver-chased case from him. It had strange reddish spots and we just wondered. . . . Being in the house of an ex-cannibal gave us an uneasy feeling.

We parted in the friendliest way from the raja and his village. As we climbed into our truck, we found we had acquired another passenger. The native Assistant Controleur had requisitioned our vehicle to take him to a village some distance beyond the place where we had tied up our boat. A murder had occurred and he was on his way to investigate it. A Batak was accused of killing one person and wounding another. We were invited to come along to watch him solve the crime and afterward have coffee at his house. Had we been alone we should certainly have gone. It would have been our first chance to assist in catching a murderer. But Dinker wanted to return home so we declined regretfully.

Piet, the young Dutchman who came along for the trip, told us many interesting things about life as a planter. We always thought a planter was a man who owned a plantation, but the word merely means a white man who works on a plantation. This young man, a graduate of a Dutch gymnasium, had applied in Holland for his present job, which was with a tobacco company, and had obtained it after competing successfully with many others in a stiff examination. The company paid his fare, and he started to work for 150 guilders a month, with a 50 guilder raise each year up to a total monthly salary of 500 guilders. This was his limit, unless he was made manager of a plantation. Many Dutch boys went out to the colony on their own and, though they usually succeeded in getting a job, were never as well paid as those selected in Holland. Every five to eight years the young planters got eight months' leave, which they invariably spent in Holland. He said all plantations needed a great deal of supervision by white men because of the quality of the labor force. Regardless of what was grown, the custom was to distribute the white employees over the entire planted area, giving each a large number of native coolies to supervise. The young men, therefore, lived in complete isolation and seldom saw a white face. Their lives were closely regulated by the plantation companies; in particular, they had to live up to the standards considered necessary to preserve white prestige. This young man—hardly twenty years old—had three servants; a houseboy, his wife who cooked, and a coolie to carry water. Their total wages and food cost him 45 guilders a month. It took all of 150 guilders a month to cover bare living expenses. The young men, who came to the Indies thinking their starting salary was ample, needed every penny they earned during the first year merely to live. Each year things got a little better but standards kept rising almost as fast as the salaries did. The life was hard and lonely. Work hours were long; from five to eleven in the morning and from one to five in the afternoon, with frequent additional night duty. They never had Sundays or holidays off, but were allowed up to two weeks' leave every year in addition to the home leave every five or eight years. If they went on a holiday in the Indies they were expected to travel first-class, which they could seldom afford. No bus rides for them.

  This young man's company supervised 1,400 coolies. About one-third of them did the planting and received 60 cents a day; the rest got 35 cents (in Java they would have been paid only from 15 to 20 cents). Usually the coolies' wives had to work, as well as children over nine years; the latter received from 10 to 15 cents. Work days lasted nine hours and there were no free Sundays or holidays and, of course, no home leave. The more enlightened companies paid tiny pensions —perhaps five guilders a month—to coolies who had worked thirty years. This was a safe enough promise for few of them lived long enough to qualify for the retirement pay. This young man's company had exactly five coolies on its pension list.

  Like all low-paid labor, the coolies needed constant supervision and kept the young overseers busy, which was probably a good thing for the Dutch boys; it gave them little time to ponder their unsatisfactory lives. There was the element of danger, too, for unhappy coolies were apt to go suddenly amok. Many a young boy died with the knife of a docile-seeming coolie in his back.

Dinker told us tales of the times when he was a young planter. He was inclined to consider today's youngsters spoiled and soft. He said that during his life as a planter, he often had to clear the forest and frequently his coolies found buried treasure. Such unexpected finds were the savings of other coolies who, like all Malays, deeply distrusted banks and felt it was safer to hide their money in the jungle. Often they did not trust even their families and, when they died, nobody knew where the money was hidden. Years later it would be found accidentally to the great joy of the coolies who located it, for there it was definitely "finders keepers."

Though reconciled to ending his days under the Dutch flag, Dinker remained a loyal Swiss at heart. He had on his car a small flag consisting of half the Dutch and half the Swiss emblems, stitched together by Mrs. Dinker. To his surprise he found that as soon as he put it on, all policemen became inordinately polite and they never reported him when he speeded a little. Later he discovered that his homemade flag resembled the emblem carried by Dutch Controleurs. "Patriotism does pay," he said with a grin.

Dinner that evening was a pleasant affair. This wasn't the tourist season so there were few guests besides George and myself. Our helpful Tarutung friend, Mr. de Jong, stopped by, and there was also Piet, who had gone to Samosir with us. Mr. Dinker entertained us with stories from his adventurous past and about life in Batak country. He did not have a high opinion of the Bataks; he thought they were lazy, dirty savages. "They are not far removed from their cannibal forefathers," he said. "I remember when I was a young man they still solved the old-age problem by eating their parents when they could no longer work. All the children and grandchildren got together and made the old ones climb a tree. Then they shook the tree vigorously and if the old folks fell down, it meant they were 'ripe' and the gods willed their death. They were then promptly cooked and eaten by their offspring. If they had strength enough to hold on to the tree, they were not 'ripe' enough and so lived a little longer." More than a hundred years ago Raffles wrote about this Batak custom, but I was amazed that it should have lasted until the end of the nineteenth century and dubious that it was so.

Since we had three planters seated at the table—tobacco (Piet), palm oil (de Jong), and miscellaneous (Dinker)—we thought it a good time to query them about the "contract" coolie. This had become a major topic since the International Labor Organization had placed the labor contract with penal sanction on its last conference agenda, and our Congress had passed the Blaine Amendment to the U.S. Tariff Law of 1930 prohibiting the import of products of convict, forced, or indentured labor unless they could not be produced in the United States in sufficient quantities. This congressional action prompted the Sumatra tobacco planters to give up "contract" labor voluntarily so that they could continue to export to us.

As soon as we mentioned the word *contract*, they were all upon us, accusing us of messing up things in typical American fashion without the faintest idea of what it was all about. We tried hard to explain that the idea of forcing anyone, under penalty of being put in jail, to work for an employer if he wanted to quit was distasteful to Americans. "Yes, but do you know anything about these coolies? Do you know that we must hire them in Java at wages twice what they are paid there; that we have to pay their passage to Sumatra and that the government makes us provide better housing, better food, better medical care for them than they could ever hope to get in their own villages in Java? This is part of the contract, too. Isn't it only fair that we should have a guarantee that the boys won't run away after the first month? These Malays always get homesick at first; they aren't used to regular work hours and aren't much use for the first half-year anyway. How can we run efficient plantations if we can't be sure of an adequate labor supply. And, mind you, these fellows badly need the money we pay them or they wouldn't have hired out to come here. No Malay leaves his village unless he absolutely must, either to pay off debts or to save money for some family need. You Americans always get sentimental about the poor downtrodden natives. What about us? We work twice as hard and without us the Outer Islands would never have been developed."

We interposed mildly that perhaps the natives would much rather the Outer Islands were not developed, if that meant large foreign-owned plantations. Wouldn't it be better for them if they could go to Sumatra as we in our country used to go West to homestead? Remembering the little *sawahs* in the cleared jungle, we said that we thought fostering individual emigration from overpopulated Java to small farms in the Outer Islands would be a better solution.

"That shows you that you know nothing of this country. How do you suppose you can produce tax revenues to support schools, health and sanitation services, and public law and order without European-owned plantations? You think we could get it from the villages? These people live in a self-sufficient economy where goods are exchanged and money is almost nonexistent. They have absolutely no money sense. They never work to pay for a future need. It would be impossible to collect enough taxes to support the government. These can only come from large-scale enterprises producing for the export market. For them you need coolies, and they won't work if they don't feel like it. Hence we must have the penal sanction contract. It's as simple as that."

Well, we said, if it comes to that, do the natives want a modern government with all those services, and—so we thought but didn't say—all those high-paid Dutch officials? There wasn't any good answer to that. They said Dutch public opinion demanded that the colonies be run with minimum governmental services for the natives. We couldn't get them to admit that the natives hadn't asked for these expensive services. It seemed to us that the crux of the problem was the inability of any industrially backward tropical country to support the machinery of a modern state. We doubted that the natives in the villages wanted or needed such a state. Undoubtedly the Dutch wanted it, and probably the young Western-trained native nationalists did too, because they visualized themselves as the rulers of a modern republic with all the personal privileges this would entail for them. We felt sorry for the natives who could not really be happy in a civilization forced upon them either by the Dutch or their own Dutch-trained intellectuals.

All through the trip we were amazed at the way the Dutch identified themselves with *onze Indië*. They regarded it more as an extension of their homeland than as a colony. Those who worked there usually put down deep roots and considered themselves as much citizens of Java or Sumatra as of Holland. When we remarked gently that we didn't really believe in colonies, they invariably came up with long explanations to the effect that Holland had acquired an empire "in a fit of absentmindedness." Like the English, they had wanted merely to trade with the islands but the ornery natives didn't want to conduct business in a proper manner; in fact, they weren't too anxious to do business at all, and the rajas had a deplorable tendency to confiscate goods arbitrarily and, in general, to make trading hazardous. Therefore, the Dutch East India Company, which monopolized the Indies until they were taken over by the government,* had to bring in troops to pacify more and more territory until the Dutch suddenly woke up to find they had a nice, big colony.

One thing wrong with this idyllic picture was the running battle between the Dutch, Portuguese, and English that had paralleled

---

*The United East India Company, as it was officially called, received letters patent on March 20, 1602, granting it a trade monopoly and the right of sovereign acts as representative of the States General of the Netherlands. In 1798 the company went into bankruptcy; it ceased to exist on January 1, 1800.

occupation of native territory. In the Malay Archipelago we came to places which the Dutch had wrested from the Portuguese and others that had seen Portuguese, Dutch, and British rule in turn. It seemed to us that the interest of the natives had not been given much consideration. It was unfortunate that they had not been allowed to develop slowly and establish a more efficient government of their own, after they had learned to farm better and had earned a little surplus money with which to buy government services. Then it would have been a natural development and the people could have developed with it. The forced grafting of European political institutions upon a primitive way of life did not look good to us. Still, we could also see the Dutch point of view and had to admit that they had succeeded in humanizing native life and doing away with some of its more brutal primitive aspects such as piracy, cannibalism, *suttee*, and slavery. We listened meekly while our Dutch friends tried to enlighten us. Like many educated Europeans, they had a tendency to patronize Americans, but we didn't hold that against them. We, in turn, had so much fun laughing at their odd customs. But being in the minority, we did this only in the privacy of our room.

After a splendid breakfast, de Jong drove off in his elegant automobile while we bustled around trying to find transportation to Pematang Siantar. We finally managed to get a car to take us there in time to catch the bus to Kabandjahe—a Batak village near the famed health resort of Berastagi. We got on the bus at eight o'clock and expected to leave on schedule. It turned out that we were to see much more of Siantar.

First the bus, empty except for us, drove to a house on the outskirts where we stopped for some time for no evident reason. Then we drove back to town and all around and through the market, with the driver's helper yelling, "Kabandjahe." We did this a number of times without drumming up much trade. After another half hour, we drove to a house to pick up two women who were scheduled for the trip. They were not yet awake. We returned for these women four times watching the slow process of their getting up, washing, breakfasting, packing, and braiding their long hair. Finally, with much noise and cackling, they were installed in the bus together with their numerous babies and bundles. We started off hopefully, but after ten minutes they started screaming and a cascade of excited words was poured over the driver. He protested weakly but soon succumbed to their entreaties and drove back to the women's house. Something had been forgotten. It looked like a dirty handkerchief. After we had picked it up, we made a detour and stopped at a church where one of the women spent some time locating the person to whom she ceremoniously gave the dirty handkerchief. A puzzling affair! It took one and a half hours to round up our passengers in Siantar. As the driver said apologetically, these women were much *susah* (trouble). The troublesome ladies were not a bit abashed and talked loudly and incessantly all the way.

Once started, we got to Kabandjahe quickly. There we stopped at the *pension* of a friendly, hospitable Bavarian by the name of Glaser. He had recently imported a wife from his home town and they had started a family. But as a reminder of the gay days of his youth, they had living with them a half-caste daughter—a serious girl who was a great help in their hotel business, although she was only thirteen years old. She was an attractive child; the best points of both races agreeably blended in her small person. But with Nazi influence growing all through the Indies, Glaser found it expedient to take the girl out of the local German school. Understandably, he had little use for Nazis. He was deeply attached to his daughter and knew what would happen to her if Holland got swallowed up in the Third Reich.

Kabandjahe is badly spoiled by periodic tourist invasions from Berastagi. Steamers from Europe and most round-the-world cruises stop long enough in Medan to allow for a trip into the mountains to Berastagi with side trips to Kabandjahe. Though signs forbidding tips are displayed everywhere, the villagers make themselves thoroughly obnoxious and one cannot rid oneself of hordes of small pests yelling *wang* (money). The village is picturesque with houses that look for all the world as I would imagine the witch's cottage in *Hansel and Gretel.* They have two sloping roofs, one on top of the other, and, on the very top of the roof ridge, a tiny toy house on stilts; we couldn't imagine for what purpose. George was curious about some large round straw barrels but, when we asked about them, everyone went into hysterics. We discovered later that they served as the WC. From the village we went to the Batak museums where we saw an interesting collection of the magic wands of the *datos,* who used them to terrify the poor, ignorant villagers. We hoped Dr. Dannert was right in expecting that these evil characters would soon be put out of work by modern education and medicine. The Bataks, we noticed, share the superstition of many South Seas races that medicine men can kill a person by making secret signs and incanting proper spells over bits off his body or clothing, such as nails, hair, or parts of his sarong. Magic wands were a necessary adjunct to such proceedings.

At Berastagi we went to the Chinese agent and engaged seats on the bus to Medan. The agent had an up-to-date grocery store and his exceedingly well-mannered young clerk conversed with us in excellent English. He told us that the Chinese all paid a fixed proportion of

Ancient Batak tombs

Batak woman

Batak village

their salaries to a fund for Chiang Kai-shek. Those who desired to pay more received medals with Sun Yat Sen's face on them. It was all thoroughly and efficiently organized. What helped make the Chinese do their patriotic duty was that they lived under a sort of Chinese sub-government that was like a state within a state. No one could prosper unless he obeyed this sub-government. Chiang therefore received much money from the rich merchants in the Indies.

We thought Berastagi not as attractive as Baguio in the Philippines, with which it is often compared. It does have a fine volcano but we preferred Baguio. As we wandered about, several taxi drivers tried to rope us in for the trip to Medan. They asked seventeen guilders but our combined bus fare was only one and a half guilders, and in an elegant new bus, too. As we stood at a corner waiting for the bus, who should come up with outstretched hands and greet us cheerily, but de Jong, who had throughout paralleled our course and usually acted as a sort of advance messenger telling people all about us. "Well, well," he boomed, "Where are you going?" "To Medan. We're just waiting for the bus." "So am I, so am I. I did so enjoy talking with you. Wish we could do more of it." Waving cordially, he climbed into his large empty car, leaving the two of us just when we were afraid we should lose control and burst out laughing. It must be some sort of pre-natal experience that gives the Dutch this complex against giving people a lift.

On the bus ride to Medan we got into conversation with a Chinese businessman who had migrated to Sumatra from British Malaya. I have never met a man so bitterly resentful. He was frank in expressing his hatred of the Dutch—that they treated the Chinese like natives. We thought; "And why shouldn't they? What makes you think you are superior to a Malay and in the Malay's own country, at that?" But this was a generally held viewpoint among the Chinese in Southeast Asia: they do not want to amalgamate with the people among whom they live and wax rich, nor do they want to return to China. It must be an unsatisfactory existence.

This Chinese merchant ran on and on about the misdeeds of the Dutch: how they interfered with business, taxed people beyond what was bearable (4 percent income tax!), asked five guilders for a permit to import a foreign car, hindered trucking by setting up weighing stations (to save the roads from being overloaded), and exploited the natives shamefully, paying them about 10 cents a day. What really made him furious was that young, inexperienced Dutchmen were paid salaries much higher than those paid Chinese or natives who could do the work as well. One hundred guilders a month, he said, was about the limit any native or Chinese could get. There was going to be a revolt some day. The Dutch needed the *veldpolitie* not so much for weighing trucks so that the roads would not be damaged as for putting down the coming revolution. (The Dutch had two policemen every hundred miles!) Comparatively, in British Malaya the taxes were lower and the government didn't bother business. We finally interrupted and asked why had he left Malaya, but our slippery friend waved this away with some excuse about family affairs. What made him so angry was that the Dutch tried to safeguard the Malays from being economically swamped by immigrant Chinese, as was happening in Malaya. They limited Chinese immigration, and we could see their point. The Malays were hopelessly outclassed by the Chinese when it came to business matters.

We knew that most of what this man said was not true or only partly true, but we encouraged him to go on unburdening himself because we were extremely interested in the way the Chinese felt towards both the white colonial powers and the natives in this part of the world where they form a large minority of unassimilated foreigners. He claimed the Chinese were on excellent terms with the natives, but what we had seen made us doubt this; nobody likes to be outsmarted by a foreigner. In these islands the Chinese fulfill the function of a middle class, for there is none within a native society composed of rajas and peasants. It would be wise if the Chinese decided to throw in their fate wholeheartedly with their countries of residence. When they marry native women, their children often become influential citizens. But when they marry Chinese girls, the entire family remains aloof and belongs nowhere. We parted from our Chinese friend in Medan, glad to see the last of his lugubrious countenance. Most Chinese are jolly and good-natured; this man was a new experience for us. I have often wondered if he was planning to lead a revolt against the Dutch.

Medan is a large, modern town, lying in the lowlands of the delta of the Deli River. It was the administrative headquarters of the government of East Sumatra, the largest such unit in Sumatra. There is also a native Sultan of Deli, who has a palace with extensive gardens in Medan. Fifty years ago he was one of the many minor rajas living the typical life of a Malay farmer. Now, without having lifted a finger, he has become a rich man and can afford to import many shiny new cars, keep a stable of race horses, and a harem of expensive lady friends. In a short period of development, Sumatra has been changed from a half-empty wilderness into a treasure house from which flows a steady stream of oil, tobacco, rubber, tea, and spices. These products have made many a minor Malay princeling wealthy. Unlike the white planters who also became rich, the native chiefs did not have to work for their guilders. They just sat back and collected rents and taxes.

In Belawan Deli, the port for Medan, our Dutch East Indies trip came to an end. The high spots were Bali and Sumatra. If we had to do it all over again, we should make few changes. We would, however, provide ourselves with a tin cup and an empty bottle to be filled each morning with water. We would also take along tissue paper for this is not often to be found. Finally, we would certainly pack some sturdy bags for bananas and other fruits which we bought by the wayside, as wrapping paper is unknown in these parts. A wool sweater would come in handy, too. We crossed the equator four times on this trip; once by water, once by air, and twice by bus. George braggingly told me he had also gone *under* the equator in the submarine *S-48*, off the coast of Peru, and he had been heaved overboard *on* the equator during a Davy Jones ceremony.

The nights in Sumatra were always cool. Having lived a year in the tropics, our blood had thinned and we shivered practically every night. One morning in Kabandjahe I had said to George: "What I'll remember most vividly about this trip is that I never got warm at night." George, on the other hand, felt that his most vivid memory would be of bananas. They seemed the safest thing to eat on the way, and at first we did not mind them. Toward the end we felt that we could never again look at a banana.

5
Malaya

As we were about to climb into a taxi in Belawan Deli to go to the dock, a sleek car drove up and there was de Jong once more. "Are you not taking the SS *Kedah* to Penang today?" he asked. And when we nodded: "I am on my way there now to say goodbye to an old friend. I shall introduce you to him and you will find that he can answer all your questions about native history." Off he went, once more in solitary splendor.

It was like a reunion at the gangplank of the *Kedah*. We found our missionary friend from the *Tjinegara*, Mr. Campbell, who was delighted when we told him how much we had profited from his advice on travel in the tropics. He said he would have to leave Penang immediately upon his arrival, but that friends of his there would take us under their wing. Then someone called to us and we saw the two American businessmen who had devoted themselves with such single-minded attention to food and business at the Kuta Beach Hotel. Travel through the Malay lands had mellowed them astonishingly; they were now almost as friendly and affable as the Indonesians, and greeted us like long-lost relatives. In Bali we had exchanged no more than a brief "good morning" with them.

True to his word, de Jong came aboard with his friend, a Scotsman with a delightful burr, a twinkle in his blue eyes, and an inexhaustible fund of information on everything in this part of the world. Mr. Campbell—he was a namesake of our missionary friend and later we introduced them to each other to see if they could find mutual relatives somewhere in the history of their ancient clan—had spent a lifetime in the Malayan Civil Service and, having retired, was on his way home to a "wee" house near Edinburgh. Before leaving the scene of his adult life forever, he had made an extensive tour of the archipelago. "You know, people don't realize that when we speak of British Malaya, the Dutch East Indies, the Philippine Commonwealth, we draw artificial barriers across what is really all *tanah Melayu*—Malay land," he said, proceeding to launch into what was obviously his hobby—Malay history. As civil servant, trader, and

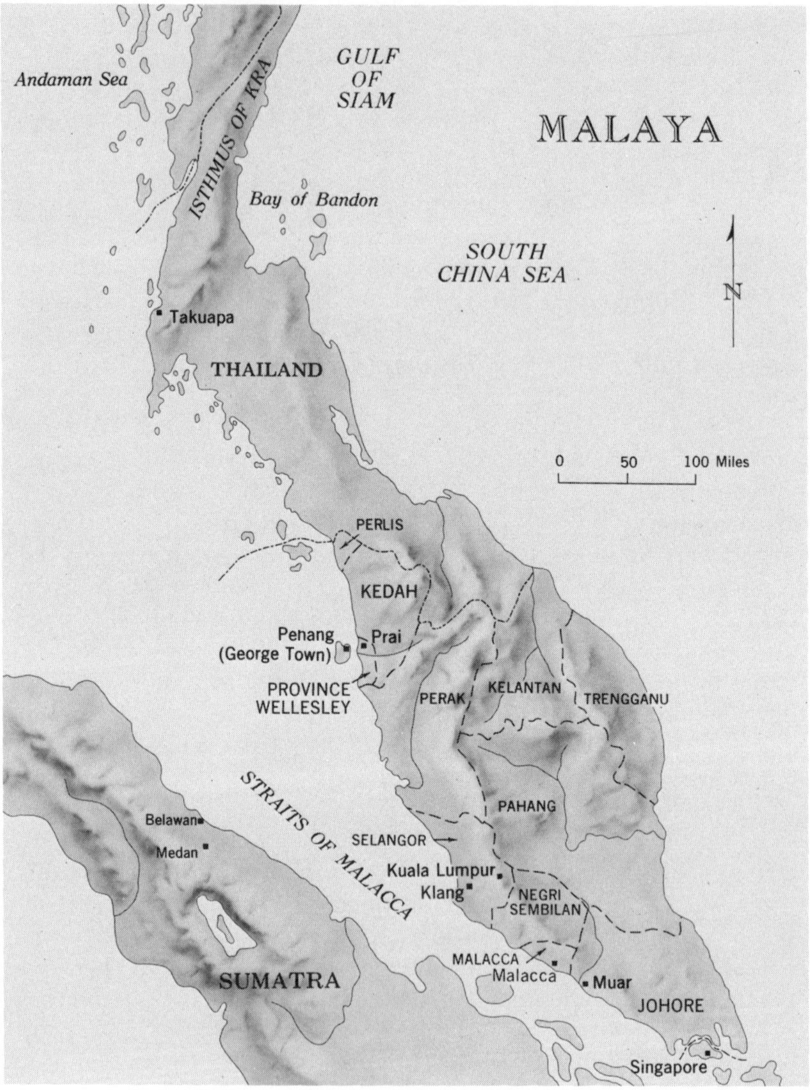
MALAYA
Andaman Sea
GULF
OF
SIAM
ISTHMUS OF KRA
Bay of Bandon
SOUTH
CHINA SEA
N
Takuapa
THAILAND
0
50
100 Miles
PERLIS
KEDAH
Penang
(George Town)
Prai
PROVINCE
WELLESLEY
PERAK
KELANTAN
TRENGGANU
PAHANG
STRAITS OF MALACCA
Belawan
Medan
SELANGOR
Kuala Lumpur
Klang
NEGRI
SEMBILAN
MALACCA
Malacca
Muar
JOHORE
SUMATRA
Singapore

planter, he had spent almost half a century in Malaya, his life thus coinciding almost exactly with the period of Britain's rule over the peninsula.* Like most white men in Malaya, he respected the industry, intelligence, and perseverance of the Chinese but reserved his affection for the Malays. He admitted that without the Chinese and the half million or so Tamils from South India, Malaya would still be an impenetrable jungle with only a few settlements along the coast and on the banks of the rivers. Nobody could have induced the Malays in that uncrowded land to leave their satisfying village life and work as coolies on rubber plantations or in tin mines; nor would the Malays themselves have produced rubber or mined tin on their own holdings.

"The trouble with the Malays," he said, "is that they have no talent for statecraft. Even when some capable man sets up a State and provides fairly good government, as did the Sri Vijayan prince who founded Malacca or the Minangkabau raja who took over Negri Sembilan—my own bailiwick—sooner or later indolence, corruption, and cruelty permeate the court. Palace intrigues and quarrels over the succession result in bloodshed and civil war, and then the Chinese merchants complain and ask us to come and take over this incompetent outfit, and another Malay State has acquired a British Advisor. The Malay State is not a State in the modern sense but simply a tax-collecting autocracy imposed on a group of villages which could get along splendidly without its expensive court.† Since it does not provide any governmental services, it is bound to lose out to foreigners who need good government so they can develop the riches of Malaya. The Malays used to consider it beneath their dignity to do the necessary hard work. Now when many of them realize that the economic life of the country has slipped out of their hands, they find

---

*The Federated Malay States (Perak, Selangor, Negri Sembilan, and Pahang) came under indirect British rule in the 1870s and 1880s; the Unfederated Malay States (Kedah, Kelantan, Trengganu, Perlis, and Johore) in 1909, by virtue of the Anglo-Siamese Treaty in which Siam ceded her claims of suzerainty over the northern part of Malaya, except for Johore, which accepted a British advisor in 1914. Besides these nine states, British Malaya consisted then of the Straits Settlements which had been acquired earlier by the British East India Company, viz., Penang (1786), Malacca (1795), Province Wellesley (1800), and Singapore Island (1819).

†Until Mr. Campbell gave us this lesson in history, I had not realized that most of the governments supplanted or brought under indirect control by Europeans in Southeast Asia were not truly indigenous at all, but were foreign importations either from India or China. Often the rulers themselves were descendants of immigrants from higher civilizations. They felt less responsibility for the welfare of the people than did the European colonial governments; at any rate, that was so after the East India Company governments were replaced by colonial administrations responsible to home parliaments.

that even if they acquire education and training and are willing to work, they can't get a foothold anywhere.

"The Chinese never let a foreigner into their business enterprises, just as they will not enter into family relationships with foreigners. Moreover, the Chinese have established such firm squatter's rights in those jobs available to non-whites in government and in European companies that nobody else can get in. They cleverly stress the alleged incapacity of the Malay for hard work and everyone believes them. Just consider this: the Malays are by far the best seamen in the peninsula, yet they do not own a single shipping line. Whenever they try to establish a business, they are met with effective boycotts by the Chinese. Soon they will be outnumbered by the Chinese—they are already a minority in their own country—and what's to become of them, I surely don't know." He sighed and shook his head. "They just haven't any luck. First, their geographic location along the spice route brought the Portuguese, then the Dutch, and finally the British—all wanted a foothold on the peninsula in order to control the spice trade. Later, when spices ceased to be important, Malaya's tin was the lure that drew us, and finally we brought them the rubber tree and now look where they are."

We were lucky to have met Mr. Campbell for, without the interesting tales he told us as we walked on the deck of the *Kedah*, we would have had a lopsided impression of Malaya. We only had a week there, much of which was spent traveling down the peninsula. After the scenic beauty of the Indies, the trip seemed monotonous—rows of dusty, greyish rubber trees, standing like soldiers. The only bit of color came from the magenta, purple, and pink saris of the Tamil women who collected rubber. But after we had heard how, in less than fifty years, rubber and tin had obliterated a way of life hundreds of years old and not without charm, the trip became interesting.

Meeting our missionary friend from the *Tjinegara* was also helpful because he introduced us to his colleagues who came to meet the boat at Penang. We were greatly touched when they adopted us in their delightfully easy and friendly American way, for we had almost forgotten that such hospitality existed. They squeezed us into their ancient Ford and took us home for refreshments and a drive around Penang.

Penang is historically interesting because it was the first British foothold on the Straits of Malacca—theretofore the exclusive domain of the Portuguese and later the Dutch. The first British ship to sail into the beautiful natural harbor was the *Edward Bonaventure*, in 1592, commanded by Sir James Lancaster, but she left after provisioning and did not lay claim to the port. Nearly two hundred years later, Captain Francis Light saw the island harbor and realized it would make a splendid port for revictualing and repairing East Indiamen sailing to and from China. Light entered into negotiations with the Sultan of Kedah and obtained a lease on the island for the East India Company. In return for a promise to supply him with material, money, and men against attack by any enemy, the Sultan leased Penang and, on August 11, 1786, Captain Light formally occupied the island. The Sultan's motive was to gain protection in his struggles against his suzerain, the King of Siam, without whose permission he had no right to lease this territory. Light, in turn, had no authority to involve the British government or the East India Company in any military operations. In 1800 Kedah ceded to England a strip of the mainland opposite Penang, which the British called Province Wellesley. Although aware of the faulty English title to Penang, Siam made no move to prevent its settlement until 1821 when it attacked Kedah, causing the Sultan to flee to Penang. The Company reneged on its promise and would not come to the Sultan's aid. In the end Kedah became part of British Malaya when Siam transferred its suzerainty to Britain in the Anglo-Siamese Treaty of 1909.

When the island of Penang was leased to Light it had a population of fifty-two persons.* The British built a town—officially named George Town but somehow always called Penang, which in Malay means betel nut—on a promontory facing the mainland. The entrance to the harbor reminded us of Hong Kong though it was not quite as grand. The harbor, however, was more picturesque. We were fascinated by the colorful assortment of praus, Chinese junks, and numerous other exotic ships that crowded the piers. It was like a scene out of Hollywood; something to do with piracy, luscious native maidens, and lusty derring-do. The lofty crown of Kedah Peak rising from a green sea of rice fields could be seen across the narrow strait separating Penang from the mainland. But when we docked, the city did not meet our expectations; it was almost 100 percent Chinese and, except for the residential sections, ugly. Not picturesquely ugly, but ugly in the garish and noisy way characteristic of cities dominated by overseas Chinese. True proletarians, these Chinese arrive as penniless coolies and by dint of heroic industry and abstinence grow rich, but they lack the exquisite sense of harmonious beauty to be found among their compatriots at home. The richer they are, the

---

*I hold no brief for colonialism, for nothing justifies ruling a foreign people against their will. Still, when native friends complained to us that all the rich and important cities in Asia had been taken over by the West, we could not refrain from remarking: "You realize, of course, that these cities—Penang, Singapore, Hong Kong, Batavia, Shanghai, Tsingtao, and others—were built by Europeans on uninhabited swampland or arid ground and that they flourished because of good government and trade with the West."

more their homes are likely to exhibit a most unfortunate blending of the worst in Chinese and Western tastes.

A striking example of what one might call "overseas Chinese architecture," is to be seen in the famous Chinese Temple, a landmark of Penang. It is overwhelming in the immensity and ugliness of numerous hideous gods cast in bronze, and it has a truly astonishing display—under glass—of all its more important donors whose generosity has been rewarded by their inclusion in a weird sort of oriental Madame Tussaud's. We wondered whether, in time, the waxen likenesses of these portly Chinese of Penang would join the 500 genii populating Chinese temples.

The other Penang landmark—the Chinese Snake Temple—also found no favor in our eyes. This uninteresting building, overloaded with carving, is famous for the gruesome prevalence of hundreds of yellowish snakes, lying, hanging, clinging, writhing everywhere —surely an astonishing feature in a place of worship. The attendant informed us that they slept during the day and wandered around at night, but we preferred to reassure ourselves that they must have been doped; otherwise, we should not have tarried an instant.

As do all major towns in Malaya, Penang has a lovely botanical garden, apparently a "must" in this country. I wonder whether this could have been an unconscious tribute to Kew Gardens in London where Henry Wickham carefully nurtured the seeds of *hevea brasiliensis* which he had managed to smuggle out of Brazil in 1876. From these seeds have grown all the rubber trees in Malaya. By this one lawless act in his otherwise blameless life, Wickham destroyed Brazil's rubber industry, turned Malaya into Britain's most valuable possession, and, not by military conquest but by unrestricted Chinese and Indian immigration, brought about the dispossession of the Malays. Surely Britain has done a grievous wrong in making the Malays a minority in their own country. Muddle-headed theorists in England may talk of eventual assimilation in a common Malayan citizenship of Hindu Tamil, Confucian Chinese, and Moslem Malay but religious and racial tolerance is not in the makeup of these three races who find intermarriage intolerable and will not even admit each other into business partnership.

On the way to the botanical garden, our trip almost came to an abrupt end. At the foot of the hill the road swerved abruptly to avoid a concrete building. The old Ford's brakes refused to function. However, since it was a missionary Ford, we made the curve miraculously.

We were amazed at the optimism of our missionary friends. After fourteen years of devoted work, they had a congregation of forty-seven. It is almost impossible to convert Moslems, for theirs is a satisfyingly simple creed, promising enticing rewards in the hereafter and making far fewer demands on the believer than does Christianity. Moreover, for a Malay to abandon his faith would completely divorce him from his village and the people with whom he grew up. There would be no place for him in the community—a dreadful fate for people who have always lived communally, not individually. It would take terrific willpower to face the isolation of such ostracism. Conversion is easier for Eurasians and heathen aborigines, and these, we were told, can sometimes be induced to abandon their old religion if a village elder, chief, or prominent member of the community has been converted. What cheered our friends and kept up their hope was a fairly recent mass conversion of a tribe in the interior of Borneo. We heard of this often later on.

Penang looks attractive only when viewed from the Hill Railway that ascends Penang Hill, whose elevation is 2,400 feet. As we moved slowly upward, the view became more pleasant, for the natural setting of Penang is lovely, lush, and green. On top of the hill there are fine walks and drives and the residence and gardens of the governor. The gardens are open to the public when the residence is vacant.

We caught the train to Kuala Lumpur that evening. There was a magnificent scene at the dock where we took the ferry to the railroad station at Prai, on the mainland. Fantastic headdresses on dark heads; brilliantly colored saris on dusky women with flashing dark eyes; a bewildering variety of picturesque costumes of a dozen nationalities; stately Sikh policemen with their long hair wound into mountainous turbans, keeping order with the quiet efficiency of an English bobby; graceful silhouettes of many kinds of native boats crowded close together, their sails flapping in the breeze; baskets and bundles of every conceivable shape and size; queer smells and strange languages all around us—it was a marvelous experience to see all this in the uncertain light provided by the city of Penang.

Prai was as far west as we had been on the Asian mainland and we had our first close look at the Tamils from India. As the ferry approached the dock, we noticed a group of young men on the deck of a native prau tied up at the wharf. They were extraordinarily handsome, with slender, perfectly proportioned bodies and finely cut faces of an aristocratic cast. Yet the color of their skin was black as coal. It gave us an uncomfortable feeling to see them clad in rags, doing the lowliest coolie work. Except for their color, they looked like ancient Greeks and could have modeled for Praxiteles. Their wrists, hands, ankles, and feet were delicate and well shaped despite the hard labor they performed. It did not seem right that they should be the lowliest of Malaya's races today. Later we saw more Tamils who had come from South India to work on the rubber plantations; though few of them were as striking as this first group, all had surprisingly European features.

Their slender women were bedecked with jewelry—bangles on arms and legs, rings on fingers and toes, earrings, and nose rings—a small gold button stuck into one nostril. Most of them wore cotton saris, but there were a few exquisite creatures clad in pastel silk saris, with gold and silver threads woven into patterns, and golden slippers on their slender feet. Even the poorest women wore jewelry.
They were sort of walking family savings banks, long experience with debased currencies having bred in the Indian a healthy distrust of paper money. It has been said that India would not be so poor if some of the gold that lies idle in the form of jewelry were invested in industrial enterprise. Yet I wonder if the Tamil coolie isn't wise in putting his capital where it not only is safe but gives him and his wife much pleasure.

We were curious to know what strange disease afflicted so many of the Indian coolies. Their foreheads looked whitish in a sickening way. Later we discovered that these devout and good men had put cow dung on their faces—the cow, as everyone knows, being sacred to Hindus. Most of them had a colored mark painted in the middle of the forehead to designate their caste. The large fat Indians who acted as officials and policemen were lighter skinned than the slender, dark Tamils. The two appeared to belong to different races.

Next morning we arrived in Kuala Lumpur, seat of the Federated Malay State government and capital of the State of Selangor. The town has some public buildings in Moorish style but otherwise not much to interest the tourist. Selangor was founded in the seventeenth century by the Buginese from Macassar, a remarkable feat of colonizing when one considers that they had only their small praus to transport themselves a distance approximately equal to that from Oklahoma City to Portland, Oregon. I shared Mr. Campbell's regret when I saw the neatly cultivated land in which the descendants of those dashing sea rovers lived.

We left almost immediately for Klang where the sultan has his principal palace. The road passes through endless rubber plantations alternating with rice fields and an occasional Malay *kampong* of thatched huts on stilts. The ordinary Malay is probably better off under the protection of the British, but I could not help feeling he deserved something better than his tame existence, particularly when we saw the palace of the sultan. We were struck by its tastelessness and newness. There was a dreadful new mosque—all onion-shaped towers and sharp rods protruding into the air and a profusion of

Native craft in Penang Harbor

Tamil woman

expensive marble. We were contemplating this structure with disapproval when a distinguished Malay gentleman greeted us politely. He turned out to be a Filipino from Zamboanga—a Moro, in fact—by the name of de los Reyes. As soon as he found out that we came from his homeland and had been to Zamboanga, he devoted himself exclusively to showing us around. He had gone to Selangor some thirty years previously as the medical attendant of the old sultan who had died recently, and he was then in charge of guarding the young sultan's seven wives. When we asked him whether they were pretty, he shrugged his shoulders and replied: "Not bad for Malay women but of course not as attractive as Filipinos." He himself was, as he put it, "not exactly married" to a local lady but his heart was still in Zamboanga. We were amused at his condescension towards the Selangor Malays. Independence is truly a heady wine. He felt himself superior to his Buginese cousins since his own country was then a commonwealth, practically independent and soon to be completely so, while His Royal Highness, the Sultan of Selangor, for all his display of wealth, was but a pensioner of the British.

Reyes took us around the palace grounds and soon we heard a droning sing-song noise coming from a small building near the mosque. This building, he informed us, contained the bones of the late sultan. For three years members of his family must take turns reading the Koran night and day beside the dead man's casket. Reyes showed us the young raja who was on duty at the moment. He sat with his feet doubled under, in a bare room, singing from an old parchment Koran. The coffin looked like a huge canopied bed and was wreathed in yellow satin. Dozens of dried and withered wreaths were piled around the small building and nobody seemed to have considered removing them after the funeral. I suppose they stayed there until they had disintegrated.

When our friend obtained permission for us to visit the royal palace, we found it full of yellow-silk-covered chairs, yellow draperies, a yellow canopy in the throne room—yellow everywhere. I recalled reading in Tomé Pires' *Suma Oriental* that in early days no one but the king could wear yellow, under pain of death, and when he traveled by land his elephant was covered up to the eyes in yellow cloth.

The palace had a bit of every Western architectural style. Its ostentation was especially objectionable when contrasted with the bareness and simplicity of the *kampongs* through which we had driven. There were many henchmen around but nobody apparently doing anything useful. The whole thing depressed us. Reyes launched upon a recital of palace intrigues and complaints about the British who had passed over the sultan's three oldest sons and made the fourth one ruler. We saw one of the brothers who had been bypassed; a fat little man in a fez, with a discontented face, doing nothing. What a comedown for those brave Buginese sailors who went there to found an empire. We wished we could have taken Reyes back with us to the Philippines, where he would have been much happier with less money and more work.

A branch line of the train runs from Kuala Lumpur to Malacca, through what is in effect one continuous rubber plantation. Malacca is a picturesque town, beautifully situated, with a romantic and bloody past. It was founded around 1400 A.D. by a Palembang prince called Parameswara (Prince Consort) from Sri Vijaya who had married a high-born princess of Madjapahit, the kingdom that had conquered his homeland. When he realized how nobly he was married, he announced his independence of Madjapahit. This proved to be a rash move because Palembang was attacked and the prince and his followers fled by sea to Singha-pura (Singapore)—the city of the *Singhs* or lions, as its Indian name implies. Within eight days, according to the account in Tomé Pires' *Suma Oriental*, the prince had the reigning head of Singapore murdered and claimed the island and the neighboring sea passages as his own. The victim was related by marriage to the King of Siam, who claimed suzerainty over Singapore. Siamese troops were sent to avenge the foul deed, whereupon the prince and his followers retreated into the Malayan jungle and spent six years at Muar. It is said that loyal *Orang Laut* (Sea Gypsies) of Singapore led the exiles to the place where Malacca now stands. A pleasant fertile land with a good harbor, it was far enough from Siam to escape punishment, yet near enough to the Straits of Malacca to ensure future prosperity through control of the sea route between India and China.* In the turmoil attendant on the gradual break-up of Madjapahit under the blows of Moslem aggression, Malacca became in a sense the heir to both Madjapahit and the earlier Sri Vijaya.† It brought much of Malaya under vassalage, main-

---

*We have a fairly detailed knowledge of the founding of Malacca because it was written down by the Portuguese Tomé Pires in his *Suma Oriental* only a little more than a hundred years after the events occurred.

†Within the lifetimes of its two first rulers, Malacca changed from the Buddhism of Sri Vijaya to the Hinduism of Madjapahit, and, finally, to Islam, which was then in the process of triumphing over all the Hinduized states of the archipelago and over the last great Hindu Malay Empire of Madjapahit. Thus, the religious turmoil of this period in Malay history was reflected in one city. The primary effect was that the old empire was splintered, and Malacca picked up nearly all the parts of the peninsula that had broken off from Madjapahit and had earlier belonged to Sri Vijaya.

Upon conversion to Islam, Malacca's ruler took the title of sultan but, as happened in most Hinduized states, the Brahmanist notions of the godhead of kings

Sultan's palace at Klang

Malacca

tained excellent relations with India, and sent tribute to China in exchange for protection against Siam. From the outset, the Malaccan rulers showed great wisdom in giving the city a businesslike administration that favored trade and commerce. Soon its harbor was filled with shipping, its streets reverberated with the strange sounds of many foreign tongues. The northeast monsoon carried Chinese junks into Malacca, laden with silk, seed pearls, musk, camphor, copper, iron, saltpeter, kettles, bowls, ironware, and ivories; it also brought Buginese and other Malay praus from the Moluccas with sandalwood, spices, and numerous foodstuffs. Indian ships came with the southwest monsoon bringing arms, silver, rosewater, dyes, incense, quicksilver, opium, and various other drugs. Malacca was the great entrepôt where goods were exchanged between East and West.* This trade and various port dues and service charges brought great wealth to the city and its rulers.

It was this prize that the Portuguese coveted when they sought the sea route to the Spice Islands. In those days when there was no refrigeration, spices were a vital necessity and worth their weight in gold. Unfortunately for Malacca, by that time its court had become corrupt and indolent, and only extraordinary courage and ability could have saved it from Portuguese conquest. Had the Portuguese arrived a hundred years earlier, they might have been driven off, but its very wealth had made Malacca too weak to resist long.

The first Portuguese ship, carrying letters and gifts from King Manuel of Portugal, anchored off Malacca in 1509—ostensibly to pay a friendly visit of state. Indian traders, experienced with Portuguese ways, warned the sultan against entering into any sort of intercourse with the strangers and urged him to kill them. A plan was made to murder Diogo Lopez de Sequeira, the admiral, but he was warned (by a woman, so it is said) and escaped, leaving 19 of his men in the hands of the Malaccans. Two years later Alfonso d'Albuquerque arrived with a fleet to free the prisoners. After some negotiating, the sultan returned the men and promised to pay damages and allow the Portuguese to build a fortress, but it was not enough. All of Malacca

---

(though contrary to Moslem tenets) survived. To this day, the enthronement ceremonies of devout Moslem Malay princes follow closely the ritual of Hindu coronations and are performed by persons who, though actually Moslem by faith, act as court Brahmans. We later found that the court ceremonies and concepts of kingship in Buddhist Siam and Cambodia showed a similar tenacity to Hinduism. *See* R. O. Winstedt, *Malaya and its History*, pp. 24-31, and H. G. Quaritch Wales, *Siamese State Ceremonies: Their History and Function*.

*Tomé Pires' *Suma Oriental* provides these details, which give a vivid picture of life in pre-Portuguese Malacca. Thanks to his diligent research, we know that as many as eighty-four languages could be heard in Malacca.

was the prize d'Albuquerque had come to acquire. He had 1,100 men; the city was defended by 20,000. Both sides had artillery and fought bravely. The Portuguese objective was the bridge over the Malacca River and, to achieve this end, a tall, heavily armed Chinese junk was sent up the river. It immediately ran aground and lay there, helpless in the path of the Malaccan fire. Whatever other faults they had, the Portuguese were brave men. Withstanding murderous fire, they worked until they got the junk free. Then they grappled it to the bridge. The Portuguese fire overcame the defense and, with the bridge gained, the sultan's forces were divided. This was the end of the fight and never since has Malacca been in Malayan hands. When I later checked Mr. Campbell's stories of Malacca against Winstedt's accounts, they proved accurate in every detail.

We were struck with the smallness of the city; it didn't seem large enough to have had so much history. We climbed up the hill to look at the ruins of the great church of Our Lady of the Mount, later called the Church of St. Paul, which the Portuguese erected on the site of the conquered sultan's palace. There, St. Francis Xavier, "The Apostle of the East," once officiated, and from there Portuguese priests went forth to spread the gospel. Propagation of the faith was almost as important to the Portuguese as were spices. The roof of the church is gone and grass grows in the cracks of crumbling walls and between broken flagstones. The view from its height is superb. We looked for a long time at the old town and across the Straits of Malacca, which had carried so many ships laden with wealth and witnessed so much bloodshed and cruelty. Chinese and Malay pirates used to dart from their hideouts in the indented coastline to prey upon the merchantmen of all nations. Not until the latter part of the nineteenth century did Dutch and British naval patrols put an end to piracy in those waters.

By a strange quirk of fate the Portuguese arrived just when Islam was taking over. It must have seemed to them that they always had to fight the Moors. The long battle to free the Iberian Peninsula from the Saracens was still a vivid memory in Portugal at the time these Portuguese sailors set out to find the sea route to the Moluccas where, again, they found themselves at war with Moslems. I suppose this explains Portuguese cruelty to the conquered Malaccans, who were rounded up, put in chains, and forced to dismantle their mosques and use the stones to build churches and fortifications. A cruel fate for devout Moslems. But sometimes the fortunes of war have a rough way of settling accounts. When the Dutch defeated the Portuguese, they tore down all the Catholic churches, except Our Lady of the Mount, which they rebuilt into a fortress. As we wandered among the old graves, we found many that showed Portuguese names on one side and Dutch on the other. In their thrifty way, the Dutch had taken the old Portuguese gravestones and used them to mark the graves of their own dead, not even bothering properly to remove the old inscriptions. There is no Portuguese graveyard left in Malacca. Such famous names as d'Albuquerque, Sousa, da Silva, Sequeira are carried on by Malacca's Eurasians who are reputed to make good government clerks.

The Portuguese controlled Malacca and the spice trade for one hundred and thirty years. One of Mr. Campbell's historical tidbits that interested us particularly was the indirect manner in which Portuguese control of the Malacca Straits led to Spanish conquest of the Philippines. These islands were discovered by Magellan in 1521 during the first circumnavigation of the globe. Portuguese by birth, Magellan had fought for his country and taken part in the conquest of Malacca but later fell into disgrace. He was accused of trading with the arch-enemy, the Moors. Piqued, Magellan renounced his Portuguese nationality and took service with the Spanish crown. It was his suggestion that the Portuguese monopoly of the spice trade might be broken by seeking a western passage to the Moluccas. He sailed as far as the Philippines* where he was killed at Mactan by natives on April 27, 1521. One of his original five ships, the *Vittoria* managed to complete the voyage.

When the Spanish ships loaded spices in the Moluccas, Portugal protested to Spain that this intrusion constituted an infringement of the Treaty of Tordesillas, which had been made between the two powers in 1494. After a brief struggle, the Spanish were forced to come to terms with the Portuguese and, by a new treaty in 1529, agreed to halt their explorations seventeen degrees east of the Moluccas.

The Portuguese might have continued to reign over the Malay Archipelago if their country had not fallen under the control of Philip II of Spain, one of whose decrees closed the port of Lisbon in 1594 to Dutch traders, thereby restraining their distribution of spices in Europe. Since the Portuguese had no facilities of their own for this purpose, they had always contented themselves with bringing the spices to Portugal and allowing the Dutch to transship them. Philip hated the Dutch because they were Protestants and they had fought him successfully, but his action was such a severe blow to Dutch commerce that he merely succeeded in driving the Dutch to take over the entire spice trade from the Moluccas to the ultimate consumer in Europe. The Dutch took Malacca in 1641, after a prolonged and bloody battle, and held it until 1795, when it was taken by the British.

*To the Spaniards, as to the Portuguese, any Moslem was a Moor; therefore, Magellan named the inhabitants of the southern Philippines *Moros*, and so they are called to this day.

Fort gateway at Malacca

They drove out the Portuguese, allowing only a handful to remain, and destroyed so much that there is little in Malacca to recall its Portuguese past—only a bit of the wall of *A Famoso*, or Old Fort, designed by d'Albuquerque in 1511, and the ruins of the church of Our Lady of the Mount. For the rest, the old parts of the town are Dutch in architecture, Chinese in population. We wandered down *Heeren* and *Jonker* Streets trying to visualize them populated by sturdy Dutch burghers, but the ubiquitous Chinese kept intruding. We visited an old Dutch gateway and the *Stadhuis*, the Dutch town hall, which had been turned into a museum of Malaccan antiquities, and thought about Malacca's turbulent past. We looked everywhere for the bridge that played such an important part in d'Albuquerque's conquest of the town, but none of the bustling Chinese we asked had ever heard of it or were the least interested in such unprofitable searches into the dead and buried past. Practical people, these, they will eventually inherit the town and all Malaya as well.

The pretty Malacca River, which meanders through the town, gives it somewhat the aspect of a Malayan Venice and, like Venice, this historical town has been passed by and become a backwater. Its harbor is too shallow for modern ships and trade now moves through Penang and Singapore.

We stayed overnight at the large and well-conducted government rest house and went to Singapore next day. While we were waiting for our train the Malaccan stationmaster came up, inquiring courteously if he could be of service. He was a handsome and dignified Indian—as were all the railroad people we encountered—and most informative. Like everyone in Malaya, he was concerned over the depression in America since we were their best customers. He asked us if we thought there would soon be an economic upturn and, urged on by us, soon launched into a lecture on rubber-tree planting in Malaya. The trees are cut or tapped daily, the coolies going around making diagonal cuts and attaching small, funnel-shaped cups into which the sap runs. Each coolie usually takes care of 600 trees. After he has cut the trees, he starts at the beginning of his route and collects the cups. At first, he said, the planters hired Chinese coolies, but being Chinese and hence shrewd, these coolies proved most destructive to the rubber trees. They figured they could get more rubber by making deeper cuts. Deep cuts damage the trees, so the planters switched to Tamil coolies and were using them exclusively. They came from South India where drought and famine keep the people in abject poverty. In Malaya they received forty to fifty cents Singapore money (one Singapore dollar then equaled about 57 American cents) a day; not much, but better pay than at home. They could live only by putting the entire family to work. Women usually had to work until shortly before childbirth. Formerly, the planters simply fired the coolies if times were bad, but that had changed and the government required that unemployed coolies be transported back home to India. We gathered that conditions were pretty bad for most of the coolies most of the time.

At Singapore we stayed at the Raffles Hotel. The room was kept cool by a large overhead fan. The city is a handsome one with fine residences, shady parks, and wide boulevards. But despite its romantic name, which immediately sets the mind to thinking of piracy, inscrutable orientals, and treasure-laden ships, it is a city devoted single-mindedly to trade and commerce. Its buildings look European, the people on the street Chinese. As in Penang, the only place where color and exotic flavor are to be found is along the wharves, which are crowded with fascinating native craft.

As a city, Singapore is young—only a little more than a century and a quarter old. There was an earlier city, so it is said, founded in the fourteenth century by Nila Utama, a Sri Vijayan prince. It was he who named the city Singha-pura (City of the Lion). But this city had a brief existence, falling into the hands, first, of Madjapahit and, later, of Siam. It was destroyed in 1377 by the Madjapahit soldiery who indulged in such an appalling massacre of the conquered population that, as the *Malay Annals* say: "Blood flowed like water in full inundation and the plain of Singapore is red with blood to this day"—a reference to the red laterite soil of Singapore. A curse is supposed to rest upon the city and explains, so the Malays say, the curious fact that it is impossible to grow rice on the island. Be that as it may, a flourishing city disappeared completely. More than four hundred years later, when Raffles looked about for a suitable port that would give the British East India Company a foothold in the Malay Archipelago, then in Dutch hands, he found the island of Singapore a deserted stretch of swampland inhabited by a few Sea Gypsies. He had a difficult time convincing the company that here was a location ideally suited to the building of a great commercial emporium and one which, moreover, would be of great strategic importance as well. The Dutch, who were and are great believers in monopolistic trade, had bullied every native raja in the archipelago into trading exclusively with them. Raffles realized that Britain needed but one advantageously situated port and a policy of free trade to make a serious dent in this Dutch monopoly. He bought the island from the Temenggong of Johore in 1819 and, immediately on founding his new settlement, proclaimed that "the Port of Singapore is a free Port and the trade thereof open to ships and vessels of every nation free of duties, equally and alike to all." And so it remained for more than a century. But the surprising thing was how much everything cost in this free port—quite different from Hong Kong, also a free port, but where one could readily indulge in a shopping spree without having any pangs of conscience, for *everything* there was cheaper than anywhere else in the world!

An even more important step—to my mind—was taken by Raffles when he proclaimed that any slave setting foot in Singapore was automatically a free man. Soon the Dutch had to follow suit and abolish slavery in the Indies. As white influence spread, slavery gradually disappeared from all Southeast Asia.

We had letters to a number of people in Singapore and were soon overwhelmed with hospitality. It was a good thing we had taken dress-up clothes with us, for we needed them. I had given careful thought to our luggage. We wanted to travel light, not only because we didn't know what unconventional modes of transportation we might have to use, but also because the baggage allowance on planes was limited and we had no money for excess-baggage charges. We did quite well to be traveling for over a month with only one suitcase and two khaki zipper bags. We had the village tailor of San Roque (back of our house in Cavite) make a khaki cover for the suitcase which served as a container for one of the zipper cases (folded flat) and our raincoats. As we bought things on the way, we filled it; bringing it back bulging with Cambodian silver, Balinese wooden sculpture, and Malayan pewter. We kept our clothes unwrinkled by packing them flat in the suitcase and putting everything else in the zipper bag. Just in case we might need them, I packed a cardboard box of dress-up clothes into the suitcase where they weren't disturbed until needed.

We worked out a fine system for dealing with the laundry problem. Our trip took us through countries where one has to change at least once a day. If we stayed several days in one place, we could get everything washed by the laundry boy. But often we stopped for only one night and didn't like to entrust our clothes to an unknown boy who might not return them on time—time not being an important consideration thereabouts. We, therefore, washed them ourselves. No sooner had we reached our room, than George would open the bags, pull out fresh changes of clothing and we would start laundering what we had worn. There was always either a breeze or a fan that dried our clothes by next morning, so we never had any dirty linen to carry about—a boon in hot countries. We could do all this in about fifteen minutes, even to placing our handkerchiefs flat against the mirror so they would dry smoothly. None of our clothes needed ironing, except perhaps a little here and there. I did this with an electric light bulb if one was available. Just turn it on a few moments until it is hot, then unscrew with a towel wrapped around your hand

and it irons quite well. I think this is a good system, allowing you to travel light, yet be always clean, and still spend no thought and hardly any time on the cleaning job.

There isn't much to see in Singapore. Friends took us to the famous New World, a huge, year-round fair where every nation and tribe has a place to produce its own kind of entertainment. The racket from Javanese plays, Chinese theatrical performances, Malayan singing, Siamese dancing, etc. was deafening. There was a cabaret with attractive taxi dancers where we stopped a while. The prettiest was Anita, a Filipino, one of the Sultan of Johore's "friends." The girls dance with you for 25 cents of which they keep half. Good ones make 200 dollars a month from dancing alone—besides other sources of income.

We were regaled with many tales about the Sultan of Johore who, though in his sixties, was still a great ladies' man. At one time he gave each of his lady loves a golden belt, and they say that Singapore positively glittered. He often shocked the British who couldn't do much with him since he had plenty of money. He behaved so badly at times that he had been forbidden to stay in Singapore later than midnight. But he had legitimate grievances, too. He gave half a million pounds to the British for the Singapore naval base. Yet, when the base was opened, he found himself seated not among the most important dignitaries but in back with all the other Malay sultans who hadn't been as generous as he. This made him angry and, I suppose, accounts for his going on a spree and having to be shipped back to Johore at midnight. That, at any rate, was what I was told; whether it is true I do not know.

I was fascinated with these scandalous rumors, for I had a special interest in the sultan. The first case in my first course on international law at Columbia University was *Mighell* v. *Sultan of Johore*. It was brought by poor little Mighell for breach of promise by the sultan who had deceived her by telling her that his name was Albert Baker. The sultan refused to make amends and rejected the jurisdiction of the British court by reason of his being an independent sovereign. Since the case was heard in 1893 it might not have concerned the same sultan; if not, his predecessor. If it was the same, it would show him still up to his old tricks; if not, then playing fast with the affections of the ladies must run in the family. Although the dignified English judge did not commit himself, you can read disapproval of such caddish behavior in the legalistic phrases of his opinion: "I must assume that the Sultan of Johore came to this country and took the name of Albert Baker, and that the plaintiff believed that his name was Albert Baker, and I will go so far as to assume for the present purpose that he deceived her by pretending to be Albert Baker, and then promised to marry her, and that he broke his promise."* Whatever made him choose the name Albert Baker?

The British govern cleverly. They are firm but the iron fist is always softly gloved. They do many things that anger the native princes, but they always follow up with something soft and pleasing. There they were without question "number one"—the most respected of all the white people. It is a curious experience for an American to find himself eclipsed. Shortly after we went to the China Station we were stationed at Chefoo from which our destroyers operated during the summer. There I discovered that the Chinese called us "number two British"—a truly shattering blow to the ego.

In Malaya the British maintain their prestige by practicing a sort of self-imposed censorship over the British community. All British firms make themselves responsible for debts contracted by their British employees. If you want credit in Singapore, you give the name of your firm and the sky is the limit. The firms naturally watch their young men and if extravagance is noticed, they are called in for a fatherly talk by the boss. The young men are particularly watched for any signs of serious infatuations. It is funny how Malaya abounds in rumors of the strange and mysterious powers over white men that native and half-caste women are said to possess. Everyone sooner or later tells you about it and, while making out that he does not of course believe in magic, your informant will invariably add: "It is strange but there must be *something* in it." And this is followed by a story of some nice young Englishman, or German, or Dane—good looks, good family, good professional chances—who ruined himself over a "black woman" (that is the term used). In some stories he takes a native mistress; when he tires of her, she casts a spell over him and he goes rapidly to the dogs—drink, debts, malaria, and a shameful end. In others he dismisses his native mistress when he returns after a trip home with a sweet white girl he has married. This cannot be allowed—the discarded sweetheart soon manages to get between the young couple; the man deserts his lovely white wife and goes back to his former mistress.

In some stories, the young man is sent away to recover from his infatuation; whereupon, he commits suicide—another promising career finished. Even at best, the dark women are said to extract every penny from their white lovers so that they are unable to save anything for their old age. Nobody ever blames the young man, for this is a town that is only too familiar with the monotony of the young

---

*Court of Appeal of England, 1893. Law Reports (1894) 1 Q.B. 149.

planter's life. Getting a girl is made easy for him. He merely tells his number one boy that he'd like a girl and one immediately appears. She lives in the household, ostensibly as a servant. The difficulty is to dismiss her. It always costs much money and, if she doesn't want to go, terrible things will happen to the young man. It is fortunate for British commerce that Malayan spells lose their potency once the ocean is between the victim and the spellbinder. When a firm observes that one of its young employees has become involved with one of these dangerous Circes, they warn him and, if necessary, move him to another post. The most tragic of all cases, but fortunately an exceedingly rare one, is when the young man insists on marrying his dark sweetheart. He is finished, professionally and socially. The British consider the half-caste the lowest in the social scale and will not accept even a light-skinned Eurasian.

The loneliness of plantation life must be difficult. It seems a great mistake for the companies not to provide more time off so that the planters can have weekends to visit each other and more short vacations to come to town. As it is, when they do get off for an annual spree, they go all out and often spend every penny they have earned. A friend told us he once traveled with some planters on home leave. On board there was an elderly lady who liked to play the piano. The planters did not approve of her technique so they heaved the piano overboard and wrote the shipping company a check for it. The offending lady was probably lucky not to have been thrown overboard with the piano.

At one party we met an English dentist who entertained us with local stories. One was about a planter who had a rubber plantation so far in the interior that it took him six days to come to Singapore. Five of these days were spent in a boat traveling downriver and stopping each night to bivouac in the jungle. One day a coolie came into the planter's house carrying the bloody head of his wife whom he had killed since he suspected her fidelity. He had come to give himself up. The nearest police station from the plantation took a half-day to reach by boat. Because the transportation of the body had to be done according to elaborate and time-consuming customs, involving much praying and frequent stops, it took two days for the planter to deliver the coolie and the body to the police, and things had become rather unpleasant. As the planter was already partway downriver and unnerved by this experience, he decided to continue to Singapore for a few drinks at the Raffles Hotel. He also took advantage of his visit to see the dentist, which was fortunate because had he waited but a few more days he would have had a bad root infection.

I commented to the dentist that it seemed to me anyone living so far from dental help would guard against bad trouble by frequent check-ups. He looked at me as if I were balmy. I don't think any of his patients ever came to see him before they had a good-sized twinge of pain. He remarked that he found it extraordinary the way Americans fussed about their teeth. "Do you know, they come in here to have me check their teeth when they stop a day in Singapore on trips around the world. Nothing on earth the matter with them. They just want me to *check.*" He shook his head.

Singapore, however, was not the only place where dentists were exposed to unusual situations. At the Cavite Navy Yard where George was on duty, the admiral frequently played golf with Paul McNutt, High Commissioner of the Philippines. On the occasion of the commissioner's departure for the United States in 1939, the admiral decided, as a friendly gesture, to gold-plate his golf clubs. He sent for George and told him he had heard that the dentist, Lieutenant Edward C. Raffeto, who later became Chief of the Navy Dental Corps, kept a cigar box full of the gold fillings extracted from sailors' mouths. He asked George to get a sufficient quantity of the gold to plate the clubs in the Navy Yard electrical shop.

The dentist was disturbed by the admiral's belief that he kept the fillings and asked George to tell him he always returned the fillings to their owners. The admiral was not convinced, but finally gave George $5.00 to buy gold wash in Manila. This quantity of gold turned out to be sufficient to plate not only the golf clubs but also all the gold buttons on uniforms of the officers on duty at Cavite—at the admiral's expense.

Our trip back to the Philippines on the *Potsdam* was short and uneventful. I was busy writing bread-and-butter letters and George brooded over an atlas, so I knew we would be off on another trip just as soon as he could get more leave.

6
Angkor

Two weeks before Christmas 1938, George managed to get enough leave so that, together with the holidays and our usual long weekends at the Cavite Navy Yard, we could have twelve days to see the ruins of Angkor in Cambodia* and Bangkok, the capital of Siam. We didn't expect to leave the tropics on this trip and, therefore, took along only George's raincoat and my white terry-cloth jacket. I had no idea that I would need wool sweaters and skirts. We did profit from the experience of our trip to the Dutch East Indies, however, to the extent of taking along a tin cup, tissue, soap, a pocket knife, and a flat bottle to be filled with boiled water each morning. Most of our friends never moved a day's distance from Manila without their medicine bag, filled with enough items to equip a small drugstore. As we were never sick, we merely took aspirin along.

We had originally planned to take one of the Philippine rice boats that make the trip to French Indo-China at irregular intervals to pick up rice in Saigon. Lack of time forced us to go more conventionally by the Dutch Orient-Java-Africa Line. The *Ruys* turned out to be an elegant steamer, not as cozy as the *Tjinegara* but equally immaculate, comfortable, and pleasant. We sat at the captain's table and enjoyed the good Dutch food.

Our trip seemed like no trip at all, so soon were we there. Though George has in many ways developed into a perfect traveler, he still suffers from a constitutional inability to see eye to eye with customs and immigration officials and his unpredictable antics are always a little nerve-wracking for me. The landing form we had to fill out before reaching Saigon asked many questions including how he

---

*In the ninth century an ancient people of Cambodia, called the Khmers, set up their capital at Yasodharapura—the present site of Angkor—which became the center of a vastly expanded Khmer Empire. Here its kings received Indian scholars, artists, and religious leaders.

made a living. He wrote "by work." On my questionnaire he put down "being married to a husband who works."

The world, after all, is divided into airtight compartments called "sovereign states" and so it is only to be expected that each "state" should feel entitled to know everything about the grandparents, parents, uncles, and aunts, as well as profession, religion, and complexion of any tourist seeking the privilege of spending his money in the national realm. But for some obscure reason George resents the personal questions he is asked to answer in writing and in duplicate, so he retaliates by putting in a lot of data which are a credit to his imagination and sense of humor. When we traveled through Japan in 1937—followed everywhere by the official spy sent to watch our doings—he kept me in a constant state of anxiety by putting the most fantastic answers on the questionnaires we filled out each night before the hotel clerk would give us the key to our room. In some, our parents were infants when we were born; in others, they were in their nineties. Sometimes we claimed to have twenty children which, given our ages, would have been quite a feat. Once, under religion, he put "Mohammedan," and when questioned by the surprised clerk, said in an offhand manner that quite a few American naval officers were converting to Islam since this was a virile religion, and, what with Japan arming herself and acting warlike, it behooved American service personnel to be prepared. When the clerk asked where he was going after leaving Japan, he said: "To Mecca for a pilgrimage." We often wondered what happened when all these questionnaires eventually reached a central office; some poor Japanese official probably went crazy.

We reached Saigon in the afternoon after sailing up the Saigon River, a tributary of the Dong Nai River, through a flat, green land. The river moves in S curves, constantly turning upon itself. We kept heading towards and away from the distant roofs of Saigon without coming appreciably nearer to our goal. On either side of the river were endless rice fields with occasional bamboo groves. We passed numerous junks and small sampans propelled by slender Annamites in loose black trousers, black three-quarter-length flopping coats, and peaked straw hats like mushrooms. The swampy shores were so close we could almost touch them. The steamer looked oversized and barely managed to turn around when it reached the dock in Saigon.

The departure of the Angkor-bent passengers on various arranged tours caused something of a mix-up, everybody rushing around trying to locate his bags, his automobile, and his guide, and trying to speak French. Eventually, they all got sorted out and off they went on a long tiring trip that got them to Phnom Penh late at night.

FRENCH INDO-CHINA

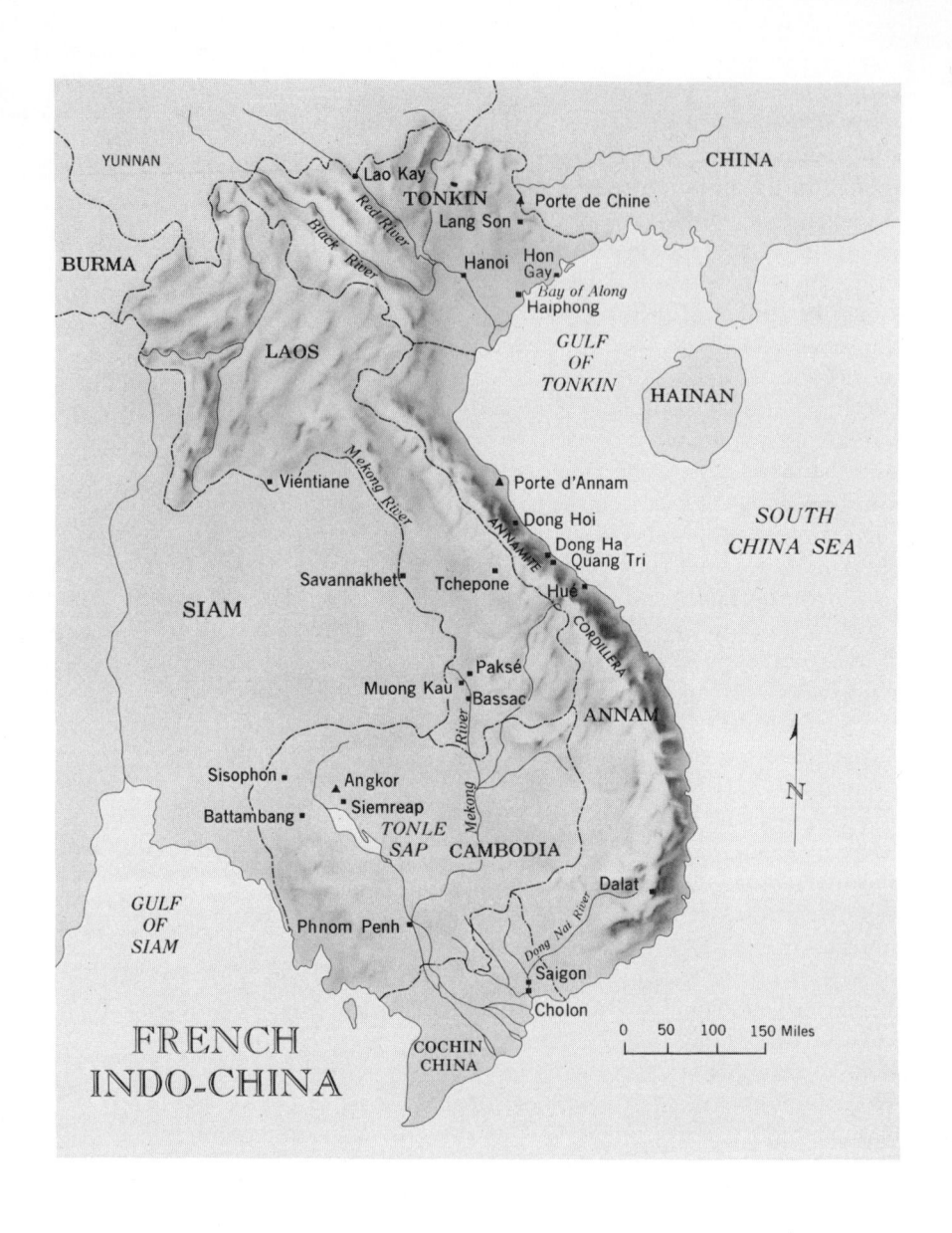

We decided we would stay the night aboard ship and start out early in the morning so as not to miss seeing the countryside. We quickly made arrangements for a car to drive us to Angkor and remain with us for our visit there. Then we set off on foot to explore Saigon.

We were amazed to find it a modern, clean city, laid out geometrically like most French towns—with broad tree-lined avenues, a park, elegant stores, cafés that were cleaner and more attractive than those in Paris, an ornate opera house, large hotels, and Frenchwomen dressed with Parisian chic. We saw efficient, native policemen, calmly directing a multitude of cars, rickshas, trucks, streetcars, creaking oxcarts, and hordes of heavily-burdened natives. The residential section, called Frenchtown, is situated on a slightly elevated plateau and consists of handsome European villas surrounded by lovely gardens. Wide avenues lined with shady tamarinds lead into this oasis of peace and quiet. As soon as you leave the European quarter, you are in the midst of the dirt and noise of the Orient. The native quarters are crowded, the houses ramshackle, and there are plenty of pitiful beggars. Many natives have no other home than the sidewalk, a small part of which they seem to regard as theirs by squatter's right. Here they slept at night on straw mats fastened between bamboo poles which were rolled up in the morning and stowed away. Then some small cooking device was set going and the family would assemble around it for its meager rations. Later the sidewalk would become a workshop or tiny business stall. Nothing distressed us more in all the vast panorama of Asiatic poverty than seeing people huddled into small formless bundles, sleeping on city streets. We never saw anything like this elsewhere in Southeast Asia, though it is common enough in Hong Kong and some other Chinese cities.

Once we passed a third-rate harbor café with shabby French soldiers drinking Pernod; a cluster of open-mouthed native country people peeking at them from behind some potted plants lined up around the tables on the sidewalk. It was evident that to these natives the French soldiers with a few piastres in their pockets were the personification of wealth.

As in all cities of Southeast Asia, the Chinese were everywhere. Their garish signs hung above small shops crowded with things for sale, and their cheerful young men pulled Saigon's rickshas which the French insist on calling *pousse-pousses*, even though they are not pushed but pulled. Sometimes we had a glimpse of the interior of one of their shops, when the owner and his employees had ceased their endless toil for a moment to sit down together in democratic sociability for a meal around a low circular table. Cholon, a little distance from Saigon, is a completely Chinese city.

The Annamites look like miniature Chinese, except that the men's teeth are black from continuous betel-nut chewing (the girls lacquer theirs), and, in their black clothes and mushroom hats, there is no mistaking them for any other nationality. The Cambodians are taller, their faces browner and cruder. They also have black teeth and they wear the Siamese *panung*, here called *sampot*.* This is a sarong that is wrapped around the waist and pulled between the legs like a diaper. It looks somewhat like bloomers. Even the prettiest woman is unattractive in this costume. Cambodians, men and women, cut their hair short so it stands up like the bristles of a brush. The Annamite women wear it as a crown around the head, wound into black or white cloth tubing.

The contrast between the native quarters and European sections of oriental port cities is always striking, but nowhere more so than in Saigon. The French do not readily emigrate from La Belle France because they feel strongly that nothing comparable is to be found anywhere in the world. If they must live for a while in the colonies, they intend to make their exile as much like France as possible. If one removed the native pedestrians, for example, one could easily take up the Rue Catinat in Saigon and set it down in metropolitan Paris, where it would fit perfectly. Nothing could be more authentically French than Saigon's government buildings, barracks, and schools. We noted that they had thoughtfully placed the Palais de Justice opposite the town jail.

As we left the *Ruys* the next morning, we found our hired car ready for us and we began the long drive to Phnom Penh. The road from Saigon to Phnom Penh, the capital of the kingdom of Cambodia, runs in a straight line through level rice fields. This is one of the three largest rice-producing areas of the world. To a visitor from the Philippines, where it is the habit of our independence-intoxicated bus and truck drivers to force a car into the ditch whenever possible, the good road manners of the Indo-Chinese were impressive. We were surprised to see all the native buses, crowded to overflowing, keeping rigidly to their side of the road; even the carabao were well disciplined. This immediately filled us with admiration for the colonizing genius of the French.

France established control over Indo-China gradually. As was the case with many other European colonies, political conquest followed upon missionary activity. Portuguese Jesuits began teaching

*The Siamese *panung* and Cambodian *sampot* are similar to the Indian *dhoti*, made familiar to the West by Gandhi. One suspects they were brought along by the first Indian migrants who moved across the Bay of Bengal. The *dhoti*, however, is made of white, gauze-like cotton, while the *panung* and *sampot* are made of opaque cotton in various colors and patterns, or of silk or brocade.

the gospel as early as 1615, but when the Société des Missions Etrangères was founded in Paris in 1659, the mission field in Indo-China was taken over primarily by the French. Under the Annamese Emperor Gia-Long (1802-1820), who was a close friend of Pigneau de Behaine, Bishop of Adran, the French missionaries were favored and their converts reached the astonishing number of 60,000 in Annam, but Gia-Long's successors (Minh-Mang, 1820-1841; Thieu-Tri, 1841-1848; and Tu-Duc, 1848-1883) turned against the missionaries and their converts, persecuting, torturing, and killing many native Christians, as well as some forty or more French priests. This led to French military intervention and eventual occupation of the entire country. Parts of Cochin China were ceded in 1862; five years later France occupied all of Cochin China and in 1884 and 1885 treaties with Annam and China (Annam's nominal suzerain) granted France a protectorate over Annam and Tonkin; a brief war in which Annam was joined by China, having been quickly won by France. In 1887, the colony of Cochin China and the protectorate Annam-Tonkin were joined in the Indo-Chinese Union and placed under a French Governor-General, who resided half the year in Saigon, and half in Hanoi.

Despite Siam's efforts to bring Cambodia and Laos, over which she had long claimed suzerainty, completely under her control, these two countries were eventually made French protectorates (Cambodia, 1863; Laos, 1893) and joined the Union, as did the Kwangchowan Territory, leased for ninety-nine years to France by the Chinese in 1899.

Since this was a devoutly Buddhist country, we met many bonzes going about their morning task of collecting rice. Yellow-robed and shaven-headed, they walked along the road without looking up, often followed by small boys learning to become bonzes by carrying their teacher's gear in neat little bundles. Often we saw them standing before a poor peasant's house, waiting for him to dole out their morning rice. In theory, they stand there only upon invitation but, since they have made it abundantly clear that dire things will befall the uncharitable Buddhist who does not gladly give them their breakfast, their rice collection amounts to a heavy tax which the peasant can ill afford to pay. There are too many bonzes in Indo-China and Siam. This is because one may become a Buddhist monk for a time and later return to secular life. Few men in these countries do not don the yellow robe for at least a few months, thereby gaining great merit. One wonders whether the lure in some cases might not be an expense-paid vacation. Those who become lifetime monks make a vow of chastity and poverty and keep it scrupulously. Besides their religious duties, the monks do some minor educational work. We gathered that they were primarily concerned with their own personal salvation, rather than with helping others in this quest. On the other hand, they are good and kindly men and not fanatics.

We often passed shallow rivers where groups of people stood immobile and half submerged, fishing. Fish is an important item in the Cambodian diet and can be caught right in the irrigation ditches that water the rice fields. Thus, one piece of land provides a harvest of protein food and cereals. Sometimes we saw a white sail moving slowly across what looked like a green rice field but was, in fact, an irrigation canal. The canals are truly multipurpose waterways, serving irrigation, fishery, and navigation. Through irrigation works, the French multiplied tenfold the acreage and yield of rice cultivation in the Mekong Delta. All six million acres of this alluvial delta land are one huge rice bowl, as is to a lesser extent the delta of the Red River in Tonkin. In fact there is a saying that Indo-China is like the carrying pole of a coolie. The narrow strip of land between the mountains and the South China Sea is the pole and the Mekong and Red River deltas are the rice baskets carried at each end.

Some 1,200 miles of rivers and irrigation canals in Cochin China are navigable, the Mekong itself being deep enough for vessels drawing sixteen feet as far up as Phnom Penh, where the delta begins. We were intrigued with the several time-honored ways of moving water into the higher-lying rice fields. First, simply by scooping it up by hand into pails; second, using a shovel-like contraption suspended from a bamboo tripod and swinging it by hand; third, by large, woven-bamboo baskets with long ropes attached at top and bottom and manipulated by two men. The men stand a short distance apart from each other, rhythmically swinging the baskets down to fill them with water and up to pour it into the higher field. Sometimes several such baskets are moved simultaneously, each with two men holding its ropes, all working in perfect harmony. The fourth method is by large wheels with bamboo buckets attached. These wheels are turned by several men on a treadmill arrangement—the water scooped up by the buckets flowing through bamboo troughs to the desired spot. Fifth, by a similar wheel operated by the current of a flowing brook or river; and sixth, by a series of such water wheels which are lined up in a row and, from a distance, look like a giant drum lying sideways on the water. We saw all of these water-moving systems on our way to Phnom Penh.

We often noticed curiously shaped roofs rising above palm and bamboo groves that reminded us of the roofs on the Minangkabau houses in Sumatra. The houses were light and airy structures consisting of triple-tiered gables at right angles to each other; the sloping roofs ended in long, curved spikes. In the center, the whole building was topped by a long tapering cone ending in a thin spire. Later, in Bangkok, we saw many palaces and temples with similar roofs. The tapering cone is a favorite motif in Khmer bas-reliefs and is the shape of the crowns worn by kings and dancing girls alike, but the multiple-tiered roofs seem to be a distinctly Siamese phenomenon, traceable neither to Indian nor to Chinese influence.* Aping the ethnologists, we amused ourselves spinning elaborate theories of racial relationships and migrations on the basis of the similarity between Minangkabau, Siamese, and Cambodian roofs. I am not sure our theories were as far-fetched as we thought at the time, or as strange as some of the ethnological theories currently in vogue. The roofs came to Cambodia from Siam—which had extensive relations with all the Malay kingdoms of British Malaya. Several of those kingdoms (notably Negri Sembilan) were founded by Minangkabaus from Sumatra. It would, therefore, seem possible that this architectural feature wandered from Fort de Kock in Sumatra, via Johore, Negri Sembilan, and Bangkok, to Cambodia.

We were intrigued by the interesting way in which Indian, Chinese, and native elements had become fused, making the Indo-Chinese Peninsula, which includes Burma, a link between these two great Asiatic civilizations. The peninsula is often called Farther India but could just as well be called Farther China. Indian influence is more marked in the west, Chinese in the east, but there is much overlapping. Moreover, Indian immigration ceased centuries ago, whereas Chinese and sinicized Annamites continue to stream westward, so that in time they may eclipse the remnants of Indian culture.

Indo-China is a bewildering maze of diverse races of whom not much is known. There were apparently several waves of migration from the north; from Tibet, Yunnan, and possibly from South China. These came roughly in the following order: Proto-Malay, Malay, Mon-Khmer, Tibeto-Burman, Lao-Thai, and finally various primitive tribes related to the Chinese who settled in the mountainous regions. In the first centuries of our era these races received the impact of Indian civilization brought to them directly by small bands of Indians

*The Siamese crown, like that of the Khmer from which it was probably copied (together with the whole concept of divine kingship brought originally from India), differs from conventional patterns of royal crowns. It consists of several highly ornamented rings, graduated in size, with a long thin spire at the top. In general outline it resembles somewhat the odd, multiple-tiered royal umbrellas which, even more than the crown, are symbols of royalty in Indianized kingdoms. Strangely enough, these royal umbrellas remind one of the *merus*, multiple-roofed pagodas, which we first saw in Balinese temples.

and indirectly by Indianized Javanese.* The Chams of Champa, an ancient kingdom in the southern part of Annam, received their civilization from Java and were once powerful, but they succumbed to the Annamites. Under Indian rulers, the Mon-Khmer founded flourishing kingdoms in Cambodia and Siam; these were eventually conquered by the Lao-Thai who, while originally possessed of a sinicized culture, later absorbed so much Indian civilization—notably a script based on Sanskrit, Indian religion, statecraft, and architecture—that Siam is today a fascinating complex of Chinese and Indian cultural elements. Indian influence also permeated Laos so that the western part of Indo-China may be said to be an area of Indianized culture.

It is surprising that Indian concepts of the deity of the king took such strong roots in countries whose indigenous village organizations were democratic. Brahman dogma held that the king was a god more or less equivalent to Vishnu or Siva and, like these gods, was subject only to the king of gods—Brahma. When Buddhism became the state religion in Cambodia and Siam, the Brahman concept of the king persisted even though it was incompatible with Buddhism. As in the Malay States where Brahmanism and Hinduism were superseded by Islam, the kings succeeded in holding their godlike prerogatives and continued to maintain court Brahmans (now Buddhist in religion) to officiate at coronations and other royal functions.

Eastern Indo-China, on the other hand, was invaded by China in the third century B.C. and remained under Chinese rule for centuries, during that time becoming a small replica of its stronger and more capable master. According to the *Annamite Annals,* China ruled Annam (called the Pacified South) for some eight hundred years: its cultural influence, however, continued long after Annam achieved independence. When the Manchus drove out the last Chinese dynasty—the Mings—remnants of loyal Ming followers retired southward and for a short period (1414-1428) re-established Chinese rule. We know little of the original Annamites. They are believed to be a

*In his *Towards Angkor: In the Footsteps of the Indian Invaders,* H. G. Quaritch Wales set himself the fascinating task of tracing the route of the Indians who colonized the Indo-China peninsula. He found that by the fifth century A.D., piracy in the Straits of Malacca had become so severe a threat to Indian shipping that an alternative route across the Malay Peninsula, from Takuapa on the west coast to the Bay of Bandon on the east coast, had to be used. At this point (a short distance south of the Isthmus of Kra) the Indians found two rivers, one running east and the other west from the watershed, which were so close to each other that only five miles of land area had to be traversed, the rest of the route being navigable. Moreover, on the Bay of Bandon they found a sheltered harbor—in fact, the best harbor on the entire east coast. Various archaeological finds confirmed Wales in his surmise that this indeed had been the main route of Indian penetration eastward from the fifth century on.

mixture of Malay, or Proto-Malay, and Chinese and were contemptuously called Giao-Chi by the Chinese—apparently because these people had a distinguishing characteristic in that the big toe was set separately from the other toes, almost as the thumb of the hand. Although eventually the emperor of Annam achieved independence, he continued to ask for investiture from Peking and sent tribute. Until 1884, when the French replaced China as the suzerain power, the tribute Annam sent to China consisted of: "Two elephants' tusks . . . two rhinoceros' horns, forty-five catties (one catty equalling $1\frac{1}{3}$ pounds) of betelnut, forty-five catties of grains of paradise, six hundred ounces of sandalwood, three hundred ounces of garronwood, one hundred pieces of native silk, one hundred pieces of white silk, one hundred pieces of unbleached silk, and one hundred pieces of native cloth."* This tribute meant less in the past because, in her vast conceit, China regarded the whole world around her as peopled by "outside barbarians" who owed tribute to the Celestial Empire. Since, for a trifling gift, the tribute-bearers were free to trade with China without paying imports and port duties, even strong and truly independent cities and states found it expedient to pay lip service to Chinese suzerainty.

It must be noted that political relationships between Asiatic kingdoms and empires can be understood only if it is kept in mind that these were not states as we conceive the term today. Practically all the rulers were essentially a species of robber barons, collecting taxes, tribute, and *corvée* (forced labor) from their subjects for their own personal use, and giving almost no public service in return. The only way in which they can be distinguished favorably from modern totalitarian rulers is that they left the customary laws and customs of the people untouched; they did not usually interfere with the locally chosen village governments. The vast majority of their subjects, therefore, lived in their time-honored ways, regardless of who sat on the throne. Often the rulers were foreigners who came from a higher civilization than that of the indigenous people. But their influence seldom reached more than a minority of the people—those who were attached to the court or who were drafted to build palaces or temples or fight the king's personal wars. Chinese political organization was in theory more beneficial to the citizen than Indian, but both introduced the notion that rulers were godlike personages before whom ordinary mortals must prostrate themselves and whose power over the lives and property of their subjects was nearly absolute. It therefore mattered little to the common man whether his ruler paid

---

*From *The French in Indo-China*, p. 240.

tribute to a foreign ruler or himself exacted tribute from others; often he did both. As a result of this political tradition, the people and governments in this area feel no responsibility towards each other, except in the small village units run on democratic lines.

During her subjection to China, Annam-Tonkin* became thoroughly sinicized, adopting China's political organization (mandarinate, emperor ruling by virtue of a mandate from heaven, Book of Rites, etc.) and, for official use, a Chinese dialect written in simplified Chinese characters. The ordinary language of the Annamites is difficult to classify since it contains Thai, Chinese, and Mon-Khmer elements. It is now written in a Latin script, called *quoc ngu*, which was invented in the seventeenth century by French missionaries. Annam's official religion is Buddhism of the Mahayana kind, brought to her from China, in contradistinction to the Buddhism of Laos and Cambodia which is Hinayana (Theravada) and came from South India.† The national costume of the Annamites is the same as that of China before its foreign Manchu rulers forced alteration in the traditional Chinese costume. In fact, Annam looks like a copy in miniature of China, especially of South China. Annamite coolies shuffle along with carrying poles loaded heavily at each end, or push creaking wheelbarrows with solid wheels, or pole boats with long single poles—exactly as in China. In the towns, Annamite houses are built in rows, with narrow streets between, just as in China. Only in their headgear do the Annamites show a spirit of independence. The girls have different hairdos and the men in Tonkin wear curious turbans with the top removed. Peasants, however, bowed over in their rice fields, here as everywhere in China, wear the same round straw hats that serve as both hat and umbrella.

It is one hundred and fifty miles from Saigon to Phnom Penh and two hundred more to Angkor. The long, dusty trip through the flat, green country might have been tedious had we not often seen signs showing an inverted capital T which meant we were approaching a ferry. Ferries are one of the most characteristic features of Indo-China. They are run by a breed of highly independent individuals

---

*The term *Annam* is often applied to the entire eastern half of French Indo-China, which comprised Tonkin, Annam and Cochin China, sometimes only to the middle part. In 1802, the Emperor of Annam took over the rule of all three territories; after 1884 they were under a French protectorate.

†Hinayana or Small Vehicle Buddhism is the religion of Ceylon, Burma, Siam, Laos, and Cambodia. It retains the teaching of the Buddha in its purest form and venerates him as a great teacher, not a god. Mahayana or Great Vehicle Buddhism is the religion of Tibet, China, Japan, Korea, and Annam. It looks upon the Buddha as one of many gods and worships numerous lesser deities and demi-gods (the Bodhisattvas). Depending on the country, it may be mixed with Brahmanistic elements, with Shinto, with the doctrines of Lao-Tse, or with Confucian concepts.

Irrigating the fields

Enroute to Phnom Penh

who can never be hurried and whose greatest joy is to cast off the moment they see a loaded bus approaching. While waiting for the ferryman to pole his boat leisurely across the water, you can sample the variety of food for sale. Native hucksters swarm about with portable food stalls exhibiting a weird assortment of edibles. Often the ladies of the neighborhood improvise a sort of cafeteria. They are seated in a row, each behind a single kind of food which they have prepared at home. First, you are given a bowl of barley soup in which a variety of vegetables and dried condiments are sprinkled as you pass along the row. Next you receive hard-boiled eggs, and finally fruit, both fresh and stewed. One pockmarked girl was especially adept and could have obtained a job immediately in any American cafeteria. She was seated beside the river and sold soup. We were intrigued with the proficiency with which she filled bowls, keeping her customers laughing by providing a constant flow of what we suspected were off-color jokes. With incredible speed the coppers handed her disappeared into some receptacle hidden inside her dirty blouse, while she reached backwards into the river swishing the used bowls and refilling them for the next customer all in one smooth movement. Never a wasted motion. There was a small piece of soap and an old can on a string to aid in making the morning toilette when you had finished eating. The river water served for drinking, washing, cleaning teeth, and finally as the sewage system. And while all this gay eating and washing was going on, two richly dressed Chinese ladies with dangling jade earrings sat aloof in the bus nibbling, in disapproving silence, on dainties of their own national manufacture. Their condescension towards the natives and determined withdrawal from the common herd were obvious.

Phnom Penh's claim to distinction rests on its man-sized mosquitoes and its lovely inexpensive silver. It is the capital of Cambodia, a shabby oriental Ruritania misruled for centuries by arbitrary kings and corrupt mandarins, beaten down by high taxes and *corvée*, a perpetual bone of contention between Annam and Siam who fought over it until 1863, when France stepped in and it was abolished. This preserved Cambodia as a protectorate with French Residents to supervise the administration and to give pin money to the king to keep him contented. In 1907 France forced Siam to return to Cambodia the provinces of Siemreap (Angkor), Sisophon, and Battambang, which Siam had stolen in 1795. There is a gaudy monument in Phnom Penh depicting three buxom ladies with simpering faces (the three provinces) bowing to a somewhat grumpy-looking seated figure representing King Sisowath of Cambodia. A small medallion shows the head of a Frenchman whom we surmised was the one who engineered the work. The monument is in pseudo-Khmer style and, like the little kingdom of Cambodia, a sad caricature of the once great Khmer civilization and empire.

We dutifully drove around the town looking at everything tourists are expected to see: the modern and hygienic new market, the museum in modern Khmer style, and the palace of the king with its silver pagoda and his old white elephant. This elephant is a sacred animal so only the king may sit on him and that only once in his life, when he ascends the throne. When tourists appear, the attendants pull the poor animal by the ear, whereupon he opens his mouth and looks at them sadly and appealingly. This is a cue to buy sugar cane at ten cents a bunch and feed him. There is a small house which has a sort of fire-escape arrangement attached to it and from there the king mounts the elephant on coronation day.

The palace throne room is lavishly gilded and there is a glittering gold throne with an impressive golden couch beside it where the king may stretch out should he become fatigued by an overly long court ceremony. It reminded us of the *lit de justice*, or "bed of justice," in which French kings once actually reclined while imposing their will on Parliament. A few of the grander officials were allowed to stand and all others knelt. It was a bed, Talleyrand quotes Fontenelle as saying, "in which justice went to sleep." There are two large golden statues of the king's father and grandfather; also a wonderful *Prah Khan* (golden sword) which, according to legend, fell on Angkor hundreds of years ago. This sword is wielded by each king on his coronation day; thereafter, it reposes in the throne room. It is comparable to the ancient sword in Westminster Abbey which is used at coronations and royal investitures. Legend says the Cambodian blade belonged to Jayavarman II (802-850 A.D.) but its appearance gives small hint of such antiquity. Sheathed in a jeweled scabbard, it is preserved in the Royal Treasury at Phnom Penh and guarded by an ancient corps of Brahmans (Baku) who claim descent from the Khmer royal chaplains.

In back of the king's throne is a smaller one for the queen, and between the two thrones is a row of chairs upholstered in gold brocade for the king's concubines. At Angkor the king had some three thousand concubines, and as recently as the middle of the last century, the Cambodian king had at least seven hundred. When we were there, the king had one queen and seventy concubines—a sad remnant of ancient glory. The French Residents ruthlessly cut down the king's subsidy and made him fire his dancing girls. His queen presented him with four children; the seventy concubines with only nineteen, which seems to indicate lack of a proper sense of duty on their (or his) part. A touching token of domestic harmony may be observed, however. In the palace temple there is a large gold Buddha, which weighs 132 pounds, donated by the king, the queen, and the concubines—all contributing.

We stayed overnight at the Royal Hotel which is the pride of Phnom Penh—and expensive. In many ways the French have an admirable talent for making themselves comfortable in the tropics. Their houses are built of cement; the rooms have high ceilings and are cool. They have trained their Annamite cooks to prepare delicious meals, and they wisely extend the two-hour midday rest period prevalent in southern France to four hours—thus avoiding overexertion. Moreover, besides Sunday, the holidays of every religion in the country are official days of rest.

In the morning we had a veritable shopping spree in the native silversmith street. The Cambodians do exquisite silver work. The Khmer motifs, to be found in stone at Angkor, appear on all the Phnom Penh silver in delicate miniature. This is the best place in the entire Orient to buy silver and jewelry.

Before we left for Angkor, we paid a visit to the Buddhist shrine on the city's only hill, the Phnom. The shrine contains four sacred statues of Buddha, supposedly rescued some six hundred years ago from the flood waters of the Mekong by a heroic woman named Penh, hence the name of the city—Phnom Penh.

The trip to Angkor was long and uninteresting. The country was flat, green, and covered with rice fields. Sometimes bamboo groves and small islands of bushes and palm trees enlivened the green sea of rice. Once we passed over an old Khmer bridge, still standing firmly on its thick brick pillars. Gifted architects that they were, the Khmer nevertheless did not know how to construct an arch. Therefore, they had to place the supporting pillars of their bridges close together so that they resembled walls. Whenever possible, the Khmers built causeways rather than bridges. The combination of highly developed artistic talent with primitive technical knowledge is typical of the Orient and always struck us forcibly. I often wondered whether it was due to the static character of oriental society in which experimentation is discouraged.

Before we left on this trip I read an article in the *National Geographic Magazine* which traced the route of Marco Polo's travels and showed graphically how much remained today as it had been then. The author remarked that any trip through Europe or America taken fifty years ago would point up the many vast changes that had occurred in that short time, while Marco Polo's tale written years ago "is largely the living, vivid geography of today."* I suppose the

---

*J. R. Hildebrand, "The World's Greatest Overland Explorer," *National Geographic Magazine*, November, 1928, p. 518.

Cambodian ferry

Khmer bridge

possibilities of variety and change are always limited when the technical bases of civilization remain primitive.

All along the way the natives politely removed their hats as we drove by. We were startled at first but soon took it with regal nonchalance. When we returned to the Philippines, we felt slighted at the lack of public acclamation when we drove into Manila.

We were grateful for the modern shower and the cool balcony overlooking a shady garden at our hotel in Siemreap, a small village adjacent to the ruins of Angkor. As everywhere in Indo-China, we first had to go through a tussle with Madame and her shifty Annamite secretary to obtain reasonable lodging, but by then we were hardened travelers and, fortified with the official hotel guide of the Bureau Officiel du Tourism Indochinois, we could usually hold our own. It seemed a pity that greedy hotel keepers nullified much of the effort and expense invested by the government in luring tourists with hard currencies into the country. In French Indo-China and the Dutch East Indies you had to be continually on your guard, but in British Malaya, the Philippines, and independent little Siam you could relax and enjoy the country and the people—in those places you never met anything but courtesy and honesty.

We spent two and a half days at the ruins, which is sufficient if you are not seasoned mountain climbers. Never had either of us done so much climbing up and down. The builders of Angkor* believed in setting their temples on the top of steep, narrow staircases, one step often rising as much as two feet above the lower one. It was thought to be good for the soul to exert oneself when approaching the deity. I am sorry to say that I mostly went up and down these stairs on all fours, but it was the only way I could see everything and I was determined not to miss a single relief or statue, they were all so fascinating.

The first afternoon, we drove to Angkor Wat (a *wat* is a temple, or religious compound) and spent three hours climbing around in it. This is without question the most imposing and the best-preserved of all the larger buildings at Angkor. It is one of the most beautiful temples in all Asia and quite distinctive, though somewhat reminiscent of the temple at Borobudur. Nothing in India is quite like it, so we must credit the ancient Khmer with having added something of their own to the civilization brought them by their Indian rulers.

---

*The city of Angkor was first built by Khmers near the present ruins during the reign of Jayavarman II (802–850 A.D.). A new capital was later built on the present site of Angkor Thom by King Yasovarman I (889–900 A.D.). This city was called Yasodharapura. For the next two centuries Khmer kings continued to expand the city, adding many new temples. Suryavarman II (1113–1150 A.D.) built the great temple known as Angkor Wat. The final walled city called Angkor Thom was reconstructed by Jayavarman VII (1181–1219 A.D.), known as the greatest Khmer builder.

One approaches the temple on a wide causeway, 1,148 feet long, built of huge square blocks of laterite faced with sandstone. This leads across a broad moat filled with lotus-covered water in which are mirrored the elegant facades of the entrance pavilions. In the evening, natives bathe in the moat and yellow-robed bonzes wander to the temple to sleep in its galleries. Along the shores grows a particularly decorative bush with white blossoms which gives the temple a lovely background. Flocks of white birds, probably of the heron family, looking for all the world like snowflakes against the old grey walls, rise periodically from the moat. When the sun sets and the rim of the sky is banked with fleecy clouds and pink and turquoise streamers—all reflected in the water—the scene is full of peace and beauty.

The temple covers an area a mile square but appears less bulky than it actually is, because of its graceful proportions. It is a step pyramid which rises in three galleries and is topped by five rounded towers shaped somewhat like lotus buds, a distinctive architectural feature at Angkor. The center tower is higher than the others, and all are so cleverly arranged that one obtains a most pleasing perspective from every angle. The setting, which is lush green jungle, makes it look a bit as one imagines the palace of the Sleeping Beauty. But also, perhaps because it stands at the end of a long causeway, intersected in the center by a wall around the temple area, or perhaps because of its symmetry and the elegance of the carved pavilions which are let into the wall, Angkor Wat reminds one a little of Versailles. I could imagine the astonishment of the French naturalist, Henri Mouhot, when he came upon the temple after a long and arduous tramp through trackless jungle. This was around 1860, and Mouhot was completely surprised because people had forgotten about the temple although it was still well preserved. Mouhot wandered about looking for some sign of human occupation but found none. He was familiar with the Cambodians living nearby in nipa shacks and he could not conceive of their being the descendants of the builders of Angkor—nor could they tell him who had built it. Yet the Cambodians are descended from the Khmers. Their writing is similar to that on the stone inscriptions in the Angkor ruins and their name *Cambodia* is merely a Western adaptation of the name *Kambuja* which, according to legend, was the name of the founder of the Khmer Dynasty, Kambu Svayambhuva. Chinese documents called it Chenla, while the French refer to it as Cambodge. Cambodians actually call their country Sroc-Khmer, or Land of the Khmer, and there is certainly no question that Angkor was built by Khmers.

In a sense Mouhot did "discover" Angkor, and his studies and reports made it known to the West. But long before him French missionaries had seen Angkor and written about it. Before them, the

Ancient stone naga on road to Angkor

Angkor Wat

Tower at Angkor Wat

Portuguese had visited this region and written about it as early as the sixteenth century. One, Christoval de Jaque de los Rios de Mancaned,* wrote that in 1570 a city was discovered in Cambodia filled with a number of buildings and surrounded by a wall four leagues in length whose battlements were covered with beautifully sculptured animals—elephants, tigers, lions, eagles, stags, and many others. Within the wall were handsome residences and magnificent fountains and inscriptions which even then the Cambodians were unable to decipher. They were particularly impressed with a beautiful bridge and mentioned the giants supporting its balustrades.

Ancient Kambuja was just another Indianized state, as were Sri Vijaya, Mataram, and Madjapahit. As in Java, Sumatra, and Malaya, Indians had come in small numbers and brought with them their civilization. They had made themselves rulers on the pattern of the princely states of India, and had forced the natives to build them palaces and temples and to fight their battles. For a time there had been splendid courts with a flowering of literature and the arts, then these Indianized states decayed or were destroyed in battle. In the Indies it was Islam that brought them to their end; in Cambodia it was the Siamese and the Chams from Champa who looted Angkor periodically. Once destroyed, these ancient kingdoms disappeared, leaving but a few ruins and stone monuments with carved inscriptions to tell of their past glory. What mystified the French, when they took over Cambodia as a protectorate in the nineteenth century, was that they could not find any living inhabitants who knew how to build as the Khmers had done. The Cambodians of that day did not even know how to decipher the ancient inscriptions, nor could they tell anything of the history of Angkor or the reasons for its final abandonment. A city, still in fair state of repair, without a single inhabitant! It seemed a mystery as inexplicable as that of the *Marie Céleste*, the ship that was discovered drifting with not a man on board and no evidence of any disaster that could have necessitated abandoning her.

Nothing in the stone inscriptions of Angkor gives a hint of decay. They recount the splendors of the various kings, and then just stop. Some experts believe that the huge population required to carry out the Khmer building program may have exhausted the soil so that in the end it could not feed the city: the soil around Angkor is indeed sandy and poor, and no rice is grown. Others think that perhaps the mouths of the Mekong became silted, with the result that in the rainy

---

*E. Cortambert and Léon de Rosny, *Tableau de la Cochinchine*, pp. 175-176, relates this account by Mancaned, written in 1606. Mancaned wrote that the city was called *Angor*, or "the city of five points" resembling five high pyramids.

season too much water backed up into the Tonle Sap—the large lake lying to the west of Angkor—flooding the city and surrounding rice fields and turning them into marshland so that the people had to move away to find food.*

I had heard, too, from various sources that cities were often abandoned after a disastrous looting or a severe epidemic. Rather than rebuild, the people seemed to prefer to build a new city nearby, as if they felt that the old site was unlucky or perhaps inhabited by evil spirits. Angkor might have been abandoned because of some such catastrophe. Possibly the little town of Siemreap was built to house those who wished to remain in the neighborhood but did not want to live in the devastated city. Perhaps the superstitious natives began to see something eerie and frightening in the abandoned ruins, which is not surprising in view of the large number of bats in the old buildings. Rumors started that the place was haunted and dangerous. Soon it was all but forgotten.

All those things may have occurred but it seemed to us that the explanation for its abandonment might be simpler. Angkor's wealth was a constant temptation to the Annamites in the east and to the Siamese in the west, both of whom attacked her whenever difficulties arose over succession to the throne or if the time seemed otherwise propitious.

Angkor was at one time a vassal of Annam from which it was wrested by the Siamese who, in turn, imposed their own suzerainty. At times Angkor regained its independence but there were frequent wars and numerous sackings of the city. The Indianized rulers and their families must have been decimated by this constant warfare and their power over the native population weakened. The kings appear to have moved the court eastward to escape the continuous Siamese incursions as long ago as the middle of the fifteenth century.† They finally settled at Phnom Penh, where they lived in greatly reduced circumstances. The French took them under their protection, gave them enough money to replace their thatch-roofed huts with small pseudo-Khmer palaces, and forced Siam to return Angkor and the three western provinces.

When we were there, the ruler, King Sisowath Monivong, called himself the ninety-seventh in the royal line and ruled over a territory almost as large as the ancient Khmer kingdom, though gently guided by the velvet hand of the French Resident.

---

*E. Robert Moore, "Along the Old Mandarin Road of Indo-China," *National Geographic Magazine*, (August, 1931), p. 159.

†C. E. Bouillevaux, *L'Annam et le Cambodge: Voyages et Notices Historiques*, p. 348.

The French government, through the Ecole Française d'Extrême-Orient, did an outstanding job of freeing the monuments from the jungle, preserving them, and making them easily accessible by building excellent motor roads that run straight as the old Khmer roads must have, right to all the principal ruins. My only criticism is that they could not eliminate the bats. There are far too many of them and they smell atrocious. Some ruins cannot be visited in the morning because of the overpowering scent of these creatures. They squeak at you as they hang from the ceiling and, as soon as it gets dark, one hates to remain.

We wandered the whole length of all the Angkor Wat galleries with Monsieur Henri Marchal's *Archeological Guide to Angkor* in hand. To the layman, the profusion of gods and goddesses and the constant intermingling of Brahmanism and Buddhism is bewildering, though Monsieur Marchal tries his best to clarify the matter. What makes his book so delightful is that it is a literal translation from the French, and the translator frequently falls into the trap of thinking that two words that sound or look alike in French and English mean the same thing. We liked particularly his use of the word *defile* which he thought was a good rendering of the French *défiler* (to march past). So he speaks at length of "personnages defiling." There are many such defiling "personnages"—kings, generals, soldiers, common people, gods, giants, monkeys, birds, and quaint animals of all descriptions. The profusion of detail is almost overwhelming. There is not a square inch of stone, so it seemed to us weary travelers, that had not been used to fashion a *naga* (the sacred serpent, in the form of a hooded cobra, worshiped by the Khmer kings as the ancestor of their race), *garuda* (a mythical half-man, half-bird sacred to the god Vishnu), a *devata* (a sort of lesser goddess), an *apsaras* (a dancing girl sent by the gods to tempt pious ascetics), or at least a few leaves and curlicues. Surprisingly, despite this overloading with decorative material, the monuments are designed with such great artistry that they give an impression of grandeur and simplicity. From a distance, the carvings look like graceful lace draped over the stone. In fact, the stylized wreaths and flowers are being used as patterns for modern lacework embroidery. The ancient Khmers were indeed masters of the chisel. All through the city, Angkor Thom, they have left on the grey stone ruins a vivid record of daily life, of busy kitchens, gossiping women, gambling men, naval and land battles, cock fights, regal processions, and elephants marching in single file by the hundreds. In Angkor Wat they carved row upon row of ravishing *apsarases* and *devatas* whose pretty faces smile at you intriguingly as you wander past. The sinuous curves of their lovely figures look as if they had only this moment stopped dancing. What struck me was that they do not look in the least like Khmers or, for that matter, like Indians; they look almost like European maidens. I wonder whether this could be an echo of the fair-skinned Aryan invaders who came from the north and developed Brahmanism in India. It is interesting that modern Cambodian girls, whose dances are exact copies of those seen in the stone carvings of *apsarases* and *devatas*, whiten every bit of exposed skin when they prepare themselves for dancing.

Though the Khmers could not build a vault, they were clever at arranging perspectives so that, looking through the doorway of an outer pavilion, one would invariably look in a straight line through a half-dozen or more doorways, each slightly smaller than the preceding one, so that altogether they gave an impression of a continuous vaulted passage.

Angkor Wat was built in the twelfth century when Brahmanism was dominant. It was consecrated to the worship of Vishnu, who has a special temple in one of the inner courtyards. To reach it one must climb thirty-eight exceedingly high steps. With the tolerance typical of Indian religions, the temple contains sculptures of many other gods, among them Indra, who, much to our amusement, was sitting sideways and cross-legged on a goose—a bird that seemed to us as quite an unsuitable mount for a major god. When Buddhism replaced Brahmanism, the temple became a shrine to Buddha without any disturbance of the religious carvings of the earlier cult. There are several miles of bas-reliefs in Angkor Wat, most of them depicting episodes from India's two great epic poems, the *Ramayana* and the *Mahabharata*. Since we had frequently come across these in the Indies and expected to meet them again in Indo-China and Siam, I looked them up before we left Manila, so as to be able to understand what all the fierce battles between men, monkeys, gods, and giants signified.

The *Ramayana* and *Mahabharata* were written probably around 200 B.C., and are still beloved wherever Indian civilization has left its mark. To us they appear as fantastic adventure stories, but to the Indians they have religious significance and parts of them are often read by the priests in temple ceremonies. Both point up the moral lesson that Good, after much strife, ultimately triumphs over Evil. The *Mahabharata* turns on the struggle for a northern Indian kingdom belonging to five Pandava brothers (representing Good). The kingdom, together with the brothers' jointly owned wife, is stolen from them by the Kurus (Evil). After taking counsel with Krishna, an incarnation of the god Vishnu, the brothers eventually regain both the kingdom and the lady. In the *Ramayana*, the more popular of the two, a young prince by the name of Rama, also regarded as an incarnation of Vishnu, is driven from his father's court by the evil machinations of a stepmother. He goes into the wilderness with his beautiful wife Sita and his brother Laksmana. While Rama contemplates becoming a hermit, Sita is abducted by the demon Ravana (representing Evil). I am a little suspicious of Sita; she may have gone along willingly—being dissatisfied with the idea of a husband becoming a hermit. However, Rama and Laksmana set out to obtain allies to help them liberate Sita. They finally succeed, aided by a troupe of monkeys who are led by their king, Hanuman. One of the favorite characters of Indian audiences, Hanuman is used extensively in dances and sculptures. At the end of the story Rama, Laksmana, and Sita return to their home, and Sita proves her innocence by walking through fire while Rama is wildly cheered as the new king. Though the basic story of each poem is simple, it is nearly buried in a bewildering mass of plots, subplots, and stories about subordinate characters. The poems are much like the *Arabian Nights* which may in fact have been patterned after these ancient Indian epics.

Of the many bas-reliefs at Angkor Wat, we liked best the panel depicting the "Churning of the Sea of Milk." For some reason not clear to us, the *devas* (gods) desired to obtain some amrita, the ambrosia that gives immortality. This seems odd for I thought gods were by definition immortal. Be that as it may, the *devas* enlisted the help of the *asuras* (demons), promising to share evenly. Amrita could be obtained only by churning the milky sea with the *naga* Vasuki, god of the waters, fastened to Mount Mandara in the sea. Seated on the mountain, Vishnu in his human form presided over the whole endeavor while the mountain, in turn, was supported by Kurma (Vishnu in the incarnation of a tortoise). The 88 *devas* and 92 *asuras* held fast to the *naga* and, using the mountain as a pivot, churned the sea. Luckily the tortoise was strong enough to hold the mountain, for the churning took a thousand years. First, the *apsarases*, then Laksmi (goddess of beauty), then numerous animals and, at the very end, the desired amrita were thrown up by the sea. As was to be expected, no sooner had the amrita been thrown up than the unholy alliance of *devas* and *asuras* collapsed and the former allies proceeded to engage in fierce battle, realistically perpetuated in stone. Monsieur Marchal did not tell how the story ended but I felt certain that eventually Good would conquer Evil, as in all Indian legends. What makes the "Churning of the Sea of Milk" particularly interesting is that its symbolism is also shown in one of the most impressive Khmer architectural ideas—the balustrades that line the causeways leading across the moat surrounding Angkor Thom. Stone giants hold across their knees an enormous snake whose fan-shaped multi-head is turned toward the visitor as he enters the city. The giants (if they were standing they would measure twelve feet in height) represent the *devas* and *asuras*. The gods are distinguished by oval faces, almond-shaped eyes, and grave, austere, and somewhat disdainful looks; the demons have round eyes and grin in what is intended to be a terrifying manner.

After dinner we returned to Angkor Wat to watch the performance of a group of local dancing girls from Siemreap. Small urchins showed us the way with lighted tapers made of twisted newspaper. The dancers' artistry was further enhanced by the superb setting. They danced on the causeway in front of the temple, which was illuminated by colored flares and looked almost undamaged in the moonlight. The small girls went through all the poses we had seen in stone on our way through Angkor Wat, so that one had a strange feeling they had just this moment stepped from the bas-reliefs. The music was an odd mixture of Indian and Chinese elements but pleasingly tuneful. Both Bali and Cambodia received their artistic inspiration from India. The Cambodian dance, however, is not primarily a flow of rhythm but a series of postures, each held for an exact number of beats. Another evidence of their common Indian past were the carved buffalo-hide puppets for shadow plays, much like those we had seen in Bali, which are made in Siemreap—otherwise, an uninteresting village.

Next morning we took a guide and did both the "big" and "little" circuits, as the guide books call them, of Angkor Thom. The city was laid out as a square surrounded by a wall from ten to twenty feet high, and a moat approximately eight miles in perimeter. There were five massive entrance gates in the wall, each surmounted by a tower from which four enormous faces looked in the four directions of the compass.* The faces were capped by pinnacles which may have been covered with gold leaf. These gates were still fairly well preserved though the gilt had gone and the massive doors had been carried away. Four causeways led from the center of the city at the Bayon, a temple whose many four-faced pinnacles dominated the city, through the entrance gates situated in the exact center of each side of the wall, and across the moat continuing on in each direction. A fifth causeway led from the king's palace, on the north side of the Bayon, through the Gate of Victory in the east wall, crossing the moat and the Siemreap River and continuing to the Eastern Baray, an overgrown morass that was once one of two large water reservoirs. This was no city growing haphazardly according to the needs of an expanding population. It was planned and laid out symmetrically as a capital to fit the splendor of Angkor's Indian court.

*Robert J. Casey, in *Four Faces of Siva*, p. 191, mentions that the faces were of Siva, the Destroyer. They were later proven to be of Lokesvara, a more benign god.

Naga balustrade at Angkor Thom

Gate of Victory at Angkor Thom

A Chinese emissary, Chou Ta-kuan, spent eleven months at Angkor, from 1296 to 1297, and wrote the only detailed description we now possess. Though a sophisticated gentleman from Peking, he was greatly impressed by the splendor of the court at Angkor Thom and the magnificence of the city's palaces and temples. I cut out a piece of his account of a royal procession and took it along with me to help my imagination "people" the ruins as we crawled about them. The following is a translation of what he wrote:

> When the King goes out, covered with iron, so that knives and arrows, striking his body, can do him no harm, cavalry head the escort; then come standards, the pennants, and the band. Maidens of the Palace, to the number of three to five hundred, dressed in flowery gowns, with blossoms in their hair and holding big candles in their hands, form a troop; even by daylight their tapers are lighted.
>
> The ministers and nobles ride in front on elephants and look far ahead; their red parasols are without number. After them come the King's wives and concubines, in palanquins, in carriages, or on elephants. They certainly carry more than a hundred parasols adorned with gold. Behind them is the King, standing upright on an elephant and holding in his hand the precious sword. . . .*

We climbed over endless ruined walls, up and down unusually steep stairways, and through miles of galleries whose walls are covered with stone carvings. At one time the Khmers must have been warlike, for scenes of daily life alternate with vivid pictures of war at sea and on land. Our guide told us that generals rode on elephants and common soldiers walked. Knowing the ponderous gait of elephants, we imagined these past battles as moving majestically and slowly like chess games.

The only advantages in hiring a guide are that it saves time and he chases away the cobras. At least he makes much of walking ahead of you and knocking with his stick on the flagstones before he lets you enter the dark, dank galleries. One of the temples—Prah Khan—is in such a state of ruin and so grown over that we were glad to have the guide along. We got there late in the afternoon. The sky was grey and it looked ready to burst into a thunderstorm. It was eerie and even a little frightening. "When it rains," said the guide, "the mosquitoes come into the galleries, the bats come down, and the cobras come out."

A good many fairy tales are told by the guides to titillate the tourists but we suspected that they were pure inventions since so little

---

*From Maynard Owen Williams, "By Motor Trail Across French Indo-China," *National Geographic Magazine*, October, 1935, p. 519.

is actually known of Angkor. As with Borobudur, there were echoes of European fairy tales. One of them reminded us of *Hansel and Gretel,* only here the poor woodcutter had twelve daughters instead of a boy and a girl. Twice the children were exposed in the woods. The first time they found their way back and the second time they were discovered by Santhomea, Queen of the Ogres, who wanted to keep them with her and who got into a terrible rage when the little girls escaped, found their way to Angkor and eventually married the king. This Khmer witch did not rest until she had revenged herself and finally succeeded in having the poor girls blinded and incarcerated on the Phnom Bakheng (the only elevation around Angkor). Luckily, one child born to the unfortunate prisoners survived, escaped, and eventually by magic returned their eyes to the woodcutter's twelve daughters.

Another story is a little like that of Undine, the mermaid turned human for love of a knight. The Khmer story is that once upon a time the daughter of the King of the Nagas, or Cobras, fell in love with Kambu, an Indian, and decided to take human form so she could marry him. These two are the ancestors of the Khmer kings. Since the Naga princess was immortal, she settled herself in the small temple Phimeanakas to watch over the fate of Angkor and there each king had to visit her daily on pain of arousing her wrath. Each king, in turn, became her husband, not an easy position for she is supposed to have been a jealous female.*

The *pièce de résistance* in the Khmer tales is the story of the leper king, which is told in various versions. On our tour we saw the terrace of the leper king, with a statue supposedly of him. Our guide pointed out to us that he was naked because leprosy eats away clothes (a novel idea), had an upturned mustache because he was proud and haughty, and a "tiger smile" to indicate that he was a cruel man. Allegedly he caught the disease because, having married four sisters, he became tired of them and dismissed them to marry a lovely girl who had caught his fancy, whereupon the mother of the sisters, who was a leper, threw herself upon the fickle husband and in due time he broke out with leprous spots. Since kings are gods and cannot possibly become lepers, the people drove him out as a faker and he had to stay on the terrace, visited at night by the four sisters who came to him through a secret passage. The passage is shown to visitors to prove the truth of the story.

Another version of the legend is more interesting. Here, a ragged leprous beggar manages to seize the throne of Angkor, marry a royal

*Robert J. Casey, *Four Faces of Siva,* gives these and a number of other fairy tales told about Angkor.

princess, and restore the power and glory of Angkor, which had already passed its zenith after several disastrous wars. In a country where leprosy is fairly widespread and poverty universal, one can see how such a story of personal triumph against all odds would appeal to the people. This beggar king is supposed to have lived in the twelfth century and is credited with having built many of the famous edifices at Angkor. His name was Neak Sedak Komlong, so it is said. He is also alleged to have invented the Khmer alphabet, patterning it on Sanskrit, and to have reformed the calendar.

It was a day of hard work for us and my knees became wobbly with all the climbing. We explored the Baphuon, a multiple-staged pyramidal temple which originally had a pinnacle built of wood and gilded or sheathed in copper, as described by Chou Ta-kuan. Between the Baphuon and the king's palace, we climbed a particularly steep wall; this was supposed to have been the secret passage (another one!) to the king's concubines. The huge swimming pool where the king watched his ladies bathe was most impressive. The retaining walls, even below the water line, are covered with sculptures. We were amused by an older, smaller pyramidal temple, farther north in the center of the palace quarter. This was Phimeanakas, the "aerial palace," where the king was expected to commune every day with the *naga* queen to ensure the prosperity of the kingdom. Chou Ta-kuan called it the "Tower of Gold," though the gold has long since disappeared. One of the staircases—the one used by the king—has very comfortable steps.

The French have cleared the ruins fairly well but sometimes they had to leave things as they were, since trees had grown into the stone walls and could not be extricated without destroying the monuments. One particular tree, called a silk-cotton tree, has especially strong roots which it sinks deep into the stone crevices; sometimes one can hardly see where the tree ends and the temple begins. All this produces an atmosphere of desolation even in broad daylight and points up the futility of man's most grandiose undertakings.

We ended an exhausting day at the foot of the little hill outside Angkor Thom called Phnom Bakheng, where an elephant carried us to the top. It was our first elephant ride and we enjoyed it. The howdah in which one sits sways rhythmically and the motion makes some people sick. Little elephant boys perched precariously on the beasts' heads and tickled them behind the ears. On top of the hill was a ruined temple erected by Yasovarman I, who built Yasodharapura, the first city at Angkor. There was a magnificent view from this temple over endless jungle-covered land, with only Angkor Wat in the distance peaking above the trees. The five towers when they were covered with gold leaf must have been a stunning sight.

Bas-relief sculpture on Bayon

Temple on Phnom Bakheng

Temple carvings at Banteai Srei

Sculptured niches at Banteai Srei

We enjoyed the view from this hilltop so much that we went back the next morning when it was still dark and climbed Phnom Bakheng once more to arrive just as the sun rose. Many monkeys chattered in the forest and we had a wonderful feeling of being all alone in a wild and untamed world. On one of the tourist folders the area around Angkor is marked as "forests full of game," and in a half circle these are listed from left to right as gaurs, wild bulls, wild buffaloes, bears, elephants, tigers, and panthers. Though we looked and looked, we could not discover what might be a gaur or a bear—nothing but monkeys.

We had been urged not to miss seeing Banteai Srei, the Citadel of the Women. It was about an hour's ride from Angkor so we hired a car which took us there over a dreadful, rutted road. We drove through several villages populated by scantily clad natives looking dull and sickly. One woman was nursing a newborn baby on one side and an 11-month-old child on the other.

Banteai Srei was the most attractive temple of all those we had seen. It was reconstructed according to the methods evolved by the Dutch at Borobudur and looks almost undamaged. Built of pink sandstone and laterite, it is a perfect little gem of a temple, covered with the most exquisite carvings, and has a silent forest for its setting. One should always see it last of all, as a special treat.

In the afternoon, we went once more to Angkor Wat and sat for a long time on the causeway, dangling our feet above the moat as we watched the modern Khmers bathing and the herons flying overhead.

7
Muang Thai

Next morning we arose in the dark and caught the early morning bus from Siemreap to Aranya (Aranyaprathet) on the Siamese-Cambodian border. The bus was speedy and comfortable, the morning air pleasantly cool. Gradually, darkness lifted and we made a sudden turn to bring us face to face with the first pink glow on the horizon. A thin sliver of moon and the morning star shone in the deep blue sky. The flat country was half-hidden in a delicate white mist floating mysteriously about. Flocks of white heron and beautiful blue birds unknown to us rose up from the rice fields and flew across the road. Far off we could see the faint outline of mountains. Once we drove through a sleeping village where no light showed in any of the houses and not even the roosters stirred. Suddenly the bus shifted to the left side of the road, as in England, and signs appeared with the quaint Siamese script instead of the now familiar French signs. Otherwise there was no change in the character of the country.

We reached Aranya, then the terminal of the railroad to Bangkok, at ten o'clock. It was hot and dusty. The train was not clean but we managed to make ourselves comfortable and started undoing the luncheon our hotel had packed for us in newspaper, wrapping paper being apparently an unknown luxury in Indo-China. The ride to Bangkok was at first through arid country with only occasional irrigated patches where rice grew. Part of the way a narrow canal paralleled the railroad tracks. In southern and central Siam, the canals are the main highways of commerce and travel. Most of the country is covered by water to a depth of several inches during the rainy season, for this is the alluvial delta of the great Menam River. Everyone in this part of the country lives on a canal or river, which may be why the Siamese are such exceedingly clean people. As we neared the Menam Plain, the country became lush and green—similar to the land we had traversed on our way from Saigon to Angkor.

Friends who had been this way before had advised us to stay at the Europe Hotel in Bangkok, and not at a Siamese hotel. We had written for reservations but found upon arrival that we had been too

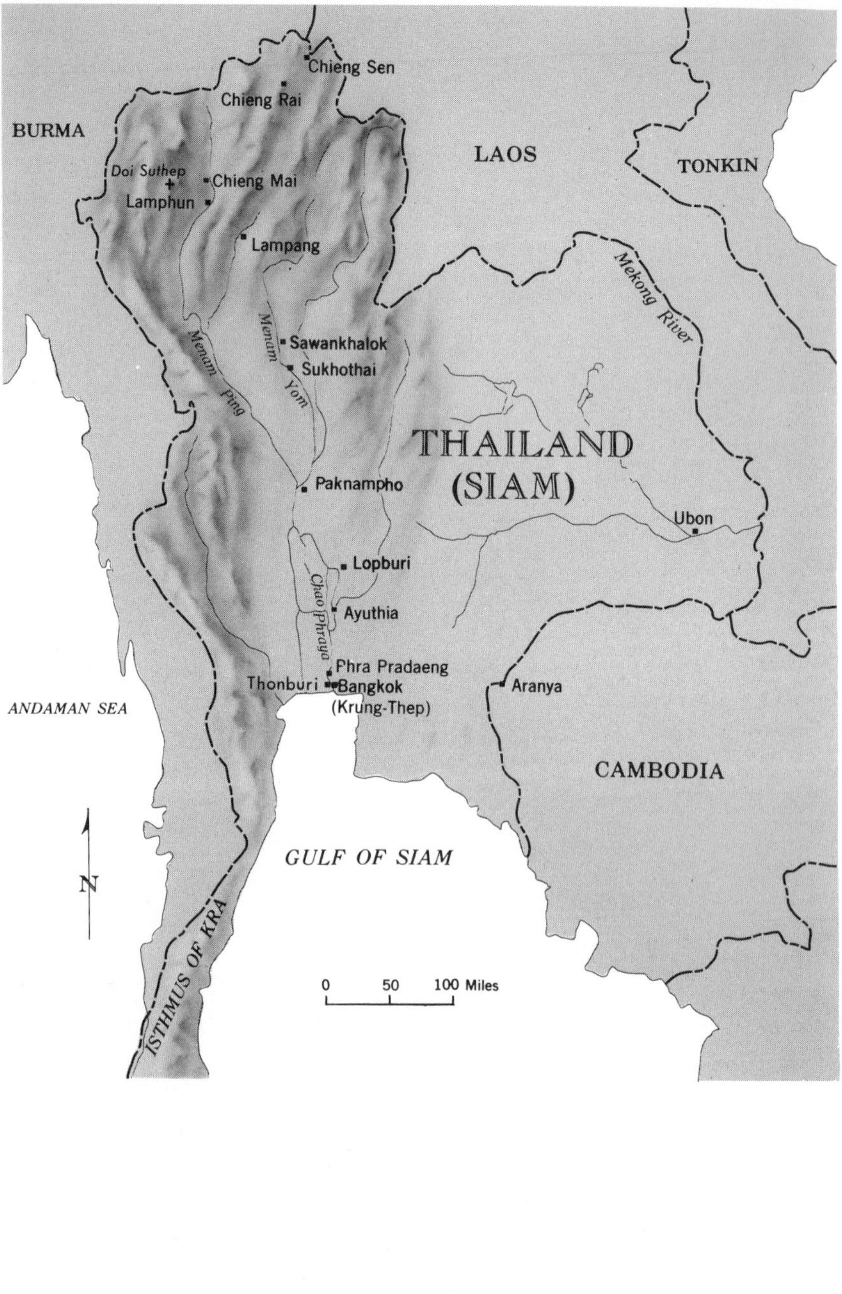

Chieng Sen
Chieng Rai
BURMA
LAOS
TONKIN
Doi Suthep
Chieng Mai
Lamphun
Lampang
Mekong River
Menam Yom
Sawankhalok
Sukhothai
Menam Ping
THAILAND
(SIAM)
Paknampho
Ubon
Lopburi
Chao Phraya
Ayuthia
Phra Pradaeng
Thonburi
Bangkok
(Krung-Thep)
Aranya
ANDAMAN SEA
CAMBODIA
N
GULF OF SIAM
ISTHMUS OF KRA
0 50 100 Miles

late and all rooms were taken. The agent of the Europe Hotel who met us at the station insisted that we go there, promising they would move heaven and earth to find suitable accommodations for us elsewhere. The proprietors of this little hotel welcomed us with lugubrious faces, acting as if a major catastrophe had occurred in our lives when they could not give us a room. Diffidently, they suggested that we engage a room at the Rajdhani Hotel and, if the food there was too bad, come and take our meals with them. As it turned out the Rajdhani was one of the nicest places we ever stayed and treated us with such courtesy and personal concern in our welfare that then and there we fell in love with the Siamese. It was a big, well-run hotel, operated by the Royal State Railways of Siam and built above the station. For just eleven ticals* they gave us a huge, high-ceilinged room with private bath—of the dimensions of a ballroom—plus five delicious meals,† while at the Europe the cheapest cubbyhole of a room without bath was fourteen ticals. This was a good example of the curious sense of superiority that afflicted Europeans in the Orient. The Europe was owned by Danes, the Rajdhani run by Siamese; hence, it was taken for granted that the former must be better than the latter, and apparently nobody except us took the trouble to investigate the truth of the matter.

We were surprised at the many modern buildings and wide boulevards in Bangkok. It has as many European-looking parts as Shanghai or Saigon, but the tall spires of its hundreds of *wats* give it a distinctly Siamese appearance. Most native life still takes place on the Menam—also called the Chao Phraya River—which winds through the city in a wide curve, and on numerous *klongs* (canals). Thirty years ago there were no roads (only mud paths) and virtually all traffic was by water. Bangkok was then in truth an oriental Venice. But now we could reach many points of interest by pedicab or on foot from our centrally located hotel.

We got up early next morning for a trip through the *klongs*. The Bureau of Tourist Information's handy booklet, *This Week in Bangkok*, contained a list of Siamese phrases. With this in hand, we were able to hire a motor boat (for one tical per hour) to take us around. We kept the boat for several hours and succeeded quite well in directing it to go where we wanted. Traveling is no fun unless you plunge right into the life of the country and experiment with the language. Smiles, gestures, and drawing pictures will always work,

---

*One *tical* contains 100 *satang* and was worth about 45 cents American then. The *tical* is also called a *baht*.

†Obviously English guests had been here and exerted their usual influence on eating habits. The Rajdhani served: morning tea in bed, breakfast, tiffin (lunch to us), afternoon tea, and dinner.

and everyone has a wonderful time helping the poor, ignorant foreigner who doesn't know how to pronounce their words. It makes for warm international relations since all people enjoy helping the stranger in their midst who desires to learn their language and customs.

The trip through the *klongs* was fascinating. There was at first a faint mist over everything, the sky showing only a pinkish hue. For a few moments we rode along silent and deserted canals and, turning a corner, found ourselves in a narrow canal with overhanging trees, so that we seemed to be in the midst of a jungle rather than around the corner from a major waterway in a city of a million inhabitants. Suddenly people began to stir and open the shutters of their houses—all fronting on the water. Everyone took his morning bath in the *klong* or river—little boys naked except for a silver shield hung in the area which sculptors usually cover with a fig leaf. One man washed his false teeth in the canal; another brushed his teeth and then scrubbed his toes with the same toothbrush. Everyone bathed modestly, using the *panung* as a general cover-all. This way, both person and clothes get clean in one simultaneous action and with little effort.

Dozens of yellow-robed bonzes came sailing along in small boats, narrow at both ends, often rowed by a faithful servant, the inevitable begging bowl conspicuously displayed. Everywhere we saw women cooking morning rice on their front porches and pious householders doling it out to the hungry bonzes. The newspaper boy rode by in a tiny canoe; the butcher passed in a large boat, a huge slab of carabao meat across the bow. Schoolboys in their olive green uniforms were on their way to school in launches; people went marketing in the family sampan and country folk came to market bringing fruits and vegetables. Occasionally we saw a police launch but it never had much to do, for these aquatic people were law-abiding and had better road manners than we Americans do.

We passed a market where masses of sampans, piled high with attractively arranged produce, were anchored. All along the *klongs* the banks were lined with small stores that had no front wall, giving them the appearance of stage settings. We saw many American canned goods but not nearly as many of them as of Japanese goods. George kept climbing all over our boat to get pictures, nearly upsetting it a number of times. The Siamese found this amusing and willingly posed for him. They have pleasant faces, intelligent eyes, olive skin, straight black hair; they are of medium height and look sturdy, though their wrists and ankles are delicate. Perhaps they are not a beautiful race but we thought them attractive and liked them from the start. They have in their bearing something of the gentlemanly manner of the Malay, combined with the alertness of the Chinese.

The Siamese would look more handsome if they changed their national costume. The *panung*, which resembles voluminous bloomers, looks good only on slender, young, aristocratic gentlemen. Older women look awful in it; moreover, they wear their hair short, exactly like the men, which adds nothing to their appearance. The story goes that this hairdo started a long time ago when Siam fought one of her interminable wars with the Burmese and, not having as many soldiers as the enemy, hit upon the idea of enlisting women to create the impression of a larger army. Ever since, the women have worn their hair that way. However, Hollywood's influence has been turning the young girls from the ancient and venerable ways, and many of them now look just like us—hairdo, grooming, slimness, and all. Those who still wear the *panung* hold it around the waist with a pretty silver-link belt.

We ended our tour with a visit to Wat Arun, also known as Wat Chang and referred to as the Porcelain Temple, which stands on the right bank of the river. From a distance it glitters and looks as if it were covered with jewel-encrusted mosaic. Unfortunately, as one approaches, the jewels turn out to be bits of glass and pottery glued to the masonry in shoddy fashion. One ought never to look closely at Bangkok *wats*. But from a distance they are magnificent. Most of them are conical in shape, though the base may be round, square, or octagonal. They rise tier upon tier in symmetrical gradation into a narrow spire at the top, the delicate tracery and the glitter of porcelain and pieces of glass giving them somewhat the aspect of a wedding cake.

Wat Arun has several galleries supported by our old friends, the *garudas*, and the god Indra on his three-headed elephant, Airavata, looks down from all four corners. It is surmounted by an elegant *prang* (a thickset, ornament column tapering to an almost rounded top) that can be seen far and wide. We climbed up as high as it is possible to go and had a marvelous view of the city which, from on high, looks like a green garden, criss-crossed by silvery *klongs* and sparkling with the *prangs* and *chedis** of hundreds of *wats* glittering in the sun. However, all this pretty greenery costs Siam a fortune because most of it is temple property.† One-fifth of the city's real estate is in the hands of the bonzes. Altogether there are a quarter million bonzes out of a total population of fourteen million—too

---

*A *chedi* is a graduated cone or pyramid ending in a thin spire. A *phra chedi* is a *chedi* that contains a sacred relic.

†*Wats* and monasteries are usually inseparable, consisting of several buildings within a square enclosure: a *bôt* (the temple proper), a monastery library, and a block of cells for the bonzes.

many for a tropical, agricultural country to support. Though they live frugally, it costs one tical a day to support a bonze. This is equivalent to the daily wage of an ordinary working man. In return, the bonzes do a little teaching (of a rather limited kind) in the temples, and that is all. They are paid extra for their services at religious ceremonies.

I confess I cannot see any justification for Buddhist monasteries and bonzes. It is true that a devout Buddhist requires their assistance in ceremonies throughout his life; such as birth, marriage, illness, planting and harvesting of crops, and death. But the purpose of the bonzes is not to serve the religious needs of the community—at least not primarily—but rather to achieve personal salvation through complete withdrawal from life. It seems strange that work is not regarded as gaining merit—only meditation and austere living. The Buddhist concept of monkhood is based on complete withdrawal from all worldly concerns, be they manual work or intellectual activity. It is true that the bonzes do not pamper themselves. Formerly they wore only tattered garments thrown away by others, but this has become something of a polite fiction, since good Buddhists leave decent habits for them to "find." They may eat only two meals a day; one at daybreak, the other at noon. Thereafter they may take a little tea but nothing solid. They do have a hungry look when you see them begging for their morning rice and most of them are exceedingly thin. When bonzes walk in the streets they must look straight ahead and curb all idle curiosity, in particular any tendency they might have to look at pretty girls, for to "have a mind on a woman" is a dreadful sin for which they must punish themselves. A proper punishment would be a pilgrimage into the jungle to meditate. On our way to Ayuthia the next morning, we saw many small white tents and were told that they were the tents of bonzes traveling north to the jungle, so it would seem that not all of them manage to discipline their eyes and minds. Before modernity came to Siam in the nineteenth century, any breaking of the vow of chastity brought death to bonze and maid. I am glad to report that by 1822, when John Crawfurd visited Bangkok, this unduly severe punishment was generally commuted to—of all things—a life term of cutting grass for the royal elephants!*

After lunch we went down to the Menam to hire a launch for the following day. We planned to go by rail to Ayuthia, and have the launch meet us there and take us downriver back to Bangkok. If you use normal tourist facilities, this costs seventy-five ticals for two persons. Armed with our Siamese list of phrases and pencil and paper,

---

*John Crawfurd, *Journal of an Embassy from the Governor-General of India to the Courts of Siam and Cochin China*, Vol. II, p. 134.

Bangkok klong

Our launch for the Ayuthia-Bangkok trip

Wat Arun

we felt we could manage on our own. It was fun looking over the various launches and picking one whose boatman looked pleasant and reliable. Then trying to get our wishes known to him and getting him to promise that he would go up the river during the night and meet us at the railroad station for the trip back. We had lots of help from people who crowded around to see the show, and everything went splendidly. By being a little adventurous, we did the trip for eleven ticals plus four ticals which we squandered as tips. The management at the Rajdhani Hotel were somewhat perturbed at our independent ways and didn't want us to come to harm as we wandered around Siam all by ourselves without knowing a word of the language. They begged us to let one of the clerks come along entirely without cost to us, so that they would not have to worry about us. They were so adamant and sincere that we had to force the clerk to accept our tip afterwards. He assured us he had enjoyed the trip as much as we and had come along as a friend. We could have managed easily without him but he was a nice person and told us many interesting things about Siam. He took his job as guardian and protector seriously and did not let us miss a single noteworthy monument at Ayuthia. Of the three of us, he was unquestionably the best dressed and most dignified.

The rest of the day we spent looking at more *wats*. There are more than three hundred in Bangkok and, after a while, they look much the same. All of them look more beautiful in photographs than in reality but occasionally, as at Wat Jetubon, commonly known as Wat Po, one comes upon a veritable jewel of a temple. This temple contained a 160-foot-long golden statue of Buddha reclining on his side, signifying his entry into Nirvana—a state of nonexistence to which all Buddhists ultimately aspire. The most notable feature about the statue was the soles of his feet on which was inlaid in mother-of-pearl the "Wheel of the Law," the basic tenets of the Buddhist religion.

That evening we went to dinner with some people who had been advised of our presence by friends in Manila. We enjoyed meeting them enormously because they lived exactly as *pukka sahibs* and *memsahibs* should—in a palace of a house surrounded by innumerable servants dressed in brocade *panungs* and immaculate white drill jackets with high collars like the white uniforms of American naval officers. At dinner one of them was at our elbow practically all the time. We ate with silken sarongs around our legs to protect us against the mosquitoes for, in all this luxury, there were no window screens and Bangkok mosquitoes are large and potent. I had read about this use of sarongs but this was the first time I saw it done. The sarong, sewed at the bottom to form a sack, is pulled on over the legs. Then all exposed areas are smeared with antimosquito lotion.

Wat Po

After dinner we strolled through their lovely garden illuminated with Chinese lanterns. "You'd better not go down there," warned our host, "that's where the cobras are." This was a shock but I became thoroughly blasé about cobras and other snakes. They are there but they mind their own business. I never saw one, except at the snake farm—which I visited a few days later.

As we had planned, the following morning we took the train to Ayuthia where we were met at the station by our boatman's boy. A little farther on, the boatman himself, scrubbed clean and looking relieved to see us, greeted us solemnly. He must have worried if we really would come and whether he had understood what we had told him. A short walk brought us to the river where we found the boatman's cheerful wife awaiting us beside the launch, which was so clean that we were sure these people must have sailed upriver and then turned to—working all night to shine it in our honor. How they could keep their eyes open during that long day was a mystery.

Ayuthia (Ayudhya), a settlement in the ancient kingdom of Dvaravati, became the capital of Siam in 1350 under Rama Tibodi. In 1767, it was sacked and burned by the Burmese. Ayuthia is now a thriving little Venice but of no significance to the country at large except as a tourist attraction. The present town is a short distance from the site of the old town. One goes to the old town by pedicab—a small carriage with an awning, pulled by a bicycle. It is comfortable and much less bothersome to one's conscience than a ricksha. Sturdy young boys do the cycling. Of the old capital city, nothing is left but crumbling ruins of *chedis* and *prangs* and a huge bronze Buddha sitting in a tumbledown temple with his unprotected head exposed to sun and rain.

After seeing these ruins, we continued our enjoyable meandering along the river and the canals in our launch—observing the people at the markets and their domestic activities. Everybody lived either in a houseboat moored to the river bank, or in a sampan. Most of the stores were houseboats with the family living in the back and the merchandise displayed on the front porch—a comfortable and cool way of life. The country people wore amusing hats, which resembled large baskets turned upside down, with a bamboo frame to hold them above the head; this gives maximum shade with minimum friction between hat and forehead. Many of the houseboats and sampans had flowers in lovely Chinese jars, and their hardwood floors were clean and highly polished. Occasionally a mother and her round-eyed child would peek at us from behind a bamboo curtain. Boys of all shapes and ages were bathing in the river and old gentlemen were taking their siestas on the front porches.

Pedicab at Ayuthia

Buddha at Ayuthia

Floating market at Ayuthia

We inspected the Elephant Kraal where until recently they used to herd the wild elephants caught for the king while he looked on from his ringside seat. They were driven through a narrow opening onto a field enclosed by an elephant-proof fence of enormous stakes driven about two feet into the ground. We were told that, once a single wild elephant has been driven into the kraal, the entire herd, trumpeting noisily, will follow him. The best elephants are then chosen and tied up, the rest driven back into the forest. Sometimes it takes two weeks to tame a wild elephant. He is herded into a narrow bamboo frame in which he cannot turn around. On either side stands a tame elephant to keep the wild beast company while a native trainer speaks soft words and makes him docile by giving him little to eat. In the center of the kraal is a small temple. We were assured that its presence had a calming effect on the captive animals, inspiring in them awe of the Buddha and thus making them more easily amenable to discipline. We asked the guide about white elephants. These are rare and, as everyone knows, exceedingly sacred and of great importance to the welfare of the country. They are albinos and not really white but merely of a lighter brown color than normal elephants. We were surprised when the guide claimed that it was not so much their color that indicated sacredness as the fact that they had thirteen toes instead of eighteen. I suspect we were being spoofed!

This veneration for the rather unattractive oddities of nature seemed strange to us, but we couldn't find anyone to give us a good explanation. It may be an outgrowth of an ancient Siamese notion that all albinos (being rare) are the kings of their respective species. Then, too, elephants seem to hold an important place in Buddhism and Brahmanism. One of Buddha's incarnations is believed to have been as an elephant. Ganesha, the guardian god of travelers, has an elephant head. Even so, I think it is odd that the king of so civilized a country as Siam should include among his many titles "Lord of the White Elephant."

Possibly the Siamese took the notion from the Khmers, as they did so much else: their script, their costume, their temple architecture, their concept of the king as a god, and others. In this turbulent part of the world, wars have been the greatest disseminators of culture. The Siamese, who once were vassals of Angkor, fought many wars with the Khmers and in the end, to stop further trouble along the eastern border, transported large numbers of Khmer prisoners to Siam and put them to work there. In the process, they incorporated a large amount of Khmer culture into their own.

When I saw the complete destruction of Ayuthia, once one of Asia's richest cities, I felt satisfied that the Siamese had got their

Elephant Kraal

Taming a wild elephant

"just deserts" for their vandalism in Angkor. We think of Europe as given to endless fratricidal wars, but for truly destructive warfare and a professional job of sacking and looting, Europe can't hold a candle to the people of the Indo-Chinese or, as the French call it, the Trans-Ganges Peninsula. At one time or another, almost every country was vassal or suzerain to every other, and few cities escaped sacking. Conquest moved from east to west, as a rule. The Chinese conquered Annam, but were finally driven out; the Annamites conquered Champa (Cochin China) to the south and Cambodia to the west, but lost out in Cambodia to the Siamese. The Siamese, in turn, often lost in battle to the Burmese, who were great pillagers of Siamese towns. The Burmese were conquered by the British. At the time we were there, of all these warring countries only Siam had preserved its independence.* Though the British and the French forced her to relinquish portions of land to the east and south over which she had claimed suzerainty, their pacification of her eastern and western neighbors gave Siam's kings their first chance to unify the country and build a modern state.

Our boatman's little boy went everywhere with us, his eyes bright and eager. He was a charming youngster, obviously the pride and joy of his elderly father and youthful mother. Sometimes he was allowed to take the wheel of the launch and then his happiness knew no bounds. At the end of the trip, George gave him a 25-satang piece whereupon he jumped into the air, letting out a yell of sheer delight. The whole family was nice: the father a dignified patriarch; the pretty young wife suitably quiet, yet obviously pleased to be on this outing; the little boy extraordinarily well behaved, but bubbling with eager interest and joy. When we started on our trip downriver, we found that they had spread hardwood boards across our half of the launch so that we could lie down. Our friend from the Rajdhani had brought along pillows on which he made us rest. I felt like Cleopatra gliding down the broad, glimmering river.

In addition to hundreds of small sampans, there were numerous teak floats on the river, as well as long trains of boats pulled by launches. One train had 45½ houseboats—the "half" being a tiny sampan at the end. On the teak floats we noticed small bamboo huts in which the guards slept. Theft is rare, perhaps because of the great weight of teak logs.

---

*The people of this country call themselves *Thai* (free), and they call the land in which they live *Muang Thai* (land of the free). The facts of history point out the appropriateness of the word *free* among the Thai, for theirs is the only country in Southeast Asia that was never under European colonial control.

In the teak forests, the trees are first ringed with an axe and none may be felled unless it has been marked by a government forest ranger, because the Siamese government tries to protect its forests against excessive cutting. The ringed tree is left for a year or two so that the sap may run out; then it is felled and pulled to the nearest creek by elephants. During the rainy season the water level of the creek rises and the log begins to move slowly downstream. Eventually it reaches one of the upper tributaries of the Menam where the teak companies maintain rafting stations. The trees have been marked with company chops so that they can be sorted out and tied into rafts, which float down to Paknampho, where the tributaries meet. Here there is a control station that collects royalty for the crown. The rafts then float majestically down the Menam to the company mills in Bangkok where the logs are cut into square puncheons for export. From the time a teak tree is ringed to the moment it reaches the saw mill, a period of approximately five years elapses, which is just long enough to season the log properly.

Most of the teak companies are British, though some are Danish and Chinese. The companies send their young white employees into the jungle where they live a rugged life supervising the cutting and transport of the trees. Some four thousand elephants are at work pulling teak logs; each elephant is worth from two thousand to three thousand American dollars. The greatest hazard to these huge beasts are snakes; an elephant will die within an hour after being bitten by a cobra.

A few miles below Ayuthia we stopped to see the royal summer palace at Bang Pa-In. During the days when Ayuthia was still the capital, the Siamese kings used this small island in the river as a cool summer resort. It was rediscovered by King Chulalongkorn, who rebuilt part of its old Thai buildings and added a touch of European architecture.

The palace grounds were surrounded by an artificial lake or moat about 130 feet wide from which a canal led to the Menam. A curved bridge, built across the moat, had statues of the seven muses and of a Swiss boy who had just shot a bird. Since we had forgotten to obtain a special permit to enter the palace, we were allowed only to peek through the windows. What we saw was a most uninteresting European interior in late-Victorian style. We let our boatman's boy peek, too. Watching that child so elated with all the marvels he saw that day gave a fillip to our own enjoyment. We took him around the palace grounds looking at a variety of buildings from a medieval water tower to a charming pavilion built in the middle of the artificial lake.

In one corner of the palace grounds was a monument which King Chulalongkorn had built in memory of his Queen who had drowned in the river on her way to Bang Pa-In in full view of numerous bystanders who could do nothing but throw coconut shells to her.* In the King's own English, the inscription read:

> To the Beloved Memory of Her Late and Lamented Majesty Sunandakumaviratn, Queen Consort, who wont to spend her most pleasant, and happiest hours in this garden amidst those loving ones and dearest to her. This Memorial is Erected by Chulalongkorn Rex Her Bereaved Husband whose suffering from so cruel an endurance through those trying hours made death seemed so Near and Yet Preverable. 1881.

We were told that the canal had been dug by prisoners, which spoiled its attraction for us. We had seen these unfortunates wearing chains around their ankles (as they also do in Indo-China and Yunnan) which must chafe them cruelly. Sometimes they pulled carts with a yoke across their shoulders like carabao. This business of chaining prisoners struck us as inexcusably barbaric but we were told they would otherwise all run away. In fairness to the French, I should add that the prisoners in Indo-China have the lightest chains.

After Bang Pa-In we proceeded steadily downstream, with only one bit of excitement to break our languorous journey—a race with another launch which we won hands down. We passed the ruins of an old Portuguese settlement and were told that, in that neighborhood, there were still many Catholic villages. Often one sees in the Orient some surprising remnant of Portugal's old far-flung trading posts. Portugal was the first European country to conclude a treaty with Siam. This was in 1516 and the treaty permitted the Portuguese to reside and trade in certain parts of Siam. Five years earlier d'Albuquerque, who had just captured Malacca, sent an envoy to Ayuthia and he was courteously received by the King of Siam. He

---

*H. G. Quaritch Wales, *Siamese State Ceremonies: Their History and Function*, p. 33, states so godlike were all royal persons believed to be that not even to save their lives might they be touched. Wales tells as an example that royal barges carried bundles of coconut shells which were to be thrown to the king or any royal personages who might fall overboard. Siamese Palace Law laid down specific rules as to what could be done in such cases: boatmen must swim away from the foundering boat; they may stretch out a signal-spear and throw coconut shells at drowning royalty; they may even let the drowning personage lay hold of one end of the spear while the boatman holds the other, but under no circumstances may he remain near the boat or touch the drowning person, on pain of instant execution. Nor may bystanders do this; in fact, should they try to aid the victim, their whole families would be executed. The rules still stand, but I suppose they would not be obeyed today; still, it would take courage to be a Good Samaritan.

was the first white man known to have set foot in the "Land of the White Elephant." The Portuguese did not try to exert political control but were content to trade. Many entered the Siamese army as mercenaries and contributed substantially to the ultimate victory of Siam over its numerous enemies.

The Rajdhani had provided such marvelous food and in such quantities that passengers and crew of our launch all had a big feast. We were amused at the rapid and decorous manner in which the boatman and his family did away with their half of our huge hamper. They seldom spoke to each other but were evidently a harmonious and contented little family. Whether our presence squelched them or they were always so tongue-tied was a puzzle we couldn't figure out. We dozed and wrote letters and filled our minds with pictures of Siamese life. The sun was hot but there was a pleasant breeze and always something to see on the river. Toward evening the ritual of the bath again took place and the water was full of slender, brown bodies, always modestly hidden by a *panung*. We passed the Siamese Navy which was unique in those days in that it did not have electricity when it was anchored since it could apparently generate electrical power only when it had steam up. "Greatest pile of junk I ever saw," was George's impolite comment.

Bangkok is beautiful when the sun sets and the sky turns pink and the first stars come out. It was dark when we finally got home and we sadly said goodbye to our skipper and his family. We spent that evening telephoning around frantically to try to get a plane reservation for George. For a while it looked as if he were going to be AWOL—his plane had run into trouble somewhere over the Indian Ocean and every other plane was full up with Christmas mail. Finally he got a place on a plane leaving the next morning for Hanoi and Hong Kong. We had originally planned to be gone only twelve days, but I was so enamored of Siam that I hated to leave. "Why don't you stay another two weeks or so," said George, handing over the rest of his money. It took little urging to make me fall in with this suggestion. As it turned out, I stayed two months.

George had luck in scheduling a night in Hanoi so he could do sightseeing there and still catch the *Conte Biancamano* at Hong Kong for the homeward voyage to Manila. As soon as he got to his cabin, he asked the Italian steward what he thought of Mussolini. The steward closed the door, looked over his shoulder to make sure no one else was present, and moved his hand across his throat. In the dining room they had two pictures on the wall; one of Mussolini, at the right, the other of the king. George started seditious thoughts by asking whether the king's picture should not be to the right of Mussolini's since he was, after all, the number one man.

They were still debating the question when he left the ship at Manila. George still uses this gambit when he visits a high-ranking official and observes pictures of superiors on the wall. He asks whether the senior ranking official should be on the right-hand side as the viewer faces the pictures or as the pictures face the viewer. Occasionally this has resulted in interchanging the pictures.

Before he departed, the Rajdhani management assured George earnestly that he need not worry about me, for they would take good care of me and see to it that I returned safely to Manila. The first thing they did was to locate a nice pedicab boy who had once worked for an American lady and spoke good English. We sort of adopted each other and did a lot of sightseeing together. After George left, the boy and I set forth to see the snake farm of the Pasteur Institute.

The snakes are milked of their venom one day each week and there is always a crowd to watch this spectacle. There are three cement-walled enclosures marked: King Cobra, Cobra, and Banded Krait—every snake a mean killer. Around the rim of each enclosure runs a narrow canal. The snakes sleep in small white hemispherical cement houses (like igloos) and are usually all inside. An attendant steps into the enclosure, lifts up each igloo and pushes the snakes unceremoniously into the canal with a stick. They don't like this and try to get on dry land as quickly as possible but he kicks them back with his foot or with a stick, which is his only weapon. Sometimes they raise their heads and hiss at him but sad experience must have broken their spirit because, despite this disrespectful treatment, they never bite him. In the beginning, the Institute used to pay a consolation fee if an attendant was bitten, but now they fine him since he is supposed to be able to keep the snakes disciplined.

After all the snakes have been rudely thrown out of their cozy igloos, a white-clad gentleman enters; the attendant then nonchalantly picks up a snake from a mass of twisting and squirming reptiles. This is quite a feat because one can hardly distinguish where each snake begins or ends. He holds it in both hands while the white-coated gentleman slides a sliver of glass into the snake's mouth. As it bites, a small amount of venom is deposited on the glass. The snake then gets a drink of milk for a treat and is thrown back into the canal where it lies, apparently stupefied. One can easily see that the snakes don't like this business at all, but there is nothing they can do. I shall never again be as afraid of snakes after seeing them in this humiliating procedure.

We had with us a number of letters of introduction, but had been too busy sightseeing to use them. After George departed I called

At Bang Pa-In

Extracting venom at Pasteur Institute

up Mr. Walter A. Zimmerman, who was in charge of the Bangkok YMCA, and for whom I had a note from our mutual friend, Anne Guthrie, of the Manila YWCA. He and his wife, Betty, immediately came over and took me to watch the children's Christmas party at the Polo Club. This was interesting because it gave me a glimpse of the life of the white community in Bangkok.

The children were all dressed like little princes and princesses. Some of them sat eating cake and ice cream at long tables, with neat Siamese nurses standing by to serve their little masters and mistresses. An extraordinarily handsome and stately attendant in an old gold silk *panung* and high-collared white drill jacket with gold buttons supervised the children who were riding on ponies. Another, equally handsome and dignified, operated a toy automobile which was almost as popular as the ponies. Every European language could be heard on the lawn where people sat at small tables in cosmopolitan groups. Most of the mothers were beautifully attired and had arrived in large cars driven by chauffeurs in colorful Siamese uniforms. Several cunning-looking young Siamese princes and princesses were there also. I noticed some interesting mixtures: a Viking-like Dane whose wife was blonde and blue-eyed but in every other respect quite Siamese; a portly German with a wife who spoke German without accent, was dressed like a typical German *hausfrau*, and moved and acted exactly like a German woman, yet her complexion, features, and hair were Siamese. Several princes were there with American, English, or Danish wives. It isn't easy for foreign wives to make their way in Siamese court circles and few of them looked contented.

From the polo grounds we went straight to the YMCA where a Christmas party of all the Protestant churches in Bangkok was taking place. This was an entirely different sort of affair. The guests were predominantly Siamese and Chinese, with a goodly contingent of bespectacled, grey-haired, missionary ladies in print frocks. The food was Siamese and spicy. The mission schoolchildren gave a nativity play and, being born actors like all Siamese, put on a splendid show. Stage fright is unknown to Siamese kids. They looked wonderful as Egyptian soldiers!

Early next morning I went with my pedicab boy for a stroll around the city. Much of it looks completely Chinese, for here, too, most of the hard work and the trading is done by Chinese. The Siamese are excellent farmers but do not care for commercial affairs. The educated ones want administrative positions so the jobs done elsewhere by the middle class are done here by the Chinese—for which they are not liked. One interesting sight was an entire street devoted to selling nothing but chickens. I saw them at all ages from the tiniest balls of yellow fluff to good-sized ones ready for the pot. The little ones are in big shallow woven baskets shaped like trays and I was told that eggs are hatched in such trays without any heat other than from the sun. The eggs are laid on chaff in the baskets, exposed to sunlight, and turned constantly. At night the chaff covers them and keeps them warm.

After breakfast, I visited the palace and the famous statue of the Emerald Buddha. I felt uncomfortable in stockings, but they are required for so solemn an occasion. This is a hardship in a city where it is so hot. Still, the Siamese are right in expecting foreigners to show respect for their royalty. A handsome palace guard with charming manners and a delightfully infectious chuckle took visitors around and, though his English was sketchy and he spoke haltingly, I enjoyed the visit because he was so enthusiastic and such a gentle, nice person. He proudly showed us the picture of the young king, Ananda, saying with a light in his eyes: "His Majesty is so kind to everyone." The Zimmermans, who knew the boy king and his mother, told me that he was a popular king. Ananda's father, Mahidol, went to a mission school, studied medicine abroad, and interned at the Presbyterian hospital in Chieng Mai. He must have been a fine person. His wife was a commoner and at first had a hard time getting her husband's relatives to accept her but everybody came to love her for her gentle nature. The Zimmermans told me that she was raising Ananda and his brother and sister sensibly. They were away at school in Switzerland when I was in Bangkok.*

The palace impressed me as much by its splendor as by its shoddiness. In this respect it resembled the Bangkok *wats*. At a distance everything looks glitteringly resplendent, but when one comes nearer, the cheap material and shoddy workmanship show up. However, the royal temple of Wat Phra Keo is impressive. Though it was begun by King Rama I in the same year that Bangkok was founded, it took so long to build that it wasn't until Bangkok's centenary in 1882 that King Chulalongkorn opened it formally. The temple was built primarily to house the fabulous Emerald Buddha, a lovely, priceless statue made of green jasper, which was discovered about five hundred years ago in the provincial town of Chieng Rai.

In the afternoon, the Zimmermans took me to another children's performance. This was given at the Wattena Wittya Academy, an excellent Presbyterian mission school. The children were charm-

---

*King Ananda was found dead on June 9, 1946 with a bullet wound in his forehead. His death was a mystery that has never been satisfactorily cleared up. The commission of enquiry could not decide between suicide, accident, or murder. He was succeeded by his younger brother, Bhumibol Adulyadej.

ing. They had written a play and staged it with near-professional skill. It was slightly reminiscent of Dickens' *A Christmas Carol* and turned upon the effect of the Christmas spirit on a nasty, stingy master who overworked his servants scandalously but finally had a change of heart and gave them time off for the holiday. The play had as a comic character (well done by a clever little actress) a typical Chinese peddler who offered his wares in funny singsong Chinesy Siamese. His talk and mannerisms threw the audience into paroxysms of laughter. Apparently Siamese playwrights always use a comic character who is Chinese. As one of the older students explained, the Chinese come to Siam as illiterate coolies, work like devils, never wash, never bother to learn Siamese or adopt the customs of the country, and leave after years of this undignified living, loaded down with wealth. This is an unfair picture but it is how most Siamese see it. They are a light-hearted people who see no point in working themselves to a frazzle. Theirs is a rich and underpopulated country.

The alluvial plain of the Menam is among the world's most fertile lands. The Siamese are good farmers who work hard for a few months to produce enough food for the family and who consider it only sensible to relax and have fun the rest of the year. They are personally clean and consider a life of all work and no play barbaric. Therefore it is not surprising that they dislike the Chinese and look down upon them. Chinese habits and manners seem uncivilized to the Siamese and they resent the Chinese hold on their country's economic life. Yet, they do not want to do the work performed by the Chinese. For one thing, the Siamese are physically not as strong as the Chinese and for this reason the latter have the rice trade firmly in their hands: by tradition, rice sacks are of a weight (200 pounds) that Siamese coolies do not desire to carry and must, therefore, be handled by Chinese. For another, the Siamese have the manners of gentlemen and also a traditional lack of money sense; so they are often exploited by Chinese merchants and moneylenders. I suspect that they ridicule the Chinese to offset an uncomfortable feeling of inadequacy in commercial matters.

There were several Eurasian children in the play—one looked exactly like her English mother from a distance, but not at all that way from close by. These children do not have an easy time. If they look more European than Siamese, they usually want to be European and then may find they are not welcome. Still, things are much easier here than in English colonies. The fact that Siam is an independent country helps raise the position of Eurasians in European eyes. Many of Bangkok's Eurasians are a Siamese-Danish mixture, a reflection both of the importance of the Danes in Bangkok and of their lack of prejudice against mixed marriages. The influential East Asiatic Company—teak and shipping—was a Danish concern and provided the only direct shipping line between Bangkok and Europe. The foreign colony in Bangkok is unusual in that the smaller nations of Europe are exceptionally well represented, a result of the wise policy initiated by King Mongkut when he decided to modernize Siam with the help of foreigners from such politically nonaggressive states as Denmark, Portugal, and Holland. The Danes are predominant in maritime matters and are credited with having created Siam's navy; the Belgians specialize in electric power stations, streetcar lines, and engineering work in general; the Portuguese have helped to modernize Siam's army; the Italians specialize in art and architecture.

There were only a few hundred Europeans and Americans in Siam, but they certainly succeeded in generating much Christmas spirit in Bangkok. Everybody entered wholeheartedly into the holiday atmosphere; Christmas packages were continually being interchanged between Siamese and their foreign friends, decorations went up everywhere, and there were innumerable parties. That evening I had dinner with the Zimmermans, from whose house one of the many bands of Christmas carolers started on their tour. Nobody knows who began the custom of caroling from house to house. The British claim that it was originally their idea and done to collect money for the lepers. The Americans maintain that they were the ones who started the custom, and they were serving cakes and refreshments with greater gusto than any other group in Bangkok. On Christmas Eve the main band of carolers started from the American legation and serenaded everybody in town—having sent chits ahead to announce themselves. Everyone kept open house and nobody got any sleep, for it would have been a grave breach of etiquette not to be ready for the carolers when they arrived. The tour ended at Wattena Wittya where early Christmas breakfast was served the weary "Carusos." Of course, almost all the singers were good Buddhists the rest of the year. Christmas had simply become a national holiday in Bangkok.

I left on the 25th by evening express for Chieng Mai in the northwest corner of Siam for I had found that the Christmas spirit interfered with my plans to interview people. I decided to utilize the holidays to see more of the country. Meeting the Zimmermans had been a bit of luck, for through them I became acquainted with several American missionary ladies who suggested that, if I wanted to see more of Siam, the best way was not to sleep at government rest houses (there were hardly any hotels outside Bangkok) but to visit around in missionary homes instead. This was the first I had heard of that delightful missionary institution—the paying house guest. Most missionaries live in isolated spots and enjoy meeting and entertaining visitors. For the weary traveler it is wonderful to find lodging in the home of fellow Europeans or Americans. But mission salaries are minuscule and could never be stretched to allow for such hospitality. The mission boards, therefore, set a daily rate which the guest puts into an envelope and places somewhere before leaving. Otherwise he acts like a guest and feels relieved to know that his presence will not cause hardship in the hospitable home. The rates are sufficient to cover the actual cost of entertaining but are exceedingly reasonable. The Wattena Wittya people sent a telegram ahead to Chieng Mai announcing my arrival, and from then on each hostess passed me on to the next one on my way.

I came to have the greatest admiration and affection for the missionaries. Even should we never succeed in converting a substantial number of Asians, the missionaries will have brought the Christian spirit of charity and brotherliness to countries where nothing like it has ever been known. Poverty and the general insecurity of life leave the average Asiatic little strength or desire to extend a helping hand to anyone not belonging to his own family circle. Since within the family—and families include far more than just kissing kin—extraordinary demands on loyalty and generosity are made, it is not surprising that its members have little interest in outsiders. All the money spent on missions and all the devoted work done by missionaries will have been well worthwhile if a little milk of human kindness has been spread about to leaven the harshness of life in this part of the world.

The Wattena Wittya ladies opened up a delightful prospect of being able to extend my vacation four times the length originally planned. By staying at missionary homes and traveling in native trucks, I would have enough money to travel clear up to the Burmese border and also to crisscross Siam and Indo-China from west to east. My missionary friends thought I should be able to manage on about three dollars (American) a day and, as it turned out, that is just what I spent, except that the trip into Yunnan by train upped the total a little. I cut it rather fine, arriving back home with only seventy-five cents in my pocket.

8
Siamese Laos

The Chieng Mai Express leaves twice weekly at 6:00 p.m. and gets to its northern terminal at 2:30 in the afternoon of the next day. I went second-class which is all right, except that you sleep in full view of the whole coach unless you can induce the porter to give you a curtain. According to regulations you are supposed to bring one along, but the Siamese don't care for curtains since they enjoy being sociable on trips, even when asleep. So it is not easy to find one for, after all, this is a Siamese country, make no mistake—no special privileges for lordly whites!

The trains are crowded. People take along their babies, water-jars, silver drinking cups, kitchen utensils, bedding, and food in huge hampers. The corridors are so full of bundles that each trip to the washroom is something of a mountaineering excursion. The coaches are laid out like our pullmans, but have straw seats instead of upholstery. At night the porter brings a thin mattress, a sheet, and a pillow. I bullied him into giving me an extra sheet for a curtain, which he brought along grumbling audibly about unreasonable foreign nuisances. The good Rajdhani had given me a blanket and a sheet so I had all the bedding one normally needs on a train. I fixed one sheet as a curtain and made up my bed with hospital corners, admired by all the women passengers who thought these to be fantastically elaborate preparations for anything so simple as going to sleep. The temperature began falling and I was glad to have the blanket. When the Rajdhani boy brought it, it had seemed like a joke because it had been hot in Bangkok that day.

I'd have been even more comfortable if I hadn't caught a cold sitting by the open window, so engrossed in the beautiful scenery that I didn't notice how cold it was getting once we passed Lopburi. After our experiences in Sumatra I ought to have known better, but I had forgotten what a difference altitude makes in a tropical country. Chieng Mai is 750 kilometers north of Bangkok and has an elevation of 800 feet. Its climate in December resembled that of a brisk fall day in Washington, D. C., and for anyone with my thin tropical blood this was enough to cause shivers. All through the northerly parts of Siam and Indo-China I lived in borrowed wool skirts and sweaters, shifting from one outfit to another whenever transportation back for the original became available. I am sure the climate in Chieng Mai must be affected by the cold winds that blow down from China during winter. The nights were always cold though in the daytime there was a warm sun.

The view from the train was lovely. The sky turned pink and darkness fell with the suddenness that always disconcerts when you first see it in the tropics. We passed quiet canals and lush rice fields. Tiny lights twinkling through the trees and the dark silhouettes of fishermen still busy at work reminded me of Chinese etchings. There was a half-moon in the sky and, as the train mounted steadily through jungle country, the air became fragrant with pine scent. Toward early morning I saw several elephants pulling teak logs, for this was teak country and Chieng Mai is the center of the teak trade. All the stations were neat and attractive. They had green hedges and, as we moved northward, I noticed that these were cut to resemble dragons which curved somewhat like the *nagas* of the Angkor balustrades. In temples, too, one saw these curved dragons instead of the snakes seen in the south. I suppose this was because we had now passed beyond the limits of Indian influence.

The Siamese call their country Muang Thai, Land of the Thai or Free, and belong to the Lao-Thai race which had its homeland in Yunnan and the Yangtze Valley. The Lao-Thai were neighbors of the Chinese, to whom they are related and with whom they fought numerous wars. They began migrating southward along the Mekong, Salween, and Menam rivers as far back as the first century of our era, establishing small kingdoms in northern Burma (where they are called Shan; the name *Siam* given to the Thai by foreigners may have derived from the Shan), and along the banks of the Mekong near Vientiane, French Laos. In the thirteenth century Kublai Khan defeated the Lao-Thai decisively and drove them out of their homeland in such large numbers that they soon overwhelmed the Mon-Khmer who had settled in present-day Siam some centuries earlier. The Lao-Thai who remained in northern Siam and did not intermingle with the Mon-Khmer retained the lighter skin and more Mongoloid appearance of the original migrants; they are today's Lao. The Thai populated southern Siam and absorbed much Khmer and Malay blood, together with the Indianized art, script, statecraft, and literature of the defeated Mon-Khmer. Both Lao and Thai are Hinayana Buddhists, but the Buddhism of the former lacks the Brahmanistic elements to be found in the south. While the Khmer *naga* appears in southern architecture and occasionally in the prows of royal barges, the Chinese dragon is much in evidence in "Siamese Laos," as northern Siam is sometimes called.

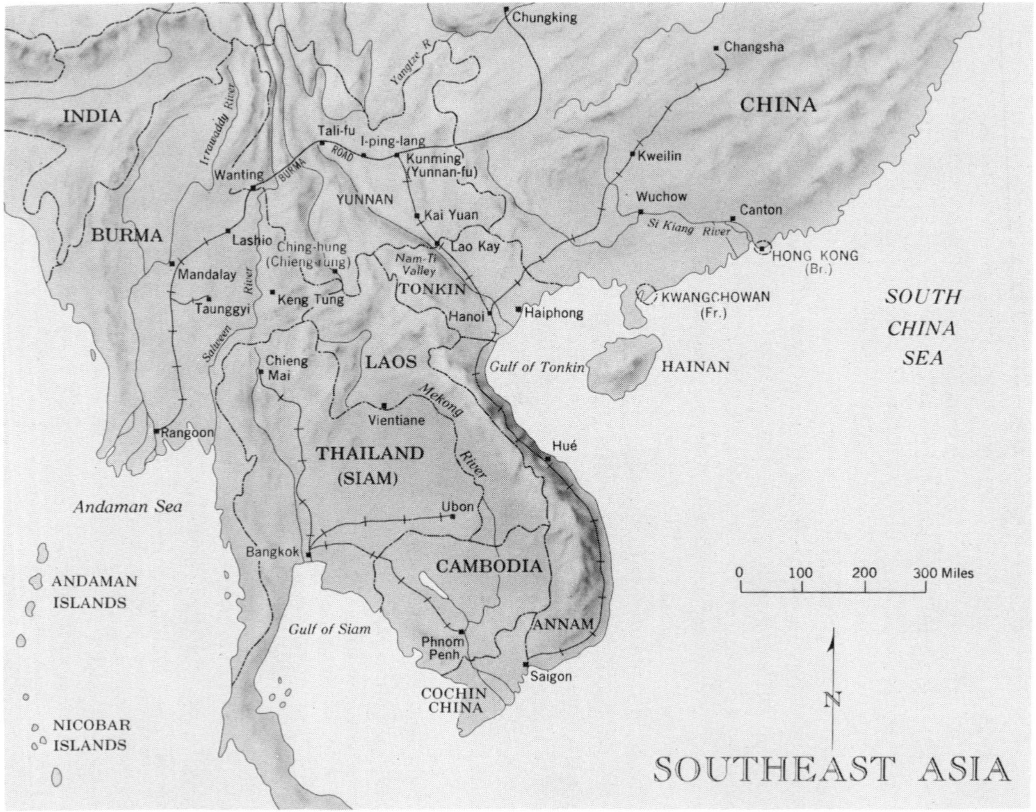

SOUTHEAST ASIA
INDIA
CHINA
BURMA
YUNNAN
TONKIN
LAOS
THAILAND
(SIAM)
CAMBODIA
ANNAM
COCHIN
CHINA
HAINAN
SOUTH
CHINA
SEA
Andaman Sea
Gulf of Tonkin
Gulf of Siam
ANDAMAN
ISLANDS
NICOBAR
ISLANDS
Chungking
Changsha
Kweilin
Wuchow
Canton
HONG KONG
(Br.)
KWANGCHOWAN
(Fr.)
Si Kiang River
Yangtze R.
Irrawaddy River
Salween River
Mekong River
Tali-fu
I-ping-lang
Kunming
(Yunnan-fu)
BURMA ROAD
Wanting
Kai Yuan
Lao Kay
Nam-Ti
Valley
Lashio
Mandalay
Taunggyi
Keng Tung
Chieng
Mai
Hanoi
Haiphong
Vientiane
Hué
Rangoon
Ubon
Bangkok
Phnom
Penh
Saigon
0
100
200
300 Miles
N

Basically the Lao and Thai are closely related. Cultural distinctions have been disappearing rapidly since Bangkok established direct administrative control over northern Siam which for centuries had enjoyed virtual independence under its chieftains. Though nominally vassals of the king, these chieftains had often conducted themselves as independent rulers, even going to war with their suzerain.

It is believed that the sinicized political organization that the Lao-Thai brought with them from Nanchao, their homeland, gave them the advantage over the Khmer, whose strong kingdoms held the early Lao-Thai migrants in vassalage. Eventually the Thai not only freed themselves from Khmer bondage but, in turn, subjected such Khmer kingdoms as Sukhothai-Sawankhalok and Angkor to vassalage; in the process adopting Khmer civilization into their own. While the Thai consolidated their positions in the south, the Lao established a strong kingdom in northwest Siam with Chieng Mai as its capital. Modern Siam may be said to have come into being when all sections were firmly united under King Chulalongkorn in 1892.

When we reached Chieng Mai I had a momentary feeling of uneasiness, but to my relief I saw a young, pretty woman and knew the telegram had arrived safely. She welcomed me kindly and said: "I am so glad you came today. You just have time to wash up before we leave for the Christmas party with the lepers." When she saw my expression, she hastened to assure me that the food had been cooked and would be served by non-lepers and that I need not worry about infection, anyway, since leprosy was difficult to acquire unless one had lived in close proximity with a leper for a long time. Mrs., or rather Dr., Mary Collier was the wife of a Presbyterian mission doctor, Douglas Collier, both being extremely active physicians.

The mission center at Chieng Mai dates back to 1867 when Dr. Daniel McGilvary obtained permission from King Mongkut to start a medical mission. It has an excellent hospital in addition to two rather famous schools—the Prince Royal College for boys, to which many Siamese princes have gone, and a girls' school. There has been a Presbyterian leper colony since 1890, when Dr. James McKean opened a leprosarium to take care of the many lepers who had been coming to the mission clinic. Dr. McKean succeeded in obtaining from the Chieng Mai *chao* (local chieftain) the grant of an island in the Menam Ping River, on which Chieng Mai is situated. Each Christmas the superintendent of the leper colony gave a tea on the lawn of his house, and all the important people, Siamese and foreign, attended. Thus, on the first day of my visit, I met everybody who amounted to anything in Chieng Mai. The Siamese were all delightfully courteous in an Old World fashion and looked dignified. Seeing Siamese and Europeans in close proximity, I particularly noticed the almost European bearing and appearance of upper-class Siamese. When you analyze it, you realize that it isn't anything in their features but it is their expressions and bearing that makes them appear more Western than any other people in Southeast Asia. They look frank and intelligent and their manners are exquisite. When we were in Japan we also noted the almost-European appearance of upper-class Japanese.

The foreigners were for the most part missionaries, though a sprinkling of British teak industry men added a touch of variety. Most of the missionaries were doctors or educators rather than evangelists. A good many were second-generation Siamese missionaries with a vast fund of knowledge about Siam, which I immediately proceeded to tap.

The Chieng Mai mission has been successful in gaining the confidence of Siam's leading families, and its influence on the men who led Siam from medieval barbarism into the modern world has been remarkable. On the train I had read a book which someone in Bangkok lent me, with the remark that I might be interested in it since its author had played no small part in the modernization of Siam. It was the story of Mrs. Anna H. Leonowens, the English governess engaged by King Mongkut to teach his numerous children.*

Born in Wales and married young to a British army officer stationed in India, Mrs. Leonowens had seen much of the Orient and was an experienced traveler when she accepted the offer of King Mongkut of Siam to come to Bangkok and teach his sixty-seven children. Major Leonowens had died the year after the Indian Mutiny and Mrs. Leonowens had to choose between taking her two small children back to the home of her unsympathetic stepfather or venturing to the then almost unknown capital of a semi-savage country. It took a great deal of courage for her to accept the job which King Mongkut offered her in the following letter:

> English Era, 1862, 26th February.
> Grand Royal Palace, Bangkok
>
> To Mrs. A. H. Leonowens:—
>
> Madam: We are in good pleasure, and satisfaction in heart, that you are in willingness to undertake the education of our beloved royal children. And we hope that in doing your education on us and on our children (whom English call inhabitants of benighted land) you will do your best endeavor for knowledge of English language, science, and

---

*Anna H. Leonowens, *The English Governess at the Siamese Court*. This book and *The Romance of the Harem* are difficult to find. The Siamese government tried in every way to prevent their publication and is said to have attempted to buy up all copies. Margaret Landon rewrote and combined the two books into *Anna and the King of Siam* on which the musical, *The King and I*, was based.

literature, and not for conversion to Christianity; as the followers of Buddha are mostly aware of the powerfulness of truth and virtue, as well as the followers of Christ, and are desirous to have facility of English language and literature, more than new religions.

We beg to invite you to our royal palace to do your best endeavorment upon us and our children. We shall expect to see you here on return of Siamese steamer Chow Phya.

We have written to Mr. William Adamson, and to our consul at Singapore, to authorize to do best arrangement for you and ourselves.

Believe me
Your faithfully,
(Signed) S. S. P. P. Maha Mongkut.

With this charming epistle in pocket, Mrs. Leonowens embarked for Bangkok in 1862.

Though he underpaid and overworked her, the king had confidence in this upright and courageous English lady and often consulted her on state affairs. Her influence on Crown Prince Chulalongkorn appears to have been great, and it may well have been her teaching that led the impressionable young monarch to initiate his reign with a decree abolishing slavery and the humiliating practice of prostration, which required anyone approaching royalty to crawl on the floor.* At his coronation in 1873, numerous other reform measures were enacted, but King Chulalongkorn like his father, Mongkut, was a curious mixture of medieval autocrat and enlightened reformer. For instance, he still treated the national revenues as his privy purse to do with as he pleased; his enormous harem cost the country vast sums. Nevertheless, his reform measures and those instituted by his father were truly amazing when one considers that up to that time, the Lord of Life, as the Siamese king was called, had such absolute power that not only could he have anyone imprisoned and executed if he so

---

*H. G. Quaritch Wales in *Siamese State Ceremonies: Their History and Function*, p. 35, traces the divinity of the king of Siam back to the Laws of Manu: "Because a king has been formed of particles of those lords of the gods, he therefore surpasses all created beings in lustre; and, *like the sun,* he burns eyes and hearts; *nor can anybody on earth even gaze on him.*" Hence anyone approaching the king could do so only on all fours, his face to the ground. By abolishing prostration in 1873, King Chulalongkorn tacitly relinquished the claim to godhead. The concept of the king as a god was brought by the Indians and, though a part of Brahmanism, survived the eclipse of that faith by Buddhism.

In contrast to the elevated position of the king, that of the people was abject; they were "considered only as the goods and chattels of the king, who had absolute power over their lives and property, and could use them as best suited his purpose. Otherwise they were of no importance whatever." (*Ibid.,* p. 21.) In King Mongkut's time, the majority of Siamese carried a number and brand below the armpit which indicated to which noble they belonged, the nobles being assigned certain government departments for which the services of the branded men were needed: each had to devote part or all of his life to the department served by his father, the servitude being

wished, but any member of the royal family could walk about the capital city or elsewhere and take whatever he fancied.

I think that Siam's smooth Westernization was due in part to the effect on King Mongkut and King Chulalongkorn of the teaching and personal bearing of Mrs. Leonowens and of the unselfish medical and educational work of a devoted band of missionaries, mostly Presbyterian. Certainly Siam obtained the services of these good people at very little cost to herself—Mrs. Leonowens was promised a salary of 100 dollars a month but seldom got it, and the missionary schools and hospitals were financed by American churches.

Dr. Collier introduced me to Dr. Manfred Oberdoerffer, a young German physician. Dr. Oberdoerffer had temporarily taken the place of the superintendent of the leper colony, who was away on leave of absence. He was anxious that one should not mistake him for a refugee; yet it seemed to me that, despite his fervently expressed patriotism, something must have driven him from his fatherland to serve the poor lepers in this far corner of the earth. I was told that he was doing exciting things in leprosy, and decided I would try later to encourage him to tell me about them.

The leper colony is reached by way of a short bridge. There are no guards or fences. The lepers go there voluntarily and seldom leave before they are dismissed as cured. There were about 550, of whom 100 were women. Men and women are strictly segregated although leprosy is not an inheritable disease. If babies are immediately taken from their leprous mothers, they have a good chance of growing up normally. Sometimes, however, babies are not removed soon enough, or healthy parents have children who are infected at an early age, and so there were many little tots romping about the island. It was heartrending to see them, still unconscious of what life held in store for them. One little boy gave a splendid performance in a solo dance. He looked so gay and was such a nimble sprite that I could hardly bear to watch him and the memory of him still haunts me at times.

The lepers lived in neat little cement houses (two to a house), with gardens in which they could raise flowers and vegetables. There were shady avenues, attractive community buildings, a river to bathe in, fields where they could grow all the food they needed, a kindly doctor, and a devoted, self-sacrificing minister. This was as good a leper asylum as any in the world, but one could not help feeling unhappy all the time one was there.*

---

hereditary. Below these men were the slaves, those born to slaves, or those who were prisoners of war or debt slaves. It was these that Chulalongkorn freed in 1873. (*Ibid.*, pp. 22-23.)

*When George was on duty in Okinawa during World War II, he had occasion to visit a leprosarium in the northwestern part of the island. It had been mistakenly

A wat at Chieng Mai (with dragon balustrades)

Doctor Hayata and family in front of holy shrine at Okinawa leper colony.

The Christmas tea party was the big event in the life of the colony and the lepers went all out to make it a success. The whole island was profusely decorated with paper lanterns and colored streamers. The patients had been busy with preparations for weeks; even their injections had been skipped in the mad rush to get everything ready on time. They had put every penny of their meager funds into beautifying the island in honor of their distinguished guests.

Some of the dances they performed were good; notably a peacock dance, a sword dance, a dance representing the fight of two make-believe tigers, and the dance of the gay little leper boy. There was also singing and, at the end, a splendid torchlight procession. The singing was not good, for one of the symptoms of the disease is a raucous voice. Fortunately, the lepers are unconscious of the harsh sounds they make. In fact, they are unusually fond of singing. Later, in the large, open-air auditorium, they gave a theatrical performance, which was loudly applauded by some one thousand guests from all the surrounding villages. Everyone was so engrossed in the play that they forgot to be careful and lepers and villagers became mixed together. It is a good thing that leprosy is hard to catch.

Next morning Cornelia Harris, the wife of the Reverend William Harris, principal of Prince Royal College, drove me on a sightseeing tour around Chieng Mai. The old part of the city is surrounded by a moat and a massive, but crumbling, wall. One enters the old town through the Elephant Gate from which the road leads to a small temple that houses rather crude statues of two huge, white, good-luck elephants. There are many temples in and around Chieng Mai, most of them badly in need of repair. Since a Buddhist gains merit only by *building* a temple, there is no benefit in putting money into repairs. It is a shame that nobody feels responsible for the upkeep of temples, because many are attractive. They are not at all like those in Angkor, except for one small temple which has only recently been discovered overgrown by the jungle. This is the seven-pinnacled Wat Jed Yod, which looks distinctly Khmer and has well-preserved carvings that are good. It sits in a pretty bamboo grove, and is again

---

bombed by our aircraft and the conditions were deplorable. George was appalled by what he saw: they had no electricity, medicines, dressings, and wore rags for clothing. What unnerved him most was watching the women washing their ragged clothes, gradually wearing away their fingers until only the palms of their hands were left—a characteristic of leprosy. Also, since there were no artificial limbs available, one man had strapped to his thigh a "leg" made of cement. The Japanese doctor, Dr. Hayata, with his wife and three children, had remained behind when the Japanese troops had left the island. They were modern saints. George sent food, medicine, supplies, bed linen, blankets, clothing, and a small electrical generating set. When I told him about the leper colony at Chieng Mai, he remarked how fortunate they were in comparison with those he had seen on Okinawa.

in use. A while ago bonzes moved in and set up their wooden huts in the temple grounds. Inside, incense rises and one can hear the chanting of the monks.

Chieng Mai has grown far beyond the original site and is now a busy market town with rows of open-front stores selling every imaginable commodity. It is famous for an exceptionally clean market, owned by a public-spirited citizen who engaged an Englishman to put it into good condition and keep it so by putting every penny of profit into new cement floors, walls, fountains, and other improvements. This was my first encounter with such interested civic pride and service in this part of the world. I inquired about rental costs and found that a tiny cubbyhole costs two satang a day; a larger stand suitable for selling fruits and vegetables rents at five to six satang, depending on location; a small bakery shop in a good place costs ten satang. The Indian stores which sell yard goods, Bombay brass, and lacquerware pay thirty ticals a month.

Some lacquer and silverware is made in Chieng Mai. The silverwork is influenced by Burmese designs and features heavily embossed work, which I did not like as well as the shallower Siamese kind. Most householders have a few round silver bowls with stylized flower designs. The Chieng Mai lacquerwork is poor, but the weaving industry makes attractive sarongs. All these things are manufactured for the home market, not for tourists. Still, word had spread that I had arrived, and when we returned for lunch we found a number of ancient ladies squatting on the porch of the Collier house with silver items spread out before them. These were all articles they had used in their own homes and few of them appealed to me. Until I left, the porch was never empty. I did buy a silver bowl and told them what I wanted most was one of the small bronze weights in the shape of an animal that merchants used in the old days.

The Siamese calendar—like the Chinese—is divided into cycles of twelve years, each having the name of an animal: the Rat, the Cow, the Tiger, the Rabbit, the Major Dragon, the Minor Dragon, the Horse, the Goat, the Monkey, the Cock, the Dog, and the Hog. A merchant born in the Year of the Tiger would have all his weights made of bronze tigers. I thought this a charming custom and wanted a tiger or a dragon. Nowadays, ordinary weights like ours are used and the old kind have become collectors' items. Only after much searching around did I finally locate one little tiger, weighing perhaps four ounces.

In the afternoon, Miss Helen McClure, the principal of the girl's academy, took me on a drive to Lamphun, said to be the oldest of all the cities of northern Siam. We traveled through lovely country with high mountains all around. On both sides of the road were broad shade trees, through which we could watch the rice being harvested. The grain is separated from the chaff by pounding the sheaves in large woven baskets or by hitting them against a bench made of bamboo logs, the grain falling between the logs to the ground. The Siamese are thus more advanced than the Bataks, whose threshing is done by women trampling on the rice sheaves while holding on to a wooden beam for support. They are not as advanced as the Japanese, who have a more efficient contraption—the sheaves being held against a large wheel which is worked by foot and rotates rapidly; strong legs are needed to turn the wheel but it works efficiently. I noticed that all Siamese houses have a courtyard with a well and a rice pounder; the latter is a wooden pestle on a long wooden stick which pounds the rice in a stone trough.

We visited friends of Miss McClure's and this gave me a chance to see the inside of a Siamese house. Those of well-to-do villagers are large, have wide verandahs, and are separated from the cookhouse, which is connected to the main house by a passage. The houses are on stilts and have beautifully polished hardwood floors. As you enter, you take off your shoes—just as in Japan—and step onto a raised platform where you squat down. The hostess immediately offers you the paraphernalia for betel-nut chewing or, if you are a foreigner, cigarettes. There is always an earthenware jug of water with a silver drinking cup which you are invited to use.

The house we visited in Lamphun was bustling with preparations for the wedding of the owner, a famous beauty who once played havoc with men's hearts but finally decided to settle down. Siamese weddings are big affairs. Everything must be brand new for the young couple. A woman who has never quarreled with her husband makes the mattress for the bridal bed. All clothes for the newlyweds must also be new. We admired all her finery and offered our best wishes to the slightly overblown Rose of Lamphun—that was the bride's name.

Until the latter part of the nineteenth century, northern Siam and Laos were virtually independent of Bangkok. They were ruled by local chiefs called Chao Luang (Big Chief), whose only obligations to the Bangkok government were the payment of tribute and triennial visits to the royal court for renewal of the oath of allegiance. This oath, or more correctly the "Drinking of the Water of Allegiance," is of ancient Indian origin and one not to be lightly undertaken by anyone harboring treasonable thoughts. Beginning with "We, the slaves of the Lord Buddha," it begs all the deities of the universe, including the dreaded evil spirits that lurk around the hapless Siamese all his life, to inflict the most fearful punishments upon the oath-taker—should he ever break the oath—among them everlasting hellfire in

Threshing rice in northern Siam

House in northern Siam

the Buddhist inferno, which is a place of fiendish tortures unimaginable even to Western man. As he swears allegiance to the king, the vassal must drink water hallowed by the priests. Not infrequently, the result has been that the vassal fell ill and died of cholera, thus demonstrating the fearful consequences of harboring traitorous thoughts!*

For centuries it was a moot question whether Laos would fall to Siam, Burma, or Annam, each at one time or another claiming suzerainty. At times, the Khmers and the Chinese entered the fray, but in the end Siam succeeded in ousting all other contenders for northern Laos. However, she failed to make good her claim to eastern Laos, which fell into French hands. For a time Bangkok ruled Laos through the Chao Luang, but when difficulties arose between the Chieng Mai Chao and the British teak men from Burma as well as the American missionaries, King Chulalongkorn decided to establish direct control through appointment of a Siamese commissioner, and pensioned off the Chao. Gradually, the Lao became reconciled to direct Siamese administration, which brought them greater security and more efficient and just government. Nowadays they do not like to be called Lao, but insist on being known as Northern Thai or Siamese. Besides their lighter skin, the principal difference between them and the Southern Thai is that they wear *sarongs* instead of *panungs*. In the old days the women of each village went in for *sarongs* with different horizontal stripes, so that on market days one could immediately tell whence each came. This is now considered old-fashioned.

I was amused to hear people in Chieng Mai speak disapprovingly of Bangkok as a wicked big city full of thieves and miscreants. However, I was told that the Lao are in fact a gentler race than the Southern Thai. Whenever you enter a shop they all bow low and raise their hands as if in prayer. If they consider you socially inferior they raise their folded hands up to the heart; if you are an equal, up to the mouth and if superior, or white, up to eye level.

The Laos script and language differ slightly from Siamese but not enough to prevent mutual intercourse. The Lao maintain close trade relations with the Burmese, whose language is similar to Lao. The Burmese here are called the Great Thai in contradistinction to the Siamese, or Little Thai. Properly speaking, this term should apply only to the Shans who live in northern Burma, the other Burmese being more closely related to the Tibetans than to the Siamese.

*H. G. Quaritch Wales, *Siamese State Ceremonies: Their History and Function*, pp. 193–198.

Next day I went by car on a delightful picnic with Miss McClure and two friends, Miss Lucy Niblock and Mrs. Elder. We drove up Mount Doi Suthep on a road that wound through forests, and had our lunch beside a cool waterfall at Huey Keo. The road was built a short time ago by some 3,000 volunteers, who constructed it entirely by hand. They were led by a Buddhist priest and did the work to gain merit. The road leads to a temple with an enormous bell which could only have been carried up that steep mountain by elephants. The view from the temple on top of the mountain was breathtaking. We sat for a while on the porch of one of the mission's summer cottages built on top of the mountain, from which there is a lovely view of the flat country below and the high mountains around. Roses grew in the garden, there was pine fragrance in the air, and it was cool enough even in the sun to wear a light sweater.

I had a fine time questioning my friends about missionary life in Siam. As did everyone I met, they eventually spoke of the changes wrought by the bloodless revolt of 1932, which turned Siam from an absolute monarchy into a constitutional government. The revolt was engineered by young Siamese who had been sent abroad to acquire Western training and found upon their return that all the good positions in the administration were in the hands of princes. Since, in the past, Siamese royalty had huge families, there was an overabundance of princes in Bangkok.* This was so, even though Siam had a sensible system of gradually reducing the rank of the king's progeny. Each generation became one step below the preceding one, so that the great-great-grandson of a king became a commoner. The same safeguard against the growth of a powerful aristocracy existed in Cambodia and Annam. Under the absolute monarchy, all the top ministerial positions were held by princes: hence, one of the first acts of the new rulers was to forbid princes to hold positions as ministers. Although this has deprived Siam of the services of many capable men, it seems to me a good policy in the long run. It would be better still if they could get themselves to go a step further and put the holding of high positions strictly on a basis of merit. One of the consequences of the 1932 revolt has been a slight lowering of the influence and position of foreign missionaries. With the stirring of nationalism and pride of country has gone an insistence that no one in Siam have special privileges. Moreover, the mis-

*King Mongkut had 67 children—a remarkable performance since he spent 27 years in a Buddhist monastery, entering at the age of 20 when he was passed over for the succession by his brother, Nang Klao. King Chulalongkorn began earlier, had 32 wives and 100 concubines who presented him with 236 children. A list of the male descendants of Chulalongkorn takes up nine and one half pages in the Siam Directory.

sionaries had firm friends in the princes and both have lost influence together. One of the serious problems for mission schools was the new law requiring that all schools teach at least thirty hours a week in the Siamese language. This was hard on the foreign colony because it meant they had to send their children to British Malaya, or India, or home. But the new government claimed that no other sovereign state permitted schools to teach exclusively in a foreign tongue. However, small study groups of not more than seven were permitted. Apart from a newly awakened nationalism, which tends to put excessive emphasis on outward forms, this law is intended to end the perpetuation of Chinese enclaves in the national body. The Chinese used to send their children to their own schools, where Siamese was not even taught as a subject. It is hoped that, under the new law, the younger generation of Chinese will eventually be assimilated. In the meantime, immigration has been made more difficult by the collection of a 200-tical fee from any foreigner who stays longer than one month.

The new government is inordinately fond of rules and regulations—possibly because so many of the young Siamese now in control studied in France, the mother country of red tape. The mission teachers bemoan the time they must spend on paper work. Each child's name must be entered into a large book and every day all his actions must be recorded therein: when he arrives in the morning; each time he begs to be excused; when he leaves and returns at lunch time; and when he goes home at night. The same data must be furnished for the teachers. It isn't clear what good all this paper work does. On the other hand, I could understand why the new regime required teachers to pass an examination in Siamese before allowing them to teach. It is probably directed at the Chinese schools. The missionary teachers suspected that an element of jealousy entered into this rule, for the new government people disliked to see foreigners excel in anything. By making the examinations difficult for aliens, they manage to fail a good many. Significantly, these failed candidates are then engaged by the government to teach in government schools at high salaries!

Also there was the matter of taxation. Miss McClure told me that she had to fill out three sets of papers for the internal revenue office: one as owner, another as principal, and a third as teacher in her mission school, paying taxes on each count and furnishing no less than fourteen photographs of herself. When it is considered that the school was supported by mission funds from abroad, it can be seen that these new rules were felt to be onerous. Actually, the government was not so much anti-mission as determined to be recognized as master in its own house. Rightly or wrongly, the new rulers felt that under the old regime aliens were favored; now they want to make sure that everyone is treated equally. As our guide in Ayuthia put it: "Today we actually put foreigners in jail if they violate our laws!" His chest expanded as he said this.

That afternoon I had tea with Dr. Oberdoerffer in front of the fireplace in his large living room. He told me his interest in leprosy began some years ago when a siege with scarlatina sent him to a sanitarium. As he was recuperating in the sunny garden, he noticed a small pavilion tucked away in a corner. One day he wandered there and met a man still in his prime but covered with nodules. The two became friends and often went walking together. The leper had led an adventurous life. As a boy—in 1910—he ran away from home and school to join the French Foreign Legion, but five years later he was weary of it and participated in an uprising. He and other rioters were caught and all were executed except this German who was sent to Devil's Island. He managed to escape, spending years in the jungles of French Guiana before he could get on a ship bound for Europe. For a while he made a good living in Germany, giving sensational talks on life in the Foreign Legion. He met a girl, fell in love, and thought that everything had finally come out right for him. Shortly before the wedding, a German doctor with experience in tropical diseases recognized a small pinkish spot on the back of his hand as leprous. His world tumbled about him.

He and Dr. Oberdoerffer had often discussed the effect of leprosy on a normal person. "It's a mutilating disease," the leper had told him, "but you can't feel proud, as you would of mutilation received on the battlefield. Suddenly your family, your race, your education, intelligence, and character aren't worth a tinker's damn for the world is no longer interested in you. You can't even hate society for pushing you into isolation because it is the disease, not society, which makes you an outcast. You are simply finished. Most people go through a period of complete anarchy, letting down completely and giving in to despair and flirting with thoughts of suicide. But, after a while, people realize that they are thrown entirely on their own resources. Usually they manage to rally and come to terms with life." Dr. Oberdoerffer's friend regained his self-respect and led a fairly contented life in his little pavilion.

Only neurotic individuals break down permanently. The greatest help anyone can give a leper is to permit him to lead as normal a life as possible and to aid him in winning back a sense of personal worth. Dr. Oberdoerffer did much work with athletics which, besides being good for the soul, help the body fight the disease. He believed that good food and healthy living account for 60 percent of all cures, 20 percent he called "normal body recovery," and 20 percent, at most, he ascribed to chaulmoogra-oil injections. He felt that it was a moot point whether a leper ever really recovers, for the disease is likely to recur whenever the body is weakened from some other cause.

When I asked him, Dr. Oberdoerffer said he thought only 15 to 20 of the 550 lepers in Chieng Mai were really unhappy—no greater percentage than would be found in any community of healthy people. Of course, nobody likes to have the disease but they have adjusted to it. When I wanted to know just how great was the danger of infection, he replied that of some 600 leper doctors, 15 are known to have contracted the disease, and it was believed that about that many more got it but kept it quiet. He admitted that there were times when he himself was seized with horror and fear of the disease. I should think anyone would occasionally be afraid to be a leper doctor!

Dr. Oberdoerffer had a novel theory on which he was working at that time, that persons whose adrenal glands do not function properly are particularly susceptible to leprosy. In support, he cited the fact that women are less susceptible than men, because their menstrual periods keep the adrenal glands in good order, and adults less than children, because the adrenal glands of the latter are not completely developed. He evolved this theory while working at a British leper mission in Nigeria, where he noticed that of two tribes living on either side of a river, one showed high susceptibility to leprosy and always in its severest form; the other seemed to be almost immune and, if a case did occur, it was invariably of the milder kind. The tribes belonged to the same race and he could find only one significant difference in their modes of life: the leprosy-prone tribe was given to eating certain plants called *colocasia, alocasia,* and *xanthsoma,* commonly known as taro; the relatively immune tribe had a strict taboo against eating these plants. They contain a highly toxic acid, sapotoxin, which Dr. Oberdoerffer believes to be responsible for weakening the ability of the adrenal glands to resist leprosy.

Dr. Oberdoerffer also noticed that when Indians emigrate to Malaya, where little *colocasia* is eaten, they contract leprosy at approximately the same rate as the Malays, which corresponds to that in India and is relatively low; when they do contract it, they are apt to get the mild form prevalent in India. On the other hand, Indians migrating to the Fiji Islands, where much taro is consumed, are prone to leprosy and contract it in its severest form. Dr. Oberdoerffer read a paper on *Regional Variation of Clinical Types in Leprosy, Seasonal Variation of Bacteriological Findings in Tuberculoid Leprosy, and their possible Causation by Sapotoxins in certain Food Plants* before the Congress of the Far Eastern Association of Tropical Medicine, in Hanoi, November 1938, which elaborates this theory.

He said it was still not known how leprosy was transmitted but apparently long and close personal contact is necessary. However, it is known which lepers are infectious and which are not. Frightfully mutilated persons are usually uninfectious, while people who look normal and have only a few nodules or a diffused mottled skin may be highly infectious. He said that sometimes the disease develops quickly; sometimes it takes years before symptoms appear. This seemed odd to me for, if it is not known how the disease spreads, how can anyone ever really know the exact moment when leprosy has been contracted.

The lepers of Chieng Mai owe Hitler a debt of gratitude, because Dr. Oberdoerffer might never have decided to devote his life to helping these poor outcasts, had he not been made to feel something of an outcast himself. I gathered that he was engaged to the daughter of a prominent Nazi when a jealous suitor raised the question of the purity of his racial antecedents. He had to undergo a trial in one of the courts especially set up to examine into the heredity of Germans whose ancestry had been questioned. Apparently the non-Aryan relative was sufficiently remote for him to be declared eligible to marry the fair maiden. By then, however, he had had enough of the whole thing and went to Nigeria to work for the lepers instead. This experience seems to have left an ineradicable impression on him. Although he ought to have known better, his conversation was loaded with such Nazi clichés as "good blood" and "bad blood," "superior races," the significance of "pure heredity," and what not. I found it pathetic that he was still clinging strongly to German patriotism, going so far as to reject out of hand the possibility of obtaining a Rockefeller grant for his leprosy studies because "America hates my country." When he left Germany in despair, he found kindness and help among Englishmen and Americans. Yet he remained truculently German—always a little superior to those who took him in.

In the evening I was invited with the Colliers to an elegant dinner party at the Harrises—black tie for the men and trailing gowns for the women. Having never had any experience with missionaries, I thought of them as narrow-minded and dowdy. This party showed me that, as I ought to have known, missionaries are like other people. Most of those I met that evening were second-generation Chieng Maiers and looked like any other American physicians and educators. Dr. Harris himself was the very embodiment of the master of an exclusive private school, and his wife had the gracious ways of a great lady. Their beautiful home was filled with exquisite silver and brass objects given them by illustrious Siamese personalities. I was green with envy at the rows of bronze weights that ran along all the walls of the living room. Mrs. Harris had a complete set of all twelve animals!

There were a number of British teak industry people at the party, Chieng Mai's white colony being about equally divided between British teak and American mission people. My partner, one of the teak men, recognized in me a complete greenhorn and entertained me with the wildest stories about snakes and tigers and other dangers in the teak forests. He claimed that snakes run from humans and never attack unless cornered; that is, all but the king cobra which will attack man when it is nesting. It is the only cannibal snake, and the larger its size, the more deadly its bite.

All the guests at the party had been closely associated with Siamese royalty and were rather critical of the new regime, though one or two admitted privately that Siam had gone about as far as was possible under a benevolent autocracy, gently led by a few trusted foreigners. Next morning I interviewed a prominent Siamese in Chieng Mai who had been active in the 1932 revolt and who tried to explain to me that the change to constitutional government was long overdue: "We were lucky to have had a succession of enlightened monarchs, for such a tremendous transformation as ours, which turned Siam from a medieval country into a modern state, can best be accomplished by an absolute ruler." But progress had begun to slow down, and it was time that Siam avail herself of the services of young men who had been trained abroad. King Prajadhipok, himself, favored a constitution but kept postponing what he had promised to do. At first he approved a new constitution establishing a limited monarchy. But he refused to sign a measure abdicating the royal power of life and death and so he resigned. Personally, I suspect his ill health may have had something to do with the decision. Like most Siamese, this man expressed great affection for the young boy king, Ananda.

Later Dr. Collier took me to see their hospital and orphanage. I shall not be able to forget the picture of the babies who had been wrested from death by the Colliers. The Lao are a gentle people but superstitions make them commit cruelties. One of the worst superstitions is that a mother who dies in childbirth remains as a *phi* (spirit) in the vicinity of the baby and is harmful to others. Such babies are therefore immediately taken to the forest and abandoned. The Colliers have been picking them up for years. Mrs. Collier showed me a room full of the pathetic little creatures—tiny, ash-grey morsels resembling nothing so much as rats. They were so emaciated from exposure that they looked scarcely human, but many have grown into plump boys and girls. They are usually adopted by missionaries, for nobody else would chance taking them.

My final day in Chieng Mai went by in a mad rush of last-minute interviews and in the end we threw things into my suitcase and ran for the train. I had heard so much of the mission at Chieng Rai, in the northeast corner of Siam, that I decided to go there, especially as I would have the company of Miss Niblock all the way. We went by train to Lampang, a 100-mile trip back towards Bangkok. There we were met by Dr. Loren Stanley Hannah, the resident Presbyterian missionary. Old-fashioned horse traps were the means of transportation in this town, so we settled ourselves amidst rugs and baggage in one of these and trotted off, with Dr. Hannah accompanying us on his bicycle. I felt like the heroine in an old-fashioned story, in which the ladies ride in a carriage and the gentlemen accompany them on horseback, conversing politely on the way. In the evening light, the landscape was beautiful and things became more storylike than ever as it grew dark. We rode up a circular driveway to a house that looked like a Southern mansion with its white pillars and large verandahs. Mrs. Hannah came down the steps holding aloft a kerosene lamp.

Inside, we found refreshments set before a cozy fire, which was welcome for the night had turned cold. In the midst of getting acquainted there was a knock on the door, and Dr. Robert L. Pendleton from Bangkok came in. He had found no room at the government rest house and was welcomed with open arms by the Hannahs. I enjoyed the casual though warm hospitality of the missionaries—home comfort with no fuss. Dr. Pendleton used to be an agricultural expert in the Philippines, but was then advising the Siamese government. He was on an inspection trip into the remote hinterland to survey possibilities of growing new crops to diversify farming and increase productivity—one of the projects of the new government. He told us that he had stayed two nights with one of the opium kings—actually, they were chiefs of small, semi-savage tribes—up in the mountains near Indo-China. The people in the mountains are the most recent immigrants among the hodgepodge of races on this peninsula, all of whom seem to have come south via the river valleys. They are closely related to the Chinese but still in a fairly barbaric stage of civilization. The opium king introduced Dr. Pendleton to his executioner—who lops off fingers, toes, hands, and ears of recalcitrant peasants who refuse to grow as much opium as he orders or who haggle over the price. The proximity to the frontier facilitates opium-smuggling. The Siamese accused the French of not cooperating properly, but the Siamese themselves were also at fault. Since they do not smoke opium, the Siamese were not overly interested in suppressing the opium trade. They were frequently scolded by the League of Nations Opium Board, but seemed to bear up well. Many Siamese officials found it difficult to resist the temptation to make a little money out of opium. Some are said to have gone so far as to force the peasants to sell them opium cheaply, on pain of having their fields burned. Occasionally the government made a raid but the principals, who lived in inaccessible strongholds along the Indo-Chinese border, were never caught.

As we walked up the stairs to our bedrooms, candlesticks in hand, Dr. Hannah warned us to step carefully over a small hole in one of the risers where a cobra dwelled in perfect amiability with the Hannah family. Nevertheless, I took my slippers into bed that night and tucked the net curtains around the mattress with special care.

The next morning, while it was still dark, Miss Niblock and I got on our Chinese bus for Chieng Rai. It had to be completely reloaded in order to make room for the two of us and even so we were tightly packed. You must always make the driver arrange everything to your satisfaction before you start on your journey, for en route he will do nothing. Bus and truck travel hereabouts is an art. You must know which drivers are reliable, which trucks are least likely to come apart on the way (a difficult decision since they all look fit for the junk yard), how best to bargain for the fare, and how to have the truck reloaded so that one survives the journey without suffering permanent dislocation of the joints. If you don't watch out, the driver will, at the last moment, sneak gasoline tins into the space where you had planned to place your feet. It is also a good idea to take along a blanket and pillow, as well as drinking water, cup, and food, though you can always buy fruit on the way. As for rest rooms, you might as well forget about such Western luxuries and be on the lookout for suitable bushes when the need arises.

At Chieng Rai we were warmly received by the Reverend and Mrs. Lyle Jerome Beebe, who also proved to be the most charming of people. After a quick wash, they led us to a wonderful fire where our stiff hands and feet gradually returned to normal. Mary Beebe, who had a delightful sense of humor, regaled us with tales of their early life, when they lived in Chieng Rung, Yunnan. Some four million Thais still live in southern Yunnan which is why the Presbyterian mission sent the Beebes from Siam to open a station in Chieng Rung, rather than establish it through the China mission. The people there speak a dialect close to Siamese, and the Beebes had no trouble talking with them.

In those days it took a long time to travel to Chieng Rung; many weeks were spent on ponies. When I was there, it was traveled by train from Bangkok to Lampang; by truck or bus to Chieng Rai; by bus from Chieng Rai to Keng Tung, in Burma, where lodging was given by American Baptist missionaries; then for eight more days by pony across the mountains of Yunnan to Chieng Rung. Overnight stays were often spent in Buddhist temples—a convenient custom found in all Buddhist countries, for to give shelter to the stranger gains merit for the temple. The Beebes said the scenery was simply stupendous, if at times a little scarifying—steep descents on either side and narrow trails; the ponies stepping gingerly with part of their load hanging precariously over the abyss.

It wasn't much use to put up curtains while they camped overnight, said Mrs. Beebe, unless a man was posted there with a gun; the natives were too curious and had no sense of embarrassment at being watched making their own morning toilette, since they had never in their life experienced privacy. Even missionaries soon lost puritan habits. The Reverend Mr. Beebe would step in front of the curtain whenever Mrs. Beebe took a bath. He would then slowly shave himself, and this always drew a breathless crowd, too fascinated to bother about the lady in the bathtub. They both became quick-change artists like theatrical people and could dress and undress without exposing an inch of skin. Their small children sat on chairs to which small roofs were attached; each chair carried by two coolies. Whenever they stopped for a rest, one coolie washed the diapers while the other helped feed the children. The diapers were hung around the little roofs and waved gaily in the wind. The long trip became something of a holiday for the Beebes and they learned to take all sorts of unexpected adventures in their stride.

Except for food, nothing could be bought in Chieng Rung except the Chinese kind of dark cotton cloth. Every four days there was a market, where vegetables and questionable beef could be purchased. For the rest of the time, the Beebes relied on chicken—that staple of oriental menus. Once a year Mrs. Beebe made a list of every item they needed and this was sent to Bangkok. Anything she forgot to put on the list she had to do without. The goods on the list were bought by missionary friends and sent by pony caravan, each animal loaded carefully with boxes of standard weight evenly balanced.
Had a pony, by chance, missed a step and lost part of its load it would have been just too bad—especially if it had been the one carrying the year's supply of flour. But nothing ever happened and, since the Beebes could not spend any money in Chieng Rung, their salaries sufficed to pay for the expensive annual supply trip.

The Beebes found Thai tribes in Yunnan who speak what must be the purest form of the language, since it is free of both Chinese and Pali expressions. The latter are of South Indian origin and came into the language of Siam through Buddhism. These tribes are called Thai Yai and live in a primitive state. They are the only Thai people who were never converted to Buddhism and the Beebes were successful in winning many of them over to Christianity.

Trying to unravel the intricate ramifications of the various races of this peninsula could give anyone a headache. Oddly enough, their names sound like a concert of tomcats. There are Yao, Miao or Meo, Kaw, Yai, to name but a few. Among the Miaos there are black, white, and flowery Miaos—this to differentiate the patterns of their sarongs—and there are also black and white Lao so designated because of the different types of tattooing favored by them. The simplest way is to remember that the civilized people (Thai and Lao) live in the river valleys and the more recent primitive tribes in the mountains. Many of these tribes I later met in Yunnan. They are more closely related to the Chinese than to the Thais, and most of them are avid opium-smugglers.

From the Beebes I also collected amusing stories of native superstitions. The Thai-Yu, for example, consider it of prime importance to have silver on hand to pay for their cremation, so they won't be left unburied, their spirits condemned to fly about forever. Even beggars will keep bits of silver in their pockets and starve rather than spend them. However, if a man has been murdered, his corpse is not cremated but is left exposed to the vultures, in order that his spirit may be able to seek out the murderer and punish him. So worried are these people about *phis* that they won't take a chance even on a tiny unborn baby: if a pregnant woman dies, the baby is removed so that it won't harm the surviving family. It seems strange that the Siamese who are extremely fond of children and kind to them should see such weird attachments between pregnant women and the *phis*. The superstition that the souls of pregnant women will turn into fierce spirits leads to cruelties in the village, but these are as nothing to what Siamese royalty perpetuated in the name of this belief. Wanton cruelty to keep the people in abject subjection is, of course, the hallmark of barbaric autocracy, as it is of all tyrannical power, witness like cruelties prescribed by modern totalitarians for the purpose of keeping subject people in awe and fear. But the elaboration on the superstition about pregnant women which the Siamese kings developed into a fine art is truly horrible.

Whenever a palace or city fortification was to be built, the king's soldiers kidnaped as many pregnant women on the street as were needed—one for each pillar sunk into the ground. By throwing the women into the holes and driving the stakes into their live bodies, it was claimed that their spirits would guard the palace and the city against all enemies. Wales gives eyewitness reports of Europeans who tell of the wailing which used to arise all over Ayuthia when word spread that the king had begun another building. It is difficult to believe that such incredible cruelties continued into the nineteenth century, but this was actually the case, and here again it was fear of European reaction which induced the kings to stop the practice.*

Not all Siamese superstitions are gruesome. One of their customs shows an amusing faith in the efficacy of names. If a man and his wife feel that their family is big enough, they will name the next child Luk La (last girl) or I La (last boy). Sometimes this doesn't work; another baby arrives, and is named Luk Lun (afterwards girl) or I Lun (afterwards boy). If the stork still doesn't stop coming, they will impatiently name the baby Luk Sut or I Sut (this is really the last girl, or boy). All names must have *Luk* (girl) or *I* (boy), a good idea in a country where men and women cut their hair and dress alike.

As do Lithuanian peasants and many others, the Siamese try to defray the cost of weddings by soliciting funds from their guests. As many as possible are invited, and the first thing they see as they enter the house where the wedding takes place is a silver bowl set out in an obvious place. Each guest is supposed to put a money gift in the bowl, the intake being later carefully counted with both families present to see that nobody cheats. Only hard money is welcome—a sound instinct that should keep any future government on the straight and narrow path of honest finance.

Parents are called "father of" and "mother of" followed by the name of the eldest child; their own names apparently forgotten, almost as if, having produced children, they had lost their own identity. Laos is full of odd customs having to do with men and women and their relations to each other. Women have a fairly good position. Often the husband comes to live in the wife's house, which gives her the upper hand. If they quarrel or if he begins to wonder whether she still loves him, the husband can test her by putting a bunch of posies on the pillow of her bed. He will know everything is still fine if the wife leaves the flowers there for three days in a row. But should she have been considering the advisability of separation, she will promptly throw the flowers out the window

---

*H. G. Quaritch Wales, *Siamese State Ceremonies: Their History and Function*, pp. 304-307.

and they then get a divorce, dividing all family property evenly. Sometimes things may go beyond flowers and an angry wife simply throws her husband's clothes out of the house, which means automatic dissolution of the marriage. Most Lao have one wife, not being able to afford more. Polygamy is customary only among royalty and the rich, though sometimes the wife of an affluent merchant or farmer will decide that the work is too much for her and engage a number two wife for her husband, thereby acquiring an unpaid servant who will be completely under her thumb.

A curious bit of etiquette is that when you speak of your lower body you must excuse yourself, saying delicately, "Excuse me, my knee hurts," or "Excuse me, you have stepped on my big toe." This rule applies to everything beneath the waist and reminds me of our own Western affectation of calling legs "limbs." Contrariwise, the Siamese consider that since the hair is the highest part of the body, it is the most important part, and dislike intensely having the hair or head touched. Old-fashioned people still object to having anyone walk on the floor of the story above them. And, of course, the more important a person is, the more advisable it would be to avoid ever looking down upon him. Mrs. Leonowens almost got into hot water one day when, while the king and she were concocting a diplomatic message, he wanted a book and, helpfully, she dashed upstairs to get it. The Beebes told me that as an outgrowth of this veneration of the hair, the word *pham* (hair) is used for *I* when Siamese speak to persons to whom they owe respect—that is, in ordinary conversation. The king, as I have said, must be addressed far more abjectly than that.

The people of Siam, though Buddhists for generations, are incurably superstitious and deathly afraid of the *phis*. All of life is one long race in which you try to outwit and pacify the *phis*. A favorite protection against evil spirits is to wind around the wrist a piece of ordinary string that has been consecrated by a Buddhist priest. Once a Christian convert can be induced to take off his string, the missionaries rejoice in a real, honest-to-goodness conversion. But I am sorry to have to say that among the devout parishioners I saw in Mr. Beebe's church at Sunday services, there were a good many with bits of twine around the wrist.

As one might expect, death is surrounded with much superstition. As are pregnant women, dead mothers are believed to turn into particularly violent *phis*; no sooner has a mother passed away than the bereaved husband makes a beeline for the nearest bonzerie to get himself purified, no matter how much he may be needed in his motherless home. The dead are always wrapped in a coat which has been turned inside out "because they are now *phis*"—not an enlightening explanation. Perhaps the Lao think they can fool the *phi* into staying inside the coat and not flying about doing harm. Though fierce, these spirits are not credited with much intelligence and a careful Lao can guard against them pretty well. A *phi*, noticing that he sits on the outside of a well-known coat, may believe he is really outside and stay put. I confess this is just my own attempt at solving this puzzle of the turned-about coat. The wrists of the dead are tied together and a small basket is woven and hung across the doorway of the house to keep the *phis* away. Now why this should do any good, I can't even guess.

Depending upon the importance of a dead person, he will lie from two weeks to six months in a coffin in his home, with priests praying daily over him and food being offered him at the regular times by mourning relatives. Bamboo pipes attached at the proper places carry off the body fluids and sweet smelling herbs reduce the odor but, even so, I imagine the atmosphere gets pretty thick after a while. When cremation finally takes place, every friend and relative puts a lighted candle or a lighted wood shaving on the pile to speed the departed on his way into the next life, for Buddhists believe in reincarnation. Evidently the Lao believe that the spirit of a dead person remains with his corpse until it is burnt to ashes. They also tie so-called "spirit streamers" to the corpse just before it is cremated so that the spirit can find its way into the sky.

Naturally all these superstitions are held only by country people and old-fashioned persons who haven't acquired a Western veneer. For example, when Chulalongkorn's fifth queen died, there had to be a long period of waiting before cremation to allow for elaborate ceremonies and preparations. Instead of following the old Siamese system, Dr. Collier was asked to embalm her and, consequently, her cremation took an inordinately long time because the body was so well-preserved. The audience is said to have become distinctly restive.

All this and much more I wormed out of the busy Beebes, making myself a nuisance with my endless questions. But these people were exceedingly kind and patient. When I said I wanted to hire a car to drive to Chieng Sen, they decided to come along with the children and have a picnic. Old Chieng Sen is now merely a teak forest with a few tumbledown *chedis* lying half-buried in the undergrowth, but once it was an important city. The word *Chieng* in a city name indicates that it is a walled city. Chieng Sen was burned down in one of Siam's innumerable wars with Burma. As is customary, a new city was built a little distance away. New Chieng Sen is an important trading center, since it lies at the point where Siam, Burma, and Indo-China meet—right on the caravan trail from China which continues into Siam as far as Chieng Mai. A few decades ago, one could still see in Chieng Mai Yunnan traders who brought tea, silk, knives, scissors, pots, and pans from China, which is only 100 miles distant from Chieng Sen. Tea caravans were still going that way on occasion but we saw none. However, we met several caravans of bullock carts, which looked extremely ancient since they had solid wheels and no iron fittings. These huge wooden wheels turned slowly with the weirdest squeaks. Their piercing noise may offend unaccustomed ears, and there are ways to lessen it, so I was told. But on long, lonely journeys, the Siamese driver likes to hear the rhythmic squeak, which he finds soothing.

At Chieng Sen we came to the upper Mekong, already a majestic river as it flows through wooded hills, forming the border between Indo-China and Siam, but not nearly as broad as in Cambodia where we had first seen it.* As the Menam is the principal river of Siam, so the Mekong is the main waterway of Indo-China, and the Salween and Irrawaddy serve the same purpose for Burma. It is down these river valleys that the many races of the peninsula came from China and Tibet. We had a fine picnic on the bank of the Mekong, the youngsters bathing in the river, while various and sundry natives watched us with unflagging attention. Afterwards we drove through tangled jungle, on what can only be described as a cow path, to the confluence of the Me Sai and the Mekong. Here is the meeting place of the three countries, marked by a rock at the center of the confluence. We drove across the international bridge and a little way into Burma. It was a delightful drive, with constant vistas of blue river, thick bamboo clusters, and bushes with fragrant white blossoms. We saw several Burmese houses which reminded me of those of the Bataks in Sumatra, because their roofs are pointed and slant towards you and the houses are set on thick wooden poles. The Burmese here are all Shans and so look just like the Siamese across the border. We had tarried too long and had to hurry back to get across the bridge before 5:00 p.m.; if you are late you must pay a fine of five ticals.

---

*The Mekong is 2,600 miles long and has its source in the mountains of Tibet. It flows southward through Tibet and western China, thereafter becoming the boundary, first, between Burma and Indo-China and then, between Siam and Indo-China. At Paksé, the Mekong turns southeastward, crosses Cambodia and empties into the South China Sea below Saigon. It is one of the longest rivers of Asia and, like the Menam, forms a vast alluvial delta covered with rice fields. The first European to sing the praises of this mighty river was the Portuguese poet, Camoens, in his epic poem *Os Lusiadas* (The Portuguese). The story is told that when Camoens returned from Macao, his ship was wrecked at the mouth of the Mekong, and he swam ashore carrying aloft a copy of his book, in the manner of Caesar with his *Commentaries on the Gallic War.*

This is the road on which the mission children set forth each year to go to Woodstock, their American school in North India. It was a long way to school. First, all the children from North Siam assembled at the Beebes' house, which they reached by train from as far as Lampang and thence by bus to Chieng Rai. Then the entire group traveled by bus through Burma, staying at night in Baptist mission homes and collecting more children along the way. It took one day to Keng Tung, and two more to Taunggyi, close to the railhead. There the children boarded a train for Rangoon and, at Rangoon, a boat for Calcutta. From Calcutta they had another long journey by rail to Woodstock. They were allowed to travel on the Rangoon-Calcutta boat as deck passengers, but were fed second-class food and could use second-class cabins to wash and dress. The Indian government charged them only eight rupees ($2.40 at that time) for the ride to Woodstock. There were usually enough missionary children to fill one third-class coach in which they slept, cooked, and ate, generally with one teacher along to supervise them. For the children in the southern part of Siam, the trip to school was much easier, for they went by train to Penang and from there by boat to Kodaikanal in South India. The children who went via Chieng Rai were already seasoned travelers—no wonder they were such poised and independent little people. I saw many of them when they had their annual three-month vacation at Christmas time. It was a joy to observe the happy family life of the missionaries. Since they lived isolated from people of their own kind, they were naturally much closer than most other families, and the Christmas vacation was truly the annual high point in the lives of both parents and children.

The schools charged only $20 per month for tuition and full board, which was approximately what the missionaries received in children's allowances. This seemed to me eminently fair, as it permitted missionaries to give their children a good education. There was little else they could leave them. Their salaries were tiny and, though they managed to live fairly comfortable and dignified lives illuminated by a high purpose, they surely did not amass any worldly treasure.

On my last day in Chieng Rai we had a serious discussion concerning the relative merits of the mail bus, which was loaded with raw hides, and the Chinese rice truck, as the means of transportation for my return trip to Lampang. The bus ran more nearly on time than the Chinese truck; on the other hand, the hides smelled hideously. Even so, we decided on the bus because we reasoned that the wind would carry the smell of the hides backward and I could always move away when the bus stopped anywhere for more than a minute. This settled, we turned to the problem of how I was to make the driver stop the car, should need arise. The Reverend Mr. Beebe wrote out a few sentences for me, in Siamese, in English, and phonetically. We laughed till the tears ran down our cheeks at his efforts to get me to produce the proper Siamese tonal effects and the peculiar raucous or rasping sounds. I kept interrupting the lesson with demonstrations of how his morning sermon had sounded to me. Mr. Beebe liked to rumble in his deep voice, and my imitation had them in stitches. Finally, I managed to pronounce three sentences to his satisfaction. After all these exertions we found next day that the mail bus was full up—my place having been taken by the owner of the hides—and that on the Chinese truck there was a Chinese gentleman from Hong Kong who spoke excellent English and was eager and willing to act as interpreter. Twice I worked up courage to say to the driver *yut tee nee*, when, bang went a tire, and we had to stop anyway to fix it.

That day we had two blowouts and three thorough searches for opium. There were police stations all along the way. After they had made us pull to a stop, swarms of police crawled all over the bus, poking with long rods into the rice sacks, uncovering the driver's seat, opening the gasoline tank, looking into packages and suitcases, and even unscrewing the mudguards to look for hidden opium. The only thing they left untouched was my luggage, although I kept teasing them to open up and look at all the stuff I was smuggling. I hopped around the searchers to get pictures and, when the Chinese passenger told them that I "would be taking them with me to America," everybody smiled and wanted to get into the picture. Later I discovered that the truck I had picked belonged to one of the most notorious opium-smugglers. Luckily for me, nothing was found that day or we might all have ended up in jail.

We had a dozen or so passengers and twenty sacks of rice. The driver told me that the General Motors chassis of the truck had cost 2,000 ticals and it had cost 200 ticals to build the body in Siam. The freight for one sack of rice was 80 satang, and the passengers paid 1.50 ticals for the trip to Lampang, and less, of course, for shorter distances. I paid 2.50 ticals but then I rode first-class, next to the driver. I never saw a truck in complete repair on any trip through this region. The dashboard never functioned; for ignition, two wires were twisted, and the doors always hung precariously on bits of wire or string. Sitting next to the driver, I had to hold on to the door on my side all day or it would have fallen off and I with it. All the passengers were companionable and helped with the flat tires and with loading and unloading the rice. Occasionally, we were

New Year's festival with ornamental towers and "spirit streamers"

Opium search

hailed and given messages to be delivered down the road, or a passenger would see a relative and we had to stop so he could chat a little. In one town the bus waited until the Chinese gentlemen and I bargained for a silver bowl and a silver-link belt.

As the afternoon wore on, I began to get worried. We were still a long distance from Lampang and by then we had only two good back tires instead of the four this heavy truck normally carried. When we had our first blowout, they tried to fix it by pasting rubber pieces inside the casing although I warned them they would only waste the new inner tube by doing the job so badly. They would not listen so we promptly had another blowout, both the new tube and the casing being torn to pieces. Whereupon, they simply removed one of the two wheels on that side. The opposite side had also lost one of its two wheels on the way to Chieng Rai and it was not yet repaired. I discovered that one front light was missing and the other looked dubious, so I had visions of our dashing around the curves in pitch darkness. Just as I feared, the last and most mountainous part of the trip was made after dark with only a feeble light from the one defective lamp.

As we rounded a sharp curve—in neutral, of course, for all native drivers save gas by driving downhill in neutral—the light gave out and in the faint rays of the rising moon we noticed a huge, lumbering shape starting to cross the road. Luckily our brakes held—we stopped only a few yards from a wild elephant who moved slowly across, paying no attention to us. We were as quiet as mice and, for a while, the driver was sufficiently subdued to keep to a reasonable speed. However, everything was soon forgotten and we careened around the curves again at breakneck speed, while I cursed and threatened the driver with dire punishment. In America, I declared, irresponsible persons would be put in jail for running in neutral, without lights, down a mountain road. In America, heavy trucks like this one had six wheels and good tires. In America, I added, a rattletrap like this one would be thrown on the junk pile, and what sort of country was this where such drivers and such trucks were allowed to jeopardize the lives of innocent travelers?

All this was duly translated by my Chinese friend. The driver looked pleased to be considered such a daredevil, and the passengers got much satisfaction from telling me how many accidents had happened on this road and how many people had been killed each time. I finally put my hand on the emergency brake and threatened to pull it unless we slowed down. This cooled our driver somewhat but I hadn't thought of this good scheme until we were almost in Lampang. What worried me was that I felt certain nobody in the bus knew first aid and if we had an accident we'd be helpless and nobody would hear of it for days perhaps. Also, I remembered gruesome tales I had heard about unemployed Chinese coolies with criminal tendencies (Chinese, of course, since all bad men in Siam are Chinese, if you believe the Thai) who are supposed to roam the interior and to think nothing of killing a traveler to get his gold fillings or of cutting off a finger rather than taking the time to remove a ring. I didn't really believe these tales, but it seemed wise to slip my wedding ring into my purse. About the fillings in my teeth I could do nothing.

Although I really was a bit scared, the trip was wildly exciting. Jungles at nighttime are thrilling, for one doesn't know who or what may be lurking about. The road ran through lovely mountain country. For a while a brook flowed alongside, gurgling pleasantly. All sorts of strange animal and bird sounds came from the dark trees as we whizzed by. There was hardly a straight stretch of more than a hundred yards, for the road kept running in sharp S curves. But finally we drove up safely before the house of Miss Lucy Starling whose guest I was to be that night. As I crawled stiffly from my perch beside the driver, she said: "You've just time for a bath. We're having people in for dinner." Twenty minutes later, washed, combed, and dressed up, I sat at a candlelit table with people in evening clothes, while deft white-clad boys glided about serving delicious food. It was quite a contrast.

Miss Starling was a missionary and one of those women who surprise you by being an experienced hostess. She had people from the British teak industry as guests. One young couple was especially interesting. The wife was blonde, fragile, and fair. She wore a green chiffon blouse and a long taffeta skirt, and looked as if she had just stepped out of a beauty parlor. Yet she told me that she always accompanied her husband into the jungle, where he spent three weeks each month supervising the cutting of trees. They took along two small huts, their wireless, a portable bathtub, cots, mosquito nets, and other supplies, and made themselves comfortable. Twice a week ice was brought out to them. Sometimes they had a week's leave and would often go to Bangkok, which seemed to them a metropolis. At Christmas they always joined associates in the teak business in some central town like Chieng Mai or Lampang for an annual get-together.

Their company allowed them a six-month trip to England after every three and one-half years. The pay was good but there was absolutely no future in this work. A man can only do it while he is young enough to stand the rough life. There are few high positions and many men to compete for them. I wondered what other work a middle-aged man could qualify for when he was too old for life in the jungle. Sickness is a problem, too, for there are few doctors outside Bangkok. The young woman's husband couldn't eat ice cream because he had a tooth cavity. He had to manage somehow for he did not have time to see a dentist. A bad case of this sort happened to the Presbyterian mission doctor, Dwight Nelson, in Chieng Rung, Yunnan while I was in Siam. He had to have an infected tooth pulled, and his native assistant bungled the job and left part of the root of the infected tooth in the gum, at the same time taking off a piece of the next tooth and exposing a nerve. Dr. Nelson had to travel eight days by pony, two days by bus, and one day by train to get to a dentist in Bangkok. There wasn't one nearer. I met him coming and going; on my way south, he was completely doped up and wouldn't have reached his destination if the Siamese hadn't guided him along.

Miss Starling was an older woman and unmarried but, when surrounded by her nine children, she had the look of a happy mother. She had rescued all these little ones from the woods where their widowed fathers had abandoned them. They had been fattened up and were round, rosy, and happy. She adopted these children and raised them Siamese-fashion, also teaching them English which would be to their credit when they started looking for work.

After only an overnight stay with Miss Starling, it was time to be on my way once again. Although my visits with these missionaries and their friends had been of short duration, I have often remembered them for their many kindnesses and the warmth of hospitality they extended to me.

9
Back to Bangkok

The next day I took the express train back to Bangkok, also known as Krung Thep (City of Angels). When I arrived at the station the following morning, the number one boy of the Rajdhani Hotel was on the platform to meet me and welcomed me like a long-lost friend. My old room at the hotel was prepared for me and nicely shined up—it was almost like coming home. I enjoyed being warm again after having shivered for so long in the cooler climate up north. Here it was so hot that one could not stay dry more than a few minutes, but I liked it. My pedicab boy was waiting for me too, and after I had unpacked, we went to the Siam Society to look up some of the books on Siam I had been advised to read. Dr. Harris had given me a letter which opened the society library for me and I spent many hours browsing happily among many books and magazines full of interesting information on Siam. I found it strange, however, that this country with its relatively high level of civilization should have almost no reliable records of its past. I was told that they were all burned in the sack of Ayuthia.

The Siamese are not an historically minded people and what records we have must be regarded as more legend than fact. What interested me chiefly was the origin of these people, who seemed to be a felicitous fusion of Chinese and Malay racial elements. Siam had lost most of her Malay subjects to Britain in 1909 when she ceded suzerainty over the four northern states of Malaya (Kedah, Kelantan, Perlis, and Trengganu). I was surprised to discover that the kingdom of Siam is of fairly recent date, at least as compared with such ancient empires as China or Japan. Though the Thai have been trickling down from their ancient homeland, Nanchao, for more than a thousand years, the great waves of migrants that conquered the older Khmer kingdoms did not arrive until the middle of the thirteenth century.

The kingdom of Sukhothai-Sawankhalok was founded by the Khmers but was eventually conquered by the Thai who intermarried with the Khmers and adopted most of their civilization. The first king of Sukhothai was crowned Sri Intaratitya but is known in history as Phra Ruang. His seizure of Sukhothai in 1238 was the beginning of a territorial and cultural expansion. Its most important ruler was Rama Kamheng, the son of the first king, who had conquered the whole of the Menam Valley. He opened diplomatic and cultural relations with China and brought back craftsmen, notably Chinese potters who set up kilns in Sukhothai and Sawankhalok. He is best known for the invention of the Thai script comprised of Khmer, Mon, and Sanskrit. After his death, about 1317, the kingdom declined in power until it became a vassal of Ayudhya, an emergent city-state to the south.

Ayudhya, founded in 1350 by Rama Tibodi, was destined to become the greatest of the Siamese kingdoms for the next 400 years. Under the reigns of three of its most notable kings, Trailok, Naresuan, and Narai, diplomatic contacts with the West were opened allowing missionaries and traders into the country. Although invaded frequently by Burma, it was not until 1767 that the Burmese were able to conquer this kingdom and totally destroy it.

The remnants of the Siamese army were gathered together by a general of Chinese origin who soon proclaimed himself King of Siam and drove the Burmese out of the country. This General Taksin established his capital at Thonburi, on the western bank of the Menam, opposite a small settlement which was to become Bangkok. Becoming insane in his later years, he was dethroned and succeeded in 1782 by one of his generals, Chakri, who founded the present capital at Bangkok and the Chakri Dynasty under the title Rama I.

Virginia Thompson's scholarly book *Thailand: The New Siam* was, of course, not then available so I had to piece together bits and pieces of information that I found in various articles in the *Siam Society Journal* and in books written by ethnologists, travelers, explorers, and diplomatic envoys, supplemented by information gained from talks with all sorts of people who knew Siam well. I spent every free minute between sightseeing and shopping in the Siam Society Library. I was particularly interested in the articles by Prince Damrong in the *Siam Society Journal,* by W. A. Graham's two-volume study *Siam,* John Crawfurd's *Journal of an Embassy from the Governor-General of India to the Courts of Siam and Cochin China, The Complete Journal of Townsend Harris,* D. McGilvary's *A Half Century Among the Siamese and the Lao,* and the scholarly works of H. G. Quaritch Wales, to name but a few.

One morning I took a fascinating trip to the Sampeng district of Bangkok, where the Chinese live. There I wandered through a long, covered street with shops on either side selling a multitude of items: crockery (similar to items I had bought in Chefoo a year before), baskets, silverware, copper utensils, knives, hardware, flowers, fruits, textiles, food of every imaginable kind, Chinese drugs, straw hats, slippers, etc. All the signs were in Chinese characters; all the passersby were of Chinese origin, and one might well imagine oneself in the Celestial Empire. This street is intersected by one of the *klongs*. A delightfully picturesque bridge connects the two sections of the street. Here one is jostled by a multitude of beggars, flower vendors, merchants, and Chinese of all descriptions, amidst a profusion of bales, baskets, heaped-up cotton goods, and piles of assorted merchandise.

I wandered around trying to find a certain kind of tempered-bronze knife which we had admired among the purchases brought back from Bangkok by friends. These thin, slightly curved, sharp knives make excellent fruit knives. Since they are made of bronze, fruit juices do not tarnish them. I finally found a street where all the stores sold these knives and girded myself to make a purchase. But even with my Siamese phrase book, I could not manage the numbers game. I therefore made a little heap of money and a little heap of knives and pointed from one to the other. Immediately a crowd gathered and got into the act. One strong-willed matron took the business in hand. As soon as she had discovered that I could not understand even simple arithmetic, she started juggling the two heaps until she had matched money and knives to her satisfaction, giving me back a good bit of the money I had put out. When I found that the knives were incredibly cheap when purchased in this fashion, I wanted more and upset the whole arrangement by increasing the heap of knives. The crowd made faces, thinking I did not want to pay the proper price. So I emptied my whole purse beside the heap of knives I had made, pushing it across to the storekeeper. In a flash the matron was upon it, gathering it in before the delighted merchant could pocket the money. She carefully counted out what she considered reasonable and returned the rest to me. I liked this manner of buying so much that I begged her to help me buy a blanket which she did, getting me one of Indian make in fluffy cotton for 25 American cents. In return, I bought her a market basket which pleased her greatly.

After lunch I had an interview with Prince Wan (Wan Waithayakon Vorawan) which had been arranged for me by Mr. Zimmerman. I was led through many elegantly furnished drawing rooms (European style) and asked to be seated. Presently a distinguished gentleman entered briskly and shook hands with me. I interposed several "Serene Highnesses" in our conversation to indicate that I knew his exalted rank and respected it. Prince Wan was considered by many in the government to be a brilliant man. This was evident since only two princes had been kept on by the new regime, namely he and his brother, Prince Sakol (Sakol Wanakon), and this for the simple reason that they were indispensable to the country. Under the new law they could not be the heads of ministries but they could be and were advisors to the ministers. Prince Wan thought their greatest value to the country was their ability to interpret the aims of the new government to disgruntled foreigners and the strange ways of foreigners to the new men ruling Siam. Accordingly, he tried to explain to me just how the new regime differed from the old. "I have a theory which explains it well," he said. "When you speak of a 'nation' you mean both a 'country' and a 'people.' So naturally we cannot have many foreigners controlling our economic life. . . . We must train our own people to do what the foreigners have heretofore done and then we shall really be an independent 'nation'."

I mildly interposed that I had heard it said the Siamese were a farming people who did not like trade, commerce, and hard physical labor, except in the fields. He replied that this was true but the people could be educated. For example, he, himself, had learned to like work. His plan was to induce foreign firms to help by taking on young Siamese and training them so they could eventually take over from the foreigners. He hastened to add, however, that Siam was big enough for both foreign and native firms.

I found his discussion of the government's plan to nationalize the teak industry delightful. At that time 98 percent of the teak firms were foreign and he felt this should not go on. The new government had set itself the goal of managing 50 percent of the teak business itself and leasing the remainder to foreign firms. While the prince approved of this as an ultimate end, he was a practical man and could see the difficulties. He therefore explained to me that, really, the law couldn't work for a long time yet, since, after all, everything depended on the elephants. Whoever owned the elephants automatically controlled the teak business. The foreigners had all the elephants so no one need be worried. It would take a long time before the government could collect enough elephants to make the law effective.

As for the Chinese monopoly of the rice trade, the prince seemed willing to let that go for a while, but indicated that eventually rice sacks would have to be made smaller so that Siamese coolies could carry them.

The next day I saw Prince Wan again and met Prince Sakol, who seemed less sanguine about the chances of remaking the Siamese. I thought he realized also that the new government was not so progressive in fact as in theory. Since his special interest lay in social problems, he probably was a better judge of men and knew how hard it is to remake human nature. He thought it likely Siam would remain primarily an agricultural country. Since the country is fertile and underpopulated, he saw no reason why it should be forced to industrialize itself. Prince Sakol appeared to be more suave and *simpatico* than his brother. He also seemed to be more typically Siamese in his lighthearted attitude towards weighty problems.

While I was chatting pleasantly with these two princes, I kept thinking what a truly amazing change had taken place in their country since King Mongkut took the first tentative steps towards Westernizing old Siam. Left to itself, the East is indeed unchanging, but once it is opened to Western thought and technique, it often transforms itself with breathtaking speed. The Siam we saw only seventy-five years after Mrs. Leonowens arrived to open her school in the palace was so different from the country she described that it was sometimes difficult to believe it really was the same nation.

I had recently finished reading a description of the audience given John Crawfurd in 1822 when he visited Bangkok as the official representative of Britain seeking permission for British traders to enter the country. After much wrangling, Crawfurd was permitted to dispense with the customary prostration before the king and to approach him with the respectful bow accorded royalty in his own country. He found it difficult to advance through the audience hall because the entire floor was covered with the prostrate bodies of Siam's highest dignitaries on whom Crawfurd did not dare step.* Yet, here I sat informally opposite royal princes who spoke as directly and to the point as any European or American and who would have felt quite uncomfortable in the Siamese court of Crawfurd's or Mrs. Leonowens' time, when speech was long-winded, roundabout, and circumscribed by innumerable rules. I simply could not envision anyone crawling on all fours and banging his head on the floor. Simplification and democratization of social intercourse ought surely to be counted on the credit side if the West's impact on the East is ever judged in the balance.

One of the memories of Bangkok I cherish is of a moonlight ride by sampan through the *klongs* with Miss Tardt Pradipasena, a charming Siamese girl I met through the Zimmermans. It is a romantic experience to glide through the quiet waters where you can still see a few late bathers. We observed people eating supper by the light of small oil lamps, and listened to Siamese music (pleasant to the Western ear) coming from houses completely hidden by bushes along the *klongs* and the banks of the Chao Phraya. Sometimes it seemed to come right out of what looked like jungle but was, of course, simply a Siamese garden. Other sampans passed quietly with their small oil lamps at the bow. Moonlight in the tropics has its special flavor; it seems to bring out the fragrance of sweet-smelling flowers and to endow houses, boats, and people with an air of mystery. When the moon shines on the *chedis* of Bangkok's many *wats* they attain a fairylike beauty; one forgets the simple materials of which they are fashioned.

*John Crawfurd, *Journal of an Embassy from the Governor-General of India to the Courts of Siam and Cochin China*, Vol. I, p. 143.

Next morning Miss Tardt went to the market with me to help me purchase a large bamboo basket (for ten satang), which we filled with various fruits and a box of crackers, as well as two empty bottles which I had the hotel people sterilize and fill with water for me. Then we went to her house and had a spicy Siamese lunch which she cooked right next to the table in the open air; quite sensible in a hot climate since everybody is comfortable and the house does not become heated from the cooking fire. We ate in the open space below the house, which stood on stilts. As is the case with all good Siamese householders, Miss Tardt kept the space underneath the house immaculately clean so that it could be used as an extra room. Her food was delicious and her conversation interesting.

I left Bangkok that afternoon on the weekly express for Ubon. This city lies northeast of Bangkok, near the Indo-Chinese border, approximately at the spot where a direct line east bisects Indo-China. I chose to go via Ubon because I wanted to cross through French Laos, even though I had been warned that Ubon and that whole corner of Siam were at the end of nowhere. I couldn't have gone there if the Wattena Wittya people hadn't sent a wire to the Christian Missionary people in Ubon, asking them to meet my train and put me up. I should have been stumped if that wire hadn't got there in time, for I am certain no one at the station could speak any language known to me.

Ubon is not Ubon at all, as one might rashly conclude from seeing it marked on the map as the terminus of the railroad. When I arrived early next morning, I saw that the train had stopped at a place called Varindr. (Luckily, Siamese stations are marked with their English names below the Siamese; otherwise, foreigners would really be lost.) This was obviously the end of the line. I couldn't see anything in Varindr, except the station and a few ramshackle buses into which the passengers were hustled with their baggage. There was a terrific commotion, then the buses dashed off at breakneck speed. While I was still wondering where we were going, the buses stopped at a river and we were ferried across in a rickety boat, poled by a ragged boatman. Not until you get to the opposite bank of the river have you finally arrived in Ubon.

I was happy when I saw Mrs. Robert Chrisman with her little girl Carol coming to meet me. I felt that now all was well, and indeed it was. I came at an opportune moment. Her husband was away at a mission meeting in Dalat, Indo-China, so there was room for me in their large screened bedroom and my arrival did not upset the household routine. These lucky people actually had one completely screened-in room—something I hadn't seen since leaving Manila. It was open to the breeze on three sides and sleeping was marvelous. I had become inured to sleeping under mosquito netting but I didn't like it. The

Chrismans had saved a long time before they could manage to install the bedroom screens. Someday they hoped to be able to put screens into Mr. Chrisman's small study, too, which did double duty as a guest room.

Nobody who hasn't traveled endless hours through a strange land, surrounded by people who, though friendly and kind, can't talk with you, and whose strange customs keep you constantly alert and on guard against tainted water and food; nobody who hasn't arrived dirty and dusty at some unknown destination, can possibly visualize how good the breakfast table at the Chrismans looked to me. That morning we had the sort of breakfast one has every day at home and takes for granted, but which looks like manna on a trip like mine. It was wonderful to be in an American home.

Ubon is a town of some 10,000 inhabitants but looks smaller. There are no notable temples, palaces, or buildings other than the bamboo and wooden houses of the Siamese. In the downtown area there were some Hindu shops but otherwise Ubon was a true Siamese town. Only two white missionary families lived there: the Chrismans, who were Christian and Missionary Alliance people, and the Abels, who were Seventh Day Adventists. There were also a French Catholic nun, who was mother superior of a native convent, and a solitary Frenchman, Monsieur Troude, who had a garage and a bus service. Occasionally, a French Catholic priest came from Indo-China to say Mass in the convent. This was the total white population. Oddly enough, these isolated foreigners had no social contact with one another. I suppose this was because in a sense they were competitors and there were so few natives willing to be converted that competition was sometimes a little bitter. I believe that the two American families had never enjoyed dinner together or with the Frenchman before I arrived, but in my honor the Abels had a party and everybody got along splendidly. I hope this initiated a new era of good feeling and social visiting!

We looked up M. Troude at once to get his advice on my connections to Paksé (across the border) and from there eastward through French Laos. He was overjoyed to find someone with whom he could speak French and promised to take complete charge of my travel plans. M. Troude is one of those middle-sized, bemoustached, middle-aged, kindly French bourgeois whom one always likes right away. He was tremendously chivalrous and courteous. He could talk with the other Americans only in Siamese so he enjoyed even my rusty French.

I stayed five days with Esther Chrisman, read innumerable books on Siam and Indo-China, listened to many interesting tales of mission life, slept marvelously, and rested from the overabundance of impressions that had rushed at me during the previous weeks. One evening we went into town and listened to the native preacher who had taken over in the absence of Mr. Chrisman. I was delighted to see that he drew a large crowd and managed to distribute several pamphlets.

On the whole, it is uphill work trying to convert Buddhists, especially for Protestant missionaries. The Catholic missions have been more successful and have a considerable congregation in Indo-China. Perhaps this is because there are superficial similarities between Catholicism and Buddhism. Superficial as they may be to a people who tend to value form more than substance and have little talent for deep religiosity, these insignificant similarities may well constitute a strong attraction. There were then thirty times as many Catholics in Siam as Protestants; even at that, the Catholics constituted only about one quarter of one percent of the population. In Indo-China, where Catholic missionaries had been active since 1615,* there were about one and a half million Catholic Annamites in a population of seventeen million. In the other protectorates (Laos, Cambodia, Cochin China), the missionaries had not been as successful.

Speaking of the success of Catholic missionaries, Mrs. Leonowens made this comment:

> When a poor ignorant Buddhist goes into his temples he sees the images of the Buddha, and he sees certain forms and prostrations practised, the burning of incense, the bowing before the well-lit shrines, and hears prayers uttered in an unknown tongue, and he knows also that the most heinous sin that can be committed by the Buddhist priest is the violation of his oath of celibacy. And if from idle curiosity he should be induced to enter a Roman Catholic chapel or church, to his surprise and delight he observes not only forms and ceremonies very nearly approaching to those used in his own temple, but also images and pictures far more beautiful and attractive than those of his own gods. On inquiring he finds that the priests of this faith also do not marry, that they have the marvellous power to absolve the transgressor from the consequences of his deadly sins, and that the only thing necessary to escape the irresistible "wheel of the law" is faith in Christ.†

The Seventh Day Adventists were resented by the other Protestant missions because they were considered to be interlopers. Realizing the waste in duplication of effort, the major Protestant denominations had gentlemen's agreements which, in effect, divided the Asiatic mission into spheres of interest. Thus Siam was practically a Presbyterian preserve, except in the east; Burma was primarily Baptist; Sumatra, a Rhënish Evangelical Mission; etc. Since there are never many converts in Buddhist and Moslem countries, this made sense. But the Seventh Day Adventists did not go along with this division.

*C. E. Bouillevaux, *L'Annam et le Cambodge: Voyages et Notices Historiques*, p. 32.

†Anna H. Leonowens, *Siamese Harem Life*, p. 184.

They specialized in excellent hospitals and were comparatively well supported because all Adventists tithed and each mission was assigned the tithes of one or more specific weeks. The other denominations accused them of winning away their own converts by giving the converts lucrative jobs.

The fervent desire of missionaries to win new disciples has unfortunately sometimes been abused by would-be Christians who have discovered that one can obtain a satisfactory living by letting oneself be converted. In China these unscrupulous characters were called Rice Christians. Father Bouillevaux reported a more astonishing variation on this theme—the so-called Coffin Christians of Singapore. The Chinese attached extraordinary importance to possession of a coffin which was often held through life as a precious piece of furniture. Some Catholic missionaries gave away coffins to pleading Chinese and found their parishes to be increasing miraculously.*

Robert and Teresa Abel were evangelists, as were the Chrismans. Since there were no Western-style medical services in the city, the missionaries had to travel all the way to Bangkok for every illness and for every baby. Under the circumstances, they needed to cultivate mutual tolerance and help one another to overcome a sense of loneliness, for this was an isolated spot in which to make a home.

I felt this loneliness as Mrs. Chrisman and I walked in the evenings on the broad grassy road in front of her house. We never ventured far. It was a bit eerie to be completely surrounded by different people with whom one had little in common. I suppose we were safer than in many big cities in the West, but we didn't feel that way. We took the Chrismans' dog along on our walks, and we locked the house securely when we went to bed. The country around us was too big and silent and unfamiliar to feel entirely comfortable at night. Mission wives are brave women. They often have to stay home when the husbands go on mission errands. What if they had a sudden attack of appendicitis? Nobody in remote Ubon would be able to help.

Next door lived a leper who had just taken a young girl to himself. His house looked much like the Chrismans'. Both stood on wooden stilts and were roomy, airy, and comfortable. He was a rich man so he had no difficulty getting permission to live there. The country hasn't nearly enough leprosaria anyway to take care of all its lepers.† The young girl had come from the country, knowing no one

---

*C. E. Bouillevaux, *L'Annam et le Cambodge: Voyages et Notices Historiques*, p. 17.

†Though leprosy was prevalent in Siam, the government had failed utterly to deal with this problem. There were only two leprosaria, the Presbyterian asylum in Chieng Mai and a Red Cross asylum in Phra Pradaeng. Probably fewer than 2 percent of Siam's lepers were in leper colonies. There were no accurate statistics as to the number of the afflicted, but estimates as high as 50,000 had been made by medical authorities.

and needing a job. She had agreed to bring him food from the market, cook, and clean house, and then lived with him. The Siamese didn't seem upset over this but the Chrismans were bothered, as was I. Since the man had money, he could live as he liked provided he remained in his house and garden and did not mix with crowds, go to the movies, shop in stores, or travel on trains or buses. He still looked entirely healthy.

M. Troude visited us every day to chat a little and to tell me about his preparations for my trip. He decided that the bus to Paksé would be too uncomfortable and that I should hire his own little ramshackle Citroën. I could never get him to quote me a price. I think he felt that business ought not to be mixed into our pleasant social relationship. At any rate, I should not have questioned anything he charged for he certainly needed a little profit. He often remarked how hard it was to compete with Chinese who work all day and most of the night, eat a handful of rice, and are satisfied with a deal where they sell for one tical what has cost them one tical. I respected M. Troude's sensibilities and agreed to settle with his brother-in-law in Paksé, who managed to fix the charges without emotional involvement.

Between discussing travel arrangements, M. Troude and I talked politics. I was amused at his way of referring to Hitler and Mussolini as the "little ones." He would say: *"Ah, ils sont bien gardés, ces petits"* (they're well guarded, these little ones). He had fought in the Great War on the Balkan front with the Russians and felt dubious about these erstwhile allies. But the British, he thought, would do. Nothing could shake his conviction that only the French really knew how to fight.

His had not been an easy life. When things were difficult in France after the war ended in 1918, he came out to French Laos to enter into partnership with his brother-in-law, also a Troude, for they were all cousins, besides being related by marriage. These two established a business in Paksé, dealing in stick lac* and gasoline. Things started slowly but eventually they did well and expanded. Then came 1929 and the market collapsed; they lost every penny saved in eleven years of hard work. Not only did the price of stick lac tumble because of the general drop in all raw material prices, but a new chemical substitute nearly ruined them; only the gasoline got them through the depression without bankruptcy. M. Troude moved to Ubon and opened a garage and there he was waiting, as he remarked, until he won the *grand prix* in the lottery. He lived in the old French Consulate, which

---

*Lac is the product of a small insect, *coccus lacca*, prevalent in India, the Indies, Burma, Siam, and Indo-China. The insect feeds on the sap of certain trees and exudes a resin called *stick lac*, from which sealing wax and varnishes are made.

had been closed for a long time and was gradually falling into ruins: a depressingly large, empty building, guarded by blue and green elephant statues almost buried in a weed-grown garden. The once-elegant brocade on the chairs in the finely proportioned rooms had tears, and from the walls hung torn, silk draperies bearing witness to former grandeur. France once hoped to incorporate all of Laos in her Indo-Chinese empire and this splendid ruin must have been part of the build-up.

Most Siamese, at one time or another, spoke proudly of the fact that only three Asiatic countries escaped European colonization, and Siam was one of them. What saved her was the jealousy between France and Britain, both intent on incorporating all of the Indo-Chinese peninsula in their colonial empires. In 1904 they finally compromised their dispute in a general settlement of all outstanding controversies, which smoothed the way for the Triple Entente against Germany. Britain was confirmed in her possession of Burma, France of Indo-China, and Siam was allowed to remain independent, though shorn of parts of Cambodia and Laos in the east, and Malaya in the south, over which she claimed suzerainty.

One day Mrs. Chrisman and I talked about "paying guests" and I discovered that these were not always desirable people. Among the problems are American college students who bum around the world. The Chrismans and the Beebes had a number of unpleasant experiences with youngsters who stayed on and on, demanding much and never offering to pay their way. Still these were not the worst guests. Once Mrs. Chrisman was visited for ten days by a British missionary lady from India who always wore dark glasses. Mrs. Chrisman's suspicions finally got the better of her and she asked the lady point-blank about her eyes. It turned out that she had trachoma in an advanced stage. This is such an infectious disease that long before we in the United States screened immigrants, we did check for this disease before letting any immigrant disembark; nobody with trachoma could enter the United States. If not treated, trachoma leads to blindness. I can well imagine how Mrs. Chrisman felt, since her little girl was then a tiny baby with whom the careless lady missionary had enjoyed playing.

Another time, one of the Swiss Plymouth Brethren missionaries from Indo-China turned up at the Chrismans, bringing his adopted native daughter. The girl had an unhealthy look about her, so Mrs. Chrisman warned her servants to scald the child's dishes. Later it came out that she had leprosy and had been ill for five years. Her adopted father wanted to take her to the Chieng Mai leper colony, but the Siamese railroad officials recognized the disease and would not let him travel unless he engaged an entire rail coach. So he had to turn around and take her back to the government asylum, which he hated to do "since it wasn't Christian." The good man never seemed to have considered the risks to which he was exposing other people. He was determined to get his child into a Christian leper colony because he loved her and wanted to shield her against the possibility of losing her faith. By delaying, he may well have ruined her chance of recovery.

I later told this story to Mrs. Homera Homer-Dixon, the missionary lady with whom I stayed in Hanoi. She said she could well believe this of Plymouth Brethren. She had once stayed several days with another of this strange sect and their unworldiness had simply amazed her. To their great credit, they shirk no danger or difficulty in their mission work and have done well by those poor creatures whom Lao superstitions make outcasts. Like all primitives, the Lao are deeply convinced that every misfortune that befalls them is caused by evil spirits. Whenever tragedy of one sort or another (mostly illness) occurs, the village witch doctor is called to determine who caused it. As often as not, he will pick some villager whom he may not like and say that this one has an evil eye, whereupon the unfortunate is thrown out of the village and has to live as best he can in the jungle. The Plymouth Brethren specialize in succoring these outcasts. They collect them and settle them in a model village built by them on a large tract of land, which they bought from the government. The Brethren live in the midst of this native village with no amenities of any sort. Their many children grow up without benefit of any schooling whatsoever.

These missionaries hold their wives in low esteem. I believe the men will grant them possession of souls, but they treat them more as if they were a species of animal fit only to keep house and bear children. The men always enter a room first, sit down first, eat first—the women following meekly. If a woman happens to be seated (and that probably does not happen too often during their busy days) and a man enters, she must rise. They think nothing of imposing the hardships of jungle living on their wives. The woman with whom Mrs. Homer-Dixon stayed had a dozen children. She had the help of an Annamite doctor for the first, but the rest were born right in the jungle with only her impractical husband around. The men look like Old Testament patriarchs, with huge beards and long hair. The children are neglected and have lice in their hair. Mrs. Homer-Dixon thought this was carrying the Lord's work too far!

Exactly one month after we had entered Siam at Aranya, I left for Paksé, thus avoiding payment of the fee of 200 ticals collected from foreigners who stay longer than that. Kind M. Troude visited me that morning to talk once more about my travel plans. They seemed simple to me, but he took as much trouble as if he had been plotting a royal tour—and then accompanied me part of the way, as a gesture of friendship. His little old car was a museum piece. There were wires strung all over it, so I kept myself closely together in order to avoid getting a shock from touching them. I am apprehensive about electrical things. The driver had to hold fast to the clutch all the way otherwise an infernal racket issued from the innards of the car. The road was one of the most impassable I had ever encountered. We drove in deep ruts with the body of the car scraping the ground. We did almost all the 130 kilometers in second gear, even though we were traveling on completely level ground. On this whole long stretch we met only one other motor vehicle—the car bringing Mr. Chrisman back from Dalat. He was surprised to be stopped by a solitary white woman greeting him with: "Mr. Chrisman, I presume." I knew he was expected.

My exit from the Land of the White Elephant was typically Siamese. These people love to practice their English on you. Ordinarily a person is stopped near the border by a customs guard on a bicycle and merely shows him his passport to check on the time spent in Siam. But not so with me. The bicycle man begged me to accompany him to the immigration office some distance from the road, where I was greeted solemnly by a young chap who brought a chair, asked me to sit down, had tea brought, and obviously considered this a proper occasion for sociability. In rather good English he questioned me on my plans, my impressions of Siam, how I thought it compared to other countries visited by me, and, of course, where I came from. Then he told me the story of his life. It appeared that he was part Malay, part Thai. The government had sent him to this out-of-the-way post which, for a man of his breeding and sensibilities, constituted a great hardship. The country people thereabouts were still pretty savage, though he was trying to civilize them. He sadly missed the amenities of Bangkok, but in a year he expected to be transferred and in the meantime he must take advantage of any chance passer-by with whom he may be able to engage in polite conversation. He said he managed to get to Ubon three times a week, otherwise he would go crazy, vegetating in this savage village. He liked movies and preferred the American kind. His favorite was Dick Powell, and how did I think he compared with Cary Grant. We discussed various Hollywood actors and actresses at length, comparing their merits. I suppose one had to consider this part of the immigration formalities. Finally I had to leave so as not to miss the ferry to Paksé. He then asked if there was anything at all he could do to facilitate my journey, and when I told him I had only large notes of Indo-Chinese money and would like some change, he sent someone to get me smaller bills and coins. This being Siam, there was no question of receiving anything but the correct change. He was the last honest person to handle money for me until I got back home.

What pleased him inordinately was to have the whole village stand around open-mouthed, watching him converse in English with the stranger. When I left he asked me diffidently if I would shake hands with him and this we did at length. I complimented him effusively on his excellent English and sympathized with his lonely life, particularly after he confided in me that he was still a bachelor. We parted the best of friends, with him walking beside the car until we came to the end of the village street. I do like the Siamese. They are polite and helpful but never obsequious. They are, in fact, indpendent people and anyone who tried to pull white superiority would not get on well at all. If you treat them as equals, however, they treat you like royalty.

The transition from Siam to Indo-China almost escaped me. At one place, a wooden barrier across the road was lifted by some people who looked into our car but said nothing. I couldn't be sure that this was all the official recognition I would get before passing under the tricolor until I saw a sign in a village saying *Dispensaire*. Evidently I was now in French Laos.

10
French Laos

We passed numerous carabao herds on our way. As soon as they noticed us, the beasts started crossing and recrossing the road. My chauffeur swore volubly, and the herders stood there open-mouthed, looking at me as if I were a circus freak. We were at the village of Muong Kau where the ferry crosses to Paksé, in French Laos, and had arrived at 5:00 p.m., only to be told that the ferry would not leave until 7:00 p.m., as it had to wait for some buses. The buses would be late since they had to wait for a boat coming up the river, and the boat had to wait for something else—I've forgotten what it was.

There, the Mekong is much broader than at Chieng Sen, though not as wide as at Phnom Penh, where I had first seen it, and runs south between high tablelands for some distance. Since I was tired from the day-long jouncing in M. Troude's car and anxious to get to the government rest house in Paksé, the driver and I went down the steep canyon road which led to the river, looking for a sampan. But one look at the rapid current of the Mekong convinced me I had better not chance it in a sampan—to the great relief of the driver who was no hero either. He didn't mind waiting because he had found many friends with whom to pass the time, while I sat in solitary splendor in the car, feeling lonely on the dizzy height of my exalted position. I had only an Annamite to talk with, whose atrocious French soon gave me a headache. It seems he was the customs man, for he asked to see my bags. I thought I might as well make use of him since he was the only French-speaking person there, so I put him in charge of my luggage and he did indeed see to it that it got safely on and off the ferry.

In compensation I had the spectacle of a magnificent sunset over the flat-topped mountains. The landscape was wild and majestic. A cold wind came on towards evening, ruffling the waters of the big river and making it look unruly and dangerous. The mountains hulked like monstrous forms over Paksé which soon disappeared in the darkness, leaving only a few tiny lights to reassure me it was still there.

While I was waiting—none too patiently—I kept thinking of a book I had just finished reading at the Chrismans', *The French in Indo-China*, which gave a brief English resumé of the famous exploration of the Mekong by a band of eleven intrepid Frenchmen and their native bearers led, first, by Doudart de Lagrée and, after his death, by Francis Garnier,* a naval lieutenant. They were the first white men to follow the course of the river into its upper reaches in Yunnan and, though their explorations took place only some seventy years before my visit, it was a dangerous undertaking, calling for great courage and perseverance. They stopped at Ubon, where they witnessed the coronation of the local king and described an anointing ceremony which may possibly have been identical to that of the kings of Angkor. Siam was strongly influenced by Khmer culture, especially in matters pertaining to royal ceremonies. At Ubon, the king divested himself of his clothes, donned a white mantle and crouched below a stone dragon—resembling the Angkor *naga* in shape—where he received ablution, the water having previously been poured into the body of the creature. Simultaneously, a bonze set free two doves to symbolize the joy of all nature in the happy event.†

I imagine this expedition may have traveled over the same route I had just traveled in M. Troude's ancient Citröen. How slow travel was in those days! The French explorers went in boats manned by from six to ten rowers, but the river was so full of cataracts and its current in many places ran so swiftly that they had to do much portaging. It took them more than half a year to go up as far as I was, and almost a year and a half to reach Yunnan, where they nearly lost their lives at the hands of Moslem princes who had just successfully revolted against the Chinese. They were turned back at Tali-fu by the Moslem princes, who would not permit them to follow the river to its source.

The expedition thus failed in this part of its assignment. But in a larger sense the report brought back by Garnier and his followers spelled failure of France's grandiose plan of erecting on the Indo-Chinese Peninsula a colonial empire to rival that of the British in India. France had occupied the mouth of the Mekong in the hope that this river, like the Ganges, would become a highway and that on it French commerce and political influence could move inland. Upon his return, Garnier reported that the Mekong was not navigable nor did it flow through rich territories where France could build a flourishing empire comparable to that of British India. In a scholarly

---

*Garnier's full report of the expedition, which started from Phnom Penh in 1866, is contained in his *Voyage d'Exploration en Indo-Chine*.
†*The French in Indo-China*, pp. 42-44.

and detailed survey of the territories traversed by the expedition, Garnier showed that most of these were jungles, many of which were extremely unhealthy and were inhabited by primitive tribes.

Feeling a bit lonesome in this rather wild country, I could easily visualize the keen disappointment of the small band of Frenchmen who found an intractable river and a sparsely inhabited wilderness, where they had expected to find an artery of commerce flowing through civilized lands comparable to those washed by the Ganges. Extraordinarily few facts were known in those days about the interior of the Indo-Chinese Peninsula. Although Garnier pronounced the Mekong route to the interior impracticable, he suggested as an alternative possibility the Red River, in Tonkin, which he thought might provide a navigable route into Yunnan. He thus turned French attention to Tonkin, which by 1884 had become a French protectorate. Garnier lost his life in connection with the capture of Hanoi in 1873.

But again France's expectations of a water route into the interior were disappointed. Jean Dupuis, a French merchant, also found that the Red River was not completely navigable. However, half a century after Garnier traveled this way, this French dream came to partial fruition with the opening of the French railroad from Hanoi to Yunnan-fu (now Kunming) in Yunnan. I often felt that Indo-China was a "prestige" colony, rather than one that was acquired in response to the needs of merchants and traders, as were the Dutch and British colonies in Southeast Asia.

My thoughts were interrupted by the arrival of the first of the two buses which disgorged an incredible number of passengers and bundles. Soon everyone was settled around small fires, eating and talking; all apparently well acquainted with each other. A while later the second bus arrived and we all rushed down to board the ferry, which became so overloaded that the water almost reached the planks on which we stood. A single oil lamp, throwing a feeble light and flickering in the wind, furnished the only illumination. Nevertheless markets were immediately set up and gambling, eating, and general jollification began. Any sort of trip is a treat for natives, and they know how to make the best of it.

We had considerable difficulty getting away from the shore since the current kept pushing us back. All the passagers gave advice, yelled encouragement, and helped push the branches of overhanging bushes back so that the ferryman could maneuver with his pole. Suddenly the pole broke and for a time it looked as if we were going to be permanently stuck. However, someone ran off to get a new pole and we finally broke loose. I was excited and a little scared; it was so unfamiliar to me. The river rushed past only an inch below my feet and all around me were these noisy people with whom I could not talk. The stars were unnaturally bright and the wind was blowing fiercely. Once we became stuck on a sandbank, water rushing in over the side. Another time one of the passengers got up and made an impassioned speech; everybody yelled approval. Meanwhile in the stern of the ferry gambling went on, occasionally interrupted by hoarse cursing. The single lamp gave everyone a sinister look and I felt small and cold.

Finally we reached the other side of the river and I arrived at the Troudes. One moment I had been shivering among a motley crowd of strange folk; the next I sat in a typically French petit-bourgeois* living room at a round table covered by a green, fringed cloth, which had an old-fashioned lamp in its exact center, and four stiff chairs set symmetrically around. There were large cabbage roses on the wallpaper and many framed family pictures on the big sideboard (vintage 1890). A venerable black, horsehair sofa was crowded into the remaining space and one had to squeeze oneself to get around the cozy little room. Monsieur Troude, who was somewhat invalided, had been lying on the sofa but arose as soon as I entered and inquired courteously how I had stood the long, fatiguing trip. Madame Troude, lively and voluble, bustled around fetching tea, rum, and biscuits, remarking how courageous (I think she meant foolish) I was to be traveling through this wilderness—*Mon Dieu*, for fun! Even though they had spent a lifetime in Laos, it was still an unfriendly alien country to them.

They had made arrangements for me to stay at the government bungalow and given instructions to the Annamite manager to put a hot-water bottle in my bed and give me the best service. Their tall son took me there and left final orders that I was to be given the number one treatment. I noticed how severely he spoke to the natives and how quickly they carried out all his orders. He assured me that this was the only way one could get them to do anything properly. The French demanded that orders be obeyed but, on the other hand, they were friendly with the natives and did not put on superior airs as do so many Anglo-Saxons. I soon found out that if I wanted anything done I had to imitate the French and yell at the natives. I didn't like this at all but I learned to do it. From the recesses of my unconscious, I hauled the necessary vocabulary, which I had learned years ago when I studied in Paris. In those days I used to be able to hold my own with taxi drivers, porters, concierges, and similar tough characters. I

---

*This French term, a "little citizen," is so much more expressive than our condescending "lower middle class." M. Troude was indeed a little citizen; poor, hardworking, kind, and considerate.

certainly never thought then how handy this knack would turn out to be in Indo-China.

Many people dislike the Annamites and say that they steal and cheat and are sneaky. I watched my possessions, of course, but I never found anything missing and I got along well with them. However, I never liked them as much as the Malays or the Siamese. Sometimes they made me angry with their shortsighted shrewdness. Porters and ricksha boys and girls would object strenuously if I gave them more than the current rate, thinking this showed I didn't know the correct price and was therefore fair game for them. It is the worst possible psychology on their part, but then I suppose it would be too much to expect them to understand such a quaint thing as voluntary generosity. In such cases, I found it useful to switch to *tu*, wag a finger at them, make a stern face, and roar as loudly as I could: *Ecoute, mon petit vieux. C'est assez, tu le sais bien. Tais-toi tout de suite ou je t'en donnerai moins.* (Listen, my little one. This is enough, as you well know. Be quiet or I shall give you less.) Sometimes I actually grabbed what I had given them and which they held towards me screaming it wasn't enough, and gave them less. That always caused consternation and surprise. All the bystanders thought it a splendid joke and laughed at their unsuccessful compatriot whom just a minute before they had been backing vociferously. I found the only safe way to pay more than the pitiful current wages was first to count out the exact sum due for services rendered and then to add an additional sum, saying it was a special gift for extra good service. That made it all right.

The government rest houses were run for the benefit of traveling French officials, but it was usually easy to find room. One bit of French courtesy struck me as exceedingly thoughtful: I discovered that each manager sent a wire ahead to the next bungalow announcing my arrival by bus or truck and giving the approximate time I was to be expected. I don't know whether they did this for everyone or merely because they regarded me as a helpless foreigner, but when I found out about this I was quite touched. The government charged two piastres (an amount equal to fifty American cents) for the room and fixed fees for meals which were served by the manager, usually an Annamite. Besides a small monthly salary from the government, the manager kept what he made on the food. The Annamite managers served excellent meals; the French managers, on the other hand, not only served atrocious food but also expected you to listen to their life stories.

Even though it was late when I arrived, the manager of the Paksé bungalow served me a delicious steak dinner, topped off with crêpes suzettes. After this dinner I retired to my room and slept marvelously. The bungalow beds were usually comfortable and often there was running water in the room, sometimes even a shower. When I awoke, I was served a tray in bed with café au lait and wonderfully crisp French rolls and butter. I decided to stay the day in Paksé and rest up for the strenuous trip across the waist of Indo-China to the east coast and Dong Ha.

I wandered about the town all morning, observing the Lao and finding them as attractive and gentle as their kin in northern Siam. The town was pretty and well-kept; its streets shady and clean. The people seemed to be about equally divided between Lao and Annamite—evidence of the relentless tide of Annamite migration from overcrowded Annam into the less populous areas of western Indo-China. The Lao cannot hold their own economically against the Annamites who have absorbed from their Chinese preceptors enough commercial acumen, perseverance, and industry to guarantee them eventful mastery of the economy of all Indo-China; i.e., all that which has not already passed into the hands of their even shrewder and more capable Chinese "uncles" (the respectful title given the Chinese by the Annamites who are otherwise not inclined to admit superior qualities in any foreigner). The Chinese, who still think of the Annamites as ex-colonials, do not return these sentiments but speak of an Annamite as "tail of a rat."

It is interesting to observe such instances of "race superiority" and of the inclination of the more advanced Asiatic peoples to colonize the weaker ones, especially since Asiatics are prone to accuse white people of being the only ones to indulge in such practices. There is a difference, however, in that neither the Annamites nor the Chinese show the slightest inclination to bring to the natives, whose economic life they dominate, any benefits to offset loss of independence. The British, the Dutch, the French, and the Americans may well pride themselves on having been the first conquerors on record to return solid benefits to subject races in exchange for taking over the government of their countries. This struck me forcibly in Laos. Here was a gentle race, living in a beautiful country, where there was ample space for anyone to grow food for his family and where nothing more was needed from government than preservation of peace and order. This the French provided. In addition, they provided the first medical service the country ever had (every village I passed seemed to have a centrally located *dispensaire*), set up the first schools, and gave the Lao fair administration of their own legal codes—government services never experienced before the French came.

As I wandered around Paksé, I kept making comparisons between French and Siamese Laos. These indigenous people are much alike and both have been gently treated by the paramount powers. Local laws and customs and local forms of village organization have hardly been touched, but internal peace has been established. Until Chulalongkorn's time, Siam demanded no more from the Lao than did France: an oath of allegiance from the local ruler, light taxes, and *corvée*. But because the Lao were racially Thai they gradually became absorbed into the Siamese nation and ceased being colonials, whereas all the beneficence of France and the lightness of her protectorate could not hide the fact that her Lao were a subject people. Had the French not interfered, all would long ago have become members of independent Siam. By incorporating Laos into Indo-China, the French exposed these people to the economic exploitation and perhaps eventual political domination of the Annamites and Chinese. The sophisticated Siamese of Bangkok may look upon the Lao of northern Siam as slightly old-fashioned country cousins, but to the Annamite and Chinese, the Lao are inferior aliens. There ought to be room in this world for gentle people who harm no one and want only to be left alone.

In Siam and Indo-China the indigenous population was subjected at approximately the same time to the violent changes in age-old ways of life that come about when Westernization is effected abruptly, but with this difference: in Siam it was done by fiat of the Siamese king; in Indo-China by persuasion of the protecting power—France. As for the outward results, the traveler moving from one country to another was not conscious of any significant difference between Siam and Indo-China. Both had governments which provided efficient administration, security under the law, and about the same amount of modern amenities in their big cities. Siam's railroads seemed to me better than Indo-China's; on the other hand, the latter had more and better roads. Possibly there was better public sanitation in Indo-China; but there were fewer signs of abject poverty in Siam. However, the contrast between the Thai, who are truly the Free as their name indicates, and the Indo-Chinese, especially the Annamites, is striking.

I don't think any traveler could help preferring the self-respecting, open-faced, clean, courteous, and honest Siamese to the Annamites, who show extreme ruthlessness and cruelty to less nimble-witted peoples in the country (Lao, Cambodians, Chams, Mois), and tend to dissimulate in relation to those more powerful than they; their vanity and love of luxury are great. Yet, often on reading reports of travelers, government missions, teachers, and educators written a hundred to a hundred and fifty years ago, I find Europeans putting the Annamites above the Siamese in character and governmental organization. The conclusion seems inevitable:

indigenous people are better off when the force that pushes them into modern life proceeds from the local sovereign, no matter how much of an autocrat he may be, than from a colonial power, no matter how benevolent it is. All the available evidence indicates that the Siamese are better men today than in the past while the opposite seems true of the Annamites.

As the county seat of the province of Bassac, Paksé had a French Resident and a number of lesser French administrative personnel. There were imposing government buildings and attractive residences, built of cement, cream-colored, with tall, narrow, green-shuttered windows. They had lofty, spacious rooms and were surrounded by lovely gardens. Many of the buildings had open balconies running around all four sides, giving them a cool and comfortable appearance. The country around Paksé is *la plus giboyeuse de l'Indo-Chine*; that is, it abounds in wild animals of ferocious disposition such as gaurs, wild boars, tigers, bears, panthers, and wild buffalo (so the travel literature tells you). Therefore, one often saw Frenchmen in shorts and topees, driving into town, their ramshackle cars (there just weren't *any* new motor vehicles in this whole country) loaded with trophies of the hunt. There was much evidence of the military. One soldier practiced bugle calls all the time I stayed in town, even at night, but it did not matter since a three-day Chinese festival, commemorating the collection of funds for a new school, was being celebrated and the noise from the merry-making Chinese drowned out the bugle sounds. The native troops were neat and trim, as were the policemen who saluted me politely. All the natives greeted me with "Bonjour, madame," giving me again the pleasant feeling of being an important personage that I had first experienced in Cambodia. Nevertheless, I already felt slightly homesick for the Siamese "Oh yes," which they say firmly and pleasantly whenever they do not understand a word of what you are saying. It sounds reassuring and I liked it better than the Annamite "Oui, madame." I suppose it is because I prefer to be among free and independent people, and for this reason I did not take to the Annamites as well as to the Siamese.

I passed a school and decided to visit it. A polite Annamite teacher showed me around. She was nearly dying of curiosity and hardly able to refrain from asking personal questions but too well-mannered to break in on my questions about the school. Like everybody else, she couldn't figure me out—a woman wandering all alone through the country. She wanted to know whether there was a monsieur and, if so, why wasn't he along. She was so friendly that we settled down to an exchange of highly personal data. I was interested to learn that they started teaching the children French right after kindergarten. Most natives I had met knew some French, which had surprised me, but I suppose it was necessary since the French did not bother to learn native languages. As spoken by the natives, French is an odd language and it took a while before I could make it out. I think it was a mistake that the French did not know the native languages, for this lack made them too dependent on their interpreters, who often became small tyrants, perpetuating injustices and collecting petty graft. However, the French told me that all this was temporary and soon all the natives would speak French and then everything would *marche très bien.*

Towards noon I paid the Troudes a visit. We had a pleasant chat, with both Troudes making witty and somewhat malicious remarks about the Siamese. The French like to poke fun at the "Sovereign State of Siam." This was not surprising since they had once expected to incorporate it into their colonial empire. Besides, as long as Siam was free, it kept alive in France's colonial subjects the dream of ultimate freedom. The Lao, whose Mecca remained Bangkok, were especially likely to have "dangerous thoughts."

A favorite story of the French, told me by M. Troude and several other French people (with slight variations and individual embellishments), concerned a visit paid a short time previously by the Siamese Navy. It appears that the Siamese admiral in command notified the French that he wished to pay a courtesy call on the French fleet at Saigon. In due time, a number of ancient craft made their way up the coast and safely reached the mouth of the Dong Nai River, where they were met by the pilot. He took them up the winding river to its junction with the Saigon River where the city is located. There, the Siamese dismissed the pilot although that was the very point where navigational difficulties really began. "You understand, Madame, the Siamese were going to show us what good sailors they were," said Monsieur Troude. "But, alas, when they tried to execute an elegant turn, the ships got tangled up with each other, there were several collisions and some ships had to be sent into dry dock. We had to rescue them. Ah, it was a sad spectacle, that Siamese Navy. But as soon as they left their ships, the Siamese officers and men had a wonderful time in Saigon. The festivities were a great success—*un succès fou.* When the time came to leave, a wind had risen and the sea was high. The Siamese admiral prudently decided to go home by train. *Il y avait trop d'eau pour lui* (There was too much water for him)," he said wickedly. I suspect the truth of the story, but it was amusing as told by the French in their lively and witty way.

The Troudes invited me to go to a party that the Chinese of Paksé were giving that afternoon for the French community, as part of the festivities celebrating their new school program. The French liked the Chinese because they were capable and businesslike and never made trouble, their community being effectively policed by their own sub-government. The Chinese built and financed their own schools, did not bother to learn either French or the local language, and did not assimilate with the people among whom they had settled. They devoted themselves wholeheartedly to making much money off the poor, ignorant natives.

George and I had visited many Chinese schools on our trips through Southeast Asia and found them generally uniform in appearance and curriculum. Each was decorated with large pictures of Chiang Kai-shek and Madame, and large Chinese flags. The children were exceedingly clean, wide-awake, and cunning. There was always a tremendous amount of athletic activity, obviously due to that all-pervading British influence, for sports were not held in high esteem in China.

As in all Indo-Chinese towns, there were a number of *cercles*, or clubs, one for each major community in Paksé. The most elegant was, of course, the Cercle Français; next in point of elegance came the Chinese club, whose membership was composed of emigrants from the same hometown or province—there it was the Congregation Hakas. Below this was the Annamite club and, at the bottom, that of the Lao.

The French population numbered about thirty. They all turned up for the party but affected boredom. Still, I noticed that they did full justice to the good food and champagne. Several dignified Chinese merchants welcomed us at the door and led us ceremoniously with many bows and smiles to a nicely decorated room. A long table, loaded with delicious petits fours and other French pastries, stood in the middle of the room. In its center was an enormous bouquet of flowers in a riotous clash of colors. The lone Chinese who sat at the table with us made a long speech in French, in which he expressed the deep feeling of gratitude of his people for being privileged to live under so just and generous a great power as France, etc. The young French Resident-Adjoint replied that great and just France loved its Chinese subjects. Whereupon a group of young Chinese girls entered and started to sing something which became more and more familiar to us. Suddenly we all scrambled to our feet. They had been singing the "Marseillaise," but it was so Chinesified that one could hardly blame the French for not recognizing their national anthem. Afterwards we all sang "Frère Jacques" with the children, drank excellent champagne, and had lively conversation; so it turned out to be a good party. As we left, a terrific explosion of firecrackers went off at the door, stunning us all. The Chinese measure the esteem in which a person is held by the noise of the firecrackers let loose upon him at festive occasions. These must have cost a great deal and testified eloquently to the high esteem in which the "just and generous power," France, was held by the Chinese of Paksé.

The mail bus was to have called for me at 5:00 a.m. next morning but nothing came until six o'clock and then it wasn't the bus but a decrepit old Ford, which took me to the garage where a number of men were tinkering with the bus. They worked on it for an hour and still it wouldn't run so we set forth in the Ford. There were so many passengers that it looked as if the car would burst. There was no road at all; a narrow strip of the plain had merely been cleared a bit and flattened here and there. Optimistically, the French marked it on their map as *automobilable en saison sèche* (open for automobile traffic in the dry season), but it was really *automobilable* only for old Model T Fords; lower-slung cars would not have been able to make it. I suppose during the rainy season one simply did not travel from Paksé to Savannakhet, for I was told that the whole plain is then inches deep in muddy water.

I never was so thankful in my life as when we actually arrived safely at the little village where the real long-distance bus awaited us. This elegant vehicle—all white, red, and blue with leather upholstery and a door which fastened with a lock—was the first and only completely intact bus I saw in all our travels through Southeast Asia from the Celebes to Siam. I could hardly believe my eyes when we drove up beside it. We stopped for a while to get our breath and exchange village gossip but eventually we got started and made good time, arriving at Savannakhet exactly on time.

I had been informed that there would be a mail bus from there to Dong Ha next day but this wasn't so. There was no public transportation out of Savannakhet, except back to Paksé. The only thing to do was to go to the market place and look over the line of trucks being loaded for the next day's trip. The least ramshackle vehicle going in my direction was a Renault, whose owner contracted to get me to Dong Ha by 6:00 p.m. for four piastres.

The truck picked me up next morning at 5:00 a.m. I was getting used to rising in pitch-darkness and fumbling for my clothes by candlelight, but there were compensations. I never tired of the thrill of driving through the dark jungle and watching it awaken slowly. It was marvelous to see the first faint light in the east and to hear the squeaks of the birds as they were getting ready to burst into their morning song. The sunrises were always magnificent. Laos is a beautiful country, fertile, underpopulated, and mostly mountainous, since it lies astride the great north-south mountain chain that runs down the center of Indo-China and is called the Annamite Cordillera.

Laos is a sort of Asiatic Eden where no one need want if he will only devote a little time to tending his rice field. There is still vacant land to be had and, therefore, the country has few rapacious landlords, for most Lao till their own fields. The Lao have few wants and value leisure above worldly goods. Their houses, built on stilts, are bare of gadgets but comfortable; their outlay for clothing is minimal for nobody wears much and the youngsters wear nothing. It saddened me to think that in time this idyllic land would be overrun by Annamites, escaping from the misery and poverty of crowded Tonkin and Annam. Then the Lao will be as dispossessed in their own land as are the Malays in British Malaya and for the same reason. These are evil effects of colonialism I find hard to condone, even though they are the result of thoughtlessness rather than of evil intent.

That day we crossed Indo-China near its narrowest part—traveling a distance of 327 kilometers. From 5:00 a.m. to 8:00 p.m. we had only one break long enough to be worth my crawling over the huge Renault motor which sat between the driver and myself; that was in Tchepone where I had lunch at the government bungalow. It was a tiring day but the countryside was beautiful, especially after Tchepone, where the road zig-zags up and down mountains, past enchanting streams, and through charming valleys where Lao villages nestle in bamboo groves. As we were climbing into the wild and uninhabited mountains where large herds of wild elephants and other beasts still lived, we saw a group of Moi natives by the roadside who looked savage and shy. The driver said that if we slowed down they would scamper into the forest so fast you could not believe your eyes. They were small brown men, completely naked, except for a G-string, or *cache-sexe*, as the French so aptly name it. They carried woven baskets strapped to their backs which were half as tall as they and loaded to overflowing. One man wore a coat of bark, the first such garment I had ever seen. Their women are somewhat more elaborately clothed—they wear sarongs.

These primitive, semi-nomadic people are scattered all over the southern part of the Annamite Cordillera. They are believed to be Proto-Malays and do, in fact, resemble the Igorots of the Philippines but are far more primitive. For one thing, in contrast to the Igorots, who are famed for their rice terraces and their excellent farming methods, they are poor farmers. They practice the soil-destroying *ray* method of planting—they clear a piece of forest land by burning (often, in the process, burning down large forest areas through carelessness) and then sow haphazardly. As soon as the soil is exhausted, they move to another part of the forest and repeat the process. They are primarily hunters who live an independent life with practically no government and nothing that could be called religion. French missionaries have had some success in converting the Mois, but they are suspicious of all outsiders, and with good reason. Both Annamites and Cambodians have always exploited them and made them debt slaves through trading transactions not properly understood by the Mois, who have no commercial talents and cannot even count correctly. The term *Moi* means "savage" in Annamese* and I was told that in the not too distant past the Annamites did not even consider them real humans; only a sort of advanced type of monkey!

Having read Father Bouillevaux's report of his visit with some of these mountain people,† I was on the lookout for any carrying the huge ceramic jars, which are one of the two most highly prized possessions of the Mois—the other being gongs. On his visit to a Moi village, Father Bouillevaux was offered wine from one of the ceramic jars and pronounced it quite as good as most of his native wines, at least those drunk by the common people. He noted that they broke their front teeth, and was told they did it so as not to look like monkeys. The good Father was also offered a slave—a young man of twenty years or so—for a handful of glass beads, a few pounds of tobacco and a little salt.

The second small group we saw carried these ceramic jars (shaped like Chinese ginger jars) strapped to their backs with rope. Each man carried a T-shaped stick on which he rested his burden when he stood and rested. This is a simple but useful device used all over the mountainous parts of Indo-China (also in China) where most transportation is by humans. The stick has a cross bar at one end which is braced under the load carried on the back, so that when one leans against it, one rests both feet and back. I couldn't find anyone

---

*The Cambodians call these people Penongs; the Lao, Khas. Though they all look alike, the Mois are not and never have been a single nation. Their villages are independent of each other and often speak mutually unintelligible tongues. Unlike the Igorots and the Bataks, who are also Proto-Malay mountain folk, the Mois engage neither in head-hunting nor cannibalism. They use poisoned arrows in hunting and frequently make war upon each other, the purpose apparently being acquisition of the treasured jars and gongs. The gongs are used to make music when there is a bibulous feast in the village.

†C. E. Bouillevaux, *L'Annam et le Cambodge: Voyages et Notices Historiques*, pp. 149-157. The book consists of three parts, two covering travels and explorations undertaken by Father Bouillevaux in connection with his missionary work (Part One covering the period 1848-56; Part Three, 1867-1874) and a third (actually Part Two) giving a history of Annam based primarily on the Annals of Annam and the Royal Chronicles of Cambodia; also on various contemporaneous reports and studies made by men like Lagrée, Garnier, Aubaret, and Msgr. Pallegoix, as well as missionary letters of the period. It is one of the most interesting and readable accounts of the history, customs, and character of the various peoples of Indo-China.

to explain just why the Mois should be so fond of these jars. They go into debt to purchase them and loot them from each other during inter-tribal wars. I finally decided that the most likely explanation was that they use them as containers for the rice wine of which they are extraordinarily fond.

Among them it is always feast or famine. When they have enough food and drink, the whole village goes on a binge; even the domestic animals are said to lap up enough of the overflow to make them stagger about noticeably. Drunkenness is their besetting sin, though it is not so regarded by the Mois themselves. My French host at the Tchepone bungalow told me that they greet each other with an expression one might loosely translate as "Let's go on a binge together." The truck driver who, being Annamite, belonged to a frugal and abstemious race, looked down with utmost contempt on the shy little people who are in fact rather unprepossessing. They are squat, broad-faced, and have black hair hanging about their heads in lanky strings. Compared with them, our driver looked very civilized, though I hadn't thought that way of him before.

Our truck had two horns: one for the ordinary uses known to us, the other to sound a sort of clarion call (1) to announce our arrival to the world at large—often in the midst of empty wilderness; (2) to greet oncoming cars; and (3) ostensibly to drive carabao off the road. As a matter of fact, the horn acted as a rallying call to all the beasts in the neighborhood, who rushed onto the road and looked at us in surprise.

Time meant nothing to driver or passengers. The trip was fun; the longer it lasted, the better. Frequent detours were made to deliver messages or pick up a few fish, which then dangled in front of the driver and were taken to "Aunt Martha" in the next village. She would likely give the driver an order for groceries to be picked up at the Chinese store five miles down the road and brought back on the return trip. Passengers often saw friends or relatives who had to be greeted, the bus stopping while family affairs were discussed. The passengers all took part in these conversations and gave advice. Stops had to be made to allow for natural functions, for a drink of water by the roadside, for loading and unloading, and also for periodic inspection of the tires. Every hour or so the truck stopped, one of the driver's helpers got off and, squatting on the ground, contemplated each tire thoughtfully for several moments. Whenever our Renault jolted a little more than usual, we stopped and a helper crawled under the car and hit it with a small hammer, while the other helper sat on the ground watching him closely. When I asked about these mysterious doings, I was told that they were afraid the tires might burst in the heat. Since the chassis of the car was made of French wood, they were afraid it might not withstand the tropical climate and might therefore also crack. I remarked that I suspected nobody really knew what they were doing, and proceeded to tell the driver the story of the American railroad worker who, having completed fifty years of service for his company, was feted upon retirement, given a gold watch, and praised for faithful performance of duty. When the speech-making was over, the old man rose and asked the president of the company would he please answer a question which had puzzled him all his life. "Why was I supposed to tap the wheels of the train at every stop?" After I explained that the tapping was done to discover whether the wheel tires had become loose, the driver saw the point immediately, and thought it such a good story that he told it at every stop.

We were supposed to reach Dong Ha by six o'clock but there had been so many delays that I began to get impatient. I tried to bribe the driver, offering one piastre if he speeded up and got us to our destination by seven. He really tried his best but the old habits of dawdling could not be overcome, even for so magnificent a sum. We arrived at eight. The passengers had taken such an interest in this novel attempt to reach a destination at a given time—several small bets were placed on the outcome—and looked so disappointed when we failed that I handed over the piastre, anyway.

The only lengthy stop that day was made at Tchepone, and that was so that I could have lunch at the government bungalow. This one was managed by a Frenchman who immediately told me that he was an *ancien combattant* (veteran) and, as such, well informed on the European situation. He proceeded to enlighten me since, as he said in a kindly voice, Americans are usually misinformed, as are many people in France, whereas out here in the colonies they kept themselves au courant and really knew what was what. He got his information from a bimonthly sheet of the Association des Anciens Combattants, a copy of which he pressed upon me. While I ate his indifferent food, he proudly told me that France was highly respected in the Orient and had made even the Japanese hand over their arms when they wanted to go through the French Concession during the Shanghai war in 1937. The Annamite soldiers had directed their guns at the Japanese and threatened to shoot if they did not hand over their arms. This story was told to me by every Frenchman I met. It is a fact, as I was told by George who had command of the minesweeper USS *Finch* at Shanghai during the 1937 war, that the French did not permit the Japanese troops to enter their Concession. I never could quite see how this evidence of Annamite prowess redounded to the glory of France, except in a roundabout way. The Tchepone Frenchman also expressed satisfaction that England had finally decided to listen to French advice and stepped up her war preparations. I never saw such self-confident people as the French there.

As usual, I was pitied because I had to stay at bungalows run by Annamites and it took willpower not to make snide remarks on the superior service given in these Annamite-run bungalows. All the Frenchmen who ran bungalows (a low occupation out there) had taken Annamite wives or *congaies* (mistresses) and gone native in a run-down sort of way. The Tchepone bungalow was filthy and the plumbing had evidently been out of order for years. Lunch was expensive and mediocre. But the worst was the bungalow at Dong Ha which was damp, run-down, and dirty. There was no electricity in Dong Ha, therefore kerosene lamps were used. When I arrived about eight o'clock after my tiring day, the damp, empty, badly lighted house looked most uninviting. I had hoped to eat dinner and go to bed immediately but this was not to be.

The French manager insisted on telling me his life story, as well as giving me considerable advice on how to travel in Indo-China. In his youth, he had been a guide, taking rich men on safaris, and he could not let pass the opportunity of telling me his hunting adventures. While I drowsily ate a poor meal, he hopped around vivaciously, demonstrating how one bags a gaur. First he was the hunter, crouching in the bushes with gun raised; then he became the gaur charging with head lowered. He showed me exactly where you shoot a gaur to kill; it's in the back of the neck. Fortunately for you, the gaur puts down his head when he charges and, thus, does not see what you are doing. You can try for his neck or step aside and hide behind a tree. Personally, I should hide behind a tree.

The only profit I derived from this show was that at last I found out what a gaur looks like. It seems that he is a sort of wild ox and is dangerous. But the Frenchman assured me that wild animals never attack humans, the only exception being old tigers who can't run well enough to catch animals and, therefore, go after weaklings like men or, better still, women. I am now excellently informed on hunting in Indo-China. This Frenchman told me many stories about the odd behavior of rich Americans on safaris. I was too tired to argue with him but felt that I really ought to defend my countrymen against all his accusations of cowardice, niggardliness, and general lack of savoir-faire. He said one man was too lazy to get up before 8:00 a.m. Apparently, by that time in the morning all the wild animals have disappeared into their respective lairs in the forest, so the Frenchman had to go out alone and shoot the American's trophies for him. "Most other rich men," he said, "were willing to get up early and shoot the animals, but this man liked whiskey and slept too much. . . . Ah, it was a hard life being a guide." When he asked me what I thought of the European situation, I arose and said firmly I was now going to sleep.

On the way to my cold, damp room I saw the good Frenchman's *congaie* fixing up the conjugal bedchamber. She had remained unseen all evening. I found only one nice object in my room—a hot-water bottle. The bed was lumpy and the furniture old and rickety. There was cold running water, and a tiny jug of hot water was brought in by the bungalow coolie. It wasn't a comfortable overnight stay but then it was short.

The next morning, while it was still pitch-dark, I was on the way to the railroad station, with the bungalow coolie guiding me. My train was scheduled to leave for Hué at 4:24 a.m. Many people were waiting at the station, huddled beneath their bundles. There was a tiny kerosene light in the stationmaster's office, where I settled down to wait for the train which was, of course, late. I learned that a typhoon had disrupted train schedules all along the coast from Saigon to Hanoi.

11
Annam

I arrived in Hué at seven o'clock in the morning. It was a sunny day but the coolness in the air reminded me that I had best do something about warm clothing. All my missionary clothes had gone back to their several owners before I crossed into Laos and I was on my own. Even in tropical Laos I had felt cold in the mornings. I started the day wrapped tightly in my terry-cloth coat, George's raincoat, and the blanket I had bought in Bangkok. I shed them, one by one, as the sun came out and it got warmer; rather like the Chinese who put on and take off layers of quilted coats, as the weather grows colder or warmer, speaking of "three-, four-, five-, six-coat weather." I had been warned that the winter months in Tonkin were often cold. It seemed a good idea to see if I could outfit myself in Hué's one French department store—Morin's.*

As it was still too early to go shopping, I told my ricksha-driver to take me around the walled Annamite town—the Citadel—until time for breakfast. He was a small chap who had carried me off despite terrific competition and my misgivings as to his ability to pull me. He was the tiniest male I ever saw. Clad in tattered brown shirt and shorts, a dirty-brown rag wound turban-fashion around his head, he won me over by the wide grin when he pulled my sleeve yelling: *"Moi, parle français, bon, bon."* His French wasn't too good, but he had unexpected talents in other directions. He dashed off with me from the station, announcing to all the world that he had a rich *Anglaise*. No amount of argument could change his notions about my nationality; he had never heard of America.

As he trotted along—in a quite leisurely fashion once we had left the competition behind—he told me in execrable French about all the things I must see and which he would arrange for me. I hadn't realized it, but when I stepped into his ricksha, I acquired a guide for the rest of my day at Hué. His nimble brain quickly planned an itinerary that did not miss a single sight worth seeing and gave me a

*The Grand Hôtel Morin Frères. This enterprise began as a small grocery store and gradually expanded into Hué's only European hotel and department store.

more vivid and unforgettable memory of this lovely town than any tourist agency could have provided. I was lucky to have found him.

Since Morin's was still closed, we crossed the delightful Rivière des Parfums (so named because its deep blue waters are bordered by deliciously scented flowering bushes) to the Citadel. This was the Annamite part of town. The European quarter and the palace of the French Resident, as well as the railroad station, were located on the opposite bank of the river, as was the town of the merchants—Annamite, Chinese, and Hindu—with its narrow streets full of small shops.

I reflected on what I had read about Hué and Gia-Long, emperor of the Nguyen Dynasty, who had conceived the plan of its citadel. After thirty years of intermittent civil wars between the leading families of Tonkin and Annam, into which Siam, China, and France interceded from time to time, Nguyen-Anh, under the name of Gia-Long, ascended the throne. His first forty years had been a time of trouble when he and a French bishop, Pigneau de Behaine, had often had to seek refuge from the rebel Tay-Son family or the Tonkinese Trinhs with the King of Siam in Bangkok or on various islands off Cochin China. Though he never accepted Christianity, his friendship with Pigneau was sincere. He sent his eldest son, Prince Canh, with the bishop to Paris where, on November 28, 1787, a treaty of alliance was signed on behalf of Louis XVI and Gia-Long in which France promised substantial armed assistance in return for certain territorial concessions in Tourane. Because of intrigues in Pondichéry where it was being outfitted, the French expedition that was to have helped Gia-Long regain his throne never was sent. Instead of the troops and naval vessels specified in the treaty, Gia-Long received only a small band of volunteers whom Pigneau managed to assemble, but they were sufficient to turn the tide in his favor, and in gratitude he wrote a letter to Louis XVI which contains the following extraordinary statement: *"Si dans mes États il pouvoit y avoir quelque chose qui pût ètre utile à Votre Majesté, je la prie instamment de vouloir bien en disposer et d'être assurée que je ne négligerai rien pour remplir ses intentions."** Freely translated this means "If there's anything I've got you'd like to have, just take it." I wonder whether Gia-Long thought this up or whether we see here the fine hand of Pigneau. Thirty years later, Gia-Long's feelings had changed considerably for on his deathbed he urged his son Minh-Mang "always to love France and the French but never to give them an inch of his territory."†

---

*E. Cortambert and Léon DeRosny, *Tableau de la Cochinchine*, p. 200.
†E. Cortambert and Léon DeRosny, *Tableau de la Cochinchine*, p. 206.

When Gia-Long finally succeeded in reuniting Tonkin and Annam under his scepter, he decided to build a capital city modeled on Peking. After careful study, the geomancers pronounced the place where the Citadel now stands as highly propitious. Gia-Long, with the aid of French officers in his service, laid out the plan for this walled city and began building it in 1805. It was completed in 1822 under his son and successor Minh-Mang. As in Peking, there are cities within cities. At the innermost center is the Purple Forbidden City, measuring about three-fourths of a mile in circumference. Around it is built the Imperial City, surrounded by a moat and a double wall approximately one and a half miles in length, with an elaborate entrance tower cut in each of the four sides. These towers are built of masonry covered with a mosaic of bits of glass and china, which is quite striking from a distance. They are double-tiered and have three vaulted gateways—the center one reserved for the emperor. I could not see the Imperial City as I had no permit, but was told I might obtain one at the tourist agency. The rest of the Citadel, however, was open.

We entered its walled enclosure through a handsome arched gateway passing through several impressive Annamite government buildings, all in Chinese style. The wide streets were laid out symmetrically at right angles to each other. The Citadel was an almost perfect square, protected by thick crenelated walls, built of hard earth and cased with bricks, the whole surrounded by water: on one side by the Rivière des Parfums, on the other three by wide canals. Connected with these was still another canal which crossed the Citadel and passed by the palace, the arsenal, and the former granaries. In olden times, barges loaded with tribute and tax money could thus pass directly to the doors of the buildings where their cargoes were to be stored.

From the Citadel we went straight to Morin's for breakfast and shopping. After much searching around, I got together a fairly satisfactory outfit. I found some grey tweed (which the Chinese store tailor promised to make up into a skirt by evening) and some matching wool (as well as knitting needles) with which I planned to knit myself a sweater. I also bought a brown wool jacket, a beret, and some woolens. I looked with distaste at the only hose they had—ugly rayon stuff which I hated to put on but which did keep my ankles warm. I can't say much for the style of the merchandise carried by Morin's.

Armed with my permit, I went back to the Imperial City where a polite and charming palace guard took me around, explaining everything in wobbly French. I wandered through a bewildering maze of terraces, gateways, stone-flagged paths, courtyards, temples, and palaces—all named in the poetic style beloved of the Chinese such as Palace of Supreme Peace, Propylaeum of the Splendor of the Moon, Gate of Bright Goodness. There were reception halls, pavilions, small ponds, lovely bits of gardens, and marble bridges curving over narrow canals. There was a Temple of the Generations where each reigning emperor prostrated himself on the anniversaries of the birthdays of his predecessors, and a terrace on which were lined nine huge dynastic urns made of bronze. Each urn stood on three legs and weighed approximately two tons. They represented the emperors of the Nguyen dynasty, to which the then-reigning emperor, Bao-Dai, belonged. One urn stood apart—opposite the row—and represented Gia-Long. There were other urns along the paths, and my guide, with a perfectly straight face, pointed out one in which he claimed people used to be boiled in oil. I suspect he was "pulling my leg."

The roofs of the buildings of the imperial palace had yellow tiles like those in Peking and there was much gilding, carving, and red lacquer all over everything. If you have seen one of these palaces, you have seen them all. There Chinese influence ruled supreme and there wasn't a trace of Indian design. Instead of *nagas*, as at Angkor, there were hundreds of scaly dragons everywhere.

The guide showed me the terrace where all the mandarins used to be lined up for the solemn ceremony of the Great Salutations. There were civil mandarins, wearing embroidered badges depicting a stork, and military mandarins whose badges showed a boar, each group graded into nine ranks of the mandarin hierarchy. As in China, the mandarins were the highest government officials venerated as direct representatives of the Son of Heaven (the emperor). I was shown the courtyard where students from all over the country met once every three years to take the final examination for the mandarinate. These were the lucky ones who had passed two previous, stiff examinations. Of 1,200 candidates only a dozen or so survived all three examinations. I was glad to hear that these strenuous tests had been abandoned in 1915 for I could well imagine the heartbreaking disappointment of the many whose grinding toil for endless years brought them only failure in the end.

This system of selecting the best educated men to govern under the emperor was an exact copy of the system in China where it had begun. It had the merit of keeping public service open to any young man gifted enough to pass the examinations; even a poor boy ordinarily had no difficulty in finding a tutor willing to teach him at nominal fees. However, the education leading to successful passing of examinations was purely literary and consisted largely in memorizing the Confucian classics and in learning to write essays thereon.

The Chinese ideal of entrusting government to cultivated men with common sense did not work too badly when government was uncomplicated. It is totally inadequate today when technical knowledge is indispensable in the public servant. Moreover, by underpaying the mandarins, yet requiring them to live in pomp and circumstances befitting the position as venerated representatives of the emperor, both China and Annam inevitably got a corrupt mandarinate which, in turn, corrupted government all down the line.

I departed after photographing my guide and his friends, who complimented me profusely on my excellent accent, a compliment that would have pleased me more had it come from someone who spoke the tongue of Corneille and Racine as it was intended to be spoken. Outside the palace entrance I found my ricksha boy who had been busily making arrangements for a trip to the famous graves of the emperors. He had hired a taxi which awaited my approval and instructions as to when to pick me up after lunch; he also showed me the ricksha he had engaged to go downriver by boat and meet us at a point fifteen miles distant, where the road ended. The ricksha would take me from there to Gia-Long's grave. I was overwhelmed with all this efficiency and approved everything promptly, thus giving my little friend much face. He had apparently decided that on this trip he would be my guide, hence too important a person to do any "rickshaing" himself. I realized that I had become his private property and was now required to follow instructions.

The visit to the emperors' graves was an unusual experience. I never before saw country so Arcadian, so peaceful, so lovely. We drove on shady avenues through a light green sea of rice fields with small bamboo islands. We crossed clear blue canals and drove past gently undulating hills covered with blossoming shrubs and leafy trees. For a while we skirted the Rivière des Parfums, which is one of the loveliest bodies of water I have ever seen, bordered by graceful willows and bamboo, Japanese lilac trees, and countless other bushes covered with blossoms in all colors. Small boats poled by tiny, toy-like Annamites in their funny peaked straw hats and flapping black coats floated up and down the river. It was a scene from a Chinese painting.

The graves of the emperors lie spread over an area some five-by-ten miles. The sites were chosen by the emperors themselves, each searching for a perfect natural setting and spending great effort in planning the construction and landscaping of his own tomb. The actual work was done by *corveé*, rather like the unpaid labor that built the pyramids of the Pharaohs. Most of the graves consisted of several handsome buildings grouped around artifical lakes with bathing houses where the emperors had picnicked with their wives and concubines. On hot days they would swim in a lotus-covered lake or wander on shady paths. It was pleasant and one could simultaneously elevate the mind with thoughts of the transience of worldly splendor.

There are a number of graves but three are especially famous. That of Gia-Long, the oldest, is distinguished by its simplicity and the stern grandeur of its setting; that of Minh-Mang for its spacious and stately beauty; that of Khai-Dinh, the most modern, for the variety and profusion of its mosaic decorations and the eerie sight of the golden statue of the Emperor, which stands in semidarkness and is lighted by oil lamps.

To get to these graves, we had to cross the Rivière des Parfums by ferry. The ferries were poled by two neat Annamites and the ride across was delightful. My ricksha boy used this occasion to scrub his feet energetically with river water. His shoes were two pieces from an old rubber tire, fastened to his feet with a rubber band around his second toe. This was a red-letter day in his life. He was terribly puffed up with his importance and dealt in the most lordly manner with the natives, shooing away beggars and tip-hungry priests, telling the ferrymen where to get off when they wanted to charge me too much, and informing all and sundry that I was a rich *Anglaise* and he my personal retainer. When not occupied with washing his feet, or bragging to the natives, he spat profusely and expertly all around him. Yet he was an excellent manager. Everything functioned beautifully. Where the road ended, the ricksha he had hired stood waiting, and even the ferries were poised to take us across the moment we arrived.

All this cost a ridiculously low price and thrown in were other personal services rendered. He carried my camera, opened it for me; if it fell down, he picked it up, spat on it and wiped it with the sleeve of his dirty shirt. When I took pictures, he held my bag and he even insisted on helping me in spots where the path across the tombs was dangerous—he being about half my size! When he noticed something he thought I ought not to miss, he pulled my sleeve, grinned, and said *très bien, très bien*. Against this avalanche of services I felt helpless. I often recall this nice young man who made my day in Hué one of the best of the whole trip.

Before we started for the emperors' graves, I had stopped at the house of the Stebbins, missionaries to whom Mrs. Chrisman had given me a letter. They kindly provided me with a warm coat and invited me to dinner. After the long afternoon in the country, I picked up my finished skirt, and repaired to the Stebbins' house. They gave me a fine dinner, and afterwards put me on a couch for a nap before I had to catch my train. By this time I was really tired. For a week I had

Row of dynastic urns

Guardians at tomb of Khai Dinh

Royal tomb of Khai Dinh

awakened every morning around three or four o'clock, had looked at interesting sights all day long until after dark, and never had obtained enough sleep. My train was delayed by another typhoon and did not leave until 2:00 a.m., so I had several hours of rest at the Stebbins'.

Dr. Stebbins thought highly of French colonial policy and felt that the natives were well treated and were more fortunate in material things than before the French took possession. Certainly they no longer received several strokes of the bamboo for the slightest infraction, as was once the custom. Crawfurd, whose description of his visit at Hué I had enjoyed reading, called the Annamites a "well-flogged" nation and described his surprise at the nonchalance with which such punishments were accepted. Hardly a word had to be said before the culprit threw himself flat on the ground, received the bastinado on his back with fortitude, and prostrated himself afterwards in gratitude for the needed correction.* Life had become a lot tamer under the French. Dr. Stebbins thought that taxes were not high, considering the benefits derived from the government in matters of sanitation, policing, education, and so forth. And, of course, any disposition on the part of the emperors to use forced labor for construction of costly personal monuments or the like would have been severely curbed by the French Resident. As for missionary work, he admitted that it was hard going. The Stebbins had much success with a class in which they taught English—this having become a fashionable language in Indo-China. They used the occasion for a little proselyting, but admitted it hadn't had considerable effect.

It was a difficult task converting Buddhists, especially in competition with the Catholic Church which, not being regarded as a mission but as the official national church, had many advantages. These, however, were bought dearly with the unselfish devotion to their church and to their native parishoners of the Catholic missionaries, not a few of them martyrs to their faith during the Christian persecutions under Gia-Long's successors.

Cortambert quotes several letters written by these heroic men which show the fortitude with which they met their end. Thus, in answer to a letter from a French friend that he was to be beheaded and would therefore be lucky enough to become a martyr, the imprisoned Abbé Gagelin replied: "My heart is filled with joy at the news that I am condemned to die. Indeed I cannot but assure you that it gives me happiness." In another letter, Abbé Cornay tries to comfort his grieving family by saying: "Do not dread the day of my execution; it will be the happiest day of my life since it will put an end

---

*John Crawfurd, *Journal of an Embassy from the Governor-General of India to the Courts of Siam and Cochin China*, Vol. I, pp. 376–377.

to my suffering and mark the beginning of my good fortune. Even my sufferings are not absolutely cruel; I am not beaten until the wounds of previous beatings have healed. I am not subjected to tortures as was M. Marchand, and as for being condemned to quartering, this will be done simultaneously by four men, while the fifth will behead me. So I shall not suffer much. Be comforted for soon it will all be over and we shall meet again in Heaven."* Similar fortitude was shown by many native Christians, making a deep impression on the populace and winning respect for Christianity.

A rather gruesome practice developed from this general admiration of the martyrs. People valued bits of clothing from these unfortunates and, seeing a quick profit, the executioners soon made money by tearing their victims' clothes to bits and selling them dipped in blood. The blood itself was also sold as it was believed to have miraculous healing qualities when taken by sick persons.

I rate the trains in Indo-China definitely below those of the "Sovereign State of Siam," much as the French may like to snicker at the country. I had treated myself to a first-class compartment in the hope of getting a good night's rest but the bed was too short, the mattress too thin, and my toes stuck out from the skimpy sheets and thin blanket. The train passes through flat, rice-growing country, paralleling the famous Route Mandarine—the only real road-building job the Annamite emperors ever accomplished.† It has since been altered to take care of motor traffic and extended to run all the way from the Porte de Chine, on the northern border, down the east coast to Saigon, and from there to the western border with Siam—1,600 miles.

Along the Mandarin Road you see all Annam on the go. Rickshas, loaded with humanity on the way home from the market, coolies carrying incredible loads on the ends of their bamboo poles, ox carts, bicycles, tricycles, Citroens, trucks, and buses—a continuous stream of people and vehicles. The Annamites do not think far enough ahead to plant trees around their houses; firewood, therefore, has to be carried long distances and you see many coolies with huge bundles of wooden sticks on their backs or on their carrying poles.

---

*E. Cortambert and Léon DeRosny, *Tableau de la Cochinchine*, pp. 212-215.

†Though Gia-Long built some irrigation works and canals and started the first public health service (making use of the services of French doctors who had introduced him to the novel idea that governments should concern themselves with the health of their people), the Annamite concept of the duties of the sovereign towards his people did not include public works but seems to have considered it sufficient for him to celebrate the ancient rites of the Nam-Giao every three years. This is a ceremony in which the emperor solemnly communicates with Heaven and renders an account of his stewardship—exactly as did the Emperor of China at the Temple of Heaven in Peking.

Every once in a while I noticed a clump of bamboo bushes with a gate, sitting in the midst of rice fields. This meant a village. These are surrounded by hedges instead of stone walls. I was told they close the gate carefully at night though it would be easy enough to walk through the hedge.

The trip to Hanoi takes sixteen hours and I was glad when I got there. I left my bags at the Station Hotel and took a ricksha to Mrs. Homera Homer-Dixon, to whom I had a letter of introduction from Mrs. Chrisman. I found her in the midst of a party for several Annamite ladies. She most cordially invited me to stay with her, and I moved over the next day.

I had heard of her on my way. She had the reputation of being the most enthusiastic missionary in the field, devoting all her time and most of her considerable private fortune to the work of the Lord. She was paid nothing for her missionary work since she had gone out on her own, and I detected a tiny bit of animosity among some of the other missionaries, because she wasn't one of the group and had, therefore, more independence. Also she was sometimes accused of being so fond of Annamites and so wrapped up in writing and preaching to them that she had almost lost contact with her own kind. Everybody thought it would be good for her if I visited her. It certainly was good for me. I enjoyed my visit with her enormously, for she was an extremely generous, warmhearted and enthusiastic person one could not help but love and admire.

Hers was a delightfully informal home. She rushed in and out and, in the midst of a conversation, she was likely to dash off without explanation, having just remembered some Annamite who needed help. She had many people in her congregation whom she supported and I fear a few exploited her kind heart. Her servants were well trained and coped in an unruffled way with unexpected guests, erratic meal hours, and sudden absences of the lady of the house just when guests arrived for a party. When her boy served meals, he was dressed in white, with a starched cook's cap on his head, and had a tremendously dignified bearing. He gently but firmly insisted on my eating two eggs *and cereal* every morning, though I protested that all I wanted was fruit and coffee. He knew no French; I knew no Annamese. But we got along marvelously just the same. Mrs. Homer-Dixon used to laugh at what she called my polite *thank-yous* and *pleases* to him which he didn't understand but seemed to appreciate.

I shared her bedroom, in which there were also two canaries. Every morning at 6:30 the bedroom door opened noiselessly and a ponderous female figure entered in the semidarkness, carrying a bucket of hot water. In her gathered skirt and with the typical

Annamite shawl wrapped around her hair in a flat turbanlike headdress, she looked like the nurse in *Romeo and Juliet*. When the ancient Annamite opened the shutters of the tall French windows, the singing of the canaries and that of the birds outside woke us in the pleasantest possible fashion.

The bathroom was medieval. It had running cold water, but instead of a bath there was only a narrow, rectangular, tiled enclosure with a wooden board across one end, on which the hot water was placed. In this enclosure one did one's ablutions. Actually, in Mrs. Homer-Dixon's clean bathroom I became used to this in no time.

Mrs. Homer-Dixon was an interesting person to be with and I enjoyed talking over my daily experiences with her and sharing hers. Her life was an inspiring story. She was born late in her parents' lives—an only child. Though Scottish, her father had been the Dutch Consul in Toronto and she grew up in Canada. When her father died, she became a dutiful daughter to a mother who became steadily more of a hypochondriac. When her mother died, Mrs. Homer-Dixon found herself exceedingly rich and totally inexperienced in the ways of the world. It is not surprising that she made an unfortunate marriage to a man who merely wanted to obtain her fortune. She tried for three years to make a go of things but finally, much against her religious principles, divorced him. I was amazed that she could speak without rancor; she was grateful to him for their daughter, a charming and pretty girl.

When you want to become a missionary, she said, you either have a general "call" to the field of missionary activity, or you experience a "call" to some specific country. One day she was listening to a speaker from Indo-China who told his audience that they were in great need of a matron for the school in Dalat, but had no money to pay her salary. Then and there she felt a "call" for Indo-China and went out at her own expense. She stayed on, despite the fact that she was never made a real missionary. The regular missionaries did not approve of her generosity to the Annamites. They said she spoiled them, and I think she did. But the natives simply adored her and she went her way unconcerned. She wrote religious tracts in Annamese and had them printed at her own expense; perhaps some of them have done good. She edited a church paper and was busy morning, noon, and night. She was a fortunate woman, for this work filled her with happiness and satisfaction. I stayed with this wonderful person both before and after my trip to Yunnan, and grew fond of her.

It took a little doing to get ready for the trip, so on my first visit I saw little of Hanoi, being too busy with passports, ticket agents, hairdressers, and a much-needed overhaul of my whole person.

12
Yunnan

My decision to see the Burma Road had been made while I sat by the fireside with Dr. Oberdoerffer, at the leper asylum in Chieng Mai. He had just finished telling me that, while attending the Far Eastern Medical Conference at Hanoi the previous November, he had wanted to take the French railroad to Kunming but was refused permission by the German Consul, who said the trip was too dangerous and his safety could not be assured. Other members of the conference were also frightened off by their respective consuls, except for one intrepid Scotsman who returned with wild tales of hardship and of encountering Chinese soldiers who shot at him and one of whom he claimed to have killed. Rumor had it that the mountainous terrain traversed by the railroad remained in the hands of untamed hill tribes who paid no attention to Chiang Kai-shek's edicts. They were said to be growing opium poppies right alongside the railroad tracks, in defiance of the central government's prohibition on opium-growing. One could never be sure these lawless people might not take it into their heads to attack the train and kidnap its passengers for ransom. Moreover, Kunming itself was a dangerous spot, as it was expected that the Japanese would recommence bombing any day; they were supposed to have discovered that they could easily fly through the mountains of Yunnan, simply by following the weekly Eurasia plane from Hong Kong to Kunming. The city was said to have built no bomb shelters, even though two thousand civilians had been killed in a raid that September. Besides, it was so overcrowded that one might easily arrive and find no bed to sleep in.

Even so, Dr. Oberdoerffer regretted bitterly not having gone to Yunnan-fu, or Kunming, as it had recently been renamed (everyone had trouble remembering the new name and all the maps still showed Yunnan-fu as the capital of China's western province of Yunnan). When he said this, I promptly resolved I would go to Kunming. All my friends in Siam thought this extremely foolish, but I had become hard-boiled about danger warnings, since everything always worked out splendidly for George and me. I remembered the uncertainty we had about Sumatra, and what fun we had there—how completely safe it had been, despite all the fearsome beasts said to be lurking in the jungle. Besides, I thought, this might be my last opportunity to see a little more of China before we returned home—the port cities were at that time out-of-bounds for Navy families. Also, like George, I tend to bridle when anybody tries to keep me from doing something on which I have set my mind. To stiffen my backbone, I immediately wrote George I would go. After that I couldn't backtrack or he'd have called me a coward.

Almost at the moment Japan's soldiers and sailors closed China's front door to the world by conquering all the port cities from Chinwangtao to Canton, China's coolies opened the back door by building the Burma Road, thus linking Chungking, via Kunming, with Lashio in Burma, whence a railroad ran south to Rangoon on the Andaman Sea. Everyone who cheered Chiang Kai-shek's gallant fight against the Japanese invaders—and that included just about every European and American in the Far East—was thrilled and excited at this feat of Chinese ingenuity and perseverance. I couldn't possibly miss the chance of seeing the Burma Road.

Mrs. Homer-Dixon, always an adventurous soul, thought it an excellent idea and immediately wrote by airmail to a missionary friend in Kunming, Dr. Evans, begging him to find a place for me to sleep and to meet my train. In this she braved the strong disapproval of Mr. Cadman, the chief Protestant missionary in Hanoi, and practically all the other missionaries there. We were invited to a tea at his house on my first day in Hanoi. As soon as I mentioned having trouble getting train reservations to Kunming, everybody there expressed deepest disapproval and urged me strongly to give up this wild idea. They said I ought not to burden the missionaries in Kunming, who had their hands full with refugees; they warned me that any day the bombing might start up again; they frightened me with stories of imminent anarchy in Yunnan, should Chiang's government collapse. By this time I was inwardly quaking though I put on a show of complete indifference to danger. Mrs. Homer-Dixon and the French railway people who handed me my ticket with a flourish laughed at these woeful predictions and told me to go right ahead. When Mrs. Homer-Dixon kissed me good-bye, I asked her spontaneously to pray for me and she promised she would, and so would all her Annamite boys. As a result everything went favorably for me and I was never even near any sort of danger.

My trip to Kunming took one night and two full days, with an overnight stop in Kai Yuan. By leaving Hanoi in the evening, one could arrive at Lao Kay on the Yunnan border early next morning. Twice a week a fast Micheline (a single self-propelled electric car) made the ride from Lao Kay to Kunming in one very long day. However, at that time it was impossible to get a seat on the Micheline since everything was booked weeks ahead. The wealthy North Chinese, who were traveling up the line to find refuge in the interior, were augmented by many Europeans going there to conclude profitable contracts for supplying the Chinese government with goods of every kind. The Burma Road had not yet been opened to traffic; hence this railroad was Chiang's only link with overseas.

Finally I could get a train reservation and I departed Hanoi. The night train connecting with the Micheline was deluxe and I enjoyed an excellent night's sleep, not only in a first-class berth (the only thing I could get) but in a first-class train completely filled with Europeans and Europeanized Chinese—a novelty for me after the kind of traveling I had done the preceding weeks. When I saw my elegant travel companions and the luxury of a wagon-lit, I felt considerably reassured; these were not people who would go on a dangerous trip— they were too rich, self-assured, and important. The man in the berth next to mine, moreover, turned out to be an Englishman who knew friends of ours on the South China Patrol very well. He immediately promised he would book me a room at Kunming's premier caravanserai, the Hôtel du Lac. He thought it rather risky for me to travel by ordinary train from Lao Kay, but dismissed all talk of danger in Kunming itself. Greatly comforted, I went to sleep.

But next morning, I began to get a sinking feeling when all the elegant wagon-lit passengers departed in the grey light of a cold morning—leaving me in sole possession of the combined first- and second-class coach, which was being coupled to the end of a long freight train with some third-class coaches filled to bursting with soldiers and Chinese refugees. At the right moment, a tall, handsome French railroad engineer got on. He immediately reassured me and promised to see to it personally that I had a pleasant journey. He telegraphed ahead to Kai Yuan, ordering dinner and lodging for me, and issued orders to the train personnel to take special care of me. He went part way with me and we had an interesting talk. As usual, the conversation soon turned to European politics, and American ignorance thereof; this man, too, was full of that French self-assurance I found everywhere in their colony. Somewhat patronizingly he spoke of England's belated awakening to the danger of Nazi Germany; he felt that since she had become France's ally, the two were invincible. For Italy, he had nothing but utmost contempt, deeming Mussolini's troops fit only for guitar-playing and suchlike artistic pursuits but as soldiers—phhht. *Vous comprenez, Madame. Le Français, c'est un soldat, mais ces Italiens.* . . (You understand, Madame. The Frenchman is truly a soldier, but these Italians). There was a military flavor to Indo-China—testimony of its fairly recent pacification by French arms. Bugle calls were heard often and many soldiers in uniform were to be seen on the streets.

While we were talking, a young Greek from the second-class compartment joined us. He was on his way to a job on the railroad and, after the Frenchman left, took over the care of my welfare seeing that I got an excellent lunch. How the tiny, black-toothed Annamite boy managed to concoct it in his little cubbyhole of a kitchen was a mystery, but then it is one of the glories of French colonial genius that they teach the natives to cook.

The young Greek spoke good French and it was obvious that his greatest ambition was to be taken for a Frenchman. The French have the same talent we have of making foreigners living on their territory want to become assimilated. They take the civilized point of view that the essence of Frenchness is French culture and the French spirit. Whoever acquires these becomes a Frenchman. The French railway inspector claimed that for this reason the French were better colonizers than the British who refused to admit into their own closed circle the "lesser breeds without the law." But I felt certain he exaggerated when he said that the French ruled by love. Nobody loves a foreign ruler. Even so, their lack of the deep-seated feeling of superiority which infuriates native people under British rule was a great advantage in winning friendship. I saw a good example of this at Lao Kay.

As the train moved across the frontier to the Chinese customs shed, the French inspector interrupted our conversation to tell me that he had a good friend there, and he hung out of the window and shouted enthusiastically at a Chinese customs official of dignified bearing. The two embraced warmly in the French manner, omitting only the kissing of cheeks which Americans and Britishers find so odd. They acted like long-lost friends and certainly on a basis of complete equality. The inspector told me that his friend was *un brave garçon* (a wonderful guy), one in a million. He liked the Chinese, he said, and compared them favorably with the Annamites, remarking that they were splendid physical specimens, *"de bonne taille, grands comme nous Français* (well set up, and tall like we French)" This rather amused me because I had never thought of the French as particularly tall and well built.

The railroad was owned and operated by a private French company but seemed to enjoy some sort of extraterritorial status. Along the right-of-way, the land was under the French flag and a good-sized area around each station in Yunnan was fenced in, flew the tricolor, and had armed Annamite guards at the entrance and exit gates. It was odd watching a train stop while guards opened a wire gate, and then steam solemnly into a fenced yard. Many Chinese policemen were in evidence all along the way. They looked neat and trim in black and white uniforms—black tunic and breeches, white facings, white caps, white leggings and, of course, the inevitable black bedroom slippers which I first observed in Chefoo and found amusingly unmartial. However, they sternly reprimanded anyone who tried to take pictures and were known to confiscate the cameras of disobedient foreigners, so it wasn't wise to judge them by the slippers.

We had a guard of soldiers on the train all the way to Kunming to protect us against bandits; rather, I suspect, to protect the ammunition and war material we carried. The Japanese were constantly putting pressure on the French to stop the movement of war supplies through Haiphong and Hanoi, but a lot of equipment kept going through. The French stated firmly that no guns were carried on their railroad, but I saw gun mountings sticking out of freight cars on my own train before I was shooed away by a slippered Chinese soldier. At that time Chiang Kai-shek had not yet won complete control over Yunnan, which enjoyed virtual independence until it suddenly became a vital factor in China's defense against Japan. There was still a good deal of mutual distrust; the Governor of Yunnan would not permit armed central government troops in his territory. The ones we saw must have been Yunnanese soldiers. Still, Chiang's influence was gaining steadily and already had become a major factor in suppressing the banditry that had formerly been rampant along the railroad right-of-way. Occasionally, a lonely French railway inspector making his tour in a rail-car might be attacked, but the trains always got through safely. Another result of Chiang's growing influence was the disappearance of the opium poppy fields which used to line the railroad right-of-way. Building the railroad to Kunming was France's final attempt to tap the riches of western China after Garnier's expedition proved the impossibility of using the Mekong as a useful artery of commerce and Jean Dupuis soon afterward reported that the Red River in Yunnam was also useless for this purpose.* These rivers are full of cataracts and change so drastically in depth, depending on the time of the year (floods in the wet season, dry river beds in the dry season), that they are nearly useless for navigation. Dupuis, however, opened an overland trade route to eastern Yunnan which he found rich in minerals.

The Hanoi-Kunming railroad, which more or less follows in Dupuis' steps, was begun in 1901, finished in 1910, and, because of hastily and carelessly drawn plans and poor engineering, cost far

*Garnier's expedition and Dupuis' findings are mentioned in Chapter 10.

more than necessary in money and lives. It is estimated that it cost the lives of some 30 percent of the coolies who were imported from China to build it.* Beyond Lao Kay it passes through lush tropical jungle, then climbs up the valley of the rushing Nam-Ti. The scenery is lovely but this region is among the world's most unhealthy. As I passed through, a serious meningitis epidemic was raging, and malignant malaria is rampant all the time. The valley of the Nam-Ti is called Death Valley.

After an unpropitious start, the railroad had begun to pay handsomely, thanks to the Japanese conquest of China's port cities. It is quite an engineering feat. From Lao Kay to Kunming, it traverses some 400 miles of stupendous mountain scenery, passes through 172 tunnels, goes back and forth from one mountainside to another, above raging torrents, on 107 viaducts and bridges. It winds in endless zigzags along the steep sides of bare, brown mountains—as everywhere in China, long since denuded of all forest growth—often at such heights that to look down from the rear end of my car made me dizzy. Every moment was filled with vistas of great beauty. After lunch on the first day you come into the Yunnanese tableland. When the sun sets, the brown mountains turn blue, red, and purple.

Normally, at the time of year I was traveling, one should reach Kai Yuan just when the light fades, but we were delayed and it was dark when we steamed through the gate in the high, wire fence around the station. The electric plant had gone out of order so I gingerly felt my way in pitch darkness to the bungalow where a comfortable, enormously wide bed awaited me. All the fixings were elegant—tiled bath, modernistic lamps, hot and cold water. Only there were no lights and the water did not run. I turned on all the taps but nothing happened. When I returned from an enjoyable dinner, the water had begun to run again. This was its only spurt of activity, however. For the rest of my stay I used the familiar Chinese pails of water carried by a coolie. In the middle of the night I awoke to bright light. For a moment I feared I had missed my train, but it was only the electric light which had suddenly turned on. Apart from these minor mishaps, the bungalow was fine. The Annamite manager was anxious to please and carted in bundles of soft comforters and a welcome hot-water bottle. Mornings and evenings in Yunnan were cold, but the days were warm and sunny, the air invigorating, and the sky a deep Chinese blue.

On the second day the scenery was even more beautiful and majestic. The people at the stations where we stopped also became

*Virginia Thompson, *French Indo-China*, p. 208.

more fascinating as we entered regions where lived the wild Chinese hill tribes, still virtually unsubdued. They all look more or less Chinese, certainly they are Mongoloid. The men have generally adopted Chinese clothes and look wilder than the Chinese, but the women wore the colorful ancient costumes of their tribes. Most of them were Lolos, in pleated short skirts (reminding me somewhat of Scottish kilts) with scarfs hanging coquettishly down their backs. They wore leggings but no shoes and decorated themselves with huge, round silver earrings, from which silver ornaments dangled. Around the head they wound a blue cloth turban, skillfully folded to resemble a high hat. The relatively few Chinese women I saw all had bound feet; the women of the mountain tribes did not. The women of one tribe, whose name I could not learn, wore long, blue, gathered skirts and a piece of blue cloth wound around the head in such fashion that their long black hair came cascading out at the top like a yak's tail.

As soon as the train stopped, small food stands selling things to eat were set up and brisk trading began. The men stood around smoking water pipes, while the women busily took in the coppers. I kept thinking that it could not be I who was witnessing such movie-type scenes. I felt like a latter-day Marco Polo and enjoyed every minute of the trip. If these people thrilled me by their weird appearance, they were no less intrigued by me. I had by now finished my sweater but was busily at work knitting a cardigan, as it was getting colder all the time. It looked to me as though nobody thereabouts had seen either a white woman or a knitter, for as I sat at the rear of the car, staring at the scene, completely entranced, the scene itself moved around my end of the train, staring at me in utter absorption, chattering, smiling, pointing to my face, my knitting, my clothes. I wish I could have talked to them for they were obviously friendly and eager to start a conversation.

The few houses I saw from the train were mud huts, though occasionally there would be a stone building with the Chinese style of carved eaves and a curved roof. The Chinese coolies who kept the railroad in repair lived in flimsy shelters of bamboo matting. Even though everything was wilder and more primitive, there were so many similarities to what I had seen of China, north of Chefoo, that I was convinced this was indeed a single nation. The Yunnanese are smaller than the North Chinese and they look Tibetan but, except for the tribal women, they are dressed much like other Chinese, and I gather that they are able to understand Peking Chinese.

After lunch on the second day, I had company. A tall, attractive North Chinese gentleman boarded the train. His home was Kunming where he had a flourishing contracting business. He was returning from a survey of the railroad, for which he was to build a tunnel. We were soon talking—French, since he had received his education in France. Although I got along well with Orientals on our trips and made friends with many, I never could understand how a white person could marry into their way of life. Marriage, to my mind, is such a close relationship that it can't possibly succeed unless both partners have similar backgrounds, education, and attitudes towards life. Even with educated Orientals I always sensed a deep barrier because traditionally their way of life has been unlike our own. Also, I had never seen one with any interesting features. But here, for the first time I met a Chinese who was attractive and who treated me with positively Gallic chivalry. I kept forgetting that he was not a Frenchman, and could quite well imagine that a white woman might fall in love with him.

He had gone to Peking five years previously and was then busily putting up all sorts of structures in and around that city. He told me proudly that the Burma Road had been built entirely by hand labor and in only five months. I found out later that he was a little carried away for, in the first place, parts of the road had been built long before Chiang Kai-shek decided to forge this link with the outer world and, in the second place, it took more than a year to build. Still, he had reason to be proud, especially since all the European experts had predicted it would take at least three years to build the road. He told me also how humanely the Chinese treated captured enemies, citing as an example the fact that numerous Japanese communists were enrolled in the Yunnanese armies and were planning the eventual overthrow of the Japanese government. The possibility that these communists might turn against Chiang apparently did not occur to him. This prosperous businessman simply regarded any enemy of Japan as his friend. He said that for centuries the Chinese had been peaceable people who looked down on the soldier as the lowest element in the human scale, but Japanese aggression had finally awakened them to the necessity of defending their country. Even the ricksha coolies of Kunming, he assured me, were now full of fervent patriotism and turned over all their earnings to Chiang on certain fixed days. Somehow I couldn't quite believe that of these tough individuals against whom Europeans and Americans can seldom hold their own. I bet they held back the *kumsha* (tip) at least!

By the time we neared Kunming my new Chinese friend had assured me he would take me safely to a hotel, if I wasn't met by missionary friends. In the meantime, another passenger had joined us. This was an Englishman whose business I never discovered. He urged me to come to the Hôtel de Commerce, where he and his wife were staying for the moment, and where there was a social room with a real fireplace; this must have been that hotel's chief attraction because all its guests bragged about it. When we arrived in Kunming, I was met by Dr. Evans who had obtained a room for me in the house of the English nurses of the CMS (Church Missionary Society) hospital. Thus, after all the dire warnings, I ended up with four different offers of lodging in overcrowded Kunming!

I was glad that Dr. Evans met me, for this was a completely Chinese city and, by myself, I shouldn't have known where to go. The city was exceedingly dusty, dirty, and crowded with assorted humanity. Trucks with soldiers in olive green uniforms were constantly rushing through the narrow streets that looked too small to hold all the rickshas, bullock carts, coolies with carrying poles, automobiles full of refugee North Chinese, soldiers, women, bicycles, and babies. I heaved a sigh of relief when we finally reached the CMS compound. Inside its thick walls all was peaceful; neat red brick houses were set midst flowers on a shady green lawn. It looked like a bit of England. I was cordially welcomed by the English nurses and invited to sit by the fireplace and join them in tea with crumpets and jam. Everything was cozy and far more comfortable than I had any right to expect. There were no bombings during the night—only a small commotion not loud enough to wake me. In the morning I found that we had another visitor. A missionary wife, who had planned to come to the hospital two weeks later, suddenly felt misgivings and had a truck rush her to the nurses' house, where she quietly produced a nice baby without once crying out, the brave woman.

After breakfast I set out to contact some of the people to whom I had forwarded letters of introduction. But first I visited the American Consul, who gave me a letter to Dr. Chiang, President of the Federal University and a one-time student of the International House in New York.* Then I got in touch with the local YMCA people—Mr. and Mrs. Roger Arnold—who were friends of the Zimmermans in Bangkok. Through them I met a number of interesting Chinese officials. The "Y" circuit is quite similar to the missionary circuit, in that once you have entered its magic circle you are passed on, finding helpful friends in each town where there is a "Y," whether run by Americans or local people. It is like one big family. I

---

*This is a handsome building at 500 Riverside Drive, donated by John D. Rockefeller, Jr. It serves as a coeducational dormitory for graduate students of whom only one-quarter are Americans; the rest are from all parts of the world. Under the motto "That Brotherhood May Prevail," which is carved above the main entrance, this miniature One World lives amiably together, producing a network of friendly ties among a growing number of people the world over. George and I resided there while he and I were doing graduate work at Columbia University in 1929.

The Micheline

Street in Kunming

was lucky in that I was privileged to operate in both the "Y" and the missionary circuits, receiving great kindness from both. One of the "Y" people told me of the long march of the students of Changsha, who preferred to walk seventy days across China to Kunming and freedom rather than remain at a Japanese-controlled university. Marching in military formation, they arrived stronger and healthier than when they set out and much better informed about their own country. It was an epic march and I wish someone had written it up.

Kunming was a strange mixture of old and new China. The newcomers regarded the Yunnanese as hopelessly backward and slow-witted, and told me that when they arrived they found conditions medieval. As late as 1935 there were only two automobiles in all of Yunnan: the only Western influence reaching the province had come via the French railroad. George, who went over the full length of the Burma Road six months later on a truck furnished by the central government, wrote fascinating letters about the country. The farther west he moved, the more medieval the country became. He observed the most extraordinary customs and a degree of poverty impossible for a Westerner to visualize. In many villages, mothers hid their children's faces in their laps when George's truck appeared for there—oh, horror—were two fearful creatures, one white, one black (the Hindu driver), and never had they seen anything so horrifying.

Kunming itself, however, was rapidly changing into a replica of a coast city, Chefoo or Amoy perhaps. One seldom saw a foreigner but there were quantities of cars and trucks, uniformed soldiers, scholarly Chinese in long silk coats, tall elegant North Chinese in fur-lined Western style overcoats with beautifully groomed, slender wives, Chinese boys and girls with fresh alert faces and books and papers under their arms coming from or going to classes at one of the many refugee universities; all these gave the town an aspect of modernity. Otherwise, Kunming was an authentic inland city with streets littered and dirty, because the individualistic Chinese see no point in wasting time cleaning up public places—in their own houses they are neat and clean enough. Sewage still floated away in numerous "Rose Creeks," as we used to call the smelliest waterways in Chefoo; there was a ripe, rural odor everywhere. Most houses were built of mud though occasionally I had a glimpse, through the doorway in a high grey wall, of a beautiful, quiet courtyard and a handsome stone house with the picturesque Chinese roof and carved eaves. Once I looked through a moongate and saw a delightful miniature lake surrounded by blossoming shrubs growing in glazed Chinese pottery jars.

The streets were narrow, paved with cobblestones, and always full of children who looked cunning despite their ragged clothing.

They wore brightly embroidered caps—the one bit of luxury on their small persons—fashioned lovingly by their mothers. Bullock carts with massive solid wheels creaked slowly through the traffic, pony caravans brought farm produce from the countryside, and there were even a few sedan chairs, besides hundreds of rickshas. Women carried on their backs large bundles of charcoal, which they brought from villages many miles distant. One of the most astonishing sights was the men carrying salt blocks. Of hemispherical shape, the blocks weighed from 100 to 150 pounds and came from I-ping-lang, one hundred miles west of Kunming. They were strapped to the coolies' backs in a manner similar to that used by the Moi people to carry their beloved pottery jars; attached to this rig was a sort of small umbrella to keep the sun from the bearer's head and the rain from the salt block. You could see these human pack animals on every road leading to the city—eloquent testimony to China's abysmal backwardness.

Kunming is surrounded by a massive old wall, broken by five large square gates with heavy iron doors, all guarded by soldiers. Soldiers indeed were in evidence everywhere. They even stood watch at the entrance gates to the university campuses. The city has many carved arches, commemorating important people or events; these are the Chinese equivalent of monuments. They look odd standing by themselves—gates without a wall on either side.

Three "Y" people—two Chinese, one American—took me to see the Federal University, a combination of three refugee universities from North China. We rode there by ricksha and noticed at once the big potholes all over the campus, and the ruined buildings—evidence of the effectiveness of the previous September's air raid. The Chinese were divided in opinion as to whether the Japanese had been trying to hit the nearby arsenal or were aiming at the students; they were accused of specializing in the bombing of hospitals and schools. Fortunately, a large student assembly had just ended and the students had all dispersed but nine persons were killed. The Federal University had moved into the buildings of the former agricultural school, but the youngsters still slept in the bomb-damaged buildings of the old campus, for there was a great housing shortage. I visited the girls' dormitories where ten girls slept in one small room on double-decker beds—plain wooden pallets without matresses or springs. A table made of boards in the center and some hooks for clothing completed the furnishings. To wash, the girls had to go to the court-yard and, if they wanted a bath, had to go into town—two to three miles distant—to a public bathhouse. Many had the delicate look of the daughters of wealthy Chinese families, but they took to roughing like ducks to water and were a cheerful lot.

Weighing salt blocks

At the old agricultural school we found truly spartan conditions. There were not enough classrooms, tables, desks, chairs, books—everything was in short supply. The boys and girls sat in unheated, bare rooms on rough-hewn hard benches; instead of a blackboard, they made do with sections of cement wall painted black. The library was a pitiful sight: rows of hand-made pine shelves all along the walls with hardly a book on them. The students had not been able to carry many books with them on the long march to freedom; what they brought along was donated to the library but it didn't begin to answer the need. They managed with mimeographed class notes and programs but, I was told, refused to lower academic standards. Many of the youngsters left beautifully appointed campuses, preferring Kunming's freedom. The government paid the living expenses and tuition of all who were too poor to pay or whose families could not get money to them from Occupied China—about two-thirds of the students. Strangely enough, the rough life seemed to agree with them. They looked sturdier and stronger than any Chinese students I had ever seen. A great deal of athletic activity was going on. Besides a heavy school program, all the boys and girls engaged in various patriotic extracurricular work—propaganda, theatricals for country folk to stir up interest in the war, first-aid classes, etc. I was impressed with their spirit. Students, as well as adults, took the war and privation without wasting time pitying themselves; without heroics but with quiet determination to hold on forever if need be.

I had a look at the school kitchens and was told that the students ate in shifts since there weren't enough tables, chinaware, or chopsticks to go around. They ate plain coolie food and did their own cooking and cleaning.

It was a lovely afternoon, sunny and warm. As we rode back to it in our ricksha, the city looked like a medieval fortress, the only modern touch being the many signs painted on the old grey walls—"Exterminate the Traitors," "Deliver the Lost Provinces," and so forth. I thought that from a distance Kunming probably looked much as it had when Marco Polo passed that way seven hundred years ago.

We passed through streets full of smelly, though lovable, humanity and visited the campus of the old Yunnan University, which looks French, as does all that part of the city between the campus and the Hôtel du Lac. From the university one has a wonderful view over the roofs of the town. From there we went to Mulberry Gardens—a vast park with temples, small lakes, bridges, dwarf trees, and flowers. We heard chanting and entered a temple where Buddhist priests were going through a series of circumambulation—bowing, walking in circles with folded arms, kneeling, chanting, and turning solemnly round and round. There were candles and a mist of

Gate at Kunming

Entrance to garden in Kunming

incense; deep, musical sounds emanated from large bronze gongs. It was an authentic bit of traditional China amidst all the bustle of Chiang Kai-shek's New Life Movement.

I visited Dr. Chiang, head of the Federal University, and several other professors who told me about university life under stress and of the long march of the students. They were charming gentlemen with polished manners but with an astonishing nonchalance towards the danger of bombing and a fierce, unacademic determination to fight the Japanese to the end. Some said the bombings were a good thing really, since there, where they were so far away from actual combat, they needed an occasional reminder to keep the people's patriotism burning brightly.

I had been thinking how little difference there is between cultivated people of scholarly minds the world over, when I was amazed at the response of these suave gentlemen to my remarks about the sack of Nanking. The horrible atrocities committed by the Mikado's soldiery had shocked the world and I said something to this effect. "Well, you know how it is," they replied. "The Japs had to fight hard to get the city and in war you have to expect a little looting and raping." It suddenly dawned on me that were the positions reversed, the Chinese might well have acted no differently. Small things like this often crop up, just when you feel completely at home with Orientals, reminding you that there still remains a great difference between their outlook on life and ours.

Next day, two of the English nurses invited me on an all-day picnic. We took baskets of food and left early while it was cool. I was glad to get out of the city. Being at heart a coward, I never lost my fear of bombing while in Kunming. Along the road to Tali-fu, we passed innumerable shallow holes dug in the ground and in hillsides. These were the bomb shelters. The Chinese told me frankly that they did not expect to do much fighting against attacking planes since it did little good and wasted ammunition. In the September raid, most of the damage had been done not by bombs but by Japanese machine-gun fire, the planes flying low and gunning the people who were fleeing the city. In future raids, the people were expected to get into these holes and there, it was hoped, remain unseen by the flyers. Moreover, the holes were expected to give safety against any bombs falling more than twenty yards away. These were grim reminders of the war, and I looked anxiously at the sky as we sped away from Kunming towards the western hills.

The country was lovely. There were rice fields like green lakes, a river turning many huge water wheels, villages hidden in foliage—all so peaceful we soon forgot the war. The hills around the city are wooded, which is unusual in China, and there was a large lake.

Scene near Kunming

Kunming is situated 7,500 feet above sea level and, though its latitude is about the same as Miami, Florida, it has a continental climate and cold winters, pleasantly dry and usually sunny. It seldom gets unbearably hot in summer. Pines and other flora give it a northern aspect; in fact, this part of Yunnan is called the Chinese Switzerland.

We were now driving on the famed Burma Road I had come so far to see. It follows approximately the ancient Tribute Road on which Marco Polo traveled east. Sections of that trail have been incorporated into the new macadamized road, but on our way we could still see parts of the old trail—paved with large stone slabs and shaded by poplars—meandering through the countryside. Most of the country roads are raised above the fields so that the rickshas, the ponies, the walking coolies, the bullock carts, and the sedan chairs which use them in preference to the new road, appear like silhouettes against the sky. You get a picture that reminds you of patterns on Chinese tapestries.

The part of the Burma Road on which we were traveling had been *automobilable*, as the French say, for years as far as Tali-fu. It was macadamized in 1933. The Burma Road was actually not built in its entirety in the previous year, as one might have believed when listening to some of its boasters. The part between Lashio, at the northern end of the railroad to Rangoon, and the Chinese border at Wanting had been an all-weather road for a good many years, and sections of the road between the border and Kunming and thence to Chungking had for a long time been usable by motor vehicles, at least during the dry season. The absence of such vehicles in formerly backward Yunnan, however, made it unnecessary to build these roads strong enough to stand up under heavy truck traffic. Much of the building of the Burma Road was, therefore, a matter of widening, strengthening, and hard-surfacing existing roads.

But there remained the stupendous engineering feat of bridging the deep gorges of the Mekong and Salween rivers, which had not been attempted earlier because the cost was all out of proportion to any profit that could have been derived from peacetime traffic. In war, of course, cost is immaterial. When the Chinese government decided to complete the road, late in 1937, an army of 200,000 to 300,000 coolies, carrying only picks and shovels and lacking any modern road-building equipment whatsoever, was used. The headmen of each village were paid a sum calculated to defray the cost of food in that particular locality (less, the farther west the road moved), and it was left to them to mobilize the necessary manpower to build the section for which they were made responsible. By the time I arrived in Kunming in February 1939, the task had been virtually completed. Without modern engineering aids, the gorges had been bridged with steel-cable suspension bridges, and innumerable culverts and bridges, built of timber, had been converted into solid masonry structures. Much of the work was done in extremely dangerous malarial regions which had previously been shunned by all natives but there, too, the building went on and the task was done. The question on everybody's mind when I visited there was the ability of the road to withstand the effects of the rainy season, during which landslides were expected to occur in many places.

I could vividly picture to myself how the construction must have looked, for something similar was going on along our way. No sooner was the road completed, than they began constructing a railroad to parallel it. From Kunming to a point about 110 miles to the west, I noticed hundreds of coolies swarming over the hills and through the rice fields, throwing up earth embankments along a broad white line that the engineers had drawn straight across the country. Some coolies were blasting tunnels through the hills, others were working on bridges and culverts. They worked in small groups, each assigned a section of the roadbed, so that the embankment along the entire 110 miles rose simultaneously. The Chinese expected to complete the railroad in four years. Work had begun a month previously and, to my untrained eye, the embankment appeared one-third finished. The coolies looked like ants as they moved about, heavily loaded with earth and stone.

I was puzzled why the Chinese had embarked on railroad construction which required import of vast quantities of rail equipment that could not be made locally. How could they have hoped to bring it in on their slender lines of communication with the outside world, which were already overloaded with war material? I had heard that another railroad, connecting Chungking with Sian-fu, was under construction. The answer I received was typically Chinese—so many high-ranking railroad officials had fled to Yunnan from occupied China, losing their well-paid jobs, that the Chinese Railway Administration felt compelled to provide them with new jobs by building the requisite railroads!

Yunnan had certainly become a scene of feverish building activities. The tall North Chinese, who strike you for some odd reason as fellow exiles in a backward land, had brought money and initiative and started all sorts of new industrial enterprises. Several International House alumni were among these industrial pioneers. One had built a new power house and was running it efficiently. Others had set up thriving factories. I heard that whoever could do nothing else, built a brick factory. Kunming was the busiest place imaginable. There was no unemployment despite the crowds of refugees. The city had three to four times its normal population and was rapidly becoming a boom town. There were even automatic traffic signals in Kunming though, as one might expect, they worked only half the time.

The good Yunnanese peasants seemed hardly affected by all this bustling life around them. They wore their traditional blue cotton clothes, usually in rags; they lived in their primitive mud huts and plowed the land in their ancient manner; they thought little of the war, for it was too far away to concern them and I suspect few knew what it was about. Meanwhile, they rejoiced in the welcome rain of coppers. The women wore strange-looking blue kerchiefs around the head or a sort of band across the forehead, resembling a horse's eyeshade. The American Consul told me that they had few manufactured goods but had plenty of food and were a healthy lot. This they had to be, for they were truly beasts of burden. One could see men and women all along the road, carrying heavy loads on their backs. It was a good thing someone had invented the T-stick so they could rest their burdens occasionally. I also saw many bullock carts and pony caravans winding slowly around the hillsides or being carried across the mountain streams on primitive ferries pulled by ropes stretched across the water.

We climbed a steep road leading to the Flower Temple, a place of great peace, beauty, and quiet, and the cleanest temple I ever saw in China. Potted cherry trees and magnolias were blooming in the courtyards. A fierce guardian image and a dragon protected each side of the entrance. Their purpose was not to frighten worshippers but to ward off evil spirits. Inside we found the usual figures of the Buddha—enormous, serene, and glittering. Since China's Buddhism is of the Mahayana kind, there were also many lesser deities in the temple. I was struck with the five hundred genii, some good, some bad; a wild confusion of gesticulating porcelain figures. The wicked ones had fiery red faces; the good ones looked serene. Some rode elephants or lions. One had elongated arms stretched straight up to heaven; he is supposed to be the one to ask for heavenly favors because he can reach them for you. Another figure had long legs like a stork. A fat goddess sat smiling in the midst of children sprawling all over her; she is the one whom Chinese women ask for more children.

Signs at the entrance to the temple said that it could accommodate no more people. Temples always act as sort of inns for wayfarers, who sleep right beside the good Buddhas. This temple was filled with refugee students sitting in every convenient niche or embrasure, their heads buried in textbooks. There was the continuous sound of a deep-toned gong: as soon as the sonorous sound produced by hitting the gong died away, it was hit again so that there

Constructing the Burma Road

Yunnanese peasant

The Flower Temple and guardians

500 genii at Flower Temple

was a ceaseless swelling and ebbing of its resonant tone—soothing to the ear.

We went on to a charming town near some famous hot springs and caves. People were sitting in the sunny courtyard of the inn adjacent to the hot springs. Several weddings were going on, as it was apparently a propitious day for such festivities. We met a number of wedding processions; the shy brides were all in pink and had pink flowers in their hair; the bridegrooms wore the traditional brown silk. One of the brides was weeping disconsolately.

We had our picnic in front of the caves, whose walls were covered with Chinese poetry. Many contented people must have preceded us at this lovely spot. We faced a river with an ancient water wheel turning slowly. Willow trees bordered the stream and early spring flowers grew on the grass beside us. Everything was idyllically rural and peaceful. It was a pleasant end to my excursion to dangerous Yunnan.

On the morning of my departure I was awakened by a cannon shot. Heavens to Betsy, I thought, they've come after all! But it wasn't Japanese bombers—merely the salute at sunrise. The Chinese were really getting to be a martial people. Everyone I had met in Kunming came to the station to see me off. Though I had known them such a short time, they seemed like old friends. In these out-of-the-way places friendships develop rapidly.

The train ride back to Hanoi was uneventful, except for the trials and tribulations of a CMS missionary couple with two small children—one a baby of thirteen months, the other two and a half years old—whom I discovered in a third-class coach. They had traveled from Chengtu by bus, a hard, long trip, taking two weeks. They were on their way to Haiphong and a boat home for furlough, knowing not a single word of French. The children were lively, the parents looked drawn and weary, but never lost their patience with the little ones. They did their own cooking amidst crowds of Chinese, bundles, and babies. It was a trying experience for them and I admired their fortitude, although I felt resentful at the comfortable mission boards in England which decreed that missionaries must always travel third-class, regardless of circumstances. At Kai Yuan we had trouble getting the children's food fixed properly. Though the Chinese always stood around in admiring circles to watch the children—they do so love children—they were inefficient in providing the right kind of baby food. I helped them as much as I could at Lao Kay and got them settled on the night train to Haiphong.

When I arrived in Hanoi early in the morning, I found Mrs. Homer-Dixon ready with a delicious breakfast. She told me all her boys had prayed for me, and obviously this had been effective.

13
Tonkin

I might easily have made myself a nuisance, since I was highly elated about my courageous defiance of the Cassandras of Hanoi, but I was saved by the arrival of Miss Nellie Jones, an American missionary from Kweilin, who visited us while waiting for her boat to America. She had just come through the Porte de Chine, the gate in the wall separating Tonkin from China, near Lang Son, after completing a dangerous journey by truck through bandit-infested country where there were neither Japanese nor Chinese law enforcement forces. Her stories were far more exciting than mine so I kept quiet.

Kweilin had been bombed almost daily for three months. When the siren blew, everybody rushed to the natural caves at the edge of town. The bombing was a great boon to the ricksha boys who pocketed one dollar Mex (worth 33 cents American in 1937, but steadily declining in value as the war progressed) for the short ride to safety. During the ten minutes that elapsed between the warning of the sirens and the arrival of the bombers, the boys put on a fantastic spurt of dashing back and forth which netted them enough to dawdle the rest of the day. Miss Jones said that people got used to grabbing babies, passport, money, and a basket of food seconds after the first wail of the siren, and soon they took the whole thing as a matter of routine.

Many Chinese worked at night and slept during the day in the safety of the caves. Others kept their stores closed in the mornings, since the raids occurred before noon, and hurried their business through in the afternoons. The moment the bombers left, everyone returned home and took up immediately where he had left off before the alarm sounded. If homes and shops were found in ruins, the owners kept right on living and doing business on the spot, while they cleared away the rubbish and started to rebuild. She thought the net effect of the bombing was to make the Chinese furious and strengthen their determination not to give in; it cost the Japanese more to bomb than it did the Chinese to rebuild. The most maddening thing, she said, was to have the bombers come minutes after the new wash had been hung in the yard. Since white clothes were the signal given by traitors to guide the bombers, the wash had to be torn off the lines immediately—a great nuisance.

So much had happened in the twenty-two years Miss Jones had spent in the China mission, that nothing fazed this intrepid lady. In the early days, Kweilin was often the prize fought over by competing warlords. When the city was beleaguered by Warlord A, everybody bought A's flag so as to be ready to welcome the deliverer, should he succeed in taking the city. Sooner or later, of course, defeated Warlord B would arrive with new troops, whereupon there was a brisk trade in B's flags, to be hung from the windows when he marched in victoriously. The citizens didn't care who took control since they were equally bad. The only truly unpleasant situation occurred when the soldiers inside the city decided their cause was hopeless and stole away to go back home, while outside soldiers remained in ignorance of this happy state of affairs, for then the bandits would take over. Disguised as country folk, they slipped into the city during the interregnum and looted it thoroughly.

Those were the days of leisurely and civilized old-style Chinese warfare. Few lives were lost because the weaker side could usually be bought off by the stronger. Missionaries were often let down from the city walls to palaver for peace. Defeated soldiers sought refuge in the mission compounds. It was never difficult to find a former student or acquaintance among the invaders who could be induced to grant reasonable terms to these soldiers. Usually, the majority enlisted under the victorious flag and the few who had had enough of soldiering could be put into hospital gowns, given bandages to wrap around head or arm for disguise, and kept in the mission hospital as "wounded" prisoners of war.

At one time Miss Jones was quite ill and was sent down the Si Kiang River to the hospital in Wuchow. The river was controlled by a powerful bandit who had a tendency to kidnap missionaries and hold them in uncomfortable captivity until the Chinese government could be prevailed upon to pay the ransom; this was apt to take weeks, but the government had to do it in the end, or lose face for not being able to protect foreigners in China. In the meantime, the captured missionaries were given little food and had to do much walking and climbing to keep up with the bandit armies. Such treatment would have been fatal to Miss Jones, who was extremely ill. Fortunately arrangements were made through friends for her to pass downriver under the protection of the bandit flag. Everyone in Wuchow was amazed when she arrived safely, and had avoided being robbed on the way. "No indeed," said she. "Why, I joined the bandits myself."

Miss Jones needed a little refurbishing, so I took her shopping in the afternoon and invited her to have tea with me at the elegant

Hotel Metropole, where an excellent White Russian orchestra played old-fashioned waltz music. Hanoi was more attractive than Saigon. Many parts of it were French, especially near the imposing opera house and along the pretty lake where flower girls sold their wares. Nearby was the Café de la Paix where one could sit all day at small tables on the sidewalk and watch the world go by.

Next day I spent a quiet and pleasant morning with Truth, Mrs. Homer-Dixon's secretary who was usually detailed to look after guests and who showed them the town according to his own personal itinerary, from which it was impossible to budge him. I felt that I had seen so many temples on this trip that I might skip some of those in Hanoi, but I found myself kept firmly to the regular tour. Truth was a gentle soul who worshiped foreigners, especially Americans. He lived a life of dignity and ease in Mrs. Homer-Dixon's office. She said he was too weak to do any real work and so she gave him this job, since he was a good Christian. He loved acting as guide.

First, we went to look at the Temple of Literature, the Van Miêu, also known as the Raven Pagoda. Like all such temples of literature in the Far East, it was a replica of the one in Kiu-Feou, birthplace of Confucius. We passed through several shady courtyards where large old trees and overgrown weeds and bushes create an atmosphere of country quiet, which is strange right in the midst of a big city. Everywhere there are greyish, moss-covered walls, stone tablets, and rows of stone tortoises (symbols of perseverance and longevity). In the center of the third court there is a quadrangular pond, the Well of Celestial Brilliance, in which bloom a few lotus. Naturally, there are Chinese gates, blue dragons, and tiled roofs. From one of the gate towers, we had a fine view of the temple grounds and the city of Hanoi. In the Temple of Confucius there is the customary tablet inscribed with his name. In accordance with tradition, there are no statues or images of any kind—only chests and tables of dark red lacquer and several stork-shaped candlesticks. The storks (symbols of wisdom and filial devotion) stand on a tortoise base. These candlesticks are seen in all Confucian temples and they can be bought on Brass Street for one and a half piastres a pair.

Next we went to see the so-called Great Buddha who is not really a Buddha but the Spirit of Huyên-Vu or Trân-Vu. Since he looks Buddhistic, visitors insist on calling him a Buddha. One may look at this great bronze statue through a red silk curtain which the priests will lift for a small consideration, while electric lights are turned on to illuminate the figure. Ponderous and mysterious, he sits in the shadows and all that can be seen clearly are his false beard and his big toe.

The Raven Pagoda

Temple of Confucius

Finally I saw the Môt-Côt, or Temple of the Column. This was a graceful little pagoda sitting on top of a thick column in the midst of a lotus-covered lake. Its construction is attributed to King Ly-Thanh-Tôn who wanted to commemorate an apparition which proved to be auspicious. The king had long wished for a son. One night the goddess Quan-Am, seated on a gigantic lotus blossom that rose out of the water of the lake, appeared to him in a dream. She presented him with a child and, surely enough, a year later the long-awaited son was born.

Tonkin seems to be full of kindly spirits. The Pagoda of Jade Island, located in the middle of a small lake called Hô Hoàn-Kiêm (Restored Sword Lake), was built in memory of just such another spiritual apparition. The legends say that during the short period in the fifteenth century when Tonkin—in fact all Annam—was under the control of the Chinese (1414–1428), a young fisherman named Lê-Loi cast his net into the small lake that is now in the center of the French part of Hanoi. Suddenly he felt a weight in his net and, upon pulling it up, discovered that he had caught a miraculous sword. He seized it instantly and proceeded to fight the Chinese, defeating them and making Tonkin and Annam once more free and independent. Whereupon he crowned himself king and became the founder of the second Lê dynasty. Clothed in his coronation robes, and girded with the miraculous sword, he offered a sacrifice to the Spirit of the Lake. During the rites, the sword rose out of its sheath into the air, turned into a jade dragon, and then disappeared into the lake. The king naturally built a pagoda to remember this event. It is still there, proving the truth of the story.

There is just this much truth in it: Tonkin and Annam were liberated from China largely through the valor and leadership of a distinguished citizen named Lê-Loi, who drove out the weak and decadent sovereign and replaced him on the throne. The Lê dynasty eventually became decadent, too, and had to fight to retain the throne against a family of contenders of the name Mac. The Lê-Mac civil wars still live in the memory of many Tonkinese and the names of the rivals can, even today, stir partisanship. Another ancient dynastic feud, which may perhaps be revived to set Annamites against Tonkinese, is that of the Cochin Chinese Annamite Nguyens and the Tonkinese Trinhs. This ended in the triumph of the Nguyens under Gia-Long, who reunited Tonkin, Annam, and Cochin China into a single empire—Annam—in 1802, as I have previously mentioned.

For a foreigner there seems to be little difference between the Tonkinese and their southern brethren—they are generally known by the name of Annamites and can be distinguished chiefly by their costume. North of the Porte d'Annam, which is about 45 miles north of Dong Hoi and was once the gateway of the ancient Annam frontier, men and women wear brown clothes and wide, flat, round hats resembling circular trays with narrow rims; south of the Porte d'Annam everyone wears black coats, black or white trousers, and small pointed straw hats that resemble mushrooms. The Tonkinese are said to be more industrious than the southerners and less beautiful, but I couldn't see any difference.

While we were wandering about, Truth told me, in his gentle voice, of the iniquities of the French. He felt that Tonkinese were good scholars who were always at the top of their class in the public schools, far outstripping the French youngsters, but that when it came to jobs, they were invariably passed over for Frenchmen and had to be content with inferior, poorly paid government positions. This was a complaint made generally by colonials with a little Western education, and no doubt they had a point. But it seemed to me their resentment went beyond what was reasonable, in that they judged the accomplishments of Western civilization superficially without understanding that it was based upon a solid foundation totally lacking in the East. Asiatics tended to think that because they knew how to operate a machine, they could also build it; or, if they could build it, that this ability was equivalent to inventing it. They often wanted to take over Western techniques without going through the process of learning and discipline that produces and maintains modern industrialism. They seldom realized that our civilization developed slowly through changes in human thought and behavior; gradual democratization of government, as education spread among the masses, enabling them to exercise the duties of free citizenship; growth of intellectual power as the mind emancipated itself from medieval superstition and conventional behavior patterns and accepted the discipline of scientific thinking.

Truth said the French claimed they had to pay their own people high salaries to compensate for the sacrifice they were making by living in Indo-China. "We have plenty of people who could do their work. We don't need them. They don't have to suffer here in exile." I was surprised at his bitterness, for he was the first Annamite I heard say anything unfavorable about the French. When I mentioned to him that my friend the railway inspector had said the French ruled by love, he laughed cynically and told me that there was much Communist unrest and that some years previously an insurrection had been planned for New Year's Day so that the shooting would not be noticed amidst the general jollification. But the French had learned of the plan and thwarted it immediately and ruthlessly. "There is no hope for us," he said sadly. "Our backbone has been broken. We have been suppressed too long."

Even at that, said Truth, the country was much better off under the French than under the Chinese, and he proceeded to tell me gruesome stories of the atrocities committed by these ancient enemies of Annam. They used to kidnap men to work their silver mines, forcing each man into a deep mine shaft where he lived out the rest of his days,* digging the silver-bearing ore and sending it up in baskets, which would be returned to him with just enough food to keep up his strength. He never saw daylight again. If he ceased sending up baskets, it was presumed he had died. A new victim would be caught and lowered into the mine, and his first task would be to bury his predecessor; thereafter he would go on digging the silver-laden earth.

When I talked to Mrs. Homer-Dixon about Truth's complaints she commented that, like all Annamites, he confused ability to get good grades at school with ability to cope with the challenge of real life. She thought the real problem was overpopulation in Tonkin and Annam, with consequent frailty of the population. Possibly this could be overcome—to the cost of the Lao and Cambodians—by migration into the less crowded parts of Indo-China. At that, the country isn't as badly off as the rest of continental Asia because the majority at least own the land they cultivate. Only in Cochin China were there many large plantations.

Truth and I set out next morning for the Paper Village, half an hour's ride by streetcar from town. I was familiar with Oriental specialization by streets (brass street, slipper street, silver street, etc.), but that was the first village I'd seen where everyone did one single thing, and nothing else. Men, women, and children participated in making paper according to such archaic procedures that I wouldn't be surprised if they had remained unchanged for two thousand years. Paper-making was known in China as early as the second century B.C. and probably, therefore, also to the Tonkinese, who were then subjects of China.

Paper was made from the bark of the wind tree, or Cây Gió. You could see the bark hanging in large bundles from the ends of the carrying poles of many sweating coolies trotting into the village. After several days' soaking in water to soften it, the bark is torn into strips and put into great clay kilns, with alternate layers of quicklime and banana leaves on top. The mixture is covered with water and cooked for four days. Then it is again soaked in water to separate

---

*This is what the early Spaniards did to the Indians of Mexico.

the outer layer of bark, from which coarse paper is made, from the inner, from which white paper is made. Both kinds of paper are finished in the same manner.

Next, the soaked bark is crushed into a pulp, which is done in small sheds all over the village. These sheds have such low roofs that you can see only the bare legs of men busily stamping the bark. When they have finished, water is again mixed with the bark, and to this is added the sap of a tree called Gô Mun, which has adhesive qualities. By then the mixture has taken on the aspect of thin pea soup. This completes the work of the men, and the women take over. They stand on either side of a tank filled with this "pea soup," holding flat, square, wooden trays with shallow rims. These they dip into the liquid, skillfully taking only the quantity needed for a single sheet of paper. With a swift turn of the wrist, they flop the trays upside down onto a pile, thus depositing a thin layer of pulp.

When the pile has reached a given height, it is carried away to the presses. These are primitive affairs which reminded me of the rice-hulling contraptions I saw in Laos. A thick upright log has been staked into the ground. It has a notch on top through which a long thick log has been passed. The pile of pulp is placed close to the upright log; then a bundle of heavy stones is attached to the other end of the crosswise log, which tapers slightly, and as it is pulled down, the log squeezes the water out of the layers of paper. If necessary a small Annamite will crouch on top of the log to add his weight to the stones. This part of the paper-making process looks like fun.

The raw paper sheets are finally peeled off the pile and dried in the sun or, if the weather is wet, in sheds heated by open fires. The end product of this time-consuming process of manufacture is a rough, pulpy sort of paper that nobody in the West would dream of using. The whole procedure seemed an incredible waste of time, but many hundreds of poor people make their living that way. I wondered what would become of them once they got pushed out of the market by machine-made paper.

Looking backward into history was one of the most intriguing features of my travels into this part of the world. It was as if the history of mankind were unrolled before my eyes—from the Stone Age, represented by the Negritos in the Philippines and the Mois in Laos, to the beginnings of Asiatic industrialization. I was glad to have had the opportunity to see this pre-industrial manufacturing process before it disappeared from the earth. It also demonstrated to me the reason why paper is treated as an expensive commodity in all of Southeast Asia.

Nearby, we saw a village where bricks were made in a primitive brick kiln, and another where a dozen weavers wove silk cloth on

Temple of the Column

Making paper in village near Hanoi

hand looms. This process I found particularly interesting because here was visible the very beginning of factory production as I had seen it described in textbooks on economics. The weavers represented the transition stage between handcraft and the modern factory. Previously a master weaver had owned one loom and worked in his small shop with the assistance of apprentice boys. Here a master weaver had in some fashion become rich enough to own twelve looms which he lined up in a room in his house, hiring men to work them at a small monthly wage (2 or 3 piastres in this case) plus room and board. The owner no longer did any weaving himself, but supervised his workers and managed the business of buying raw materials and selling the finished product. He was an industrialist in embryo. By assembling his workers in one room, instead of giving out work to be done in the workers' homes, he was able to effect savings through greater efficiency of production. From this to the modern factory only one additional step was needed: acquisition of power looms. The weavers were working at top speed, banging down with the right foot and yanking the thread out hard by hand. They worked from dawn to dark in crowded, unsanitary surroundings, yet this kind of work was considered preferable to farming and carried greater prestige. Each man had a small boy to help him and, perhaps, to learn the trade by watching. The lengths of finished silk were stretched out on the meadow behind this miniature factory, and held taut by bamboo trestles. The silk sold for about 20 to 30 American cents a yard and was inferior to the machine-made product. Soon the little industrialist, who looked as ragged and dirty as his workers, would have to switch to power looms or go bankrupt.

If the manufacturing activities of these villagers were primitive, their plumbing was even more so. I felt that I had reached a new low as I gingerly stepped around neatly placed little heaps in the outdoor latrines of the Paper Village through which winds the path connecting it with the outside world. At times, villagers were seen squatting with thoughtful expressions on their faces and total lack of embarrassment. Nearby ran a small brook where other villagers were washing vegetables for the market in Hanoi, tying them into neat bundles which might easily give the unwary housewife a wrong impression of their cleanliness. The Annamites have many admirable qualities but cleanliness is not their strong point. Even the silk-clothed, dainty women who trip around Hanoi on high-heeled slippers lack that well-scrubbed look around the neck and ears which we in the West require even of unwilling boys.

Many of the young Tonkinese girls are pretty. Their delicate, oval faces with large, long-lashed eyes are set off attractively by their peculiar headdress. They twist their long, black hair into a rope, encase it in white or black-velvet tubing and, starting above the right ear, wind it counterclockwise around the head so that it forms a crown. Formerly, the girls allowed a long strand of hair to hang out of the casing to show they had so much that it couldn't be confined. Around the neck, they wear silver necklaces, which are actually neckrings, i.e., stiff round rings embossed in front and tapering off towards the back. These are peculiar to the country and may well have been copied from similar neckrings worn by the primitive Man-Coc mountain tribes. Most girls wear these silver neckrings, but occasionally you see one who has a rich husband (or a French protector) and has been given a gold neckring. I thought them so attractive that I bought one for myself—silver, since I have no rich husband.

To Western eyes, the beauty of Tonkinese ladies is impaired by their black-lacquered teeth and their constant betel-nut chewing. Black teeth are beautiful to the Tonkinese, who consider white teeth ugly, and call them "dog's teeth." It is said that during the Chinese conquest of the country there was much unrest, and that sporadically underground conspirators would start local revolts. The Chinese found it difficult to identify traitors because it was often hard to tell who was Chinese and who Tonkinese, so they decreed that for easier identification the Tonkinese blacken their teeth. Later, as I mentioned before, the miraculous sword appeared and Lê-Loi freed Tonkin. But by that time the Tonkinese were so proud of having driven the Chinese out that they had come to regard black teeth as a badge of honor and clung to the custom. In this they resembled the Chinese themselves, who long refused to give up their pigtails—a custom originally imposed upon them by the Manchus after they had conquered China. The lacquering of teeth requires a period of silence lasting several hours; girls are apt to tease each other and induce the quiet sitters to laugh or speak, so that the lacquering has to be done all over again.

In recent years Tonkinese women have been making great strides towards Western-style chic. Many now keep their teeth white, this being no longer considered a sign of easy virtue, as previously it was. Many use rouge, lipstick, and face powder and wear high-heeled shoes. With their dangling jade earrings, these modernized ones are distinctly attractive, as the French gentlemen are only too anxious to acknowledge. Malicious gossip indicates that the French in Indo-China were engaged in a perpetual triangle: Monsieur paid court to another man's wife; Madame had a French lover. But Monsieur also had a *congaie* which gave him the advantage in this game. The poor Tonkinese men were left with a greatly reduced supply of pretty girls for brides. No wonder Truth was bitter toward the French.

Since I was about to leave the betel-nut chewing peoples of the world for good—having been among them from Moroland in the Southern Philippines, all through the Malay Archipelago, up the Malay Peninsula, and through Siam and Indo-China—I was delighted to hear Truth's story of how the custom arose. This is the legend, as told in Tonkin.

Once upon a time there were twin brothers who were extremely close to each other. But, as often happens in stories, one day they met a beautiful girl with whom both fell in love. She did not know which one she should marry for, in Tonkin, younger sons and daughters may not marry until the older ones have. It would, therefore, have been improper for her to fall in love with the younger brother. But she could not determine which was the older, nor would anyone tell her. In order to discover the firstborn, she resorted to ruse. One day she brought them two bowls of rice, but only one pair of chopsticks. Then she hid behind a curtain and watched. When they had finished eating, she came out blushing and smiling and pointed to one brother saying she loved him and wanted to marry him. He was the one who had eaten first.

The young pair lived happily and so great was their devotion that they completely forgot the twin brother, who had lost both his love and his brother. This made him so sad that he no longer considered life worthwhile and he became a wanderer. Finally he came to a wide river where there was no ferry to take him across. This was the final straw and he could not further endure his fate so he sat down and died of a broken heart. The gods turned him into a shaft of limestone.

After a while the two lovers came out of their trance and noticed the absence of the twin brother. Remorse shook the young husband and he immediately set off to find his brother, coming in due time to the same river, where he sat down and contemplated his thoughtlessness toward his brother. This broke his heart and he died and was turned by the gods into an areca palm.

The young wife waited and waited but, as neither the husband nor the twin brother returned to her, she went after them, came to the river, sat down thinking sadly of her wasted life, and also died of a broken heart. The gods turned her into a betel vine growing between the limestone and the areca palm and embracing both as she climbed upwards.

Eventually the story of these unhappy young people reached the ear of the emperor, who decided to look for them. He set out with an army of retainers, at last reaching the same river, where he sat down beside the limestone shaft, while his men built a raft to cross the river. Accidentally, he rubbed a nut from the areca palm against a leaf from the betel vine and touched the limestone with his hand. He noticed the deep red juice on the rock, and in a flash the whole sad tale was revealed to him. He decreed that, in memory of the three unhappy young people, all the inhabitants of the country should rub limestone, areca nut, and the betel vine together and chew the mixture. Since everyone liked the pleasant feeling this left in the mouth, it became the law of the land and was enthusiastically obeyed throughout the realm.

On my last day in Hanoi I had a quick look through the interesting museum of the *Ecole Française d'Extrême-Orient,* a treasure house of statuary, jewelry, tools, weapons, etc. from Indo-China, Burma, Siam, and China. In the afternoon, Mrs. Homer-Dixon had a tea party for Annamite ladies, whom I enjoyed meeting. All of them knew a little French so we were able to carry on an interesting conversation, primarily about the comparative ways of life in America and Annam.

Next day I went by train to Haiphong, arranged with the China Travel Service for passage to Manila via Hong Kong, stored most of my baggage with the clerk, and boarded the launch *Sacric* for the five-and-a-half-hour trip to Hon Gay, which is the starting point for visiting the famous Bay of Along. Besides its fantastic beauty, the bay has at Hon Gay extensive coal mines that lie close to the surface and were mined in much the same way as they were once mined by the Chinese—the coal was simply scooped up and carted away. The *Sacric* was a small boat, but the *commissionaire* (this was the title given to captains of such launches) made me comfortable, gave me a cabin, and saw that I was served a good dinner. We reached Hon Gay at 10:30 that night, docking right in front of the Hôtel des Mines, where I stayed for a day.

In the morning I hired a motorboat to take me around the bay. At first, the day was grey and the curious rock formations were interesting rather than beautiful, but when the sun came out, the deep blue water against the hundreds of islands of steeply rising rock formations—some covered with pines and green shrubs—was breathtaking. The craggy rocks are of fantastic shapes. Some rise from the water in perfect cones, others form graceful arches, still others contain mysterious grottoes or tunnels. Many islets consist of a single huge rock, with small trees perching precariously in the crevices; some are fairly large and wooded. The boat takes you through tunnels into unexpected small lakes surrounded by green slopes, and glides through narrow passages, past caves with stalactites and stalagmites, and innumerable bays and quiet inlets. Climbing through the caves is hard work. The guide goes ahead with a torch, revealing rock walls covered with Chinese characters. Wherever the Chinese

Lengths of handwoven silk

Bay of Along

visit natural-rock formations they are irresistibly driven to carve poems on rock—a more civilized way to memorialize your visit than our carved initials. Wild boars, monkeys, and sheep inhabit these wooded islands and can often be seen if you let the motor idle and glide around a corner unexpectedly—it would have been better had I made this trip by sampan, many of which dotted the water with their brown mat sails looking like bat wings.

The Bay of Along has a sinister reputation. Until recent times it was the haunt of Chinese pirates, whose junks would steal silently at night to a Tonkinese village, surprising the sleeping people. These raids were made primarily for the purpose of kidnapping pretty girls, for nothing else of value can usually be found in a Tonkinese village. Whenever the French coast guard vessels succeeded in catching up with the pirates, they always found a peaceful fishing boat with no girls on board. This was so because, if capture became imminent, the pirates slit the girls from top to bottom and dropped them overboard. The slitting was done in order to keep the bodies from bobbing to the surface later on. The Tonkinese say that the bottom of the Bay of Along is "paved with the beauty of Tonkin." The French had stopped this practice when I was there, and the Bay of Along was safe, though I suppose it still is a haven for smugglers, the fashion having changed from girls to drugs. In the old days, Tonkinese girls fetched a high price in the markets of China, as they were considered prettier than Chinese girls.

When I boarded my little *chaloupe* for the return trip to Haiphong, I was welcomed heartily by the *commissionaire,* clad in an eye-catching, purple dressing gown. He was a small chap with clear, blue eyes, white hair, and a beautiful white, curly moustache. He had exactly five teeth—I counted them. His old-world courtesy and chivalry were a pleasant contrast to the manners of the owners of the Hôtel des Mines, whom I thought robbers. I had my old cabin back and ate a delicious dinner with him. We sat on deck and feasted our eyes on the ever-changing spectacle of the thousands of islands in the bay. It took an hour to pass through them. All the while I reported to my host what I had seen in the past two months. To my delight I found him to be a Frenchman who approved of my travels; he thought them broadening. *"Ca change les idées,"* he remarked, waggling his head.

This was the end of my trip. I took the Jardine Matheson steamer *Taksang* to Hong Kong, where I boarded a Dollar Line ship to Manila.

Epilogue

We traveled with no purpose except to enjoy ourselves. We found it was more enjoyable to visit strange peoples and countries if we knew something about them beforehand. So we read books and steeped ourselves in the history and ethnography of each country we were to see. We talked with everybody who could help us understand the people among whom we were to travel. We discussed native psychology, character, history, aspirations, and attitude toward Europeans and Americans.

Our relations with the native peoples we met were pleasant and friendly because we had no feeling of superiority. Being strangers, generally ignorant of the language and customs of the country yet traveling mostly in the native manner, we were in fact less capable of coping with life than they were, and this immediately brought forth extraordinary kindness and helpfulness on their part. Villagers quickly sense a basic friendliness if it is deeply felt by the foreigner, and their hearts go out to him. Once a stranger becomes a friend, his lapses in etiquette are easily forgiven. We met these people on a level where our problems were often the same as theirs: finding shelter at night, food by day, and getting to a given destination by some sort of transport. There is nothing in all this that would have justified us in feeling superior—quite the contrary.

But we were conscious that, although we were equals, we were very different. We came from a Western culture strongly based on technology—which we have not yet mastered—and a political tradition that has evolved over centuries. In our relationship with these people we cannot let ourselves forget that at the moment they lack our history of scientific curiosity, our inventiveness, our willingness to try new things, our adaptability to changes in environment, our deep-rooted sense of social responsibility. It is more difficult for them to master the machine than for us. To them the machine is part magic, part slave; an attitude shown in their lack of concern in keeping tools and machinery in good condition.

Similarly, in the development of government, the history of Southeast Asia has been different from that of the West. Not one of the peoples of Southeast Asia has ever had native government even faintly resembling the state as it has evolved in the West. Indigenous political organization never grew beyond the confines of the village or tribe; everything above has been foreign importation. Any government above the village or tribal level has always been arbitrary, tyrannical, and unrelated to the needs of the people. Occasionally there has been an enlightened ruler who concerned himself with the welfare of his people, but they are exceptions. Normally, kings have collected taxes and *corvée* and given little in public service in return. They have kept themselves aloof from their people by claiming to be the shadow of the gods on earth or the lord of life, demanding abject prostration from all who approached them. To the people they were distant objects of awe; the government of princes, kings, and emperors—a burden that must be borne, lest one be cruelly punished. Wars were special tribulations which were of no concern to the people who suffered the consequences—they were personal feuds of the rulers. The concept that governments are servants of the people and that, conversely, people owe a responsibility to their government is a Western notion, novel and strange to the peoples of Southeast Asia. It would be demanding too much if we expected them to have a sense of civic responsibility just because they have achieved political independence.

There is a native democracy in the villages of all the countries of Southeast Asia. These people place a great deal of emphasis on time-honored forms of courtesy—in fact, one of the most difficult barriers to mutual friendship that Western people have to surmount is native inability to distinguish between form and substance. Much of the friction between East and West has been due to the Westerners' ignorance of Eastern form and the inability of the East to make allowances for such ignorance. To an extraordinary extent—almost impossible for the Westerner to understand—the peoples of Southeast Asia lack a realization that customs necessarily vary among different peoples and that their own are not the only proper ones.

We came away from these people recognizing that their future would be troubled, for the tide of change was sweeping them toward social and political problems to which there could not be any easy solution. All that we could hope was that the kindness and the dignity of these individuals whom we saw as friends would survive.

Bibliography

Baum, Vicki, *Tale of Bali*. Garden City, New York: Doubleday, Doran & Co., Inc., 1937.
Bouillevaux, C. E., *L'Annam et le Cambodge: Voyages et Notices Historiques*. Paris: Victor Palmé, 1874.
Casey, Robert J., *Four Faces of Siva*. New York: The Bobbs-Merrill Company, 1929.
Cortambert, E., and de Rosny, Léon, *Tableau de la Cochinchine*. Paris: A. LeChevalier, 1862.
Covarrubias, Miguel, *Island of Bali*. New York: Alfred A. Knopf, Inc., 1937.
Crawfurd, John, *Journal of an Embassy from the Governor-General of India to the Courts of Siam and Cochin China*. 2 vols. London: H. Colburn, 1828.
French in Indo-China, The. London: T. Nelson and Sons, 1884.
Garnier, Francis, *Voyage d'Exploration en Indochine, Effectué Pendant Les Années 1866, 1867 et 1868*. 2 vols. Paris: Librairie Hachette et Cie, 1873.
Graham, W. A., *Siam*. 2 vols. 3d ed. London: A. Moring Ltd., 1924.
Harris, Townsend, *The Complete Journal of Townsend Harris*. New York: Doubleday, Doran & Company, Inc., 1930.
Hildebrand, J. R., "The World's Greatest Overland Explorer." *National Geographic Magazine*, November 1928.
Landon, Margaret, *Anna and the King of Siam*. New York: The John Day Company, 1944.
Leonowens, Anna H., *The English Governess at the Siamese Court*. Boston: Fields, Osgood & Co., 1870.
―――, *The Romance of the Harem*. Boston: J.R. Osgood and Company, 1873.
―――, *Siamese Harem Life*. London: A. Barker, 1952.
Lockhart, R. H. Bruce, *Return to Malaya*. New York: G. P. Putnam's Sons, 1936.
McGilvary, D., *A Half Century Among the Siamese and the Lao*. New York: Fleming H. Revell Co., 1912.
Moore, E. Robert, "Along the Old Mandarin Road of Indo-China." *National Geographic Magazine*, August 1931.
Pires, Tomé, *Suma Oriental*. Translated into English by Armando Cortesao. 2 vols. London: The Hakluyt Society, 1944.

Thompson, Virginia, *Thailand: The New Siam*. New York: The Macmillan Company, 1941.
———, *French Indo-China*. New York: The Macmillan Company, 1942.
Wales, H. G. Quaritch, *Siamese State Ceremonies: Their History and Function*. London: B. Quaritch, Ltd., 1931.
———, *Towards Angkor: In the Footsteps of the Indian Invaders*. London: George G. Harrap & Co., Ltd., 1937.
Williams, Maynard Owen, "By Motor Trail Across French Indo-China," *National Geographic Magazine*, October 1935.
Winstedt, Sir Richard O., *Malaya and its History*. London: Hutchinson's University Library, 1953.

Index

Adat. See Law, Customary
A Famoso, 117
Albuquerque, Alfonso d', 113-115, 117, 173
Allegiance, Siamese oath of, 192, 194, 235
Along, Bay of, 294, 296
Ananda, King (Rama VIII), 178, 200
Angkor Thom, 124*n*, 140, 141, 143-144, 145, 147, 148-152, 185
Angkor Wat, 140-141, 145-148
Annam: history, 129, 132-133, 134, 247, 286; Chinese influence, 132-134, 249-250; religion, 134; overpopulation, 234, 288
Annamites, 234, 255; physical features and dress, 125, 128, 132-133, 134, 287; ethnic origins, 131-133; language, 134; mannerisms, 233, 234, 235, 254
Aranya, 157, 226
Architecture, styles of: *meru*, 17; *stupa*, 54; *prang*, 161; *chedi*, 161*n*
Asoka, 54*n*
Atjeh, Raja of, 53
Ayuthia (Ayudhya), 167, 169, 172, 205, 215, 216

Badung, Prince of, 23-25
Bali: temples, 16, 17, 19, 26, 28, 38, 39; volcanoes, 16, 17, 39; physical structure of villages, 16, 41; crops, 17, 37; Dutch rule, 23-25; size, 25; natural barricades against invasion, 42; religion, 42; Indian colonization, 43

Balige, 83; Rhënish mission, 83-88
Balinese people: village life, 16, 17, 20-21, 34, 37-38, 41; religious beliefs, 17, 19, 26, 31, 33; artistry, 19, 22, 30-31, 34-38, 39; physical features and dress, 20-21, 30-31; mannerisms and customs, 20-22, 23-25, 42; cremations, 31-33; Indian influence, 43-44
Bangkok, 159-161, 165, 177, 178, 215, 216-217, 219; administrative control, 185, 192, 194; founding of, 216. *See also* Wats
Bang Pa-In, 172-173
Banteai Srei, Temple of, 156
Bataks, 43, 192; conversion by missionaries, 42*n*, 81, 83-84, 86, 88; ethnic origin, 75; physical features and dress, 78, 83, 84; houses and villages, 83, 89-90, 96, 208; cannibalism, 83, 84, 92; education and health, 84-86; marriage customs, 86-87; stone sarcophagi of, 89
Batavia (Djakarta), 45*n*, 67, 105*n*
Batik, 50
Berastagi, 95, 96
Besakih, Temple of, 31, 38-39
Betel-nut, 12, 22, 128, 192; legend, 293-294
Bhumibol Adulyadej, King (Rama IX), 178*n*
Bongkasa, 26
Borobudur, 51, 53, 54-57, 140, 151, 156
Brahma, 19, 132
Brahmanism, 146, 187*n*; court Brahmins, 52, 111*n*, 132, 137;

301

concepts, 53n, 54n, 111n, 132, 187n
Britain and British people: colonial policy, 48n, 57n, 94–95, 106, 118–119, 121, 225, 234; acquisition of Malay States, 103, 104–105, 115, 215
British East India Company, 57n, 103n, 105, 118
Buddha, 54, 56, 134n, 146, 169; images, 56, 57, 137–138, 165, 167, 178, 222, 277, 284
Buddhism: expansion in Malay Archipelago, 43, 53, 54; in Cambodia and Siam, 54n, 132, 134, 146, 183; in Annam, 134; Mahayana, 134, 277; Hinayana, 134, 183. See also Sri Vijaya
Buddhists: monks, 129–130, 141, 160, 161–162, 191, 230, 271; converting to Christianity, 222–223, 254
Buginese, 11, 108
Buleleng, 13, 15, 42
Burma and Burmese people, 54n, 131, 167, 171, 183, 194, 208, 216, 225
Burma Road, 258, 259, 260, 265, 268, 275–276

Cambodia, 131; capital, 128, 136, 144; French protectorate, 129, 136; early kingdoms, 132, 141, 143–144; religion, 134; Siamese incursions, 143, 144, 171
Cambodian people, 128, 138, 141, 143, 148
Cannibalism, 75n, 83–84, 90, 92, 95, 241n
Carabao, 28, 48, 71, 73, 128, 229, 242
Celebes, 10–12
Chakri, General (Rama I), 178, 216
Champa and Chams, 132, 143, 171, 235. See also Cochin China
Champlain, Samuel de, 7

Chao Luang, 192, 194
Chao Phraya River, 159–160, 219
Chiang Kai-shek, 9, 98, 238, 258, 259, 260, 262, 265, 273
Chieng Mai, 182–183, 185–186, 190–191, 208; Presbyterian Mission Center, 185–186, 188, 198–200
Chieng Rai, 178, 202, 203, 209, 212
Chieng Rung, 202, 203, 214
Chieng Sen, 207–208, 229
China: war with Japan, 1, 5–6, 80, 256, 258, 259, 260, 262, 263, 265, 269, 273, 282; religion, 54n, 134, 277; government organization, 96, 134, 249, 255n; architectural influence, 106, 183, 248–249, 264; trade, 113, 218; suzerainty of, 129, 132–134, 234, 286; cultural influence, 132, 134, 148, 216
Chinese people: business acumen, 9, 64, 98, 103, 104, 105, 179, 234; unassimilation of, 98, 99, 106, 179, 196, 238; dominant influence, 98, 104, 105, 117, 127, 131, 177, 179; bandits and piracy, 114, 283, 296; laborers, 117, 263, 264, 265, 275–276; education, 196, 238, 249, 269–271; physical features and dress, 264, 268, 277
Chou Ta-Kuan, 150, 152
Christian and Missionary Alliance, 220, 221
Chulalongkorn, King (Rama V), 172, 173, 178, 185, 187–188, 194, 195n, 235
Church Missionary Society, 266
Cochin China, 129, 130, 134n, 247, 288. See also Champa and Chams
Coen, Jan Pieterzoon, 45n
Column (Môt Côt), Temple of the, 286
Confucius, 284
Confucius, Temple of, 284
Conrad, Joseph, 12
Coward, Noel, 37

Dances, 30-31, 34-36, 38, 39, 145-146, 148, 188, 190; *gamelan* orchestra, 30, 34-35, 39
Deli, Sultan of, 99
Den Pasar (Badung), 23-25
Djembrana Plateau, 41
Djokja, 47n, 48, 50-51, 61
Djokja, Sultan of, 50, 57, 59
Dong Ha, 243, 244
Dupuis, Jean, 231, 262
Dutch East India Company, 94
Dutch government: colonial policy, 1, 23-25, 42, 48n, 57n, 59, 81, 85-86, 93-95, 98, 119, 234; merchant marine, 6-7; trade monopoly, 11, 94, 104, 115, 118; tourist trade, 4, 13, 15, 20, 42, 47
Dutch people: resemblance to other nationalities, 3-4; language, 4, 7; customs and mannerisms, 7, 10, 47, 65-66, 78, 79; colonial service, 5, 63, 90-91

Ecole Française d'Extrême-Orient, 145
Elephants, 110, 137, 150, 152, 169, 172, 183, 212, 218; sculptured, 143, 145, 190

Felatehan, 45n
Filipinos, 8n, 10, 47, 51n, 64, 75. *See also* Igorots, Moros
Flower Temple, 277
Fort de Kock, 69, 73, 131
Fort Rotterdam, 11
France: colonial policy, 48n, 136, 234-236, 237, 247, 254, 261, 287-288; acquisition of Indo-China, 128-129, 136, 171, 194, 225, 231, 247; search for trade routes, 230-231
French people: influence of, 128, 261; mannerisms, 128, 232-233; missionaries, 128-129, 141, 254-255

Funeral rites, 78, 89, 110; *suttee*, 23, 42, 95; cremation, 31-34, 207

Garnier, Francis, 230-231, 241n, 262
Gaurs, 244
Germany and German people: resemblance to Dutch, 3; Tsingtao defense, 62-63; in colonial service, 63; Nazi influence, 63, 85, 96, 199; missionaries, 81, 83-88
Gia-Long, 129, 247-248, 249, 250, 251, 254, 286
Gilamanuk Bay, 41-42

Handicrafts: Macassar, 11; Bali, 31, 37-38; Java, 48-49, 50; Cambodia, 138, 148; Siam, 191, 216; Tonkin, 292
Hanoi, 231, 284-285, 294
Hanoi-Kunming Railroad, 260, 261, 262-263
Hinduism: caste system, 21, 43, 53n; expansion in Malay Archipelago, 43-44, 52-54; influence on art, 22, 43, 50, 132. *See also* Brahmanism, India, Madjapahit
Hon Gay, 294
Hué, 246-249; emperors' graves, 250-251

Igorots, 17, 43, 75, 78, 84, 240, 241n
India: epic poems, 35-36, 50, 146-147; colonization and influence, 43-44, 131-132; concept of princely state, 52, 111n, 143. *See also* Brahmanism, Hinduism, Madjapahit
Indo-China: religion, 54n, 128-129, 132, 134; migration into, 54n, 131, 132-133, 234; racial elements and cultures, 131-132, 204, 215; political relationships, 133-134, 171. *See also* France
Indo-Chinese Union, 129
Indra, 146, 161

International House (New York), 266n
Islam, 41, 42, 49-50, 52n, 53, 54, 75n, 76, 111, 114, 132, 143

Japan and Japanese people, 3, 7, 54n, 64, 125; siege of Tsingtao (1914), 62-63. *See also* China
Java-China-Japan Line, 1
Java and Javanese people, 47, 48, 64, 75, 132; handicrafts, 48-49, 50; religion, 49; dress, 49, 50-51, 59; temples 54-57; Dutch rule, 59; potentates, 59. *See also* Madjapahit
Jayavarman II, 137, 140n
Jayavarman VII, 140n
Johore, Sultan of, 120

Kabandjahe, 95, 96
Kedaton, 30
Kedah, Sultan of, 105
Khmers: ancient kingdoms of, 124n, 140, 152, 215; sculpture, 131, 143, 145, 146, 147, 150, 152; cultural influence, 169, 183, 185, 215-216; as architects, 138, 140, 141, 146, 147, 148; vassalage, 144, 185; legends, 151-152
Klang, Sultan of, 108, 110
Klungkung, 38
Klungkung, Dewa Agung of, 23, 38
Koninklijke Nederlandsch-Indische Luchtvaart Maatshappij (KNILM), 9, 67, 69
Koninklijke Paketvaart Maatschappij (KPM): steamship line, 4, 6; tourist services, 13, 15, 20
Kota Gedeh, 48, 50
Kotanopan, 78, 79
Kra, Isthmus of, 132n
Kuala Lumpur, 108
Kublai Khan, 52, 183
Kunming (Yunnan-fu), 258, 266, 268-269, 271, 275, 276-277; Federal University, 269-271,

273. *See also* Burma Road, Hanoi-Kunming Railroad
Kuta Beach Hotel, 19-20, 34, 39
Kwangchowan Territory, 129

Labor, forced and indentured, 173, 254; contract, 92-93; *corvée*, 133, 136, 235, 250
Lagrée, Doudart de, 230, 241n
Lampang, 201, 212-214
Lamphun, 191, 192
Lancaster, Sir James, 104
Languages and scripts: Dutch, 4, 7; Malay, 8-10; Sanskrit, 43, 44, 132, 152, 216; Javanese script, 75; Lao and Thai scripts, 132, 183, 194, 204, 216; Annamite, 134 (*quoc ngu*); Khmer script, 143, 152; Siamese, 210
Lao Kay, 259, 260, 263
Lao people: ethnic origins, 131-132, 183, 185; physical features and dress, 194, 204; mannerisms, 194, 235, 240; superstitions, 200, 204-205, 206-207, 226; marriage customs, 205-206; under French administration, 235
Laos, 134, 192-193, 239-240
Law, Customary, 51, 52, 86, 87, 90, 133
Legends: *Ramayana* and *Mahabharata*, 35-36, 50, 146-147; at Borobudur, 56-57; white monkey, 60-61; at Angkor, 137, 141, 147, 150-152; Phnom Penh, 138; in Tonkin, 286; betel-nut, 293-294
Leonowens, Mrs. Anna H., 186-188, 206, 219, 222
Leprosy, 88, 151-152, 185, 188-190, 197-199, 223, 225
Light, Captain Francis, 104-105
Literature (Van Miêu), Temple of, 284
Louis, XVI, King of France, 247

McGilvary, Dr. Daniel, 185
McKean, Dr. James, 185

Madjapahit (Hindu Malay Empire), 52–54, 54*n*, 111, 118, 143
Magellan, Ferdinand, 115
Mahabharata, 50, 146
Malacca, 103*n*, 111–117
Malacca, Straits of, 43, 53, 104, 111, 114, 115, 132*n*
Malay Archipelago: language, 8*n*; racial elements, 8*n*, 75; pre-colonial influence, 42–44, 76; early political organization, 51–54; colonial rule, 94–95, 115, 118. *See also* Madjapahit, Malay people, Sri Vijaya
Malay people: language, 8–10, 43; race and origins, 8*n*, 75; influence of colonization, 42–44, 51–52, 76, 94–95; conversion to Christianity, 106–107; migration of, 131. *See also* Balinese people, Bataks, Igorots, Java and Javanese people, Minangkabaus
Malaya (Malay States): acquisition by British, 103, 105; suzerainty of Siam, 103*n*, 105, 215; Penang, 104–106, 107; Selangor, 108; Malacca, 111–117; religion, 132. *See also* Rubber, Trade
Mancaned, Christoval de Jaque de los Rios de, 143
Mandarin Road, 255
Manuel, King of Portugal, 113
Marco Polo, 54*n*, 138, 264, 271, 275
Mataram (Moslem Malay Empire), 53, 53, 143
Medan, 99
Mekong River, 130, 183, 208, 229; exploration of, 230–231, 262
Menam River, 157, 179, 183, 208; life on, 167, 171–172, 173, 175. *See also* Chao Phraya River
Meru, Mount, 19
Minahassa, 10, 42*n*
Minangkabaus, 70, 75, 83, 85; houses and villages, 72, 73, 76; physical features and dress, 73, 78; matriarchy, 76, 87

Minh-Mang, 129, 247, 251
Missionaries, Christian: schools of, 84–86, 178–179, 196, 209; medical services of, 86–88, 185, 188, 198–199, 200; devotion and work, 106–107, 181, 202–203, 222–223, 256–257; early missionaries, 128, 129, 141, 241*n*; persecution of, 129, 254–255; influence on royalty, 186, 188
Mois, 235, 240–242, 269, 289
Moluccas (Spice Islands), 53, 113, 114, 115
Money, American equivalent value: guilder, 3*n*; kepeng, 21; Singapore dollar, 117; tical, satang, and baht, 159*n*; piastre, 233; Mex, 282
Mongkut, King (Rama IV), 180, 186–188, 195*n*, 219
Monkeys, 26, 73, 147, 156, 296
Moros, 10, 11, 52*n*, 115*n*
Moslems, 106–107. *See also* Islam, Moros
Mouhot, Henri, 141
Muong Kau, 229

Nam-Ti Valley, 263
Nanchao, 185, 215
Nang Klao, 195*n*
Narai, King, 216
Naresuan, King, 216
Netherlands. *See* Dutch government, Dutch people
Netherlands India Tourist Office (NITOUR), 42, 47, 67
Nguyen Dynasty. *See* Gia-Long
Nommensen, Ludwig, 84

Opium, 113, 201, 202, 210, 258, 262
Orang Laut. See Sea Gypsies

Pajakumbuh, 72
Pakanbaru, 67, 69, 78
Paksé, 208*n*, 229, 236, 238
Palembang, 53, 67, 111
Paper, making of, 288–289

Parameswara (Sri Vijayan prince), 111
Parfums, Rivière des, 248, 250, 251
Pematang Siantar, 95
Penang, 103n, 104-107
Philip II, King of Spain, 115
Philippine Islands, 8n, 51n, 53, 88, 101, 289; discovery of, 115. *See also* Filipinos
Phimeanakas, Temple of, 152
Phnom Bakheng, Temple of, 152
Phnom Penh, 128, 130, 136-138, 144, 229, 230n
Phra Ruang, 215
Pigneau de Behaine, 129, 247
Piracy, 11, 42, 53, 95, 114, 132n, 296
Planters and plantation life, 90-91, 93, 117, 122, 172, 213
Plymouth Brethren, 225-226
Porte d'Annam, 287
Porte de Chine, 255, 282
Portugal: control of trade routes, 11, 94, 104, 113, 114-115; conquest of Malacca, 104, 113-115; missions and missionaries, 128, 143; trade in Siam, 173-174
Prah Khan (Cambodian Sword), 137, 150
Prai, 107
Prajadhipok, King (Rama VII), 200
Province Wellesley, 103n, 105
Puntjak Bukit, 73

Raffles, Sir Stamford, 57, 92, 118-119
Rajdhani Hotel, 159, 165, 174, 175, 182, 215
Rama Kamheng, 216
Rama Tibodi, 167, 216
Ramayana, 35-36, 50, 146-147
Red River, 130, 231, 262
Rest houses, 79, 82, 83, 117, 233, 263
Rhënish Evangelical Mission, 84-86, 222

Rice: *sawahs* in Bali, 17, 37, 39; irrigation methods, 64, 130; harvesting, 192; world production, 128, 130, 179
Rubber: 99, 104; seeds smuggled out of Brazil, 106; tapping of trees, 117

Saigon, 127-128, 208n
Saigon River, 125
Sakol Wanakon, Prince, 217, 218
Salween River, 183, 208, 275
Samosir, 89
Sangeh, Sacred Forest at, 23, 26
Sanur, 23, 31
Sawankhalok, 185, 215-216
Sculpture: Bali, 17, 19, 26, 31, 38; Java, 56; Sumatra, 73, 89; Cambodia, 136, 143, 145-146, 147-148, 150, 152; Siam, 172, 183, 190, 230; Annam, 249, 251; Yunnan, 277; Tonkin, 284. *See also* Buddha
Sea Gypsies (*Orang Laut*), 28, 111, 118
Selangor, 103n, 108
Selangor, Sultan of, 108, 110
Sequeira, Diogo Lopez de, 113, 115
Seventh Day Adventists, 4, 221, 222-223
Shadow plays, 22, 148
Shanghai, 5-6, 105n
Shans, 183, 194, 208
Siam: religion, 54n; claims of suzerainty, 103n, 105, 111, 129, 171, 194, 215, 225; incursions and conquests, 105, 136, 143, 144, 169, 171, 194, 207; influence on architecture, 131; shorn of land, 136, 144, 225; early kingdoms, 167, 185, 191, 207, 215-216; independence of, 171; modernization of, 180, 186-188, 219, 235; government administration, 192-194, 195-196, 200, 218, 235-236

Siamese people: ethnic origins, 131-132, 169, 183, 185, 215, 230; physical features and dress, 160-161, 167, 186, 194; mannerisms, 160, 169, 179, 182, 218; handicrafts, 191; marriage customs, 192. *See also* Lao people, Thai people
Sibolga, 80
Siborongborong, 82
Siemreap, 140, 144, 148
Silk, making of, 289, 291
Singapore, 103n, 105n, 111, 118-119, 120
Siuhan, 88
Siva, 33n, 132, 148n
Snakes: *nagas* (sculpture), 145, 147, 152, 183, 230, 249; cobras, 150, 167, 172, 175, 200, 202; snake farm at Pasteur Institute, 175
Société des Missions Etrangères, 129
Spain, 51n, 115
Speelman, Admiral Cornelis, 11
Sri Koemala, 23-24
Sri Vijaya (Buddhist Malay Empire), 52-53, 111, 118, 143
Suicide: *puputan* in Bali, 23-25, 38, 42
Sukhothai, 215-216
Sumatra, 53, 67, 71. *See also* Bataks, Minangkabaus, Sri Vijaya
Superstitions and beliefs: Balinese, 19, 31-33; Batak, 84, 88, 89, 96; in Malaya, 121; at Angkor, 144; Siamese and Lao, 192, 200, 204-207, 226; in Annam, 255; in Yunnan, 277
Surakarta (Solo), Susuhunan of, 42, 57, 59
Suryavarmin II, 140n
Suttee. *See* Funeral rites

Tafelhoek, 28
Taksin, General, 216
Tali-fu, 230, 273, 275

Tamils, 103, 106, 107-108
Tampaksiring, 39
Tarutung, 79, 80, 82
Tchepone, 240, 242, 243, 244
Teak, 172, 183, 218
Temples and shrines: Bali, 16, 17-19, 26-28, 38-39, 41; Java, 51, 54-57; Sumatra, 76; Malaya, 106; Cambodia, 138, 140-141, 145-148, 150, 152; Siam, 161, 165, 169, 178, 190-191, 195; Yunnan, 271-272, 277; Tonkin, 284-286. *See also* under name, Wats
Thai people, 53, 171n, 194, 202, 204, 235; ethnic origins, 131-132, 183, 185, 215-216; religion, 183. *See also* Siamese people
Thieu-Tri, 129
Thonburi, 216
Tirta Empul, 39
Tjandi Mendut, Temple of, 57
Tjinegara, 1, 7, 15
Toba, Lake, 78, 89
Tonkin, 129, 132, 134, 247, 286, 288
Tonkinese, 287, 291-292, 296; village industries, 288-289, 291
Tordesillas, Treaty of, 115
Trade, 10-11, 12, 43, 94, 118, 173, 207-208; control of spice trade, 53, 104, 113, 115
Trailok, King, 216
Trees: banyan, 16, 26; cinnamon, 76; rubber, 106, 117; silk-cotton, 152; teak, 172, 183
Triple Entente, 225
Tsingtao, 62-63, 105n
Tu-Duc, 129

Ubon, 220, 221, 230
Utama, Nila (Sri Vijayan prince), 118

Villages and dwellings: Celebes, 10; Bali, 16-17, 36, 41; Sumatra, 72, 73, 76, 83, 89-90, 96; Cam-

bodia, 130-131; Siam, 167, 192; Burma, 208; Laos, 240; Yunnan, 264; Tonkin, 288, 289, 290; village government, 37, 51-52, 86-87, 90, 93-95, 133, 192, 298
Vishnu, 19, 49n, 132, 146, 147

Wan Waithayakon Vorawan, Prince, 217-218
Wats, 140, 161, 165, 178, 219; Wat Arun, 161; Wat Po, 165; Wat Phra Keo, 178; Wat Jed Yod, 190-191. *See also* Angkor Wat

Wattena Wittya Academy, 178, 181
White Monkey, story of, 60-61
Wickham, Sir Henry, 106

Xavier, St. Francis, 114

Yasovarmin I, 140n, 152
Yasodharapura, 124, 140n, 152
Yunnan and Yunnanese people, 262, 264, 268, 269, 273, 275-277. *See also* Burma Road, Hanoi-Kunming Railroad